Winged Warriors

For Jackie with love,
for Hannah, the first reader,
for Matthew and Dionne and especially for
Joaquin

Winged Warriors – The Cold War from the Cockpit is also dedicated to
Ron Etheridge, Ian Johnson, Paddy Thompson, Roger Lane, Jerry Yates,
Keith Holland, John Sheen, Steve Wright, Mike Smith, Alan Grieve,
Stan Bowles, Neil Anderson, Ian Gristwood, Kieran Duffy, Norman Dent,
Max Collier, Richard 'Wes' Wesley, Hylton Price and Rod Leigh;
and to countless more, all of them warriors.

Winged Warriors

The Cold War from the Cockpit

Paul McDonald

Pen & Sword
AVIATION

First published in Great Britain in 2012 by
PEN & SWORD AVIATION
An imprint of
Pen & Sword Books Ltd
47 Church Street
Barnsley
South Yorkshire
S70 2AS

ISBN 978-1-84884-748-4

Typeset by Concept, Huddersfield, West Yorkshire.
Printed and bound in England by CPI Group (UK) Ltd, Croydon, CR0 4YY.

Pen & Sword Books Ltd incorporates the imprints of Pen & Sword Aviation,
Pen & Sword Family History, Pen & Sword Maritime, Pen & Sword Military,
Pen & Sword Discovery, Wharncliffe Local History, Wharncliffe True Crime,
Wharncliffe Transport, Pen & Sword Select, Pen & Sword Military Classics,
Leo Cooper, The Praetorian Press, Remember When, Seaforth Publishing and
Frontline Publishing.

For a complete list of Pen & Sword titles please contact
PEN & SWORD BOOKS LIMITED
47 Church Street, Barnsley, South Yorkshire, S70 2AS, England
E-mail: enquiries@pen-and-sword.co.uk
Website: www.pen-and-sword.co.uk

Contents

List of Plates

Every effort has been made to trace copyright owners and obtain permission for the photographs in the book; however, the provenance of some is uncertain. If there have been any errors or omissions we apologize and will be pleased to make appropriate acknowledgements in any future editions. A number of photographs are UK MOD Crown Copyright and have been released under the new Open Government Licence (OGL). Their publication in this book does not imply any endorsement or official sanction for the book. Photographs not credited are from the author's own collection.

Plate Section 1 (mono)
1409 (Consett) Squadron, Air Training Corps, 1964.
  (*UK MOD Crown Copyright 1964, OGL*)
Graduation Parade RAF Henlow, 1971. (*Studio Five, Thetford, Norfolk*)
Award of RAF Wings, 1972.
Canberra B2 WK119, 1973.
Canberra TT18 WJ721, 1973. (*UK MOD Crown Copyright 1975, OGL*)
In front of Jet Provost, 1972. (*UK MOD Crown Copyright 1972, OGL*)
Guard of Honour, 8 June 1974. (*www.DorchesterLedbetter.co.uk*)
No. 7 Squadron, 1975. (*UK MOD Crown Copyright 1975, OGL*)
Malta's Grand Harbour, circa 1918.
Canberra PR7 WH 773, 1976. (*UK MOD Crown Copyright 1976, OGL*)
XIII Squadron crews, 1976. (*UK MOD Crown Copyright 1976, OGL*)
Kiev and an RAF F4 Phantom, 1978. (*UK MOD Crown Copyright 1978, OGL*)
Forgers on *Kiev's* lift, 1978. (*UK MOD Crown Copyright 1978, OGL*)
Kara Cruiser, 1978. (*UK MOD Crown Copyright 1978, OGL*)
XIII Squadron, 1978. (*UK MOD Crown Copyright 1978, OGL*)
Kiev head-on, 1978. (*UK MOD Crown Copyright 1978, OGL*)
Kiev in very heavy seas, 1978. (*UK MOD Crown Copyright 1978, OGL*)
Kiev bows out, 1978. (*UK MOD Crown Copyright 1978, OGL*)
Eric Androvardi, 1986. (*UK MOD Crown Copyright 1986, OGL*)
Changing the Guard at the Tomb of the Unknown Soldier, East Berlin.
RAF Linton-on-Ouse, 1944.
Jet Provost Farewell, 1993. (*UK MOD Crown Copyright 1993, OGL*)
Air Vice-Marshal Chris Coville and crews, 1994.
  (*UK MOD Crown Copyright 1994, OGL*)

Preface

I was inspired to start writing so that our son Matthew and our daughter Hannah would have something to add to their many memories of growing up as part of an RAF family. Hannah followed in my footsteps and joined the RAF. Very soon she saw active service overseas as an air traffic controller, twice in Basrah in Iraq and once in Afghanistan engaged in 'hot' conflicts so different from the Cold War that had been my experience. Matthew's life, with his American wife Dionne in their Los Angeles home, is far removed from the experience of his youth living on various RAF stations. Their son, Joaquin, will grow up in California where little will be known about a distant RAF and a Cold War long consigned to the history books. So it is largely for them that I began to write what has become *Winged Warriors – The Cold War from the Cockpit*.

The more that I wrote the more I remembered about the postings and about the places but mostly I remembered the people with whom I served. And then I would come across yet another log-book entry which would re-kindle long forgotten sorties and some forgotten faces.

I joined the Royal Air Force in 1971 and served as a pilot until 2005. My route to a fast-jet cockpit was untypical: I was a working class 'Geordie' brought up in Consett in County Durham. I did not go to university but I had been an air cadet. Even so, it was to take three visits to the Officers and Aircrew Selection Centre at RAF Biggin Hill before I was accepted for training and that was as a navigator. I became a pilot because of a shortfall of pilot candidates.

Winged Warriors charts a path over many obstacles and challenges before I could wear an RAF brevet. I then spent fourteen years on operational flying tours abroad ranging from low level photo reconnaissance on NATO's vulnerable southern flank to tours on Tornado strike/attack squadrons in NATO's Central Region, only minutes from responding in full measure to an anticipated Soviet onslaught. All of this was at the very height of the Cold War. For four years I was at the heart of the RAF's flying training system, training young men and women for a war that we hoped would never occur. Thankfully, because of the West's posture of deterrence, nuclear war against the Warsaw Pact was avoided, but other 'lesser' wars were not.

I also had some other memorable tours: I was privileged to be a member of the Directing Staff of the prestigious Royal College of Defence Studies in

Belgrave Square, London. From 1998 to the days preceding Gulf War II, I was an adviser in Kuwait. I was a 'fly on the wall' in the Kuwait Air Force HQ and the only 'Brit' in the Kuwaiti War Room to witness at first hand *Operation Desert Fox*, the air war against Saddam Hussein's Iraq in December 1998.

During my thirty-four years regular service I visited and operated from some fascinating and intriguing places: Germany, Italy, Malta, Iran, Canada, the United States of America, Pakistan, East Berlin before the Wall came down, Israel and Palestine, Jordan, Syria, Egypt and Cuba. There were also meetings with Royalty and Heads of State including one with Yitzak Rabin, the Prime Minister of Israel, only a few short weeks before he was so cruelly struck down by one of his own.

The now long-forgotten Cold War was not just a hyphen between the Second World War and conflicts in the Gulf and Afghanistan. It dictated the lives of many people throughout the world for forty-five years. I hope that *Winged Warriors* goes some way in describing a Service and part of its history, and what that Service was called upon to do during the Cold War and the latter part of the twentieth century. It is also about a generation of RAF aircrew, many of whom gave their lives in preserving peace. And it is those aircrew who stand out for me, true warriors in every sense of the word, blessed with an irrepressible sense of humour regardless of circumstance, a humour that was typically British and very typically RAF.

I have tried to offer an open and honest account of my perceptions and my fears, my actions and my mistakes, from a flying career that spanned 5,000 flying hours in single or twin-engine RAF aircraft. While the tale touches on many aspects of military service, it is not about war or war-fighting; it shows that military service is about real people and their highs and lows, ordinary people who sometimes found themselves in extraordinary circumstances. And it is about training and tragedy.

The views and opinions expressed in this book are those of the author alone and should not be taken to represent those of HMG, MOD, the RAF or any government Agency.

Acknowledgements

There are a lot of people that I would like to thank for their support during the writing of this book. My wife, Jackie, who lived the reality of RAF life and then suffered a 'double-whammy' as I re-lived it again over many, many months; our daughter Hannah who read the very first draft in less than twelve hours and then strongly urged publication. Hannah also continued to read and comment on further drafts between long arduous shifts at Camp Bastion in Helmand Province, Afghanistan. Meanwhile Matthew made many helpful suggestions from California often reminding me of incidents when we lived at Leeming and Laarbruch and Linton. He also asked those important questions about things that I had described that perhaps only an airman would understand. I hope that I have explained them.

Matthew collated many of the photographs used in the book and designed the front cover. The photograph on the front cover captures the very essence of the Cold War and its *Winged Warriors* and I am especially grateful to Jayne Fincher for allowing me to use her late father Terry's dramatic photograph of the 'Bruggen 40'.

Some thirty years after the event, it was also Matthew who found someone on the UK Airshow Review Forum who had been at Strathallan on 12 July 1980 to witness and to photograph a very special formation. I am very grateful to Derek Ferguson of Handforth in Cheshire for allowing me to use his unique photograph of a Vampire, Meteor, and Mosquito flanked by a Hurricane and a Spitfire. Through the same Forum, Mike Hall also offered some excellent photographs of that so very graceful but ultimately doomed RAF display team, The Vintage Pair.

Thanks are also due to Mike Napier, the Honorary Secretary of the 14 Squadron Association for providing additional information and also for allowing me to use some of his personal photographs including the striking photograph, taken by the late Flight Lieutenant Alan Grieve of 'his' aircraft: 14 Squadron's 'BB' over the Aegean in February 1986.

I am also grateful to Air Commodore Terry Jones, the former Station Commander RAF Linton-on-Ouse, for his support and for allowing me access to the Station archives. Also thanks to Alan Mawby, Linton's Historian, Flight Lieutenant Dave Williams, the Corporate Communications Officer, and to Gary Wort and Ron Blenkinsop of the Photographic Section (Babcock) for their help and support. I would also like to thank Geoffrey Lee of Planefocus Ltd for his permission to reproduce two of his excellent photographs.

A number of photographs have also been reproduced which are Crown Copyright and these have been released under the new Open Government Licence. Thanks go to Nicola Hunt of MOD Abbey Wood for her advice in this regard.

I would also like to thank Sir Christopher Coville, Sir Roderick Goodall, Vaughan Morris, Mike Pilkington, Graham Pitchfork, Tom Eeles, John Whitmell, Mike Dineen, Bill Ramsay and Doug Steer for their support and inputs. I am also most grateful to Frederick R Galea, Honorary Secretary of Malta's National War Museum Association, for his very helpful suggestions. Thanks also to Steve Clarke of the Air Historical Branch for his guidance and to the late Peter Coles and to my editor Ken Patterson, as well as Jon Wilkinson and Laura Hirst and all at Pen and Sword.

Finally special thanks are due to Patricia Leigh for her permission to refer to her late husband Rod's final farewell.

North Yorkshire
March 2012

Prologue

I looked at my watch again. It hadn't stopped, but it must have been the fifth or sixth time that I had looked at it within the last twenty minutes. It seemed as if we had been airborne for hours, yet my ever-faithful RAF aircrew watch showed that only ninety minutes had elapsed since *that* take-off. We continued our search, scanning the distant horizon, but there was no sign of our elusive quarry.

Fred, as was normal for him on low-level sorties, had unstrapped from his ejection seat and come forward. Some navigators preferred to sit on the fold down rumbold seat, alongside the pilot on the right, but Fred much preferred to crawl down the narrow, claustrophobic tunnel to lie flat and look out of the Perspex nose of the twenty-five year old Canberra PR7. A navigators' lot on Canberras was all about mastering claustrophobia; if Fred had remained in his ejection seat, he had a bulkhead to look at directly in front of him and only two tiny windows through which he could occasionally snatch fleeting glimpses of the outside world as it moved swiftly past. Above his head was the frangible hatch through which his ejection seat would travel if he had to use it in earnest. If he had remained strapped in his ejection seat, Fred would have been no help to me on this sortie; I needed another pair of eyes, not that I ever had to ask Fred to come up front. Of course if we had a problem he would have to look sharp reversing down the tunnel feet first, so that he could then get up, turn around, and move to the rear of the cockpit behind my ejection seat. Then turn around once more, before quickly strapping into the double harness of the Canberra's elderly Martin Baker ejection seat. We often practiced doing just that; you never knew when you might have to opt for a Martin Baker let-down.

We flew on, varying our height between 250 and 2,000 feet, both of us scanning as far as we could see, but to no avail. It was blowing quite a gale outside, and had been all morning. The sea was running very high, with deep rolling waves and white surf being lifted and thrown across the wave tops by the gusting wind. I shivered inwardly at the thought of having to eject in such conditions. Despite being in the relatively warm environment of the Mediterranean there would be little chance of survival for long, even if we could board our tiny single-man dinghies. With the wind as it was, boarding our dinghies would be a very big 'if'. There were no search and rescue helicopters based in Malta. The nearest were in Italy, but we were a lot closer to Libya.

I reflected again, as I had done many times that morning, on the decision to launch us. Our mission must have been considered to be very important, although in the end the final decision to take-off had been mine. And if anything went seriously wrong, the final responsibility would also be mine. I was the aircraft captain. Aircraft captaincy could sometimes be a lonely place.

We simply must find her. Visibility was good, but it quickly reduced to only a few hundred yards in the frequent squalls which passed by. Could we have missed her? We were in the area that the intelligence staffs had suggested, but there was no sign of her at all. Could the intelligence have been wrong? It wouldn't have been the first time. We pressed on.

Nor would she be on her own; she should also have her faithful escorts, a Kara and a Krivak. How could all three of them hide from us? But there was not a sign. In fact we hadn't seen a single ship since our take-off. Perhaps our maritime brothers were a little wiser than we had been, venturing so far from land on a day such as this. If our quarry had any sense she would have sought shelter from the fierce north-westerly gale in one of the nearby bays in Tunisia or Libya. We continued our search as I hauled the heavy PR7 around the sky, looking far and wide, to see if we could spot a silhouette against the skyline that might give us a clue as to where our target might be.

The day – Wednesday, 22 March 1978 – had begun like any normal working day for an operational crew on XIII (PR) Squadron, based at RAF Luqa in Malta. Fred and I lived a few doors apart in the small town of Balzan. We often shared cars, sometimes driving through the main site of RAF Luqa before crossing the runway to reach XIII Squadron HQ. It always brought a wry smile to my face when one of the Armed Forces of Malta Super Frelon helicopters took off and flew slowly past our dispersal, directly opposite the International Airport Terminal. The helicopters had come from Libya, which had close links with Malta's ruling Labour Government under Dom Mintoff. We were unsure of the nationality of the pilots.

It had been one of those rare wild and windy nights in Malta, and even at 0700 hours as we drove across the runway, the wind had not abated. We had both remarked on the windsock, which showed the wind's direction and approximate strength. It had been horizontal. It was also at 90° to Luqa's Runway 24/06, which was the worst it could be for aircraft operations. It was gusting too. We both agreed that there would be no chance of flying and an 'early stack' was most likely on the cards. Perhaps we would be able to call in at the Officers' Mess on our way home for one of the Maltese barman's renowned brandy sours, or for a refreshing glass of the Maltese lager, Cisk. In that, we were not far wrong, we would indeed enjoy a Cisk in the bar that day, but it would be a lot later than we anticipated. The day would turn out to be one of the most difficult, and the most exciting, of our operational careers until then, or since.

That morning everyone at the Squadron was pretty relaxed, having come to the same conclusion: there would be no flying that day. The flying programme had been 'scrubbed', and as XIII Squadron was the last operational squadron based in Malta, there would be little else happening on the airfield. We could see that the International Airport was a hive of inactivity too, with all civilian take-offs and landings having been cancelled – even profit could not argue with Mother Nature that morning. The weekly RAF VC10 aircraft from RAF Brize Norton had also been diverted to the Italian Air Force Base of Sigonella in Sicily.

Strong winds weren't necessarily a problem and it was possible to take-off and land with a wind speed of 40 knots, providing that the wind was not too far off the runway direction. But if the wind is across the runway it becomes more difficult, and is at its worst when it is at right angles to the runway direction. Gusting winds are even more troublesome. It is relatively simple to work out the headwind and the crosswind component. For most aircraft, including the Canberra, the maximum crosswind component for take-off and landing was 25 knots. On 22 March the wind was from the north-west, 90° off Luqa's runway. With an average wind speed of 30-40 knots, and with gusts to 50 and 60 knots, it was well outside our limits. So Fred and I adjourned to the crewroom for a coffee and a chat with the boys as we looked forward to that beer in the bar on the way home, and perhaps another on one of our respective balconies overlooking San Anton Gardens and the President's Palace.

But the calm was soon shattered. That most irreverent of squawk boxes on the crewroom wall burst into life and interrupted the calm stilling our conversation, 'McDonald and Stokes, report to Operations!'

Fred and I looked at one another and wondered what we had done, what had been found out. Nothing immediately came to mind, so with a shrug and joint looks of resignation we headed upstairs to the Operations Room. We were met at the top of the stairs by my Flight Commander, who was the Acting Squadron Commander at the time. With a smile he said, 'It looks like there may be a job for you two, you may be getting airborne. Grab your hats; I'll see you in my car.'

Fred and I looked at each other in amazement, and soon found ourselves in the Squadron Commander's RAF Ford Escort Estate heading back across the runway. The windsock was still horizontal – we looked at one another even more questioningly. If anything, the wind was actually stronger than it had been earlier, but my Flight Commander was keeping his thoughts to himself. No doubt all would be revealed when we entered that very private inner sanctum of Operations Wing, the Station Intelligence Squadron.

It was *Kiev*. The very latest and immensely powerful addition to the Soviet Union's already impressive navy. She was thought to be heading west once more for the final time, having completed sea training and trials with the Soviet Black Sea Fleet, and was now thought to be on her way to join the

Soviet Northern Fleet at Murmansk. My first thought was 'so what?' What was so special about *Kiev* today of all days? She had first entered the Mediterranean in January, and I had already flown two full missions photographing her from every angle and height imaginable. While this would probably be the last opportunity for us to get more photographs of *Kiev*, didn't we have enough already? What about the weather? Didn't the somewhat extreme wind conditions scotch any thought of getting airborne? Apparently they did not.

It soon became apparent that it wasn't about getting airborne despite the weather – it was about getting airborne because of the weather. The gale force winds and the very high seas meant, according to the Intelligence staffs, that it might just be possible to get some photographs of parts of *Kiev*'s hull that were normally underwater. My eyebrows lifted a little at this. The Station Intelligence Officer was not a pilot and I am not sure whether he fully understood what I would have to do to our ancient and heavy aircraft to achieve such photography. Our low-level cameras were not mounted horizontally, but at an angle of 15° below the horizontal, and they were fixed. And he wanted photographs of parts of the hull that were normally below the waterline?

He went on. He was particularly interested in what looked like some sort of gate that was low on *Kiev*'s stern. If we just happened to be flying past the stern as it came out of the water because of the sea state we might, just might, be able to get a picture below the waterline he thought. There were lots of 'ifs' and 'maybes'. I toyed with the idea of inviting him to come along for the ride, but dismissed the thought almost as soon as it occurred - he would get in the way. All I would be able to do was try and manoeuvre the aircraft to be in the right place at the right time. We would also have to fly at very low altitude, perhaps at 100 feet or less, to try to get the shots that he wanted. This was no easy matter as the Canberra PR7 was a heavy old beast and it did not have powered flying controls. So this would be a very physical mission. And of course all of our low-level cameras were pilot operated too; once we had found *Kiev*, Fred could do little except watch. To cap it all, the Intelligence staff had no real idea of where *Kiev* or her escorts were, the last sighting having been the previous day with *Kiev* and a mighty Kara cruiser and a Krivak escort heading in Malta's direction. It was suggested that we search to the south of Malta, toward the Libyan and Tunisian coasts, where *Kiev* may seek some shelter from the gale that we could still hear blowing outside. Seeking shelter from the gale sounded like a very good idea to me.

There was then some discussion about the wind and the difficulties that it would present during take-off and landing. I was glad that aspect got a mention. I wasn't particularly uncomfortable about taking off in such a strong crosswind; we could sit at the end of the runway with the engines running at high power for as long as necessary, listening to read-outs of the crosswind component from air traffic control. I could then release the brakes during a lull and go for it. Landing though, might be a different matter, and I said so.

It was then announced that the long-disused airfield at Hal Far would be reopened for us for landing. It had a 6,000 foot runway, the minimum safe length for a Canberra, but crucially it pointed virtually straight into the prevailing wind. While it was 1,500 feet shorter than Luqa's runway and it began virtually at the cliff face, it should not be a problem. Runway sweepers, crash crews, an ambulance and air traffic controllers would also be despatched from Luqa, just as soon as the decision was made for us to launch. I was a little taken aback by all this; Hal Far had been disused for years, clearly our mission was considered to be of the highest importance. It also seemed that all eventualities had been carefully considered and each one had been covered. But no pressure was exerted on us whatsoever. That was the way of this particular Flight Commander; he was a good man to work for.

As we drove back across the airfield I reflected a little on what had been said. It was quite an accolade to have been selected for this mission, after all, XIII Squadron had upwards of a dozen operational crews available that day. Fred and I had been crewed together since we arrived on XIII Squadron nearly three years earlier, in August 1975. Fred was on his fourth flying tour and his second on Canberras. I was on my second tour and had close to 1,500 flying hours on Canberras. We also were pretty competent as a constituted crew, and had a deserved reputation for being able to get the job done and come back with the goods - usually. But I also figured that there was something that had been left unsaid during our briefing. Since the withdrawal of the Nimrod squadron from Malta, XIII Squadron was the only RAF source of real intelligence in the Mediterranean, and we too would be withdrawn to the UK within six months as part of the UK's final withdrawal from Malta. Was the presence of *Kiev* today seen as a last opportunity for XIII, and the RAF in Malta, to once again prove our worth?

Fred and I were quiet on the journey back to the Squadron. As we crossed the main runway the wind had not abated. It was clear that the go/no go decision would be ours. If we were prepared to go, my Flight Commander was sufficiently confident in our ability to authorise the sortie. A glance at Fred, and a nod from him, was all that was needed. The mission was on.

The aircraft chosen for the task was WT530; and it was fitted with a 12-inch F95 low-level camera on the starboard side, and 4-inch F95 on the port, both mounted in the forward camera bay. We would not be using any of our many other cameras on this sortie. There was very little else to cover in the pre-flight briefing except a reminder to include the codeword 'X-Ray' when we returned to Luqa if we felt that we had photography that merited immediate exploitation. My Flight Commander then signed the authorization sheet and I signed afterwards as aircraft captain. A few minutes later Fred and I strapped into the aircraft and then a towing vehicle arrived - the wind was too strong for us to attempt to taxy.

We were towed to the end of Runway 24 with the aircraft control locks fitted to prevent any movement of the aircraft controls in the frequent gusts of wind. Even the engine intake blanks were fitted, to prevent any 'debris' being blown into the engine intakes. Malta had a bit of a reputation for 'debris'. We were positioned well to the left of the runway centreline, not pointing down the runway, but at an angle of 30° into wind. The control locks and blanks were then removed and we started the engines. Once the after start checks had been completed, our groundcrew moved to one side of the runway to watch and to wait. I checked in with air traffic control and we were cleared to 'take-off at your discretion'. I accelerated the engines to the maximum continuous RPM of 7600 and then held the aircraft on the brakes. We were then given a continuous read-out of the crosswind component from the Visual Control Room on top of the air traffic control tower. I could also see that we had something of an audience on the balcony of the XIII Squadron HQ outside the first floor Operations Room.

When the crosswind component dropped momentarily below 30 knots I released the brakes, applied full power, and with a big boot of left rudder the aircraft slowly turned onto the centreline and off we went, lumbering up the gentle incline of Runway 24. Slow accelerations on take-off were a feature of the Canberra PR7. At 48,000 pounds all-up-weight, the PR7 was a heavy old beast, even without wing-tip fuel tanks fitted. Thankfully, as it was March, the outside temperature was quite moderate, on hot days take-offs concentrated the mind. The take-off was surprisingly uneventful. Shortly afterwards Fred unstrapped, and crawled forward into the nose of the aircraft. We then began our search.

All of that had been nearly two hours ago and we continued to search in vain. Finally, with about thirty minutes of fuel remaining Fred suggested that we swing toward the east of Malta, and then head north-west between Malta and Sicily before calling it a day. I agreed. While this was not the area suggested by Intelligence it would be our last throw of the dice.

We could tell by looking at the sea that it was still blowing a gale, the conditions outside looked very bad. Thank goodness I wasn't a sailor – even the hardiest of sailors would have been uncomfortable on a day like today. Soon we were within twenty-five miles of Malta. We were on the point of giving up when we spotted something ahead. Was it our quarry?

As we got closer, it was apparent that it was not, but it was definitely a warship – and it was Soviet. It was also struggling, not making any headway at all, simply pointing into wind and maintaining steerage. It was a Soviet destroyer, of the Krivak class, and we knew that she was one of *Kiev*'s escorts. She was pointing north-west so, after taking a few photographs, we headed in the same direction. The trail was getting warm. Then we found the Kara class cruiser, and she too was making very little headway. The Kara was a magnificent looking vessel with so much firepower crammed into her 580 feet. Capable of well over 30 knots, even she was struggling with the high seas often swamping her low stern and helicopter deck. But the trail was now getting hot, we had to be close.

A few miles further on, even closer to Malta, we found her. We learnt later that RAF air traffic controllers at Luqa could see *Kiev* on their radar and had done so since long before we had taken off. She was virtually on the centre-line of the approach to Runway 24, about twenty miles out. Of course they had no idea what the vessel was, nor did they know the precise nature of our mission until after we were airborne. Only when we began to fly around *Kiev* itself did they realize that the blip on their radar screen was the target that had been eluding us for so long.

Kiev was an amazing sight. Over 900 feet long with a displacement of 42,000 tons, she was the pride of the Soviet Navy and was a credit to her designer. She was also very heavily armed. No doubt conditions below decks would have been cramped for the majority of her crew of 1,612. Conditions below deck on that day must have been grim indeed, as even the might of *Kiev* was being dwarfed by the enormous waves crashing over her.

We had no time to lose and immediately set about taking as many photographs as we could. We had very little fuel left and we needed to have some reserve in case it took us a while to get down. We concentrated on the stern but also made numerous low runs alongside and over her deck. The Soviets totally ignored us, they had their hands full. With luck our 12-inch F95 camera should produce some good quality close-up shots, but all I could do was try and put our aircraft in the right place, I couldn't point the camera, and we wouldn't know anything of our results until after landing when the film negative was eventually rolled out on one of our large light tables. The flying was exhilarating but it was also tiring, and we had little time to enjoy the thrill of the very low passes that we made, sometimes even below deck level. Fred said nothing throughout, nor did he need to.

In no time at all we had used up all of our film and we headed back to Malta, by now only two or three minutes flying time away. I was confident that we would have the 'goods' so included the crucial word 'X-Ray' in our recovery radio call. That would ensure that our skilled team of 'photogs' and photographic interpreters would meet the aircraft on landing at Hal Far and get the film exploited within minutes.

As we approached Luqa and Hal Far, the wind if anything was even stronger than before and we were told to go immediately to Hal Far. I very much looked forward to this and approached Hal Far from over the sea at 250 feet and 420 knots. We flashed over the cliffs and then over the runway before I broke to the left and upwards, closing the throttles, selecting air-brakes out, and also opening our large flare (bomb) bay to reduce our speed. Fred was by now back safely strapped into his ejection seat. I turned finals at 1,000 feet and began a descending turn onto the final approach rolling out at about 300 feet with the speed now reducing toward 110 knots. That's when I realized that we had a problem, a big problem. We couldn't land.

For most of the time that we had been airborne we had been flying at speeds of between 300 and 350 knots and visibility through both the canopy and through the Perspex nose had been good. But as soon as we slowed down to approach speed for landing, I had to raise the nose of the aircraft to maintain the correct approach path. We were also heading directly into sun, toward the cliff, with the threshold of the short runway starting just beyond the cliff face. While there was no crosswind problem, I simply couldn't see anything. The lower part of the canopy was completely encrusted with salt; it was totally opaque. At higher speeds this had gone unnoticed. I overshot, and Fred scrambled back into the nose to see if he could talk me down onto the runway. I hadn't asked him too, he just came forward. Fred was not short of guts. But the lower part of the Perspex nose-cone was just as bad. I tried a couple more approaches at higher speeds but it was hopeless. In order to see the runway I had to fly so fast that I couldn't put the aircraft on the ground. Fred wisely crawled back out of the nose and strapped himself into his ejection seat. I overshot and explained my problem to air traffic control. What were we going to do now?

Chapter 1

'Bonny Lad'

County Durham, 1949–1971

Throughout my RAF career I was known as a Geordie, someone born on Tyneside within sight of the river. And I was, on 16 April 1949, in Newcastle. But I wasn't actually called 'Bonny Lad' until 1988 whilst flying Tornados with 14 Squadron, at RAF Bruggen in West Germany, before the Berlin Wall came down. It was Squadron Leader 'Herm' Harper, destined to succeed me as 14 Squadron's Executive Officer (Deputy Squadron Commander), who 'christened' me in jest and it stuck! My parents actually lived near the steel town of Consett. So, while I was unquestionably a northerner, I was only a Geordie by an accident of birth.

*   *   *

North-west Durham was known as 'Little Ireland' because of the number of Irish immigrants who settled there in the middle of the nineteenth century. By the early part of the twentieth century, Consett was known for its iron and steel. It soon had a large steel mill which dominated the skyline and became a navigational beacon for generations of RAF pilots but only until the mid-1980s: the steel mill did not see out the Thatcher years. Consett survived the death of what was virtually its only industry after the coal mines had gone, but even now, the local telephone directory is still littered with 'Mc's' and 'O's' linking the area and its people with the country of their forbears.

Both sides of my family were originally from the south of Ireland and the majority left in the middle of the nineteenth century to seek a better life. Some settled in the USA, but most came to County Durham. My father was a steelworker and I grew up on a large council estate in the shadow of the iron works and its 'slag heaps'. My family had few links with the military and none with the RAF. My maternal granddad was a retired coal miner and he lived with my parents for the last fifteen years of his life. I will always remember his constant counsel.

'You must get your tickets lad.'

He meant that I must get some qualifications, but it took me far too long to recognize the wisdom of his words.

From the age of ten, I increasingly spent holidays in Ramsey, near Huntingdon staying with my mother's youngest sister and her husband. These visits started something that would grow into my ambition to join the

RAF. My uncle had grown up alongside RAF Catterick in North Yorkshire, where a squadron of Spitfires had been based during the Battle of Britain. There were also many RAF airfields near Ramsey, some active like Wyton and Upwood, some disused like Warboys, and I always found these to be fascinating places. A seed was sown.

At the age of eleven, I left the small local primary school and headed off to a brand-new grammar school at Hebburn-on-Tyne, some twenty miles distant. There was little at school that 'lit any fire' within me and I was often counselled to work harder. I didn't and it showed. And then coming home one day, someone mentioned the Air Cadets. For me, the Air Cadets and 1409 (Consett) Squadron was to be a life changing experience.

*   *   *

I enrolled in July 1964, and was issued with a uniform known as 'Hairy Mary's' because of the coarse uncomfortable material. The shirts had detachable collars with press studs. We paraded on Monday and Friday evenings, and studied air-related academic subjects which lead to examinations and the award of basic, leading, and senior cadet badges. There was rifle shooting, and I soon earned my ATC Marksman Badge with the .22 rifle, and later my RAF Marksman Badge with the Service-issue .303 rifle. Marching was a key feature of every parade night, and with no parade square, the locals were very familiar with the twenty or so cadets being shouted at as they tried, with varying degrees of success, to keep in step and to avoid 'tick-tocking', marching in such a way that your right arm and leg moved forward together while your left arm and leg went backwards – that was always an amusing sight!

Every year, the Squadron attended a large Wing Parade at RAF Catterick. Just before the Wing Chaplain lead the parade in prayer, I heard for the first time the command 'Roman Catholics and Jews, fallout'. This wasn't because of any prejudice on the part of the Air Cadets but at the request of the religions concerned. On my first such parade I and some others 'fell out' as ordered, marched off to the trees which surrounded the parade square, took off our berets and promptly 'lit up'. That did not go down well with the Parade Warrant Officer!

My first annual camp was at RAF Kinloss, Scotland, in 1964 and it was here that I flew for the very first time, in a Shackleton. We visited all the various sections on the station, and it confirmed that RAF life was the life for me. The seed sown a few years earlier in Ramsey began to germinate. The Air Cadets most definitely 'lit the fire' that school never did. In 1965 I attended my second camp, this time at RAF Manston, in Kent, a former Battle of Britain fighter station with a Spitfire at the Main Gate, and it was here that I had my first flight in an RAF Chipmunk. While at camp I found out that I had not done well during my crucial school examinations, and had also failed Maths, so essential for entrance to the RAF. Such was the price of being a 'minimum worker', but I still hadn't learnt my lesson. In December 1965 I resat three of my examinations, and failed them all! My careers' master told me to forget my ambition to join the RAF as an officer; it simply would never happen.

However, cadet life provided me with the excitement that I thrived on. We held regular navigation exercises, some overnight, and I also began gliding at RAF Catterick, Yorkshire, and at RAF Ouston in Northumberland. By now I was a cadet corporal, and in May 1966 I embarked on a Gliding Scholarship Course at RAF Ouston, flying two types of open-cockpit glider, the tandem-seat Kirkby Cadet Mark III and the side by side Sedburgh.

For take-off the gliders were attached to a winch cable and at a given signal: 'take up slack' followed by 'haul out', a powerful engine at the other end of the grass strip wound in the cable at great speed, hauling the glider into the air. We would rarely achieve more than 1,000 feet and then it was a matter of turning downwind before making the finals turn and landing. Each flight usually lasted only two or three minutes. The course, over four or five consecutive weekends, culminated in three solo flights, and the award of those coveted gliding 'wings'.

I frightened myself silly on my first solo as the absence of my 16-stone instructor made an incredible difference to the launch height. When I made the finals turn I was much higher than I had ever been before, and completely forgot what to do in such circumstances. I simply put the nose down and hurtled earthwards. Luckily, I landed near the area known as the jet extension, out of sight of the instructors. I hit the ground hard, bounced, and finally landed heavily, but in one piece. Thankfully, none of the staff witnessed my awful arrival. When they drove up, I was very still and quiet, 'alone and palely loitering'.

Whether or not my instructor noticed my sickly pallor, I don't know, but I was told to stay in the cockpit, was towed back to the launch point and with a cheery 'don't land there again' ringing in my ears, off I went. My second solo was marginally better, and my third was almost acceptable. So that was it, I was 'winged' at last. That day, 26 June 1966, was the last time that I flew a glider until 2008, although it wasn't the only time that I ended up gliding; but that's another story.

In the summer of 1966, I thankfully passed mathematics, so my ambition, my sole ambition, was back on track, for the moment. I was also selected for an Overseas Camp at RAF Wildenrath in Germany. By then I was a cadet sergeant, and I applied for a flying scholarship. This was a highly sought after award which would result in a thirty-hour flying course and the award of cadet 'pilot's wings', a very rare brevet in those days. First, I had to attend the Officers and Aircrew Selection Centre at RAF Biggin Hill in Kent, for medical and aptitude testing lasting three days. RAF Biggin Hill: what a name, what a history, what a place to intensify my hopes and dreams. The tests were identical to those for selection as an RAF pilot. I was successful, much to my delight and that of my Squadron, as I was only the second cadet from Consett ever to receive such a coveted award.

My flying scholarship was scheduled to take place at Carlisle Airport during the Easter holidays of 1967, during which I would celebrate my eighteenth birthday. My paternal granddad paid an additional £40, a lot of money in those days, for five extra flying hours so that I could gain a Private Pilot's Licence.

There seemed little point in delaying my application for the RAF. In February 1967, I was invited back to Biggin Hill to repeat the earlier tests and to undergo the all-important leadership tests. My choices of branch were subject to some discussion as I had listed navigator as first choice, then pilot, followed by air traffic control, fighter control and RAF Regiment; I wanted a commission in the RAF above all things. At an early stage I was told that I had more aptitude for pilot training than for navigator and I was invited to reverse my first two choices, which I duly did. After that I had to wait a few weeks to hear the results.

Just before my course at Carlisle, I received a letter from the RAF saying 'No!'; I had failed the leadership tests. I was devastated! What on earth was I going to do now? I had no other 'strings to my bow'. It looked as if my careers' master had been right after all. So, what next? I couldn't go to university, as I was studying only two Advanced Level subjects (for university I needed three), and teaching held out no appeal whatsoever. But as my course at Carlisle was rapidly approaching, all of that could wait.

On 22 March 1967 I arrived at Carlisle Airport for a four-week residential course, living in a dormitory full of like-minded cadets from all over the UK. The course included intensive ground school and then thirty-five hours flying, mostly in Cessna 150 and Cessna 172 aircraft, but with one flight in an Auster to practice aerobatics and spinning. There were navigation sorties around the Solway Firth, and east toward Newcastle, flying over my home before landing at Sunderland Airport. Later I had a solo flight west, then south skirting the Lake District, to land at RAF Woodvale. On the way back I landed at Blackpool and parked outside the public viewing area before heading back to Carlisle. I felt ten feet tall and it probably showed!

I thoroughly enjoyed the flying and it convinced me that I should never have made navigator my first choice when I had applied for the RAF. Of course, with the RAF's rejection that was all over with. With my new 'wings' and a Private Pilot's Licence awarded at the age of eighteen, a few weeks before I passed my driving test, it was back home to reality and to thoughts of what to do next. Even an article in the local newspaper: 'Pilot Paul could fly before he could drive a car' – did little to lift my spirits.

*   *   *

I was accepted for a Town Planning Course at college, conditional on two passes at Advanced Level. Unbelievably, I still had not learnt the lesson about being a 'minimum worker' and passed only one. However, opportunities sometimes come unexpectedly, and I was contacted by a school friend who had had a similar lack of success, and asked if I would be interested in working for his uncle who had his own firm of estate agents. The pay would be poor, but the prospects were good. And I would get a firm's car. A firm's car! At eighteen years old! That sealed it for me, and for almost four years I would work in different offices throughout County Durham, primarily as a sales negotiator and valuer.

At the squadron, I had been promoted to cadet flight sergeant but follow-ing my rejection by the RAF my enthusiasm and previous motivation had been badly dented. There was also pressure from work where some saw my position as a cadet to be at odds with my 'adult' life. I left the Air Cadets on 4 April 1968, and it was a decision that I have always regretted. I was probably thinking more about thwarted ambition and damaged ego, than about what the Air Cadets had done for me. I had achieved a great deal and had grown up with a very real interest and, as the second most senior cadet on the squadron and one who had achieved so much, I should have stayed to pay back a little of what I had been given, by helping to develop the younger cadets. The Squadron Commander, Flight Lieutenant Jack Harwood, took it very well when I handed in my uniform, but I think that he was very dis-appointed. He was right to be so.

* * *

By the summer of 1969 I realized how wrong I had been to leave the Air Cadets, and I rejoined as a civilian instructor. As soon as I was twenty-one, I applied for a commission in the training branch of the RAF Volunteer Reserve and was successful, so from 11 August 1970 and for two nights each week, I was back in uniform as a pilot officer on 1409 Squadron. Within a few months I attended a week's Initial Administration Course at RAF Upwood in Huntingdonshire, where it came as a bit of a shock to be referred to by the regular RAF officers as 'Dad's Army'. After all, I was only twenty-one years old! Who was I meant to be – a modern day equivalent of Private Pike? Their superior attitude disappeared at breakfast one morning when one member of our course entered the dining room. Like me, he was a pilot officer, but there the likeness ended. He was Polish, wore an RAF pilot's brevet and three rows of medal ribbons. Few RAF officers in those days could boast a single medal.

To all outside appearances I was doing well. I was often running my own office, valuing houses and negotiating sales and mortgages, but I wasn't going anywhere, nor was I well paid. Unless I did something soon, that would be my future. On 28 November 1970, I applied once more for the RAF, some four years after my first application. This time being a pilot was very much my first choice. I was invited back to RAF Biggin Hill. Following the aptitude tests I was told that I had achieved the level required for pilot but, as I had undergone the tests previously, a weighting factor had been applied and I had not made the cut for pilot. I was offered navigator training instead, which I accepted, although I still had to pass the leadership tests which had been my undoing in 1967. In December I received the letter that I had hoped for: I was to commence officer training in February 1971. I was in!

A few days before I reported, as I arrived home from work, my granddad said that 'an air force fellah' had called to see me. My granddad wouldn't let him in the house and kept him at the front gate! I assumed that the visitor had been one of my colleagues from the Air Cadets, but I was wrong.

'He only had one eye', said my granddad, 'and he left you this card.'

The visitor was a navigator, the squadron leader in charge of the RAF Careers' Information Office in Newcastle. Turning over the card, it read, 'The RAF wants to know if you would like to be a pilot. I said "yes", please call me.'

Chapter 2

Per Ardua ad Astra, at Last

Officer Cadet Training Unit, RAF Henlow, 1971

I was directed to report to the Officer Cadet Training Unit, RAF Henlow, on Sunday 7 February 1971. At about 3.00pm, or 1500 hours as it was from now on, I arrived at Hitchin Railway Station along with a motley crew of young men, all dressed similarly in jackets and slacks, wearing shirts and ties, and trilby hats! We stood out I think. The trilby hat was an essential item of dress. How else could you salute an officer when you were in civilian clothes other than by raising one's hat? Until we were issued with our uniforms, this would be our daily 'garb' and the sight of dozens of young men being marched around Henlow in their trilbies must have raised many a wry smile from onlookers. There were some young women on the course too, but at least they didn't have to wear a trilby!

Eventually a 3-ton truck arrived and we climbed aboard. This was no easy task, as it only had a rope suspended from the roof, so it needed a degree of deft footwork and momentum to clamber aboard without completely losing one's composure, or trilby. Not for the last time, my cadet service came to the fore and I was soon seated comfortably looking down, probably for the last time, on those who still struggled below. The journey to Henlow took about thirty minutes and we were soon deposited outside one of the elderly and austere barrack blocks that were to be our home for the next four weeks.

I became Officer Cadet T.P. McDonald, a member of Black Squadron, which with Blue Squadron formed 246 Course. Those amongst us who had university degrees were student officers. My lack of a degree was significant as far as salary and rank were concerned, not that salary meant a great deal to me then, I was in. Even as an officer cadet, I was earning more than I had as a trainee surveyor.

A number of my colleagues had never been away from home before, not even for a night, and even living in four-man rooms came as a great shock to some. We lost our first 'voluntary withdrawal' the very next morning.

The sixteen week long course comprised of a preparatory course of four weeks, for those joining straight from 'Civvy Street', then a main course, when we were joined by airmen and airwomen hoping to be commissioned. My course doubled in size after four weeks, and the intake of such experience provided a real boost to those who had no real knowledge of service life. My Flight Commander, Flight Lieutenant 'Dickie' Lees, would be both our mentor and our judge, but it would be our RAF Regiment Drill Instructor, Sergeant Gosling, who would be crucial to the many things that we needed to master. Not only did he teach us 'square bashing', but he was responsible for discipline and gave us guidance on domestics, such as how to get the best crease into one's uniform (still the horrid 'Hairy Mary's' of my cadet days), how to 'bull' our boots, make a bed properly and a bed pack, and how to polish the linoleum floors. We would see Sergeant Gosling every day and despite his occasional fierce voice, we all quickly learned to respect him, and to like him too. Room inspections and kit inspections were regular and rigorous, but these held no fear for me as they were so similar to cadet life. Marching was also straightforward, but for some it was a nightmare. Rifle drill was new, and as for shooting, I had always been good at that. Most of all, I revelled in the lectures on RAF history.

There was lots of physical training and many of the facilities were across the road which divided the station. We usually double marched in 'ranks of three' to the gymnasium, passing the large factory-type sheds which had seen so much activity during Henlow's earliest days when aircraft and engines were being produced. It was in one of those sheds that Frank Whittle had worked on his jet engine in 1933. Henlow was in the original list of RAF stations when the RAF was formed in 1918 and it is one of only seven that remain open. By the 1930s, Henlow was the RAF's fourth largest station.

We soon underwent leadership tests and these became more and more challenging. A typical exercise involved getting a team across an area of 'shark-infested custard' using pine poles, ropes and oil drums. These exercises could be amusing unless it was 'your lead', but how you performed as a team member was often just as important. The inevitable tripod would be built, and for years afterwards whenever anyone was faced with a challenge, there would be a cry of 'build a tripod'. Map-reading and night exercises followed, all leading to the eight day, and six day Camps in the Stamford Military Training Area near Thetford in Norfolk, the same area that was often used to film scenes for *Dad's Army*.

The pressure was most definitely on during these camps. My lead came after 'cries for help' were reported from some miles away. I assembled my eleven colleagues and off we went at the double. After about three or four miles of alternate double and quick marching, we found our 'casualty', with both legs 'broken', at the bottom of a tree lined hollow, the sides of which were 'mined'. There just happened to be a few pine poles lying around, and some rope, so the inevitable tripod was quickly built. I lead some of my team to the bottom of the hollow, from tree to tree, and made an improvised stretcher. This was attached by rope, stretched high into a tree, then to our tripod at the top of the hollow. It was then a matter of hauling the stretcher upwards keeping it clear of the ground. It was great in theory and it almost worked, but as the stretcher moved ever closer to the top of the slope, the rope sagged lower and lower until, inevitably, it touched the ground only inches from the top.

That was the end of the exercise but not of my lead, as I had to get the flight to another location in good order. By then our spirits were low and, as it was a very hot day, most of us had removed our outer combat clothing. As everyone was so slow in getting ready I grew impatient trying to chivvy them along. Finally, all was ready, except one black scarf lay discarded on the ground. I asked everyone to check their kit. No one took a blind bit of notice! I raised my voice, becoming increasingly exasperated and told everyone two or three times to sort themselves out, all to no avail. Finally my equally exasperated Flight Commander intervened.

'McDonald', he said. 'It's yours!'

My lead had actually gone well and I felt no further pressure as we moved toward graduation. As each month passed we also moved barrack blocks, each with slightly better rooms, until finally we were accommodated in the Cadets' Mess. Being fitted for our uniforms – No. 1 Home Dress and No. 5 Mess Dress (Mess Kit) – certainly contributed to the feeling that we would make it, but not everyone did, with some being re-coursed to try again, more voluntary withdrawals, and some who didn't make the grade. It was a hard course and much too short. These days the officer training course, now at the RAF College Cranwell, lasts about twenty-eight weeks.

There was nothing in the syllabus that I found demanding but I struggled with a lack of confidence, and this was to be an issue, on and off, for years to come. Many of my colleagues had been educated at private schools which seemed to instil a self-confidence that I could never emulate. I was always conscious of my poor academic record, and my lack of sporting prowess. Many ex-airmen seemed to be very comfortable with who they were, whereas I was still unsure and concerned, perhaps overly so, about my northern working-class upbringing. When I first stepped into the Mess, I had stepped right out of my comfort zone. There were guidance notes of course, and a book by a retired group captain by the name of Stradling on service customs. It covered such vital things as how to have your name printed on visiting cards, and when you should call on the Station Commander's wife to 'leave one's card'. Not much help there then! I adopted the practice of watching and listening to others. We did have a 'practice' dining-in night so at least we could work out which wine glasses to use, and in which order to use the cutlery. I also learnt that sometimes what I felt on the inside was much less important than what I showed on the outside, and I developed a knack of displaying a calm exterior which sometimes masked a complete jelly.

On 24 June 1971 I was commissioned as an acting pilot officer. For the graduation parade, the junior courses had been assembled, while we formed up out of sight to be inspected for the very last time by Sergeant Gosling. Once he had completed this final and meticulous inspection he called us to attention, and then slowly looked at the assembled squadron. He then came very smartly to attention and saluted us. This was the first and only time that he had ever done that. He then turned and marched away; it was a very poignant moment, we never saw him again.

We were quickly marched on to the parade square to music played by the RAF Central Band. Our Reviewing Officer was Air Vice-Marshal Michael Beetham, later Marshal of the Royal Air Force Sir Michael Beetham. Later, we removed the white bands from our service dress hats and the white tabs from our lapels which had marked us out as officer cadets, or student officers, rather than officers. Now we were the real thing, apparently. For the aircrew candidates amongst us, we were embarking on a long road and it would take over two years before we made it to our first flying squadrons. Our numbers would be much diminished by then. And the years afterwards would take their toll too.

Academic Training Squadron, RAF Church Fenton, 1971

The pilot candidates amongst us soon converged on RAF Church Fenton in North Yorkshire for an Aviation Medicine Training Course. This would be followed by a Maths and Science course which preceded a thirty hour Elementary Flying Training course on the Chipmunk. As I held a Private Pilot's Licence, I was horrified to hear that I would miss the Chipmunk course and go straight to Basic Flying Training on the Jet Provost at RAF Leeming. I hadn't flown anything for four years and all I could see in front of me was an incredibly steep learning curve; I was not wrong.

It was tremendously exciting being fitted with flying kit; it felt as if we were 'real' pilots. We also experienced the ejection seat rig. Having strapped into a live ejection seat, but one with reduced cartridges, we ejected up a vertical ramp at great speed. It was very exhilarating, but the rig was withdrawn from use because of the back injuries it caused! We were issued with the new 'all-in-one' flying helmets which were so heavy that we were advised to wear them in our rooms to get used to the weight. What a sight we must have been, wondering around the corridors of the Mess, complete with helmet, oxygen mask, and visors down, thinking that we were fighter pilots!

I soon came down to earth with a thump when I began the maths and science course. The staff were horrified to learn of my struggles to get a very mediocre pass at mathematics, and that I had not studied physics at all. I struggled, in fact I was 'selected for further training'; in other words I was re-coursed. Thankfully, some one-on-one tuition did the trick.

I also experienced being Orderly Officer for the first time. Normally a straightforward duty lasting twenty-four hours, it involved saluting the RAF Ensign at dawn and dusk, and carrying out various key checks at the Guard-room. My stint had been going well until I arrived at the Guardroom at 2200 hours. Whilst there, a break-in at No. 2 Officers' Mess (which was locked at night) was reported, and the Orderly Sergeant, who seemed to know what he was about (they usually did!), set off with the Orderly Corporal to investigate saying, 'Best you come too Sir!'

Once inside the Mess, we headed toward the kitchens, where we could hear voices. The sergeant opened the door to find three people, all male, in civilian clothes making bacon and eggs. They had no right to be there so the sergeant promptly arrested them! I was merely an innocent bystander! When they duly gave 'name, rank and number', I realized that I was outranked! The motley crew were Royal Navy officers. I let the sergeant get on with it which, as I was to learn, was often a good thing to do. A report was duly made and all three were reprimanded by the Senior Naval Officer. Thankfully my time at Church Fenton was coming to an end, as I am sure the RN contingent planned something dire for me, and I had to watch my '6' for a few days longer. But this wasn't the end of the matter, although it would be twelve years before the subject came up again.

No. 3 Flying Training School, RAF Leeming, 1971–1972
I arrived at RAF Leeming in September 1971; it was a thriving station and had been since it first opened in 1940 as a bomber station. After the Second World War it became a night fighter base. There was a Meteor as 'gate guardian', and a Javelin in front of the Officers' Mess. Little did I realize that in four years, my front-line operational aircraft would be older than both and that in nine years I would be displaying a variant of the Meteor!

No. 3 Flying Training School was one of three Basic Flying Training Schools, the others being No. 1 Flying Training School at RAF Linton-on-Ouse, and the RAF College Cranwell. I was one of thirteen students, twelve RAF and one from the Royal Jordanian Air Force, on 51 Course, which would last for eleven months. On one of the senior courses was Steve Pepper; we would meet again as colleagues in the Tucano Simulator some thirty-seven years later. The course involved 135 flying hours to RAF 'wings' standard on the Jet Provost Mark 3 and the Mark 5. We would then be streamed to fast-jet, rotary or multi-engine Advanced Flying Training.

The course began with full-time groundschool and then 50/50 groundschool and flying. Once the exams were out of the way it was full-time flying. I surprised myself by only failing aerodynamics at the first attempt, but I was to find aircraft technical something of a struggle for the next thirty years!

My first flight was on 16 September and I loved it; even the underpowered Jet Provost Mark 3 was exhilarating. My first solo was from the Relief Landing Ground at RAF Dishforth on 10 November 1971. I didn't find the flying easy, especially at the beginning and struggled to keep pace with my colleagues, all of whom had benefited from thirty hours on the Chipmunk. I also tended to be inconsistent.

A lot of time was spent 'circuit-bashing', practicing take-offs and landings, sometimes at RAF Dishforth, or more often at RAF Topcliffe, where we would often detach for the day. Sometimes we would travel there in a 3-ton truck to meet the aircraft when they landed from their first sortie. Also on the truck would be our student record books, called RAF Form 5060, and despite being told never to look at them none of us could resist the temptation. I wish I hadn't looked at mine! I can still remember the comment, 'McDonald forgets one third of what he is shown.'

*   *   *

Heavy snow during the winter of 1971/2 resulted in our talents and skills as junior officers being put to slightly different use – with shovels helping to clear the main runway. Later our survival exercise saw us in the hills above Semer Water to the south of Wensleydale. There was lots of walking, map reading and survival shelters to be built using parachutes, but it was also great fun and culminated in a most effective 'beat-up' of our camp, by a Jet Provost swooping up and down the valley.

There was so much to learn: effects of controls, straight and level, climbing and descending, medium turns, steep turns, maximum rate turns, maximum possible rate turns, stalling, aerobatics, spinning, emergency handling, and of course circuits, lots and lots of circuits.

There were normal circuits, low-level circuits, flapless circuits and glide circuits, and then practice forced landings. Normal circuits were flown at 1,000 feet. After take-off the aircraft was accelerated to 140 knots and climbed to 500 feet. A normal circuit then involved a climbing turn using 45 degrees of bank to 1,000 feet and the aircraft was rolled out downwind on the reciprocal heading of the runway used for take-off. Drift had to be applied to the downwind heading and then the pre-landing checks were carried out with the undercarriage lowered and flap selected to the take-off position. Abeam the 300-foot point, which was a mile on the centreline of the runway, a 30-degree banked turn was initiated to roll out on the centreline maintaining 115 knots throughout. With full flap selected, the aircraft was pointed at the runway threshold and the rate of speed decay was controlled with the throttle to achieve a threshold speed of about 90 knots. All of this of course whilst making various radio calls and looking out, often for up to three other aircraft in the circuit. Low-level circuits were flown at 500 feet and glide circuits at 1,500 feet. Glide circuits were taught in order that we could develop the judgement necessary to be able to fly forced landings, landing without an engine, whether for practice or for real.

Over the next few weeks, I made steady, if slow progress and I cleared the first hurdle, the Spin and Aerobatics Test, on 14 February 1972.

The course included physical training and drill and there were graduation parades, in which everyone was involved, every two months. Survival training and dinghy drills also began to play an increasing part in our training and inevitably my weakness in the water was soon uncovered – I had never been able to swim. The dinghy drills themselves held no fear for me, not then or later, and I became quite adept at getting from the water into the single-man life raft that was fitted to our ejection seats. After a few swimming lessons I managed to achieve the very minimum of standards, called the 'Y' standard, which was one length of the pool anyway you like with no time limit. In those days that was judged sufficient; it wouldn't be good enough today.

The dinghy drills in Northallerton Swimming Baths were much enjoyed by the locals who would often watch us leaping into the pool in our flying suits wearing our life saving jackets. These jackets were referred to as 'Mae Wests' in those days, after the controversial American actress well known for her double entendres; she had other attributes too. Attached by a chord to the jacket were our single man life rafts which we inflated once in the water. The physical training instructors would take great delight in overturning our life rafts so that we could go through the whole process once more. After-wards, we would call at a café in the main street of Northallerton. We would be in uniform and the sight of RAF blue in many towns and villages in the early 1970s was entirely normal and welcomed. But things were changing, and the very real threat to UK service personnel from the IRA meant that we would rarely be seen in uniform in public for thirty years.

The mid-point of the course came with the Basic Handling Test which I passed on 18 April, two days after my twenty-third birthday. Then we moved onto the much more powerful Jet Provost Mark 5 which was capable of 300 knots at low-level. It had a pressurized cockpit and could reach 35,000 feet, which seemed to be incredibly high at the time. Soon we began advanced instrument flying, night flying, formation flying and more demanding low-level navigation. I began to perform rather better, but I was still inconsistent.

It was soon my turn for another spell as Orderly Officer. We always hoped during this duty that we would not have to deal with any defaulters, airmen who had been charged with some misdemeanour. It was a great relief when I was told that there weren't any defaulters on that particular day. So at 1800 hours it was a confident young acting pilot officer who strode purpose-fully to the Guardroom to impress the duty staff with how well he could check the key register. A young airwoman at the counter smiled as I came in. I recognized her as one of our flight line mechanics who regularly strapped us in to our ejection seats and met us when we taxied back, come rain, hail or snow. This particular girl was very attractive with striking auburn hair. But I had a job to do that evening, especially as I noticed that the Orderly Sergeant was none other than our Drill Sergeant. After checking the key register, I was just about to leave when he said to my great surprise, 'There's just the one defaulter, Sir!' He went quickly on, 'defaulter! attention!'

As I looked around in vain for some miscreant airman, to my horror, I realized that it was the young airwoman who came to attention.

'Outside,' shouted the sergeant, 'quick march, left, right, left, right'

With that the girl quickly marched out to the front of the Guardroom facing Station HQ, where the Orderly Sergeant announced, 'Defaulter ready for your inspection, Sir!'

How were you meant to inspect a girl? I did my very best and slowly looked her over. But I became increasingly embarrassed as I looked her up and down, at the front and sides and back. I thought that I had better say something otherwise it would look as if I was just staring at her, which of course I was.

'Why are you on defaulter's parade?' I said, in my most officer-like voice.

She instantly went bright red, and the sergeant coughed a couple of times before saying, 'She's been a naughty girl Sir.'

This was awful, and I desperately tried to think of something to recover the situation. I had an idea, find out what extra duties she had to undertake before reporting back to the Guardroom at 2200 hours. Well, that was the theory, but sadly the words that I heard coming out of my mouth were, 'And what are you doing tonight?'

She giggled. The sergeant closed his eyes momentarily before sighing deeply. He then about turned and slowly walked back to the Guardroom, shaking his head. I beat a rather hasty retreat to the Officers' Mess, a slightly less confident acting pilot officer.

*   *   *

Life in the Mess was pretty formal: after 1900 hours suits had to be worn on Mondays, Tuesdays and Thursday evenings; on Wednesday and Friday evenings we could relax a little and simply wear a jacket and tie! In those days we had a batman, not a personal one, but someone who looked after the rooms along one 'wing' of the accommodation. They would also bring a morning cup of tea.

'Happy Hours' from 1700 hours on Friday were rarely to be missed. Everything in the bar was charged to your Mess bill which had to be paid by the tenth of the subsequent month. It was a very serious offence not to pay your Mess bill on time, or worse still, to pay with a cheque which subsequently 'bounced'. If a Mess member was killed in an accident, his or her Mess bill was 'written off', to be paid by all Mess members. Therefore, on the evening of their death all drinks in the bar would be charged to their Mess bill. Over the next few years we all came to realize that this was a good way to say farewell, and also to come to terms with something that would never be very far away.

Dining-in nights were a regular feature of Mess life. The Mess was run by a senior officer called the President of the Mess Committee. This was a secondary duty that the incumbent would hold for six months. One of the President's duties was to preside at Dining-in Nights. The most junior officer dining would be appointed as Mr Vice and it was his task to call the diners to attention for the Loyal Toast. At the appointed time the Mess President would bang his gavel, stand up and announce, 'Mr Vice, the Queen'.

Mr Vice would stand and reply, 'Ladies and gentlemen, the Queen'.

At that point everyone would stand to attention, the National Anthem would often be played, and everyone would say, 'The Queen'.

Her Majesty would then be toasted. Mr Vice, often at his first dining-in night, would usually be sat next to more senior colleagues who would do their very best to ensure that his glass was never empty, this would sometimes have amusing consequences. At one dinner, after the Mess staff had cleared the tables, one of the doors to the kitchen had accidentally been left open and noise from the kitchen could be heard in the dining room. An increasingly irritated Mess President eventually banged his gavel, pointed at the offending door, and said, 'Mr Vice, the door!'

A slightly inebriated Mr Vice rose unsteadily to his feet and announced, 'Ladies and gentlemen, the door'.

Naturally, everyone responded by standing to attention and toasting the door!

A 'tradition' after dining-in nights at Leeming was to head off across the airfield to Londonderry Lodge, an all-night transport café often full of lorry drivers. What on earth they must have thought when this bunch of 'posers' pitched up in the early hours of the morning wearing Mess kit for bacon and eggs, doesn't really bear thinking about.

* * *

A lot of my early worries on the course had begun to disappear. Despite some inconsistency, and 'testitus', I had begun to find my feet and was growing increasingly confident, not only about graduating, but also about being selected for fast-jet training.

Soon the day of my Final Handling Test arrived, the culmination of the whole course. These tests all followed a similar format: a departure from Leeming to find a particular point either on the North Yorkshire Moors, or in the Dales, descend to 250 feet for ten minutes of low flying and navigation and then climb to medium level to demonstrate turns, stalling and aerobatics. Sometimes you would have to climb higher, up to 15,000 feet or more to demonstrate a spin and spin recovery. Then it was back to Leeming for circuits. Emergencies would be simulated, one of which would result in a Practice Forced Landing. All of this took place in a sortie that lasted barely an hour.

I was soon heading for the start point of the low-level route, which had been selected by the examiner. And then it all went wrong. I couldn't find it. It was a very small lake, more of a pond I would call it, but try as I might I couldn't find it. I went back and forward to no avail. My morale plummeted as I knew that a failure was guaranteed. After what seemed like an age, but was probably only a few minutes, the examiner suggested that we climb and continue with the rest of the sortie. I should have just got on with it, but I knew that the sortie was a 'fail' and I suggested that we return to base. Big mistake! The examiner insisted on carrying on. The rest of the trip was OK, not as good as I was capable of, but satisfactory. It was a fail of course, but I got 'taken apart' during the debrief by both the examiner and my instructor for having 'given up'. They were quite right too. Giving up was not in the tradition of being an RAF pilot.

I flew a remedial sortie before another test which went well. I would get my 'wings'. Then there was the aerobatics competition for which I was entered along with two others. I didn't win! A few days later I was selected for fast-jet advanced flying training on the Folland Gnat at No. 4 Flying Training School, RAF Valley, on the island of Anglesey in North Wales. Graduation and the Wings Parade soon followed. I was placed eighth out of the thirteen on my course. While I still had a long way to go to reach an operational squadron, it was a boyhood dream come true. Shortly afterwards I met Jacqueline (Jackie) and we soon began dating regularly.

In 2004, when our daughter Hannah, a RAF air traffic control officer, returned to RAF Northolt after her first operational deployment to Basrah in Iraq, she found a bottle of champagne waiting to welcome her back from the occupant of the adjoining room in the Officers' Mess; he was a Group Captain, my examiner of thirty-one years earlier.

With eight weeks to wait before my course I volunteered for a holding posting to one of those stations hosting an Air Cadet Camp in order to get some flying on the Chipmunk. RAF Upwood was only a mile or two from my aunt and uncle's home in Ramsey near Huntingdon. But some research on my part was lacking. I reported for duty at Upwood to find that there was no camp and no Chipmunks! I was to be attached to a unit called ELOS.

'What's ELOS?' I asked.

To my horror I found that it stood for English Language for Overseas Students. What on earth was I meant to do at an English Language School? Apparently, I was to talk to a course of six Kuwait Air Force pilots coming to the end of their language training and about to start another flying course before returning to Kuwait. They were all first lieutenants; I was a pilot officer (the equivalent of a second lieutenant), therefore their junior, with the shiniest, cleanest 'wings' in the world! My task was to cover the sort of flying language in use in the RAF such as phraseology and procedures. I got on well with them and at the end of my stay they took me out to a nightclub in Cambridge where they were welcomed as regulars! I never imagined for one minute that I might meet any of them again.

Aviation Medicine Training Centre, RAF North Luffenham, 1972

Before going to Valley, another visit to the Aviation Medicine Training Centre was necessary. The unit had now moved from Church Fenton to RAF North Luffenham, in Rutland. For most aircrew, North Luffenham was one of the

RAF's crossroads, and over the next twenty-five years, I visited there some seven or eight times as I changed aircraft types or completed refresher courses. These days, North Luffenham is an Army barracks on the very edge of Rutland Water, which was opened in 1976, but thankfully the nearby village of Edith Weston survived, along with its pub which provided a pleasant alternative to Mess routine.

The course covered oxygen systems, hypoxia, hyperventilation, decompression sickness and the like. In one of the decompression chambers we experienced an explosive decompression from 10,000 feet to 40,000 feet. The degree of discomfort depended very much on whether we had visited the Wheatsheaf the night before, and for how long. We also experienced hypoxia by being disconnected from our oxygen supply; seeing and experiencing the symptoms at first hand was interesting and useful.

After the three day course, we set off on the long drive to RAF Valley. During the last part of the journey, the road wound its way through the beautiful mountains of North Wales until it entered the A5 pass, a very steep sided part of the valley with almost vertical sides. At one point the pass bends to the right through 90 degrees before dropping down toward the coast. I would follow this route often in the months ahead, but not by car.

No. 4 Flying Training School, RAF Valley, 1972–1973
RAF Valley was untypical of many RAF airfields: the airfield and the main working area was to the west and adjoined the sand dunes, whereas all of the accommodation was further inland, separated from the station. The Officers' Mess, or Alcatraz as we called it, stood out stark and white, an unattractive three storey 1960s building. Still, we were not there to admire the architecture.

The station originally opened in 1941 as RAF Rhosneigr after the village immediately to the south; it was re-named RAF Valley on 5 April 1941. For the next two years it was a fighter station, but by 1943, with enemy air activity over the western UK greatly diminished, RAF Valley became a terminal point for transatlantic flights by American aircraft which came in ever-increasing numbers. In 1951, RAF Valley became one of the RAF's principal flying training stations.

* * *

Our twelve-strong course was made up of graduates from Leeming, Linton-on-Ouse, and Cranwell, all joining No. 4 Flying Training School which had four flying squadrons: 1, 2 and Standards Squadron all flew the Folland Gnat, whereas 3 Squadron operated the Hawker Hunter from the western side of the airfield next to the sand dunes. There was also a flight of Whirlwind Search and Rescue helicopters from 22 Squadron. Within a few weeks, I would be picked up by one of these following an emergency landing.

Frequent visits by Lightnings, Phantoms and Harriers caused us to gaze enviously, and hope. However, it would be a few weeks before our first trips after the inevitable groundschool, learning about an aircraft that was far more complex than the Jet Provost. There was also a flight simulator, so our various checks and drills and many of the sortie profiles could be practiced long before we got airborne. Most checks had to be learnt by heart and often a mnemonic would be used to help remember them. I only flew the Gnat for about eighty hours but, some thirty-seven years later, I can still remember the mnemonic for a hydraulic failure. The drill had to be completed quickly and accurately if the aircraft was to remain flyable.

The Gnat was a complicated aeroplane. It was also tiny, you could almost step into it from ground level, but it was very fast and could achieve over Mach 1 in a slight dive. Low-level navigation was flown at 420 knots, but 500 knots could easily be attained at low-level. For the moment, all we could do was watch longingly from outside groundschool during our coffee breaks where, as usual, there were examinations and where, as usual, I failed one at the first attempt. Soon we were on 2 Squadron for our first flights in a fast-jet.

*   *   *

Our first ever 'sea drill' involved half of our course being taken out beyond Holyhead Harbour by an RAF Marine Craft Unit launch. We were all wearing our 'Mae Wests' with our dinghies attached; we strapped into a parachute harness and then jumped off the back of the launch, sometimes with a little help. The launch was travelling at speed and we were dragged behind to simulate having ejected and were being dragged by the parachute. Then it was a matter of releasing the parachute harness, hauling in and inflating the single-man life raft, and then clambering aboard. After about an hour a 22 Squadron Whirlwind arrived to winch us up; we all tried desperately to attract the attention of the crew in order to be first to be picked up, as it wasn't exactly warm. We were then lowered back onto the launch before returning to Holyhead, having been fortified with a rum ration to brighten up a cold November day.

The rest of our course were scheduled for the following week, so we all 'over-egged' events to try and put them off. Not that we needed to; when the Whirlwind arrived to pick them up, its engine failed and it crashed into the sea! The crew leapt out just before the helicopter sank into deep water! Our colleagues were aghast. Another helicopter was duly scrambled to pick up the first crew, but our colleagues were left to be picked up in slow time by the launch. So it was a much longer afternoon, but their stories were far more interesting than ours.

Air-sea rescue from Valley had not always been straightforward. In August 1942 an RAF Blackburn Botha force-landed in rough sea off Rhosneigr beach. The crew sadly drowned along with eleven other people, including airmen from RAF Valley, who attempted to rescue the crew. Two young boys from

Rhosneigr put to sea in a sailing dinghy in an effort to reach the crew but their dinghy capsized. The boys were fortunately rescued by spectators from the beach who roped themselves together and waded out to them. For their bravery the two boys were awarded the George Cross.

* * *

We soon met the senior course who seemed to be so confident and knowledgeable. We asked three questions, the same three questions that are still asked on RAF pilot training courses, two are 'public' and one was kept private: 'What is the "chop" rate?', 'Who is the instructor to avoid at all costs?', and the one question you kept to yourself 'Who is the "natural pilot" amongst us?'

The chop rate, or failure rate, at Valley was high, about 40 per cent, and our course would be no exception. And who was the instructor to avoid at all costs? Well, that was easy; it was one who I would be allocated to of course! And as for the last question, looking back what a silly question that was. What on earth was 'natural' about what we were trying to do? While some people took to certain aspects of flying more quickly than others, over the years I began to realize that there was no such thing as a 'natural'. It was all about hard work and perseverance. Student pilots still wonder about the answer and hope that they might be the one.

* * *

We were issued with a cumbersome immersion suit which everyone called a 'goon suit'. This was a bulky outer garment with rubber neck and wrist seals and rubber socks. It was made of ventile cloth which allowed air to flow through but became waterproof when wet. We wore these during winter because survival time in the water following an ejection was only a matter of minutes if not properly dressed. We also wore white long-sleeved vests and long-johns, thick aircrew socks, a green roll-necked aircrew shirt, anti-G trousers (which inflated when pulling G), and finally, a green woollen aircrew jumper, all under the immersion suit. Add to that the 'Mae West', aircrew gloves and a flying helmet, and the young warrior was ready to fly. That was just as well, as he certainly couldn't walk very far wearing that lot!

My first flight was on 4 December 1972, but it was my second a few days later that has long been fixed in my memory. During a stalling exercise when I selected the undercarriage down the nose wheel indicated red, meaning that it was unlocked. The instructor calmly said, 'Well, if we can't get it to lock down, we won't be landing.'

I distinctly remember thinking what did he mean? How would we get down if we weren't going to land? Oh, my word! He meant that we would eject! On my second trip! The Gnat had a very narrow undercarriage and many instructors considered an attempted landing with one or more of the wheels unlocked to be too risky. Thankfully, we got the nose wheel to lock down properly, but it was quite an introduction to the Gnat.

*   *   *

During a sortie with a different instructor, after completing general handling above Snowdonia, he took control and we quickly descended to low-level. We entered the A5 valley from the south flying very low and very fast. It was very exhilarating as, unlike the Jet Provost where the instructor sat next to you, the Gnat instructor was completely out of sight sitting behind. All you had was the nose of the aircraft in front and the thin fuselage on either side. As we approached the 90-degree turn to the right to follow the A5 pass, the instructor descended further and accelerated. We were now very low indeed. I began to look to the right to anticipate the turn when, without warning, the instructor turned the aircraft left, towards the vertical face of the valley wall! He then continued to roll the aircraft left, upside down, until he had completed a 270-degree roll and was now facing the direction that the valley turned. Such a manoeuvre is called a Derry Turn and it is often included as part of an aerobatics sequence; it is never flown whilst practicing low flying. I have to admit that my horror at what the instructor did has grown over the years; at the time, I have to admit that it had been rather exciting.

A few days later I flew with a different instructor to practice maximum rate possible turns. Physically these were very demanding and involved descending from medium level in a very tight spiral, accelerating all the time with the G increasing, up to the aircraft limit of 6G. Even with my anti-G suit inflating around my legs and tummy, I had to brace very hard to avoid greying out (losing vision), and blacking out (losing consciousness). At the end of one of these turns we were at about 5,000 feet when I rolled the wings level and applied full power. It was then automatic to complete a full power check of RPM, jet pipe temperature and oil pressure. But there was something wrong. The engine wouldn't accelerate beyond 58 per cent RPM with full throttle; we should have been able to get 100 per cent. Try as we might we couldn't get any more power. We could maintain straight and level flight but we could not climb; if we turned, which we had to, we lost even more height. We were south of Snowdonia and couldn't get over the mountains so Valley was out of the question. We made a distress call, a PAN call, on Guard the emergency UHF frequency (243.0), and requested an emergency landing at RAF Llanbedr on the west coast, next to Cardigan Bay. The forced landing pattern was immaculately flown by my instructor and a 22 Squadron Whirlwind arrived soon afterwards. I thoroughly enjoyed the unexpected flight back to Valley, sitting on the floor of the helicopter with my legs dangling out of the open door watching the world go by. And the whole experience was well worth a beer in the bar that evening.

*   *   *

A lot of time up to first solo was spent practicing take-offs and landings. We already knew never to press on with a poor approach but to overshoot and try it again. On another dual sortie, I had completed general handling before returning to base at low-level. The instructor told me to fly a final low-level circuit to land, but my final approach was poor and I overshot. He immediately took control, flew a very tight 360-degree turn and landed. As we taxied back to dispersal the engine stopped, we had run out of fuel.

I went solo on time but my performance became increasingly erratic. It was 'closed book' reporting so I never had a real understanding of how I was actually doing, but I knew that my marks were inconsistent.

The one thing that I disliked about the manner of teaching, and testing, was the habit of many instructors not to say anything about the sortie until the sortie debrief and this often after a long wait. It would take at least twenty minutes to taxi back to the flight line, shut down, hand the aircraft over to the engineers and walk back to flying clothing. Then change out off the uncomfortable goon suits before going upstairs to make tea or coffee, including one for the instructor, and then hang about in the Operations Room until the instructor deigned to come back and find a briefing room for a 'chat'. This process before you actually found out how you had done could take an hour, and I hated it.

The all-important Progress Check concentrated on general handling and practice emergencies. I thought that mine had been OK, not brilliant, but OK. The sortie debrief began well, but then the examiner focused on some aspects that he didn't like. I thought that I had flown them in the way in which I had been taught but he didn't like them, and said that they were wrong; he then announced that I had failed! I was stunned.

Normally after a test failure, the student is placed on 'Review', given an instructor change, and a remedial package normally of three sorties before a re-test. To my relief, I was told afterwards that this was deemed to be a 'technical' failure and that I would not be placed on Review. So a quick re-test followed two days later, which I passed. I had lived to fight another day.

*   *   *

My instrument rating test soon followed. We wore a special hood for instrument flying attached to our helmet so that we could only see the instrument panel. A typical rating test began with an instrument take-off and climb, climbing turns, a practice diversion to another airfield for a self-positioned instrument landing system (ILS) approach using the Gnat's offset computer, an overshoot and climb to return to base, steep turns, recoveries from unusual positions, and then an approach using a tactical air navigation beacon (TACAN), for a precision approach radar (PAR) to land. It was a very demanding sortie and could last up to an hour and a half.

Instrument Rating Tests were all flown with instructors known as Instrument Rating Examiners. For my test the practice diversion was to Warton in

Lancashire. When I got there I was meant to use the Gnat's offset computer to fly toward the extended centreline of the runway and then intercept a radio signal known as the localizer. Then, when established on the localizer, home in toward the runway until the correct glide path was achieved, indicated by another type of radio signal. At that point, the localizer and glide path are followed until about one mile from the runway so that a visual landing could then be made. My problem was that not only did I fail to intercept the localizer, I never even found it! Not even a fleeting glimpse! So there was no way that I could complete the approach. Without the ILS, the test would be an automatic fail. Oh dear! I had at least learnt from my previous mistake and I did not give up! But my morale plummeted into my boots and I knew that there could only be one possible outcome. The examiner said that it was the worst Instrument Rating Test that he had ever flown with anyone throughout his career! It was quite a notable first then!

I was placed on Review, often a precursor to suspension from training. I was also given an instructor change and three additional remedial sorties before a re-test, known by everyone as a 'chop-ride'. Another failed test would mean withdrawal from fast-jet pilot training, but I wouldn't be the first of my course to go, we had already lost four out of twelve.

My new instructor, an experienced and well-regarded A2 Qualified Flying Instructor, immediately set to work to get me back on track. An A2 category is awarded by the Central Flying School and recognizes that the instructor is 'an above the average pilot and instructor'. But I was still erratic and even failed one of the three remedial sorties, which was almost unheard of.

My chances of passing the re-test were marginal at best and my suspension was considered to be a near certainty. I actually felt the same way. Although I didn't know it at the time my Flight Commander had completed my suspension paperwork, such was his certainty about my chances. All that was needed would be my Squadron Commander's signature and it would be all over. My re-test could well be my last sortie in the Gnat, my last ever sortie in a fast-jet.

The test profile was as before but the practice diversion was to RAF Pershore near Gloucester. I had never worked so hard in an aircraft. At the end of the sortie, as usual, nothing was said as I trooped behind my examiner back to the squadron. I then hung about waiting to here the news. Eventually he summoned me for the sortie debrief. Things did not look good. He looked at me sombrely and then immediately looked out of the window saying, 'No! … No! … No!'

He paused, looked at the papers on his desk, and looked outside again, before saying, 'No! … No! … No!'

That was it then, I feared the worst. Then he said, 'No, there is no way that I can fail you on that'. He paused for a while before going on, 'it's not a good pass, but it is a pass'.

I was speechless. What a way to find out that I hadn't been 'chopped' after all! So I lived again to fight another day, just.

From then onwards I concentrated on the applied aspects of flying the Gnat: low-level navigation, night flying, formation flying, and advanced general handling. I began to enjoy it much more, especially the low flying. I certainly wasn't a 'star' but I was holding my own and I had begun to respect my new instructor a great deal.

*   *   *

One of the RAF aircrew 'bibles' is the Low Flying Handbook, which amongst many other things included details of all areas that had to be avoided by low flying aircraft. New avoidances and sensitive areas were also briefed at the daily meteorological briefing. During my course, the same place was mentioned every day but not the reason why it had to be avoided. I eventually found out, and it proves that the RAF does have a heart. The location was a farm that was frequently over flown much to the annoyance of the farmer. He felt that the aircraft were often too low, too noisy, and that his complaints were always ignored. So one day he got out his ladder, a bucket of whitewash and a brush and climbed up onto the roof of his barn to paint in huge letters the words *'PISS OFF BIGGLES'*

Unfortunately his action did not have the intended result. Soon an RAF pilot spotted the sign, so he told all of his mates and they came and had a look too. Within days RAF aircraft from all over the UK, and from Germany, were altering their routes to overfly the farm to have a look. The exasperated farmer had no choice but to climb back up his ladder, with a fresh bucket of whitewash and repaint the roof.

By then the RAF Police had heard of the story and they called to talk to the farmer. They explained how difficult it was for a layman to estimate accurately the height and speed of a fast-jet flashing across the skyline. Right in the middle of the interview all conversation was drowned by the sound of an aircraft and everyone ducked as an aircraft flew overhead very, very low, and very, very fast. So from that day on, the RAF ensured that this farm was subject to a permanent avoidance by RAF aircraft.

*   *   *

We all had our hopes and dreams of the type of aircraft we would like to fly if we passed the course and progressed onto the next stage of fast-jet pilot training which was the Tactical Weapons Unit (TWU) at RAF Chivenor, flying the famous Hawker Hunter. The TWU course was very demanding and the staff had a harsh reputation. I wanted to fly the Buccaneer but I was also a realist: I knew that I had little chance of success at Chivenor, I had simply been too inconsistent and it had taken me far too long to settle down on the Gnat.

On the evening before our postings were decided by the rather poorly named Role Disposal Board, there was a knock on the door of my room in the Officers' Mess. It was my instructor. There had been a staff meeting earlier to agree recommendations for our future. He was uncomfortable, so I broke the ice by saying that I knew I was unlikely to get very far on the Hunter. He seemed relieved and explained that that was his conclusion too. He said that I would be recommended for Photo-Reconnaissance (PR) Canberras, although it was rare for first-tourists to be posted to Recce Canberras. The last first tour pilot to be posted to Recce Canberras had been on my senior course both at Valley and Leeming. He was killed in a Canberra PR9 crash at RAF Wyton in 1977.

If there were no PR slots for me, I could go to Target Facilities Canberras, providing there were places. While towing targets was hardly an aspiration of mine, at least the Canberra was a single-pilot aircraft. If there were no Canberra places, then I would be off to the Vulcan as a co-pilot. Despite the Vulcan being a magnificent aircraft, the prospect of a tour as a co-pilot for all aspiring fast-jet pilots was pretty dire. But beggars can't be choosers. The next twenty-four hours passed very slowly but then I got the news that I had hoped for: Canberras, not photo-recce, but target facilities.

In March I passed my Final Handling Test achieving the highest mark on my course. It was a nice way to finish but it was far too late to change the outcome for me, not that I would have wished for a change. My new instructor had judged me right; I needed time to consolidate before being considered again as a potential fast-jet pilot. Little did I realize that I would have to wait ten years.

*   *   *

I graduated from No. 4 Flying Training School in early April 1973. Of the twelve budding fighter pilots who had begun the course so enthusiastically six months earlier, there were only seven of us left, five having been 'chopped'. Of those seven, two went to Canberras, one became a first-tour instructor ('creamed-off' as it was known), and the other four went to the Tactical Weapons Unit (TWU). Of those four, only two actually made it to the fast-jet front line; not the greatest of success rates, but no one had ever said that life as an RAF fighter pilot would be easy. As far as careers were concerned, one other on the course reached the rank of squadron leader.

*   *   *

After some leave and a four-week outdoor activities and survival course at Grantown-on-Spey, I was told to report to 3 Squadron at Valley for a twenty-five hour refresher course. Surely that was a mistake? They operated the Hunter.

The Hunter T7 had side-by-side seats and dual controls, whereas the single-seat Hunter F6 was very powerful, with about 50 per cent more power than the T7; it could almost reach the speed of sound at low-level. The Squadron Commander was Squadron Leader Etheridge and I flew my second sortie with him. Sadly, he and his Jordanian student were killed in an accident at RAF Shawbury on 2 November 1973.

I thoroughly enjoyed the Hunter and felt under much less pressure than I had felt on the main course. When it came to my first solo on the Hunter F6 on 11 June, I vividly recall the short briefing I received from the authorizing officer, 'Make sure that you know where the air speed indicator is before you release the brakes!'

It was very good advice! When I selected full power there was an almighty roar from behind me, and as soon as I released the brakes the aircraft shot forward and accelerated very quickly. At 500 feet I had to turn hard to continue the climb and up I went at 420 knots which was an incredible speed for the climb.

My final sorties on the Hunter involved a dual low-level land-away and overnight stop at RAF Chivenor. Afterwards the instructor said everything had been fine, there were just a couple of points that I needed to remember before starting my course at Chivenor.

'But I'm not going to Chivenor,' I said, 'I'm going to Cottesmore.'

'Why are you going to Cottesmore?' he asked.

'For the Canberra operational conversion course,' I replied.

'So why are you doing a Hunter refresher course?' he asked.

It was then I discovered that a mistake had been made and that I should have been sent for a refresher course on the Jet Provost (JP), at RAF Manby! But I didn't care, I was now qualified on the world famous Hawker Hunter, an achievement that would become increasingly rare as this wonderful aircraft was gradually withdrawn from service.

Chapter 3

Per Diem Per Noctem

No. 231 Operational Conversion Unit (OCU), RAF Cottesmore, 1973

In June Jackie and I got engaged. I was also promoted to flying officer and, after a short visit to the Aviation Medical Training Centre at RAF North Luffenham, I joined 231 Operational Conversion Unit (OCU) at RAF Cottesmore, near Stamford.

Originally an RAF airfield, its aircraft were moved to RAF Market Harborough in 1943. This was to make way for the USAAF, whose transport aircraft had their HQ in Exton Hall adjoining the delightful village of Exton with its village green and old coaching inn. The US 82nd Airborne Division soon became familiar with Cottesmore, and on 5 June 1944 a total of seventy-two Cottesmore aircraft dropped the 82nd near Sainte-Mère-Église in Normandy. Cottesmore was also used during Operation Market Garden, the ill-fated Arnhem operation. In the 1950s it became a Canberra base and later a home to Victor and Vulcan bombers before the Canberras returned. By 1973 it had three Canberra squadrons and an Argosy squadron.

In 1973 the Officers' Mess was crammed, and my course lived in tiny rooms in a wooden hut, about 200 yards from the Mess. My Flight Commander was my former Henlow Flight Commander, Dickie Lees. During groundschool the reality of our chosen careers struck home. A lecture from one of the staff navigators was interrupted and he was told that he was required to fly that night replacing a navigator who had reported sick. That evening the news spread that a Canberra had crashed and the crew had ejected. Our lecturer had been taken to hospital but his pilot had been killed. During a night simulated asymmetric overshoot, control had been lost and although the crew ejected, by the time the pilot's ejection seat operated, the aircraft was already rolling fast and was almost inverted; there was insufficient height for his parachute to deploy. The navigator thankfully only suffered compression fractures of the spine which were typical injuries caused by the older type of ejection seat fitted to the Canberra.

* * *

Simulated asymmetric flying is when one engine, referred to as the 'dead engine', is throttled back to flight idle; the 'live engine' is then used to control the aircraft's speed. Between 1950 and the mid-1970s, on average, one Canberra fatal accident occurred each year whilst the crew were simulating flying on one engine. Only six months before the Canberra was finally withdrawn from service in 2002, two pilots (both former instructors at Linton) were killed at RAF Marham following simulated asymmetric flying.

With the wing-mounted nature of the Canberra's engines, when only one engine is in use, control of the aircraft is retained by pushing the rudder toward the 'live engine' to keep the aircraft in balance; this is vital. The more power that is applied to the 'live engine', the greater the amount of rudder needed to maintain balance. However, there is insufficient rudder authority if the 'live engine' is at, or close to, full power. If too much power is applied, or it is applied too quickly, and this can easily be done during an asymmetric overshoot, rudder authority can be lost and the nose of the aircraft will yaw rapidly toward the 'dead engine'. As a result, more lift is produced by the wing which is yawing forward which forces that wing to lift upwards, causing the aircraft to roll toward the 'dead engine'. During the roll, the nose drops and effective control is lost. This can occur very quickly and, if it happens close to the ground, there is rarely sufficient height to recover. I would spend a lot of time thinking about, talking about, and practicing asymmetric flying during the next five years and I would also have some anxious moments doing it 'for real'.

The Canberra's Rolls Royce engines were robust but they were old technology. They did not have any acceleration control to make sure that both engines accelerated at the same rate. Moving the throttles from flight idle to mid-power required finesse, but once at mid-power, the throttles could then be moved more quickly. Because of this we were only allowed to complete a roller, or touch and go, in the dual control T4 with a Qualified Flying Instructor as aircraft captain in the right-hand seat. When in the other marks of Canberra, all approaches, even on two engines, had to be to land or overshoot.

Nevertheless, the Canberra was a lovely aircraft to fly and it had been brilliant in its day. It first flew in 1949, the year of my birth, and when it was introduced into frontline service it heralded a new generation of bomber aircraft. Throughout the 1950s and 1960s many variants equipped dozens of squadrons, twenty-two within the UK alone, and it had been exported to many other countries. By the 1970s, most had been withdrawn from the RAF's frontline, and by 1973 only two PR squadrons remained in frontline service: 39 Squadron at RAF Wyton near Huntingdon, and XIII Squadron at RAF Luqa in Malta. The remaining five squadrons were second-line squadrons which flew training and support missions.

* * *

My instructor for the majority of the course was one of the RAF's characters – Flight Lieutenant Mike Dineen. Tall, sporting a huge handlebar moustache, he had a very quick sense of humour. On one sortie, as we were returning to Cottesmore weaving our way around some quite large thunderclouds, the air traffic controller, trying to be helpful, suggested, 'You might wish to hold off before landing as there is a shower down here.'

Quick as a flash, Mike replied, 'That's true!' There was a deathly silence from air traffic control.

The first sorties on the conversion course were flown in the dual-control T4 which had two pilot's ejection seats side by side and one seat behind for the navigator. Thereafter, apart from test sorties, all flying was in the Canberra B2 which also had three ejection seats, one for the pilot, and two others behind, side by side for one or two navigators.

The course was straightforward, even asymmetric flying was fine, providing that you remembered the basics and 'kept your eye on the ball' to keep the aircraft in balance. The ball is on the turn and slip indicator and if it moves out to one side the aircraft is not in balance and is beginning to slip; the further the ball moves the greater the rate of slip, and it is an indication that control of the aircraft may about to be lost if flying on one engine; whilst asymmetric, it was essential to keep the ball in, or very close to, the middle. We practiced the technique often and also practiced engine failures after take-off and engine failures during the final approach. The only thing that we were not allowed to practice, because of the earlier accident, was asymmetric flying at night. Typically, the first time that I would experience asymmetric flying for real was not long in coming and, of course, it would be at night.

As we approached the end of the course in October, our postings were announced; I was to go to 7 Squadron at RAF St Mawgan in Cornwall.

No. 7 Squadron, RAF St Mawgan, 1973–1975
RAF St Mawgan was originally opened as a civilian airfield in 1933. It was requisitioned at the outbreak of the Second World War and named RAF Trebelzue, before being renamed in 1943 and taken over by the USAAF. In 1951 it reopened as an RAF Coastal Command base used for maritime reconnaissance using Lancaster and Shackleton aircraft. In 1971, it became the home of the new-into-service Nimrods, which were soon joined by 18 Group's only Canberra squadron, 7 Squadron, operating three variants of the Canberra: the B2, TT18 and T4. The squadron's motto was *Per Diem, Per Noctem* – By Day, By Night.

The squadron was commanded by a wing commander navigator, and had two flight commanders, both squadron leader pilots, and two Qualified Flying Instructors, one of whom was the Training Officer. It had thirty-six aircrew officers: eighteen pilots and eighteen navigators, although we did not operate as constituted crews. Many of the navigators were experienced on the Canberra but few of the pilots, who were a mix of first-tourists like me, or former V-Force co-pilots. Unusually at the time, all of our ground crew were civilians, provided by Airwork Services Limited.

Our role was to act as targets, or to provide targets, for the RN, the Army and the RAF Regiment. As silent targets we primarily used the Canberra B2 and flew a variety of profiles in order to be tracked by radar. The Canberra TT18 was fitted with a winch beneath each wing, from which we could deploy either a sleeve-type target on a 5,000-foot cable for live surface gunnery practice, or a Rushton target on a 2,400-foot cable as a target primarily for ground-to-air missiles. Only very occasionally did we have to remind the gunners that we towed the target, we didn't push it!

The missiles used against our Rushton targets were the RN Sea Cat or the British Army or RAF Regiment Rapier. I soon got used to the language of our type of work: Wembury Sleeve, Portland Rushton, Manorbier Silent and the like. The first word identified the range in which we worked and the second described the type of target being towed; with no target, we were 'silent'. The ranges were normally permanently active danger areas that all aircraft were required to avoid, as, when we were towing, our manoeuvrability was limited. However, on one of my early sorties in Wembury Range south of Plymouth, just as the RN commenced firing live 4.5 inch shells at our target, a Chipmunk aircraft flew directly over us, missing us by only a few hundred feet.

Much of the flying was routine, but at least I was building up important flying hours and gaining experience. Some sorties were more demanding, notably the Templeton Silent in South Wales where we flew pair's attack sorties at low-level. For Rapier firing, the Rushton target had to be flown at 500 feet above the sea. This meant that the aircraft had to fly at about 2,400 feet, as the cable drooped down to the target. If we turned, the cable would droop even more and the Rushton would descend, so it was important to climb at a particular rate whilst turning to keep the Rushton at a constant height. If we got it wrong, the Rushton would hit the water and both it and the cable would be lost. At the time, each Rushton cost about £12,000 and the cable was £2 per foot. So get it slightly wrong and £36,000 worth of equipment was lost.

I arrived on 17 October 1973 and my first trip was the following day. Thankfully, it was a little less exciting than that of one of the squadron's first tour navigators.

On his first day he was crewed with one of the experienced pilots for an air test on an aircraft that had just undergone lengthy servicing. An important part of the flight test was to check the critical speed of the aircraft using each engine in turn. This involved identifying the speed below which control would be lost when flying on one engine at full power. The speed had to be within set limits. For the test, the aircraft was flown as low as possible but high enough to allow for a safe recovery. During this particular check a failure occurred within the latch mechanism of the rudder and it jammed at full deflection. The aircraft yawed violently and rolled rapidly, descending toward the sea as the pilot desperately tried to regain control.

He stopped the descent only a few hundred feet above the sea by using different power settings on each engine. He then discovered that some of his trim controls were working in the opposite sense. While he gently regained height he had a great deal of difficulty in turning the aircraft and headed off into the Bristol Channel with his wings near vertical. Another aircraft, flown by the Training Officer, was vectored towards him and when he saw the aircraft's plight he suggested that the crew should abandon the aircraft. The pilot felt sure that he could recover the aircraft and by experimenting with his engines he was able to turn the aircraft around and head back to St Mawgan.

However, a safe landing was far from assured. Brake pressure was delivered to each wheel by using the rudder; with the rudder jammed, all of the braking would be on one wheel only so the aircraft could not be kept on the runway. The undercarriage would need to be retracted once the aircraft was on the ground and this could be hazardous. Canberra ejection seats had a limited capability on the ground; unlike the rocket seats fitted to more modern aircraft, the minimum speed for a safe ejection at ground level was 90 knots. So once the undercarriage was retracted, ejection would not be a safe option. It was agreed that the navigator, on his first trip, would eject and the pilot would bring the aircraft in on his own. The navigator's ejection was straightforward; he was unhurt, and walked to a nearby road where he waved down a passing car. He explained to the elderly lady driver that he was an RAF officer who had just parachuted from his aircraft and could she possibly give him a lift to St Mawgan, or to a phone box so that he could call the police? She declined and drove off at speed!

Meanwhile, the pilot flew a textbook approach and landing, but as expected, as soon as he tried to slow the aircraft down, it swung off the runway at high speed and onto the grass. He retracted the undercarriage and the aircraft sunk onto the grass and slewed around. It was a magnificent piece of flying from start to finish and the pilot was awarded a well deserved Air Force Cross for gallantry.

*   *   *

On most days, within fifteen minutes of morning briefing, there would be one or two bridge schools going in the crewroom and I soon learnt the basics. The Boss wasn't too keen though, and he soon banned playing cards from the crewroom. That was quite a blow!

I was introduced to secondary duties by being put in charge of squadron rations. This was the irksome duty of trying to make sure that there was something available to eat in the crewroom for those crews airborne at mealtimes. What tended to happen was that those who weren't due to fly scoffed the food. I vowed to try and put a stop to that. I discovered what the guys thought of my approach when I arrived home just before Christmas 1973 to find a package had been waiting for me for some weeks. It contained a very old bread roll with a used tea bag as filling! The note inside, signed by everyone on the squadron, was addressed to 'Das Fooden Fuhrer' from 'Das Fooden Scoffers'.

*   *   *

Night flying took some getting used too. If it was a clear night, with a moon and a well-defined horizon, it was little different to day flying. If the weather was poor, much of the sortie could be spent flying totally on instruments so the fact that it was at night made little difference. However, most sorties involved a mix of visual and instrument flying and the transition from one to the other, and back again, was often sudden. With no moon visible, dis-orientation was never far away. Over or close to towns on clear nights, it was normally easy to tell which 'way was up', but over open countryside with some lights on the ground and no definite horizon, it was possible to mistake the stars for lights on the ground and vice versa. So the technique was to blend visual flying and instrument techniques together using whichever was appropriate at the time. Even completing a simple 360-degree turn could mean flying half of it visually and the other half on instruments. Many of us considered night flying to be something of a 'dark art'.

In January 1974 I flew a night check with my Flight Commander and it went very well. The only aspect that we did not have time to cover was night asymmetric which was to prove a little unfortunate. Almost inevitably, my first real incident as captain of an aircraft would occur when it was par-ticularly dark, and of course it was just bound to involve asymmetric flying.

On 24 January 1974 I flew a day-into-night general handling sortie to the Scillies to practice an approach to the runway at St Mary's. On our way back an unusual noise could be heard coming from one of the engines. Which one? Surprisingly, it was sometimes difficult to identify the troublesome engine unless an engine instrument could offer a clue. Thankfully, in this case, the engine instruments showed the jet pipe temperature of one engine to be 60 degrees higher than the other. All was clearly not well. What to do I wondered? The Training Officer was airborne so I asked his advice. He agreed that something was amiss and suggested that it would be best to shutdown the 'hot' engine; better that than allowing it to possibly seize, which could result in a much more difficult approach.

I was very comfortable about the idea, or I thought that I was, until the moment that I actually closed the high pressure fuel cock and the engine stopped. My heart then leapt into my mouth, and I had a great deal of difficulty even speaking. I felt acutely embarrassed, and had to switch off my microphone now and again as I thought that my navigator would hear my heavy breathing and my quivering voice. I even had trouble transmitting the distress call, a PAN call.

I asked for radar vectors for a precision approach radar, as a long straight-in approach was recommended when on one engine. During the descent I regained my composure a little, although in the descent the 'live engine' was at low power so I did not have an asymmetric problem at that stage. Once I levelled off I had to increase power on the 'live engine' to maintain speed and it seemed to need a lot more power than I expected. It was bound to, of course, as the B2 was heavier than the T4, while the other important factor was that the 'dead engine' was exactly that, it was shut down and produced no thrust at all; during simulations it would have been at flight idle. As we got closer and closer to the glide path I began to feel that I was beginning to lose control; the speed kept reducing, I needed more and more rudder, and it was so dark, so very dark; it was absolutely pitch-black with even the stars obscured by cloud above us. As we flew over Bodmin Moor there were very few lights on the ground either. I couldn't believe that my navigator hadn't noticed that all was far from well but he sounded his normal confident self. I was barely in control of myself, let alone the aircraft and was having to work desperately hard.

As we were handed over to the Talkdown Controller for the final approach, I almost completely lost control. I could feel the aircraft beginning to go, and I glanced at the all important ball which was supposed to be in the middle of the turn and slip indicator. It wasn't, it was well out to one side and the aircraft was way out of balance. I pushed hard, very hard, on the rudder pedal to get it back. I was just in time, in another second the aircraft would have departed from controlled flight. And then the Talkdown Controller began giving his final instructions. I recognized his voice.

At the same time, I was able to reduce power on the 'live engine' as we started to descend on the glide path. This eased the pressure on my leg that had been holding almost full rudder up to that point. The controller lived in the Mess and had a room near mine; we had also met in the bar a couple of times. And he recognized my call sign, so he knew it was me. He was so calm and his clear voice, the voice of a friend, was exactly what I needed during those last few miles to touchdown. As we landed, I breathed a huge sigh of relief and thanked him over the radio. Looking back, I think that it was him that got us safely down that night, not me. But, alas, the drama was not yet over.

We stopped at the end of St Mawgan's single 9,000-foot runway and shut down; the Canberra could not be taxied on one engine. As we got out, I was mightily relieved although I said little; I was barely capable of speech. My navigator gave me a big smile and a cheery 'Well done mate!' I couldn't reply.

The fire crews arrived quickly and the fireman driving Crash One, the lead vehicle, offered to give us a lift back to the squadron. We clambered on board but did not notice that one of the other firemen accidentally put the bag containing the aircraft's ground locks onto his vehicle along with our flying helmets and other assorted paraphernalia. Without the ground locks the ground crew were not allowed to tow the aircraft, so there it stayed blocking St Mawgan's only runway, while various Nimrods and Canberras flew around in the overhead waiting in vain for the runway to be reopened.

Crash One set off at high speed down the taxiway with us on board. The vehicle had a long front seat, the driver was on the right, my navigator was in the middle and I was on the left. Except that I hadn't closed the door properly. As we turned sharply to the right, the door flew open and I fell out!

My navigator's reactions must have been very finely tuned that night. His left hand shot out and he grabbed part of my immersion suit; by then I was halfway out of the door, almost parallel with the ground, and my head was only inches above the tarmac. I was hauled back in. What else can go wrong, I wondered?

But there was more. It was a much shaken Flying Officer McDonald who entered the Operations Room about twenty minutes later. The Duty Authorizer was fulsome in his praise – an asymmetric landing for real on my first night sortie as captain. I was hugely embarrassed and could barely look him in the eye. Then there was a loud crash as the door into the Operations Room was flung open. It was the Station Commander. He threw his hat from the door, and it landed perfectly on top of the operations desk, something that in thirty-four years I have never been able to master. Then he turned to me and with a piercing stare said, 'It was you, was it?'

'Yes sir,' I said.

'Well done,' he replied, 'now, would you care to explain to me why you have put our only runway out of action for the last thirty minutes?'

*   *   *

It is strange how reputations can sometimes be built on very tenuous foundations. Mine undoubtedly was that night and I only ever shared how I had felt with one other, and that was months later. He listened carefully before saying not to worry, that how I had felt was normal but few pilots ever truly admit to what they actually felt inside during an incident. He went on to tell me how, when he was a young fighter pilot flying Vampires in Germany he had suffered an engine failure at night. The Vampire only had one engine and at night the drill was to eject. Against all the rules and advice he made a successful glide landing. And the reason he didn't eject? He was too frightened.

*   *   *

Up until now I had been successful playing the 'grey man' in my short career, the one that no one really noticed. That way, I figured I would be able to buy myself some time and actually learn a little about my trade. But to be successful as a 'grey man' you must not get noticed by senior officers and I had been. And, I was about to get noticed again.

On the way back from Wembury Range in a Canberra TT18, I flew what I thought was rather a 'punchy' run-in and break at St Mawgan. But as I pulled hard over the airfield there was a very loud bang and the aircraft yawed markedly but then quickly recovered. My heart stopped momentarily as I thought that an engine had seized. But air traffic control told us that one of our sleeve targets had broken free from its canister under the wing, the cable had immediately snapped as we were doing over 300 knots, and the long, orange target fell to the ground gently fluttering in the breeze. It fell into the Station Commander's garden. Luckily one of our navigators saw this happen, jumped into his car and rapidly retrieved the target before anyone became aware of exactly what had happened. I had got away with it! Or I thought that I had until the next edition of the station magazine appeared which had a brilliant cartoon depicting the sleeve target falling into the garden, and a terrified Station Commander leaping over the fence to get out of the way.

Not long afterwards I had to write a formal letter to the Station Commander. It was nothing to do with the incident and looking back it is strange to realize that my letter was not only the 'norm' but it was expected. It began 'Sir, I have the honour to request your permission to marry Miss J.M. Brooks of Leeds ...' It ended, 'I remain your obedient servant.' It was a bygone era. Thankfully the Station Commander gave his approval.

By now, the Station Commander knew exactly who I was and he directed that, given my background with the Air Cadets, I was to be the Air Cadet Liaison Officer for eight weeks of summer camps from late June; in other words, from virtually the day I returned from honeymoon! While those weeks would prove to be hectic, it was great fun working with the Air Cadets once more. Later, a new station commander arrived, a very keen poker and bridge player. On his first visit to the squadron, he presented the Boss in the crewroom in front of everyone with four brand new packs of cards. Bridge was back on!

*   *   *

In February 1974 I had my first overseas trip, sharing the flying with another pilot; we flew from St Mawgan to Gibraltar to refuel and then onto RAF Luqa in Malta. After another quick turnaround, we flew on to RAF Akrotiri in Cyprus. There I was introduced to kebabs, Hero's Square in Limassol, and to the local brew Kokinelli. This was a particularly rough red wine; we referred to it as the fourth tread of the grape. In those days it was served free of charge with kebabs, but now it is actually bottled and sold! I flew the leg back to Malta, and while my landing at Luqa wasn't the best I'd ever done, it certainly wasn't my worst. But it was sufficient for one of the three demijohns of sherry that we had bought to fall over and crack. The entire contents gradually seeped out into the cockpit midst calls from the other two guys of 'that one's yours!' For months afterwards, whenever anyone flew that particular aircraft it had the most delightful of smells and everyone felt so happy after their sortie.

*   *   *

We regularly took part in an exercise called the Joint Maritime Course, or as we preferred to call it, 'Find the Fleet Week.' Normally we would deploy to RAF Kinloss to act as part of 'Red Forces', against 'Blue' RN ships defended by 'Blue' RAF Phantoms and Lightnings. The high-level parts of these sorties were usually very long and very boring, although with no autopilot it was always hands-on flying. The low-level attacks against the RN cruisers and destroyers always made these sorties worthwhile as the RN never complained about the heights at which we flew. They wanted realistic training which I hope proved valuable a few years later.

At high-level we would often be intercepted by fighters against which we had no defence at all except to fly very high and very slowly, much slower than the fighters, and then we would turn very tightly into any incoming attack from behind. These tactics would count for little in a shooting war, but on exercise it was fun as the fighters would often try to intercept and then fly alongside us. In theory we were limited to 48,000 feet because of our oxygen system, but the aircraft was capable of much higher altitudes. Even at 48,000 feet the fighters would struggle and it was always amusing to watch a Lightning or Phantom come past with its nose high up in the air, close to the stall, desperately trying to slow down and fly alongside us, which they could never do. We often tried to see how high we could reach; on one sortie I reached 53,000 feet in a Canberra B2. I didn't dare try for higher, although I'm sure that I could have made 54,000 feet if I had had the nerve. It was not a very bright thing to have done.

During one such exercise in March 1974, operating from Kinloss, I stayed in the bar for far too long. It had long since closed but I ended up staying up talking, sitting on the stairs leading up to our rooms until almost 0200 hours. I had to be up at 0530 hours with a take-off scheduled when it was still dark at 0630 hours. I was up on time, if a little jaded. I realize now that I was verging on the overconfident. Whilst taxing I felt something warm and sticky beginning to trickle down my neck and it slowly began to creep inside the neck seal of my immersion suit; one of the glycerine ear pads in my flying helmet had burst. Eugh! But there was no time to change it so on I pressed with only one earphone working. Whilst flying at low-level about midway between Kinloss and Denmark, the oil pressure on one of my engines fell to zero. That was all I needed!

We had little choice but to shut the engine down before it seized solid and then head home. It was now daylight and I began a gradual climb through the thick cloud back to the mainland. I made a distress call and diverted to RAF Lossiemouth which was closer and had a longer runway for our forthcoming asymmetric landing. As we got closer, air traffic announced that they could not give us a radar approach but, as the aircraft was now fairly light, I said that I would descend below cloud and complete a visual approach. That was OK, but as we cleared cloud, I realized with a shock that the canopy was covered in ice. The Canberra's engines were very susceptible to engine icing and a special type of descent had to be flown if we were forced to penetrate icing conditions. There was a real risk that the ice could limit the amount of power available or even result in a compressor stall within the engine. I hadn't even considered the possibility! A compressor stall within our remaining engine could have had disastrous consequences. I was clearly not on top of my game.

I tried to concentrate on preparing for the asymmetric landing. Lossie-mouth soon came into view and I approached the airfield at 1,000 feet. But something didn't seem right. I was pointing down the runway but the run-way heading which I had set on the compass was about 30 degrees off. Why was that? And then it dawned on me! Stupid boy! It wasn't Lossiemouth after all but a disused airfield about eight miles further down the coast. You idiot! As we finally approached Lossiemouth we passed the Search and Rescue helicopter that had been scrambled to meet us. Thankfully we didn't need it, although the asymmetric visual circuit that I flew would not have earned any applause, it was a complete shambles, and so was I. When would I learn that there was no room for 'macho' in my line of work?

*   *   *

It was raining first thing on the morning of Saturday 8 June 1974, but it soon brightened up and a team from 7 Squadron arrived in good order, resplendent in their No. 1 uniforms with white gloves and swords. They formed the Guard of Honour for our wedding. We had a wonderful day with a very enjoyable reception. During photographs, the guys obviously recog-nized that I was beginning to wilt and an officer was duly escorted across the lawn in the middle of the photographs carrying a very welcome pint of beer. After our honeymoon we stayed for a few days with one of the squadron pilots in Truro before moving into our first home in St Columb Minor. Little did we realize that this would be the first of seventeen homes that we would share during my RAF service.

*   *   *

We had a greater degree of freedom in our flying which was often denied our fast-jet colleagues. We often flew at weekends when the rest of the station was quiet, and this would sometimes give us the opportunity for that run-in and break at the end of a sortie, just that little bit lower and faster than we would ever have got away with during the week. Or perhaps we could hold the aircraft down after take-off just a little lower than normal, a couple of feet of the ground and then zoom for height at the end of the runway. But the squadron executives didn't miss much. One Monday, one of my Flight Commanders stopped me and asked, 'Paul, would that have been you taking off at about 1 o'clock yesterday?'

'Yes, sir, I think it might have been,' I replied.

'If I see you take-off like that again I will kick your a***!'

That was it, nothing more was said. No formal or written warning, just a fairly straightforward poke in the eyes! I took heed.

*   *   *

The early 1970s also saw an increase in practice alerts and exercises. These would usually be called in the early hours of the morning and because we lived off-base, an airman was despatched to our married quarters to sound the alert by using a wind-up air raid siren circa 1940. Unfortunately, our married quarters adjoined a local authority housing estate and some of the residents complained. At the beginning of one exercise the airman concerned found himself arrested by the local police for creating a disturbance!

These exercises could be especially demanding as we had civilian ground crew and they were not called in outside their contracted hours. When we arrived we had to service the aircraft ourselves before we could fly. If the exercise carried on into the evening, and they often did, then we were on our own once more. The exercises were in preparation for an annual evaluation called a TACEVAL (tactical evaluation) when an outside team arrived, at no notice, to test the station's ability to fulfil its war role.

Our war role was called LOPRO, meaning low probe, but thankfully we never had to fly it for real. We worked with one the resident Nimrods which, as well as operating against submarines, were used to track ships and in particular battle groups. They would do so from a safe height and distance outside the missile engagement zones of the very capable missile systems operated by the Soviet Navy. The Nimrod would maintain a radar plot of the various ships and from time to time would task a Canberra to probe ahead and identify which, amongst the many radar contacts, was the Soviet capital ship. Our job was to fly in as low as we dared, as fast as we could, to identify the ships from as far away as possible, and then pass back the information in code. Given the capability of Soviet missiles against low flying aircraft this was quite a task and I often wondered about the staff officer who dreamt up this 'kamikaze-type' mission. After all, the marks of Canberra we were operating had a maximum speed of 365 knots, or just over 400mph.

I was given the secondary duty of teaching ship recognition and I devised all sorts of methods which, hopefully, would allow our crews to identify Soviet warships by their profile from as far away as possible. Soon the various classes of warship, like the Sverdlov, Kara, Kresta I and II, Kashin, Kynda and Krivak, became everyday names. My growing knowledge of these ships was to have enormous benefit later.

*   *   *

The early months of 1975 saw us regularly towing our Rushton targets near the Hebrides so that the RAF Regiment could practice firing their new surface-to-air missile, the Rapier. On one sortie two missiles were accidentally launched against the target; a high ranking observer from the Middle East thought it was a very good idea as it doubled the chance of hitting the target. Little did he know that only one of the missiles could be guided; the other one could have gone anywhere!

*   *   *

Sometimes there would be quiet days and on one such day I had to complete a compass swing on the far side of the airfield. This was a tedious affair, taxiing around the compass bay as various readings were taken by the two navigators and the compasses adjusted. This particular one took almost two hours and I was very bored. I realized that there hadn't been a single aircraft movement on the station since we began. I looked across to the air traffic control tower. All was quiet. Was that a newspaper that I could see being read by the local controller? I came up with a cunning plan which was quickly agreed with the two navigators. We all had separate transmit buttons on the radio so we launched into a rapid series of calls.

'Black Section, check in,' I said.

'Black 2,' said Nav 1.

'3,' said Nav 2.

'Black 4,' said Nav 1 with a different accent.

Then it was my turn again:

'St Mawgan Tower, Black Section, four Hunter aircraft thirty seconds to break!'

There was pandemonium in the tower, as newspapers and no doubt cups of coffee were cast aside. We could see that the local controller had leapt to his feet and was peering through binoculars at the approach to the runway in use. Nothing! Then he looked the other way. Still nothing! The binoculars then slowly began to move around in our direction and then they stopped. A few minutes later as we taxied past the tower I gave them a friendly way. They were a good bunch, and they all waved back. Or was that a fist? Or was it something else?

* * *

On our annual confidential reports we could indicate our preferences for next posting. I was doing well and was a pair's leader and was hoping to have another crack at fast-jet flying. I still wanted to fly the Buccaneer which was my first choice. Photo Reconnaissance Canberras with 39 Squadron at RAF Wyton was my second choice. I was posted not to Buccaneers or to Wyton, but to XIII Squadron in Malta. I was slightly disappointed at not getting Buccaneers and I wondered how Jackie would react to the news. I needn't have been concerned as she was delighted and promptly ran out of the house to tell some of our friends and neighbours! Over the next few months I was very conscious that I should not do anything at work that could in any way call into question my posting. But I very nearly did.

* * *

I had flown to West Freugh in Scotland accompanied by two navigators. We were to fly two trials sorties, before and after lunch, in a weapons range over the sea. The morning sortie went well, and we landed at West Freugh to refuel. The Range Controller telephoned and asked us to get airborne much earlier than planned for our next sortie if at all possible. We were happy to oblige and were quite capable of seeing off our own aircraft as the civilian ground crew were still at lunch. I quickly climbed aboard to start up, while the navigators did the external checks and removed the aircraft ground locks.

Within minutes we were airborne. But what was that red light? A nose wheel red? This indicated that the nose wheel may not have locked up on retraction. It was probably just a microswitch; we often had trouble with those. Could I just ignore it and carry on? But something rang a warning bell.

'Did either of you remove the nose wheel locking pin?' I asked.

'I didn't,' said one, 'I removed the ground locks on the right.'

'I didn't,' said the other, 'I removed the ground locks on the left.'

Oh, no, I thought, what a disaster! With the pin fitted the nose wheel could not be retracted. There was no way we could conduct the trials sortie or even fly back to St Mawgan with the nose wheel down as our speed had to be kept very low. We had to remove the pin, but that could only be done on the ground. And we were in a Canberra TT18 that was more than 4,000lb above maximum landing weight. It would take nearly an hour to use the fuel to get us down to our maximum safe landing weight. Also West Freugh's 6,000-foot runway was a little on the short side for a heavyweight Canberra and there was no headwind to help slow the aircraft down, nor was there a barrier at the end of the runway to stop aircraft in the event of brakes failure.

The trials sortie would have to be abandoned, and the embarrassment would be huge. What a way to end my first tour which had gone so well, far better than I had ever expected. What if my posting was cancelled? All of these things flashed through my mind in a matter of seconds.

Was there another way? What if I landed above maximum landing weight? I felt sure that I could 'hack it'. Could one of the navigators then get out and remove the nose wheel pin? We could still make our range slot and no one need ever be any the wiser. The runway was a bit short but I was sure that I could hack it. I put the idea to both navigators and they were up for it. So that's what we did, and I asked the air traffic controller to be 'discreet' about our intermediate landing. We made our range time and then flew back to the St Mawgan.

Over the years I have often thought about what we did that day, and I cringe. When we took off the second time, our brakes would have been very, very hot after the previous landing with such a heavy aircraft. What if something had gone wrong during that second take-off and we had tried to stop? The brakes would have given up quickly, there was no headwind to help slow the aircraft and, with such a short runway and no barrier, we would have gone off the end very fast. There is little doubt that the navigators would have ejected, and me too, probably, providing that we were going faster than the minimum safe ejection speed on the ground of 90 knots. And for what? It had been an understandable error of omission not commission, and I am sure that it would have been considered excusable. But what I did that day was not just inexcusable, it was crass stupidity. And was everyone none the wiser? It was only kept quiet until the day I left 7 Squadron. Did I learn from it? I hope so.

*   *   *

My last trip on 7 Squadron was on 29 July 1975 and at the end of that month I was delighted to see that I had been rated 'above the average' in my flying log book. My tour formally ended on 6 August 1975 after one year and ten months; I had flown 506 hours. We were then on our way to a very different life in Malta and to XIII (PR) Squadron. What would that hold for us we wondered?

Chapter 4

We Assist By Watching

XIII (Photo Reconnaissance) Squadron, RAF Luqa, 1975–1978

Malta had long been strategically important for the UK. Midway between Gibraltar and the Suez Canal, the island's capital, Valetta, boasted a natural well-sheltered harbour. Malta was vital for the Allies during the Second World War and much has been written about its valiant stand against incessant bombing and the award of the George Cross to the island. The RAF contribution was crucial, beginning with Faith, Hope and Charity, three obsolescent Sea Gladiator biplanes that were crated as spare aircraft for RN aircraft carriers. Many RAF squadrons came to be based there both in defence and later in attack. RAF Luqa became the primary bomber airfield as British and Commonwealth forces fought for air supremacy, which would lead to naval control of the Mediterranean, and ground control of North Africa. Air combat over Malta was some of the most ferocious of the war, and a series of airfields were built on the small, rocky island at Ta'Qali – a fighter airfield, and Hal Far – a Fleet Air Arm airfield, plus satellite fields at Safi, Qrendi in 1942 and for a very short while on the island of Gozo during 1943.

The film *Malta Story*, starring Alec Guinness, contains many similarities with the lives of a maverick RAF airman and an English dancer, the little known Adrian Warburton and the vivacious Christina Ratcliffe. Christina, a RAF controller at Lascaris War HQ, was awarded the British Empire Medal in 1943. When 'Warby' disappeared on a sortie from England in 1944 he was the RAF's most highly decorated photo-reconnaissance pilot; there was speculation that he was trying to return to Malta to see Christina. He was found nearly sixty years later in the wreckage of his aircraft in Bavaria when I was the UK Senior National Representative at the NATO HQ at Ramstein. On 14 May 2003, 'Warby' was afforded full military honours and buried in the beautiful Durnbach Commonwealth War Graves Cemetery, which I visited in 2004. The service was taken by Ramstein's RAF chaplain, Squadron Leader the Reverend Alan Coates, and the Chief of the Air Staff was represented by my Boss, Air Marshal Sir 'Rocky' Goodall. 'Warby' was the sort of character that so often shines in war and Tony Spooner's book, *Warburton's War*, makes fascinating reading.

Ever-faithful Christina stayed on in Malta working as the civilian secretary to a succession of RAF Luqa's station commanders. She also ran The Café Christina in Valetta. She never married and her last few years were unhappy ones. She became withdrawn and died alone and penniless in her flat in Floriana in 1988 not knowing the fate of her beloved 'Warby'. She was not discovered for several weeks. But for the involvement of Frederick Galea, Honorary Secretary of Malta's National War Museum Association, Christina's grave would have gone unrecognized by many. In 1993, she was reburied in the Santa Maria Addolorata Cemetery in Pawla and her marble headstone reads CHRISTINA OF GEORGE CROSS ISLAND. Her personal and very well-written story was reproduced by Frederick Galea in *Carve Malta on My Heart* and more recently in *Women of Malta*.

*   *   *

After the war, Luqa remained an important RAF base, and it also served as Malta's main civilian airport. In 1975, it was one of the last surviving air-fields of the RAF's Near East Air Force. By then, withdrawal from east of Suez was complete and the bases in Cyprus were the UK's most easterly outposts. Since the Nationalists had been ousted from decades of power by the Maltese Labour Party, under Dom Mintoff, the UK's days in Malta were numbered. Disagreements between the Maltese Government and NATO had resulted in a large NATO HQ moving to Naples, never to return, and during 1973 all of the UK's armed forces had been withdrawn at short notice. They returned some months later, but with a firm date for final withdrawal, 1 April 1979.

The Commander of British Forces in Malta in 1975 was a RN two-star officer, a rear admiral, and his deputy as Air Commander Malta was an RAF one-star, an air commodore. Two RAF squadrons were permanently based at RAF Luqa: 203 Squadron operated the Nimrod in the maritime patrol role, and XIII Squadron operating the PR Canberra. The motto of XIII Squadron, *Adjuvamus tuendo* – We assist by watching, is so very apt.

*   *   *

On 27 August 1975, when I arrived, XIII Squadron was operating both the Canberra PR7 and the PR9. How I wished to fly the PR9, but it was not to be as they were being withdrawn to the UK and replaced by more rather elderly PR7s, which had been built in 1953. The PR9 was a magnificent aircraft, much more powerful than the PR7 with hydraulically operated flying controls and an autopilot. It was also capable of reaching 60,000 feet, which was and still is pretty remarkable. The PR9 was kept in service until 2004 and it was used to good effect in Afghanistan. The Canberra did sterling work for over fifty-five years.

Despite its age, the PR7 was a pretty useful aircraft. It was heavier than the marks of Canberra that I had previously flown but it had more powerful engines. It also carried extra fuel, but we did not operate with wing-tip fuel tanks fitted. This lack of wing-tip tanks increased our limiting speed to 450 knots. The PR7's range was just short of 1,000 nautical miles at low-level and 2,500 nautical miles at high-level. The additional weight and the more powerful engines meant that the PR7 was more difficult to handle on one engine after take-off, especially in hot weather. RAF Luqa's runway, at 7,500 feet long, was also 1,500 feet shorter than St Mawgan's.

All marks of Canberra had a safety speed, the speed at which the aircraft could be climbed in the event of an engine failure after take-off. We referred to the gap between lift-off speed and safety speed as 'the graveyard zone'. The PR7 had the widest 'graveyard zone' of all the marks of Canberra, with a lift-off speed of 130 knots and a safety speed of 175 knots. It was for this reason that most Canberras were held almost level after take-off, to accelerate as quickly as possible through 'the graveyard zone' before entering a climb. Faced with an engine failure in 'the graveyard zone', the navigator could eject but, as soon as the pilot moved his hands from the controls to the ejection seat handle, the aircraft could roll quickly making ejection a marginal option at best. Other options had to be considered, especially on hot days when it took much longer to accelerate.

One option was to put the aircraft straight down onto the ground with the wheels up. Another, when taking off on Runway 06 at Luqa, was to try and descend into Grand Harbour and gain enough speed to be able to climb. Taking off on Runway 24 was more problematic as it was a few miles before the cliffs could be reached; if you made it that far you could then descend over the sea and increase speed. In some circumstances skill and experience counted for little; in 1980 the crew of a Canberra were killed at RAF Akrotiri in Cyprus following an engine failure below safety speed. The pilot, Squadron Leader 'Paddy' Thompson, was probably the RAF's most experienced Canberra pilot and I had been examined by him a couple of times when he had been the CFS Agent on Canberras.

The PR7 had two ejection seats, but for much of our work the navigator unstrapped and crawled forward into the Perspex nose; this was essential for all high-level photography. For low flying, the navigator could either lie in the nose or sit on a collapsible seat, called the rumbold seat, to the right of, and just behind the pilot; all the navigators became pretty adept at getting back and strapping into their ejection seat in a hurry. For some sorties, a third crew member could be carried and he would sit on the rumbold seat; he would have a parachute which could be attached to a chest harness. In the event of having to abandon the aircraft, he had to jettison the small door on the right and jump out. Abandoning at low-level or just after take-off was not an option. I flew sorties on this seat a number of times. Its use was banned at the end of 1978 following a fatal accident and the loss of the third crew member.

The squadron had eighteen crews and a total strength of about a hundred. We operated in support of both NATO and CENTO (the Central Treaty Organization). The latter comprised of the USA, UK, Turkey, Iran (under the Shah), and Pakistan. We could be deployed in support of either organization and regularly exercised with both. Our NATO Forward Operating Base (FOB) was the Italian Air Force base at Villafranca just outside Verona.

For normal training we spent most of our time over Sicily and Southern Italy flying low-level training missions, but we would often climb up for high-level vertical and oblique photography of the Sicilian and North African coastlines. We were also perfectly placed to photograph Soviet ships and others, especially 'merchant' ships heading for Libya. The Soviet Black Sea Fleet was also particularly active and on most days one or more of its ships, or submarines, would be within our reach. Just to the south-west of the Italian island of Lampedusa, and close to the coast of Tunisia, the Black Sea Fleet had a mooring buoy, and a Soviet submarine or escort would often be found there for weeks on end. This fleet played an increasing part in our sorties, especially after the Nimrods were withdrawn from Luqa. I was well up-to-speed in identifying Soviet warships.

I flew my first sortie on 10 September. A major changeover of crews had taken place during the summer with a third of the crews being replaced. Many of the pilots were of a similar background to me, having just completed a short tour on second-line Canberra squadrons. We had no first-tour pilots so there was a lot of collective experience. All the new crews began with a short convex (conversion course) of about fifteen trips so that we could master the art of photo-recce. I was crewed with Fred Stokes, a very experienced navigator who had completed two tours on Victor tankers and one tour on Canberras. We would be crewed together for three years, and flew more than half of our sorties together.

The convex was demanding and we normally flew one sortie each day lasting two to three hours. The aircraft only had very basic air cooling in the cockpit so it was often very warm work, especially during the summer. Even though many of the PR7's cameras dated back to the Second World War, they were still capable of outstanding photography.

For low-level work, there were three pilot-operated F95 cameras, one of which was an optional forward facing camera in the nose; the other two were obliquely mounted in the forward camera bay facing right and left. The focal length of these was 4 inches, although a 12 inch F95 could be fitted for closer and more detailed oblique photography. The other cameras were for medium or high-level work and were operated by the navigator. There was a huge F52 PFO (port-facing oblique) camera, also mounted in the forward camera bay, which could have a 36 inch or a 48 inch focal length. It was used for photographing targets while standing-off some distance; coastlines or border areas were typical targets.

Sighting the oblique cameras was something of an art. A long tape measure, a ladder, a 'Nav Bag', a straight edge and a chinagraph pencil were required. On the ground, the navigator would measure an appropriate distance laterally from the nose wheel and place his 'Nav Bag' at the right distance for the focal length of the camera involved; the pilot would then draw a line in chinagraph on the inside of the blister-type canopy in line with the bottom of the 'Nav Bag'. The navigator would then climb up the ladder and draw another line on the outside of the thick canopy so that both lines were in-line with the bottom of the 'Nav Bag'. High tech or what? But it worked!

In the rear camera bay, we also had a vertically mounted F49 survey camera, and two F52 36 inch cameras mounted almost vertically, but in such a way that the photographs overlapped one other to give a stereoscopic image of the target. A night camera could also be fitted for taking vertical photographs from low-level while a series of flares were dropped from the aircraft flare bay. We had no defensive or electronic counter measures equipment and were therefore vulnerable in all but the most benign of environments. We could only rely on height, and would usually plan to fly very low if we were in a hostile environment.

Most sorties during the convex involved a low-level departure from Malta, before heading north to the southern coast of Sicily for about an hour's low flying taking photographs of three targets. Then we would climb up to above 30,000 feet to practice high-level photography. After that, back to low-level over the sea for photography of shipping before recovering to Luqa for circuits.

Prior to each sortie there was extensive pre-flight preparation. We had pre-planned low-level routes on 1:500,000 scale maps covering Sicily and Southern Italy. We also had an extensive target library of various installations that had been photographed and they all came complete with measurements and detailed assessments. We were given the grid references of three targets of different types but without any detail except for the type of target. The targets could vary from bridges, communications facilities, military installations, industries, ports or harbours, airfields, electrical installations, hydroelectric plants, dams, etc, but that would be all that we knew. It would be our task to photograph the target and come back with a detailed description. Both the photographs and our descriptions would be assessed by skilled photographic interpreters and we would be given an overall mark for the sortie. For the next three years every sortie that we did would be assessed in this manner.

For the best results, we had to pass alongside the target taking a series of photographs using one of the low-level F95 oblique cameras. Ideally, the target should appear about one third up from the bottom of the frame. Either four or eight frames per second were taken. When viewed through a stereoscope, the interpreters could measure the target very accurately. The visual description also had to be detailed. For a bridge, for example, what type (rail over road, rail over river etc)? How many spans? How many tracks? Electrified or not? Construction, length, width, plus many others. It was much more complicated than just dropping a bomb on it! We were allowed twenty minutes planning time for each target.

The attack runs were planned using Italian 1:50,000 maps which were circa 1942, so they were well out of date. There were many occasions when we hurtled round a corner in mountainous terrain expecting the target to be a tiny road bridge only to be confronted by a gigantic six-lane motorway bridge that was actually above us! During the planning, we would mark the target on the map with a triangle. Then an initial point would be marked with a square and joined to the target. We would normally aim to 'miss' the target, putting it on one side of the aircraft, so that it could be photographed obliquely. The initial point, about sixty to ninety seconds from the target, would be a feature that could be identified easily at low-level from some distance away. The route from the initial point to the target, normally a straight line, would then be very carefully studied so that it could be flown extremely accurately at 420 knots (even nautical miles per minute).

Many targets only became visible at the very last second. Not only were our maps very old but they were also in very short supply. All our work had to be completed in pencil so that it could be rubbed out after the sortie and the map used again. Nor could we tear the maps to make them less bulky. So not only did we have to learn to become neat at drawing but we also had to become pretty adept at folding maps too! For some targets we could be tasked with a line search and would sometimes use the nose camera to follow a road or railway line, manoeuvring very hard to keep the 'line', the road or railway, directly in front of the camera. All the low flying was exhilarating stuff but it was often exhausting. The PR7 was a very physical aircraft. And, of course, throughout all of this the navigator would not be in his ejection seat, but either lying in the nose or sitting on the collapsible rumbold seat alongside the pilot. Rather him than me!

For medium or high-level vertical work, the pilot had to fly as directed by the navigator as only he could see what was directly below and ahead of the aircraft from his position in the nose. It was vital that the pilot kept the wings absolutely level, even one or two degrees of bank would ruin the photographs. This meant that the aircraft could not be turned in the normal manner using the ailerons to bank the aircraft but had to be 'flat-turned' using rudder whilst keeping the wings absolutely level. This technique took some mastering. High-level oblique work was even harder as the targets, usually coastlines, weren't straight; they turned, so the aircraft had to be turned at the same rate using rudder while again trying to keep the wings level. The difficulty was that when using the rudder to turn, the aircraft also tried to roll. To stop the roll, the pilot had to apply opposite aileron i.e. left rudder to turn left, right aileron to stop the aircraft rolling left. This was fine for short periods but if the 'flat-turn' was prolonged, and they often were, you could quickly end up with full rudder in one direction and full aileron in the other! This was a nightmare to fly and very, very physical! But Fred and I gradually mastered these new skills and following an 'Op Check' we were duly declared fully operational.

*   *   *

Tragedy came to Malta on 14 October 1975. Whenever there was a strong gusting westerly wind, wind shear was often caused by the large hangar upwind of Runway 24's threshold. A Vulcan, with a crew of seven, touched down short, bounced, and then hit the concrete lip of the runway. One undercarriage leg was ripped off and the other was pushed upwards penetrating the fuel tanks. As the captain initiated a go around he was unaware that his aircraft had caught fire. While positioning for an emergency landing, the fire warning lights illuminated and he ordered his crew to bail out. Only the two pilots had ejection seats, the rear crew had to rely on parachutes. Within seconds the aircraft exploded, one wing coming completely off. Only then did the pilots eject. The other five crew members died, so did a Maltese lady in the village of Zabbar and a number of people were injured. It was a truly tragic day for the RAF and for Malta.

*   *   *

Exercises frequently took us away from Malta. Sometimes we were only away for a day or two, sometimes for a couple of weeks. With our NATO FOB at Villafranca, we would soon get to know the beautiful city of Verona well and it has been one of my favourite cities ever since. My first trip there was during the convex; in all I would visit Villafranca seven or eight times during my tour. This was all so very different to a Wembury Silent, or a Portland Rushton on 7 Squadron.

Now operational, Fred and I were invited into the 'vault', a strengthened room with no windows and a steel door. This was the home of the Squadron Intelligence Officer (SQUINTO). Here we were briefed on our war role and we had to spend many hours each month studying the targets that we were likely to be tasked against in the event of war with the Soviet Union and the Warsaw Pact. Just writing those words – the Soviet Union and the Warsaw Pact – seems to be a leap into the past, yet for all of us throughout the 1970s and 1980s the prospect of war was very real. Historians often refer to the Cold War as the war that NATO won without having to fight, but it nevertheless produced a lot of casualties. We certainly took the threat very seriously and trained extremely hard. Aircraft accidents and fatalities were all too regular, but thankfully we were not touched by any during my tour on XIII Squadron.

Our prime targets were in Rumania and after studying them for some time, Fred and I decided that we didn't like the pre-planned route so we re-planned it. The new route had us departing from Villafranca at low-level, crossing the Adriatic Sea, and then following the valleys through what was then Yugoslavia until we reached the Rumanian border and then on to the targets. Even flying as low as we dared, I didn't rate our chances highly, unarmed and unescorted.

Each year we operated for a week from RAF Wyton in Huntingdonshire, practicing low flying in the UK. Our first detachment was in January 1976.

In March we did our first night photography, which was called night flashing; not the best choice of phrases but it aptly described what we did. We flew from the lighthouse on Gozo toward our target, an RAF Marine Craft Unit Launch positioned south of Malta. As this was for training, the launch had a light on top at which we could aim. We released a series of flares (hence the word flashing), and took nine photographs aiming to get the target in the centre of the fifth frame. We completed two attacks but weren't able to view the photographs until the following morning when it became clear that they were the subject of a great deal of interest. To begin with we couldn't understand why. On both runs, our target was right in the middle of the fifth frame; that was pretty good going for our first attempt, we thought. Alas not. On looking more closely it was clear that our second attack was not against the launch but against a Maltese fishing boat! Apparently, the flares that we used also attracted sharks, so after the first attack the cunning Maltese fishermen positioned their boat a little closer to Gozo, then switched on a light on top of their boat and simply waited. They certainly caught us!

* * *

In April 1976, the squadron deployed to Pakistan to take part in Exercise Shabaz, a CENTO exercise which involved the UK, USA, Pakistan, Iran and Turkey. We deployed to the Pakistan Air Force (PAF) base at Masroor, on the western outskirts of Karachi. I flew there non-stop in an RAF Belfast transport aircraft which had an amazing range and a huge carrying capacity. But it would have been more appropriately called the Belslow! The journey took forever, and we were of course travelling in 'cattle class' amongst the freight, on the most uncomfortable canvas seats ever made.

At Masroor we operated from the PAF's 7 Squadron which also flew a variant of the Canberra. Masroor was highly operational with fully manned anti-aircraft guns strategically placed all over the airfield; of course it had not been that long since Pakistan had been at war with India and tension between the two countries was always high.

Although it was nearly thirty years since the end of British rule, there was still much evidence of the UK's earlier involvement. PAF uniforms were identical to our summer khaki drill uniforms and the PAF used the same officer ranks as the RAF. To book transport, a PAF Form 658 was submitted, the RAF used a RAF Form 658, and many other forms and procedures were very similar to our own.

On our way to our hotel in Karachi we drove through one of the poorer districts of the city, a shanty town of slums and hovels, and it was obvious from the appalling smell that there was little or no sanitation, with many people simply living, sleeping and in some cases dying on the street. It was truly awful and the conditions brought into sharp focus the contrast between our lifestyle and that of these very poor people. Yet within a short distance there were beautiful cricket grounds with local teams playing in immaculate whites. And of course our hotel was luxurious. Elsewhere in the city, the bazaars were fascinating and we spent many an hour browsing and bartering, or trying to, but we were dealing with experts.

Within forty-eight hours of arrival every single one of us was affected by tummy trouble to varying degrees. Many were somewhat limited by the 'thirty second gong'! This was not so good when you were strapped to an ejection seat for four hours at a time. A USAF F111 squadron from the UK had also deployed to Masroor and they arrived with everything – absolutely everything – that they would need to be totally self-sufficient for the duration of their time in Pakistan. They brought all their own food so that they would not risk tummy trouble and even brought their own bottled water. While this said a great deal about the US airlift capacity, within forty-eight hours of arrival they were also subject to the American version of the 'thirty second gong'!

The rules for the exercise varied greatly between Iran and Pakistan, and it was clear which country was just 'playing', and which one wanted effective training. The Iranians would not allow us to fly below 10,000 feet so it was very easy for them to pick up our aircraft on radar and to claim 'kills', especially with their surface-to-air missiles. The Pakistanis, however, were altogether different and cleared us to fly down to 250 feet anywhere within Pakistan, even over cities like Karachi. Such an authorization would have been unheard of in the UK. As far as Karachi International Airport was concerned, as long as we called up on the radio one minute before crossing the centreline of the main runway, they would direct any civilian passenger aircraft to get out of the way! Can you imagine that sort of thing happening over London, crossing in front of a Boeing 747 approaching Heathrow? It would be chaos.

The USAF F111 squadron had more restrictive rules, although this was not unusual for the USAF, and one of their pilots was sent home for flying at 500 feet over Masroor. One morning in the lift in the hotel a USAF pilot asked me, 'Say, what sort of height are you guys cleared down to over the city?'

'250 feet,' I replied.

'Is that so,' he said, 'yesterday I was on my balcony as one of your Canberras flew past the hotel; I was looking straight down at him.'

'Really?' I said.

'Yes,' he went on, 'and I am on the 4th floor.'

*   *   *

My first sortie was a high-level recce of the Iranian Air Force base at Bandarabbas on the northern side of the Arabian Gulf. The sortie lasted four hours, and we were intercepted by Iranian F4 Phantoms. The F4s had very 'dirty' engines and we could see their smoke from many miles away, so we could then turn to make their task of intercepting us so much more difficult. The following day we flew a similar sortie, this time against the Iranian base at Mashad in north-eastern Iran. It was another four hour sortie and we eventually landed at Tehran International Airport. We had about an hour on the ground to refuel before taking off again and after checking the weather forecast for our return I went outside the Met Office for a quick cigarette. So there I was, a rather unkempt RAF flying officer in a sweaty flying suit, no hat, having a quiet smoke when guess who came round the corner? An RAF Air Marshal in his very best uniform and he was looking for me! I almost wet myself on the spot! But all he wanted to do was to shake my hand and have a chat. He was Air Marshal Sir Alfred Ball, the UK Permanent Military Representative to CENTO, and he had flown in for a high powered CENTO meeting. As he and the many other senior delegates were walking along the red carpet to meet their hosts, he spotted our aircraft, exclaimed 'that's a XIII Squadron Canberra' and promptly hurried off to find the crew. He was a delightful man and didn't seem to mind my casual turn-out in the slightest.

Our flight back to Masroor that afternoon also lasted four hours, making a total of eight hours flying that day. As it was all 'hands-on' flying, it was quite tiring. Add to that the planning time and the time spent refuelling the aircraft, which we did ourselves, and it was easily a sixteen-hour-day. The following day we flew back to Malta, thankfully in a Canberra this time. The first leg was from Masroor to Tehran and then on to RAF Akrotiri in Cyprus. For this leg, we had to overly Turkey, as Syria, the Lebanon and Israel were very much 'no-go areas'.

*   *   *

We deployed to Villafranca ten days later to take part in Exercises Dawn Patrol and Dashing Impact. A lot of planning had been completed while we were in Pakistan but, unbeknown to anyone, much of it would never be utilized. Fred and I flew to Villafranca in a C130 Hercules with a couple of other crews, our groundcrew, and lots of ground equipment. Although we were hosted by 28 Squadron, an Italian Air Force F104 Starfighter squadron, we had to be self-supporting in the processing of film and the production of prints so we brought our own large reconnaissance exploitation laboratories which were about the size of a caravan.

On the evening of 6 May 1976, we were having dinner in the Officers' Club when the shutters on the windows began to rattle. To a man, the assembled RAF officers all put their wine glasses back down on the table! The Italian stewards, also to a man, ran out of the building. We soon realized what the stewards had so instantly recognized: we hadn't drunk too much Valpolicella, we were experiencing an earthquake. It subsided almost as quickly as it had begun with no apparent damage, so we all picked up our glasses once more. We shrugged it off as just a tremor as the Valpolicella was rather good.

During the night, however, a different picture emerged and it appeared that there had been considerable damage and loss of life in several towns and villages in north-eastern Italy, only 120 miles from where we were. The following day the Italian authorities asked us to photograph the extent of the damage. When the first aircraft returned it was clear that the destruction and turmoil caused by the earthquake was widespread with many collapsed houses, blocked roads, and fallen bridges. One of the worst cases was that of a factory where the walls had fallen outwards leaving the roof to pancake onto the occupants. Elsewhere, the side of a mountain had slid into a valley. There were many thousands of casualties and many people had lost their lives. Exercise Dashing Impact was immediately cancelled and the troops involved were diverted to help. It was then realized that the presence of XIII Squadron with our survey capability was potentially an invaluable aid and the Italian authorities soon requested that we provide more extensive photographic cover of the devastated region.

The area in question measured about 1,000 square miles. It was north of Udine, bounded to the east by Yugoslavia and to the north by Austria. Some flights would need to go very close to international frontiers, so arrangements had to be made with the countries concerned. Interestingly, Yugoslavia, a key member of the Warsaw Pact, was very quick in approving our flights; the Yugoslav Government said that we could even cross the frontier as long as we had initiated a turn before doing so. In fact, Yugoslavia was actually quicker off the mark in approving our flights than the UK.

It was decided to carry out a photographic survey of the area to a scale of 1:10,000 using the F49 vertical camera. The terrain was to present problems, so did the weather. In order to achieve the correct scale, we had to fly at 5,000 feet above ground level. This presented no difficulty in the flat triangle of ground immediately north of Udine, but the terrain to the north of Osoppo, the worst hit area, was a succession of mountains and high ridges rising to 8,000 feet with valleys descending to 500 feet. For the photography, the area was split into segments to be flown at different heights. Each flight line was drawn 1,750 yards apart and would require extremely precise flying by the pilot and very accurate visual tracking by the navigator to ensure that there was no loss of cover. For Fred and I, and a couple of the other crews, this would be our very first survey flying and we were very keen to do well.

Fred and I flew sorties on 12 and 14 May and we produced very good results. We got very close to the Yugoslav border and we could see contrails high above us to the east; no doubt Yugoslav fighters were keeping a close eye. By the end of 14 May, the squadron had produced excellent photography and had achieved 70 per cent coverage of the whole area. Three further sorties were to be launched on 15 May to complete the task and Fred and I were delighted to be selected for what was to be the most difficult sortie of all.

The next morning we had to be up very early and it was still dark as we drove toward the airfield. We strapped into our aircraft in complete silence and said little even as we taxied and took off. Once airborne, Fred unstrapped, crawled down the nose, and lay on his stomach; this was his normal position for low-level navigation and for survey photography. The route wasn't that difficult and it was now also daylight. I flew south to the

River Po then followed it east until it joined the Adriatic. Then a left turn to follow the coastline to Venice before another left turn onto a northerly heading took us to Udine. We then prepared for some work, some very real work. And this was going to be hard, very, very hard.

The area that we had to cover formed an inverted 'V' pointing into the mountains. The mountains on either side of the 'V' rose very steeply up to 5,000–6,000 feet or more. The lines that we had to cover went horizontally across the inverted 'V', and we had to fly at exactly 5,000 feet above the ground so that the scale of the photography would match that which had already been completed. The cloud was extensive and also just above 5,000 feet – so the mountains on either side of the lines we had to fly were in cloud – and we would be flying just below the base of the cloud in the valley. This was always going to be the most difficult area to photograph, which was why we had been pleased to be selected. But no one could have foreseen how difficult the cloud would make the task.

We began. I flew up the valley, as close as I dared to the mountains until just before our line, then turned sharply and rapidly rolled the wings level. Fred called 'camera on' and we flew across the valley keeping the wings absolutely level and making heading adjustments with rudder only. We flew toward the sheer mountain face at the other side of the valley. At the last possible moment Fred called 'camera off' and I threw the aircraft into a tight turn to exit the valley to the south. Once clear, we turned around and repeated the whole process from the other direction gradually working our way northwards. It was the most physically and mentally demanding flying that I had ever done and I had no idea how well or otherwise we were doing; it was entirely down to Fred's judgement to decide whether we were on the line and when to turn the camera on and off. As we worked our way north the valley got narrower and narrower and it became more and more difficult. Eventually, Fred called 'camera off' for the final time and I was mightily relieved to head south back to Venice.

The photography had taken us over three hours to complete, and the whole sortie lasted nearly four hours. I was exhausted. But how would it turn out? When we got back we waited in silence while the film was developed and then the negatives were rolled out across the large 'light' tables in the exploitation laboratories so that the Photographic Interpreters could make an initial assessment. It was important that we had achieved all the required overlaps between photo frames and that there were no gaps between our lines. Then the result was announced. It was perfect. No missing coverage at all; a far better result than many of the earlier sorties flown in good weather without the high ground problem or the weather that we had faced.

Later, the long awaited result for the squadron's overall performance was announced, 98.5 per cent coverage, with only a few cloud-covered mountain peaks being 'lost'. This was a remarkable achievement and once the coverage had been assessed, the film was handed over so that a photographic mosaic could be constructed. This allowed the Italian authorities to divert assistance to the correct area since several villages were completely cut off. Subsequently, it helped them to reconstruct towns and communications in the most suitable locations. About 1,000 people died in the earthquake of 6 May 1976, and almost 160,000 people were left homeless.

* * *

Every crew spent one week each year in Germany operating from II Squadron's HQ at RAF Laarbruch. Our first visit was later in May 1976. At the time, II Squadron was operating the two-seat F4 Phantom in the ground attack/reconnaissance role, but it was in the process of being replaced by the single-seat Jaguar. Also based there was the aircraft that I had always hoped to fly, the Buccaneer. With so many fast-jets, the elderly Canberra was viewed by many with some amusement and in a slightly deprecating manner which was always irritating.

One XIII Squadron crew managed to balance the books without actually having to say a word. As they had enjoyed four or five detachments to Laarbruch, they put on a barrel in the Officers' Mess to thank Mess members for their hospitality. As the Mess began to fill up, lots of young fast-jet aircrew looked with some amusement at the large invitation, which included a picture of a Canberra, but on reading further they became a little more reflective. Their world revolved around constant exercises, the occasional trip to the UK, then to Sardinia for weapons training and back again to the harsh exercise regime that was RAF Germany. Around their invitation, the XIII Squadron crew had placed 'luggage' labels giving the dates and places that they had visited on duty during their tour in their 'ancient' aircraft: UK, Germany, Italy, Gibraltar, Sicily, Cyprus, Egypt, Sudan, Kenya, Turkey, Iran, Pakistan, Oman, Gan, Singapore, Hong Kong etc. Maybe there was something to be said for flying our venerable aircraft.

* * *

During July and August we had trips to Brindisi in Southern Italy, Villafranca, and Gibraltar. We called at Gibraltar again on 9 September to refuel while delivering one of our aircraft for major servicing at RAF St Athan in South Wales. Later that month, I became one of the squadron's test pilots responsible for air testing aircraft that had been subject to an engine change or a period of prolonged servicing. This was interesting work and it increased markedly my experience flying the Canberra on one engine as each engine had to be shut-down in flight during an air test to make sure that it would re-start normally. Invariably they did, but one or two didn't!

* * *

In October the squadron deployed to Mashad in north-eastern Iran for a two-week exercise. Fred and I stayed back at RAF Luqa, but it wasn't long before we headed to Iran but with a small challenge en route. We had to deliver urgently needed spares as a number of aircraft were unserviceable. It would be a four-day round trip and we were to fly WH779. We soon discovered that there were no high-level airways charts to cover the route from Tehran to Mashad; the squadron had taken the complete stock with them. The Authorizing Officer told us to pick up maps at RAF Akrotiri and emphasized the importance and urgency of delivering the spares as quickly as possible. Also, we were required to pick up a senior officer from the Air Staff in Cyprus and take him with us for the overnight stay in Mashad. We flew to Akrotiri on 11 October and headed straight to Station Flight Planning to find that there were no maps there either! The squadron had been there before us. We were very conscious, perhaps too conscious, that the squadron was desperate for the spares that we carried. But what could we do? Then Fred's ingenuity came to the fore, if that is the right word to describe it. When I now think back to what we did it makes me shudder.

We had airways charts to cover the route from Cyprus north through Turkey then east into Iran and as far as Tehran. Our charts ended there. We knew the latitude and longitude of Mashad and we were also aware that the airway from Tehran to Mashad was a straight line. So, Fred attached a blank piece of paper to his chart and projected the airway to the north-east plotting the position of Mashad using the latitude and longitude. That was it. We had nothing else, and no other maps of any description to show us the topography. But, as we planned to fly at about 45,000 feet we were unlikely to bump into anything, although we knew that we would lose radio contact for a while over the mountains

The Canberra PR7 was equipped with HF, UHF and VHF radios but had no radar, and only very basic navigation aids and there would be few if any beacons to help us on our way. We set off from Cyprus on the morning of 12 October and it all worked to plan. Midway between Tehran and Mashad it did go fairly quiet for a while and the terrain below us was mountainous, desert and barren. As we got closer to our estimate of where Mashad was, we began a gradual descent but we were still unable to raise Mashad on the radio. We were flying over very high mountain ridges that were orientated north-west to south-east with wide, deep valleys between. At last we were able to speak to Mashad and as we crossed over yet another high ridge we saw a river in the deep valley beyond with an airfield on the far side which had a 12,000 foot runway running parallel to the river. There was a large town on its left, Mashad. We were there.

The Squadron Commander was delighted when we arrived but we didn't mention anything about our planning, certainly not then, and not to him. Soon we checked into the Intercontinental Hotel in Mashad and I went down to the bar for a cooling beer. It was here that the story of our planning came out. Initially no one believed that we had flown without an airways chart. Then someone said, 'But you did have a topo, didn't you?'

A 'topo' is a topographical chart showing all the terrain and features.

'No' I replied, 'Just Fred's bit of paper.'

There was what can only be described as a deathly hush amongst the assembled crews. One of the navigators left and came back a few minutes later with a topographical map. He gave it to me and asked me to describe from the map the last few miles as we approached Mashad:

'High mountainous ridges, orientated north-west to south-east; a wide deep valley with a river and an airfield beyond with a 12,000 foot runway parallel to the river and a town to its left,' I said.

Then he asked me to describe the terrain beyond Mashad to the north-east, 'It's much the same. There's a high mountainous ridge orientated north-west to south-east. Oh, and on the far side of the river there's an airfield with a 12,000 foot runway parallel to the river, and a town on the left! That's a coincidence,' I said.

He then asked me what the dotted lines were on the high ridge that separated Mashad from the terrain to the north-east. It was a border, an international border; the border between Iran and the Soviet Union. What if we had pressed on for a few minutes longer? What if we had been unable to raise Mashad on the radio? And what exactly would the Soviets have made of us and our aircraft with its seven different cameras, some of which were capable of photographing targets many, many miles away? We flew back the following day via Tehran and Turkey to Cyprus, and then home. We had an airways chart covering the whole route, and a topo.

*　*　*

Our sorties often concluded with twenty to thirty minutes over the Mediterranean Sea looking for any ships that might be of intelligence interest. These could be Soviet warships, especially submarines on the surface, or Soviet cargo ships with deck cargo on their way to Libya. Often missiles and their launchers which couldn't fit into the hold would be on deck covered by tarpaulins and we would do our best to get some close up photographs. If we ever thought that we had got something of intelligence interest then we would include 'X-Ray' in one of our radio calls so that the Photographic Interpreters would meet us on landing to get the film exploited immediately.

I became the Recognition Training Officer; this was largely down to the knowledge that I had acquired teaching ship recognition on 7 Squadron. With the new job came a much wider task as we had to become proficient in recognizing a wide range of Warsaw Pact and NATO ground equipment, such as tanks and armoured personnel carriers, as well as aircraft and ships. Every Friday afternoon was reserved for ground training, which included a recce test. There was always fierce competition to head the 'leader board' displayed in the planning room.

On 26 October, Fred and I had another night stop at Villafranca and on 8 November we headed off to RAF Wyton for another week's worth of low flying in the UK.

On Sunday 28 November, our son Matthew put in an appearance just before midnight. I celebrated with a large glass of single malt. I didn't hear the telephone or the frantic knocking on our door a few hours later. I arrived at work the next morning at the normal time of 0730 hours to find that it was a scene of frantic activity. Everyone was unshaven, sitting around in their 'war' flying suits, with tin hats and respirators – a TACEVAL. A full Station alert exercise had been called during the early hours but I had slept through the call-out!

'Where have you been?' was the cry.

But I didn't really care! The exercise lasted all week and we had to stay at Luqa throughout. I was given special dispensation to visit Jackie in hospital for an hour each evening.

A few weeks later I was promoted to the exulted rank of flight lieutenant, almost six years after I had been commissioned.

*   *   *

Apart from overnight trips to Villafranca in March, April and May 1977, I had no detachments until early July when the squadron again deployed to Villafranca for ten days. I was crewed with another navigator, Tony, who had previously flown PR Canberras in the sultry heat of Singapore; our crewing together for this exercise was to prove fortuitous.

Flying at low-level in the summer was often too hot, whereas we would often be too cold at high-level. Sorties which involved both could be a challenge. On this exercise all the flying was at low-level, so we wore minimal clothing under our flying suits. On 27 July 1977 Tony and I were programmed for a sortie in the early afternoon. Our aircraft hadn't flown that day and had been sitting in the sun on the tarmac all morning. Temperatures were above 30°C, so we were not unduly surprised to be sweating more than normal when we got airborne and for quite a while afterwards. I had already selected the cabin temperature control to fully cold as a matter of routine, but the airflow into the cockpit was a little on the low side. This wasn't particularly unusual in some aircraft. I held my wrist over one of the small air vents at one stage to make sure that we were getting air, which we were, although it was impossible to tell whether it was warm or cool, I could only tell that there was air flowing into the cockpit. Unlike Fred, Tony preferred to sit on the collapsible rumbold seat next me rather than lying down the front looking out of the nose. This preference of his may well have saved our lives that day.

As we approached the initial point for our first target, Tony didn't seem particularly sharp. If I had been flying with Fred, both of us would have had separate target maps which we would refer to. As Tony was sitting alongside me I could just as easily glance at his, so I didn't use mine at all, although I was familiar with the target run. The initial point stood out very well, it was a unique series of three bridges, and from there we were to head west.

We arrived overhead on time and set off towards the target. But then Tony began to 'rabbit on' about a railway line that he said we should be following. But I was sure that we were only meant to follow a railway line for a short distance from the three bridges before it swung away to the left, and I said so. Tony repeated that we were meant to be following a railway line. I got quite cross, which was unusual for me in the air, and looked at the map that he was holding. There was no railway line; as I thought it had swung away to the left. But Tony was obviously well 'behind the drag curve', so I swung the aircraft sharply around and headed back to the bridges. Once overhead them again I told Tony to restart his clock as we were at the initial point. He said that we couldn't be as we had already passed it! I completely lost my temper, something that I had never done in the air. But Tony restarted his clock, although he soon started to talk about the mysterious railway line that was on his map but that he couldn't find on the ground. I pointed at his map and shouted, 'Where's the railway line?'

'It's there,' he said, pointing at his map.

But the 'railway line' that he was pointing at was actually the pencil line that he had drawn from the three bridges to the target. I was totally exasperated.

Tony became increasingly flustered. I then looked at him closely. Even above his oxygen mask and behind his visor I could see that he was deathly white and sweating very heavily.

'I don't feel well; I can't get my breath,' he said.

After a short while he then said, 'I think it may be heat exhaustion; I had something like this when I was in Singapore.'

And with that he moved back and strapped himself into his ejection seat.

I had no choice but to turn the aircraft around and head back to Villafranca, but I was very cross, thinking that Tony was a complete wimp! I tried again to feel the airflow coming into the cockpit by holding my now ungloved hand over one of the air vents. I could feel air flow but was it cold, or was it warm? It was very hard to tell. But it didn't seem to change regardless of what I did with the temperature selector. I then began to feel increasingly unwell. I couldn't focus. I couldn't concentrate. I had to keep shaking my head to try and focus on what I was doing. I also began to have difficulty breathing. I was in a spot of trouble.

I flew a long straight in visual approach to Villafranca, but with a great deal of difficulty. Tony hadn't spoken since he had gone back to his seat. Air Traffic Control knew that there was something wrong as we were returning from our mission so early and they asked if we had a problem. I said 'yes' but I couldn't put into words what was wrong; it took everything I had just to fly the aircraft.

I landed on Villafranca's long runway which pointed north-east. At the end of the runway the taxiway veered slightly off to the left toward our dispersal and I followed it, but then stopped. The squadron dispersal was only a couple of hundred yards away but I couldn't continue; I couldn't actually do anything. Our groundcrew knew that there was something wrong and came running. The engines were still running but I wasn't capable of shutting them down. They got us out in a state of near collapse and one of the engineers climbed in and shut down the engines. A young medical orderly attached to the squadron quickly diagnosed severe heat exhaustion and dehydration. He treated us with fluid and salt and later said that Tony and I each drank about half a gallon of water in the first ten minutes. We recovered very quickly. It was estimated that our core body temperatures were within half a degree of the point at which we would have fallen unconscious, perhaps another one or two minutes in the air.

The fault was very simple: the cold air unit had failed. Our medical orderly received a flight safety award for his diagnosis and treatment and there was a lot of publicity about the incident on the flight safety net. We were very fortunate indeed that Tony had experienced something similar before. More discord between us could have had very serious consequences and if there had been even the slightest delay in returning to base, I could easily have become incapacitated before landing. It certainly highlighted the insidious way in which heat exhaustion can affect the human body and produce confusion and disorientation. Another two minutes in the air and we could so easily have ended up as a smoking hole in the ground. Even the most meticulous Board of Inquiry would be unlikely to focus on the cold air unit, so what would have been put down as the most likely cause? Aircrew error? Would that have been a likely fall-back option in those days? I was glad that I had been crewed with Tony that week and we gently helped to rehydrate ourselves during the early evening sitting on the wide piazza facing the Roman amphitheatre in Verona. But I have often thought about that day in July 1977.

*   *   *

Another trip to RAF Akrotiri followed in July, and then, on 3 August, Fred and I set off to play our part in the Kenya Survey. This was part of the Overseas Aid programme that had begun in the 1950s. It involved a photographic survey of the entire country for mapping purposes and the majority of it had been completed long ago. But there were still some gaps, and every year a couple of PR Canberras flew out to Nairobi to try and fill them in. By 1977 there were only three widely separated areas left to complete. So off we set to do our bit: two aircraft, two pilots and four navigators.

Our first flight of just over four hours was from Luqa to Khartoum in Sudan. Then it was on to the Kenyan Air Force base at Eastleigh, the military airfield on the eastern side of Nairobi. In total we flew seven hours that day.

The survey flying this time was relatively straightforward, although the sorties were long, averaging three to four hours. Having two navigators helped a great deal. We flew three sorties and were meant to fly a fourth, but that one didn't go quite as planned. The runway at Eastleigh was 9,000 feet long but it was also nearly 5,000 feet above sea level. I hadn't given this aspect enough thought and was about to discover at first hand that the height of the ground has a significant effect on aircraft performance, especially when the aircraft is at or near to its limits.

To begin with the take-off roll was normal; Fred was strapped into his seat, and another navigator, John, was sitting alongside me on the rumbold seat wearing a chest parachute. As we accelerated the RPM on one engine began to fluctuate wildly, the engine governor had failed. We weren't going any-where. I aborted the take-off at about 90 knots and stopping on such a long runway should not have been a problem, normally. To begin with I braked normally, but it had little effect. I gradually increased pressure on the brakes. We began to slow but at a very slow rate. I could see out of the corner of my eye that John's head was being forced forward as we at last began to slow. But by now I was braking as hard as I could and the end of the runway was getting ever closer. I wasn't at all sure that we would be able to stop and the overrun looked far from inviting; there was no barrier. By now the top half of John's body was even further forward than mine as I desperately tried to bring the aircraft to a standstill. We stopped with about three or four yards to go. We all breathed a collective sigh of relief.

Within seconds the Kenyan Air Force crash crews were on the scene. This was very impressive especially as their vehicles were circa 1950! But when the crews got out of their vehicles they were wearing shorts only and then pro-ceeded to rush around, like the Keystone Cops from 1920s silent films, trying to get into their fire-retardant coveralls. Luckily the brakes hadn't caught fire.

The reason that we had trouble stopping was simply because of the height of the airfield. Although our indicated air speed when I aborted was only 90 knots, because of our altitude, our true airspeed was nearly 130 knots which was very close to the maximum speed at which a safe abort could have been carried out. Not that we could have done anything else except abort as the aircraft certainly could not have got airborne. If we had been travelling a lot faster, Fred and I could have ejected of course, if we had been quick, but that would have left John.

An engineer was duly despatched from Luqa via Rome to Nairobi Inter-national with the appropriate spare to fix our aircraft, which delayed our return for a few days. We finally set off on 11 August and our flight from Eastleigh to Cairo was the longest that I was ever to fly in a Canberra: five hours and five minutes. We spent about an hour on the ground before another two and a half hour flight to Luqa.

* * *

After another ten days at Villafranca in the autumn, I returned to the welcome news that our second child was due in June. By then preparations were well underway for the final withdrawal of British Forces from Malta.

The resident Nimrod Squadron, 203 Squadron, soon disbanded and XIII Squadron would redeploy to RAF Wyton in October 1978. RAF Luqa would close on 1 April 1979. For some time, a new and longer 'civilian-only' runway had been under construction at Luqa. However, politics meant that we were never to operate from the new runway. Only in a dire emergency and following a 'mayday' call could we consider landing on the runway.

*   *   *

In November 1977, Fred and I spent another week low flying in the UK from RAF Wyton and this was followed in early December with a similar week in Germany operating from RAF Laarbruch. During the same month we had a number of visits from Rolls Royce engineers as we had been experiencing more than our fair share of problems with our elderly Rolls Royce engines resulting in an uncomfortable number of asymmetric landings. While I hadn't had any more problems than anyone else, I flew a lot of the air tests once the faulty engine had been replaced.

On one particular day Jackie had arrived at the squadron to pick me up and, as she was early, she went into the crewroom and chatted with some of the crews. After a while the crews all drifted off leaving Jackie on her own, but they came back after about ten minutes. When she mentioned this, they said that they had gone onto the roof to watch me land as I was coming back on one engine. They explained that if they were witnesses to an accident they couldn't act as members of any subsequent Board of Inquiry!

The Rolls Royce representatives, along with the inevitable staff officers, tried to reassure us that the faults were simply coincidences, that they were isolated and not part of a trend. For our part, we listened unconvinced. Given the number of problems that we had experienced there was an increasing risk that faults could develop in both engines during the same sortie. As far as we were concerned, there was a trend, and that trend was that we were having more than our fair share of engine faults.

*   *   *

During the squadron's final eight months in Malta, we embarked on a hard exercise routine to prepare the squadron for redeployment to the UK. Little did we realize that from an intelligence point of view the next few months would also be an extremely important period for a squadron that had been deployed overseas since 1942. And for Fred and I it would bring our most successful sortie, the results of which were still displayed in XIII Squadron's HQ at RAF Marham some thirty-three years later.

*   *   *

We attended an intelligence briefing about a new class of Soviet warship. Called the *Kiev*, she was the USSR's first aircraft carrier and had been launched in 1977 initially as part of the Soviet Baltic Sea Fleet. What was intriguing from an intelligence point of view was uncertainty about whether the Soviets had any fixed-wing aircraft capable of operating from a carrier. Was *Kiev* really an aircraft carrier or was it just a bigger helicopter carrier similar to the Moskva Class which had been around for some time?

The reason for our interest was that *Kiev* had left the Baltic for the Atlantic before passing into the Mediterranean. It was thought to be heading our way to exercise with the Soviet Black Sea Fleet. It was known to have Hormone B helicopters on board but it also appeared to have two fixed-wing aircraft on deck near the stern of the ship. These were of an unknown type and they had not been moved since the ship had first been spotted; they were also covered by some form of tarpaulin. Were they real or were they just models meant to waste NATO intelligence analysts' time?

On 6 January 1978 Fred and I were tasked with the first sortie to find and photograph *Kiev*. Our aircraft was WH779 which had seen us safely to and from Mashad in Iran. Normally, aircraft carriers had to be avoided by 2,000 feet and two miles, but on this and other occasions a 'Nelsonian eye' was adopted by our masters. *Kiev* was being escorted by two other warships, a Kara cruiser and a Krivak destroyer. The Kara was an immensely powerful warship armed with an array of weaponry including surface-to-surface and surface-to-air missiles as well as guns. The Krivak, slightly smaller than the Kara at about 405 feet, was also very capable. All three had passed through the Straits of Gibraltar the day before and were thought to be approaching the area south of Sardinia. Fred and I flew at high-level from Malta toward Sardinia before dropping down to begin our search. The weather was fine with some broken cumulus cloud but very good visibility. After a surprisingly short time we spotted something vaguely military heading toward us. We had struck lucky. No sooner had we arrived than all three ships altered course and headed directly into wind. For an aircraft carrier to do that normally meant one thing, they were about to launch their aircraft.

The earlier speculation that the fixed-wing aircraft were just models was quickly dispelled when they took off! I did my best to get some decent photography, even to the extent of flying in formation as the Soviet aircraft, the Yak 38 Forger, came into land, but the dear old Canberra became quite 'floppy' during the approach as the Soviet aircraft could fly a lot slower than I could! Over the next few days a number of other crews were also tasked against *Kiev* but it was immensely satisfying to have been first. But more, and better, much better, was to come.

On 27 January, I flew another sortie against *Kiev* as she passed through the straights between Malta and Sicily. This time I was a little more adventurous, flying much lower and closer to get as many close-up photographs as possible flying across the deck before banking very steeply to try and photograph down the open lift into the hangar deck. This involved applying about 70 or 80 degrees of bank as we came across the deck at about one hundred feet above the ship. But we got the pictures.

While we were there an RAF F4 Phantom arrived to have a look at *Kiev*. The Phantom was from a squadron that was on detachment in Malta. I suggested taking a photograph of the Phantom while he was flying overhead *Kiev*; he would then have something for his squadron's photograph album, and his own, when he got back to the UK. We set everything up over the radio and suggested the height that he should fly between us and *Kiev* in order to get a decent shot. As I headed toward *Kiev* I kept looking behind on the right to watch for the Phantom overtaking us. Then there was a flash as the Phantom flew past. Yes, he was on the right hand side but instead of approaching from behind with an overtake speed of about 60 knots; he came from ahead! We had a combined closing speed of about 700 knots! Inadequate briefing!

So we re-briefed and our next attempt looked more successful. Back at Luqa we all gathered around the light table to look at the results. There was one picture showing *Kiev* in full and with the Phantom high up on the right over the stern. Not perfect but good enough! But just as we were congratulating ourselves there was a cry from the photographic interpreters who pushed us out of the way to look more closely. They had spotted something that we had not. We had been concentrating so hard on our 'happy snap' that we had failed to notice that the Phantom was being tracked by the forward twin 76mm guns and the rear SA-N-3 surface-to-air missile launcher. What was even more important was that SA-N-3 had missiles actually on the launcher. These had never been seen mounted on one of *Kiev*'s launchers until then. While the photograph was a bit of an intelligence scoop, it was also one that amused our interpreters no end. But if it was an intelligence scoop they wanted I would give them a much better one, but they would have to wait a few more weeks.

* * *

At the time, there was a lot of political 'conflict' in Malta between the ruling Labour Party, under their Prime Minister Dom Mintoff, and the Nationalist Party. Dom Mintoff had actually had been interned by the UK during the Second World War for his very strong anti-British stance. Early in 1978 all of the Maltese doctors went on strike and this was to last until after the UK left the island. To keep the island's hospitals running, the government brought in all sorts of doctors from all over the place, Libya and the Palestine Liberation Organization being some of the more notable contributors. This would not normally have affected us except that as part of the rundown, the RN Hospital at Mtarfa would close on 1 April 1978, a year before the final UK withdrawal and two months before our next baby was due. Arrangements were made for natal care at a private nursing home in Attard called St Catherine's and the Station Medical Centre at RAF Luqa was also modified so that it could provide some basic hospital care but, as the RAF doctors no longer had any confidence in the Maltese medical services, complications could only be dealt with in the UK. Little did we realize that this would have potentially very serious repercussions for us.

*   *   *

And then there was that sortie on Wednesday 22 March 1978.

I looked at my watch again. It hadn't stopped, but it must have been the fifth or sixth time that I had looked at it within the last twenty minutes. It seemed as if we had been airborne for hours yet my ever-faithful RAF aircrew watch showed that only ninety minutes had elapsed since *that* take off. We continued our search, scanning the distant horizon, but there was no sign of our elusive quarry.

Fred, as was normal for him on low level sorties, had unstrapped from his ejection seat and come forward. Some navigators preferred to sit on the fold-down rumbold seat, alongside the pilot on the right, but Fred much preferred to crawl down the narrow, claustrophobic tunnel to lie flat and look out of the Perspex nose of the 25-year old Canberra PR7. A navigator's lot on Canberras was all about mastering claustrophobia; if Fred had remained in his ejection seat he had a bulkhead to look at directly in front of him and only two tiny windows through which he could occasionally snatch fleeting glimpses of the outside world as it moved swiftly past. Above his head was the frangible hatch through which his ejection seat would travel if he had to use it in earnest. If he had remained strapped into his ejection seat, Fred would have been no help to me on this sortie; I needed another pair of eyes, not that I ever had to ask Fred to come up front. Of course if we had a problem he would have to look sharp reversing down the tunnel, feet first, so that he could then get up, turn around, and move to the rear of the cockpit behind my ejection seat and then turn around once more before quickly strapping into the double harness of the Canberra's elderly Martin Baker ejection seat. We often practiced doing just that; you never knew when you might have to opt for a Martin Baker letdown.

We flew on varying our height between 250 and 2,000 feet, both of us scanning as far as we could see, but to no avail. It was blowing quite a gale outside and had been all morning. The sea was running very high, with deep rolling waves and white surf being lifted and thrown across the wave tops by the gusting wind. I shivered inwardly at the thought of having to eject in such conditions. Despite being in the relatively warm environment of the Mediterranean there would be little chance of survival for long even if we could board our tiny single-man dinghies. With the wind as it was, boarding our dinghies would be a very big 'if'. There were no search and rescue helicopters based in Malta; the nearest were in Italy but we were a lot closer to Libya.

I reflected again, as I had done many times that morning, on the decision to launch us: our mission must have been considered to be very important, although in the end the final decision to take off had been mine. And if anything went seriously wrong, the final responsibility would also be mine; I was the aircraft captain. Aircraft captaincy could sometimes be a lonely place.

We simply must find her. Visibility was good but it reduced quickly to only a few hundred yards in the frequent squalls which passed by. Could we have missed her? We were in the area that the intelligence staffs had suggested but there was no sign of her at all. Could the intelligence have been wrong? It wouldn't have been the first time. We pressed on.

Nor would she be on her own; she should also have her faithful escorts, a Kara and a Krivak. How could all three of them hide from us? But there was not a sign. In fact we hadn't seen a single ship since we took off. Perhaps our maritime brothers were a little wiser than we had been venturing so far from land on a day such as this. If our quarry had any sense she would have sought shelter from the fierce north westerly gale in one of the nearby bays in Tunisia or Libya. We continued our search as I hauled the heavy PR7 around the sky looking far and wide to see if we could spot a silhouette against the skyline that might give us a clue as to where our target might be.

*   *   *

The day had begun like any normal working day for an operational crew on XIII (PR) Squadron, based at RAF Luqa in Malta. Fred and I lived a few doors apart in the small town of Balzan. We often shared cars, sometimes driving through the main site of RAF Luqa before crossing the runway to reach XIII Squadron HQ. It always brought a wry smile to my face when one of the Armed Forces of Malta Super Frelon helicopters took off and flew slowly past our dispersal, directly opposite the International Airport Terminal. The helicopters had come from Libya, which had close links with Malta's ruling Labour Government under Dom Mintoff. We were unsure of the nationality of the pilots.

It had been one of those rare wild and windy nights in Malta, and even at 0700 hours as we drove across the runway, the wind had not abated. We had both remarked on the windsock, which showed the wind's direction and approximate strength. It had been horizontal. It was also at 90 degrees to Luqa's Runway 24/06, which was the worst it could be for aircraft operations. It was gusting too. We both agreed that there would be no chance of flying and an 'early stack' was most likely on the cards. Perhaps we would be able to call in at the Officers' Mess on our way home for one of the Maltese barman's renowned brandy sours, or for a refreshing glass of the Maltese lager, Cisk. In that, we were not far wrong; we would indeed enjoy a Cisk in the bar that day, but it would be a lot later than we anticipated. The day would turn out to be one of the most difficult, and the most exciting, of our operational careers until then, or since.

That morning everyone at the Squadron was pretty relaxed, having come to the same conclusion: there would be no flying that day. The flying programme had been 'scrubbed', and as XIII Squadron was the last operational squadron based in Malta, there would be little else happening on the airfield. We could see that the International Airport was a hive of inactivity too, with all civilian take-offs and landings having been cancelled – even profit could not argue with Mother Nature that morning. The weekly RAF VC10 aircraft from RAF Brize Norton had also been diverted to the Italian Air Force Base of Sigonella in Sicily.

Strong winds weren't necessarily a problem and it was possible to take-off and land with a wind speed of 40 knots, providing that the wind was not too far off the runway direction. But if the wind is across the runway it becomes more difficult, and is at its worst when it is at right angles to the runway direction. Gusting winds are even more troublesome. It is relatively simple to work out the headwind and the crosswind component. For most aircraft, including the Canberra, the maximum crosswind component for take-off and landing was 25 knots. On 22 March the wind was from the north-west, 90 degrees off Luqa's runway. With an average wind speed of 30–40 knots, and with gusts to 50 and 60 knots, it was well outside our limits. So Fred and I adjourned to the crewroom for a coffee and a chat with the boys as we looked forward to that beer in the bar on the way home, and perhaps another on one of our respective balconies overlooking San Anton Gardens and the President's Palace.

*   *   *

But the calm was soon shattered. That most irreverent of squawk boxes on the crewroom wall burst into life and interrupted the calm stilling our conversation.

'McDonald and Stokes, report to Operations!'

Fred and I looked at one another and wondered what we had done, what had been found out. Nothing immediately came to mind, so with a shrug and joint looks of resignation we headed upstairs to the Operations Room. We were met at the top of the stairs by my Flight Commander, who was the Acting Squadron Commander at the time. With a smile he said, 'It looks like there may be a job for you two, you may be getting airborne. Grab your hats; I'll see you in my car.'

Fred and I looked at each other in amazement, and soon found ourselves in the Squadron Commander's RAF Ford Escort Estate heading back across the runway. The windsock was still horizontal – we looked at one another even more questioningly. If anything, the wind was actually stronger than it had been earlier, but my Flight Commander was keeping his thoughts to himself. No doubt all would be revealed when we entered that very private inner sanctum of Operations Wing, the Station Intelligence Squadron.

It was *Kiev*. The very latest and immensely powerful addition to the Soviet Union's already impressive navy. She was thought to be heading west once more for the final time, having completed sea training and trials with the Soviet Black Sea Fleet, and was now thought to be on her way to join the

Soviet Northern Fleet at Murmansk. My first thought was 'so what?' What was so special about *Kiev* today of all days? She had first entered the Mediterranean in January, and I had already flown two full missions photographing her from every angle and height imaginable. While this would probably be the last opportunity for us to get more photographs of *Kiev*, didn't we have enough already? What about the weather? Didn't the somewhat extreme wind conditions scotch any thought of getting airborne? Apparently they did not.

*   *   *

It soon became apparent that it wasn't about getting airborne despite the weather – it was about getting airborne because of the weather. The gale force winds and the very high seas meant, according to the Intelligence staffs, that it might just be possible to get some photographs of parts of *Kiev*'s hull that were normally underwater. My eyebrows lifted a little at this. The Station Intelligence Officer was not a pilot and I am not sure whether he fully understood what I would have to do to our ancient and heavy aircraft to achieve such photography. Our low-level cameras were not mounted horizontally, but at an angle of 15 degrees below the horizontal, and they were fixed. And he wanted photographs of parts of the hull that were normally below the waterline?

He went on. He was particularly interested in what looked like some sort of gate that was low on *Kiev*'s stern. If we just happened to be flying past the stern as it came out of the water because of the sea state we might, just might, be able to get a picture below the waterline he thought. There were lots of 'ifs' and 'maybes'. I toyed with the idea of inviting him to come along for the ride, but dismissed the thought almost as soon as it occurred – he would get in the way. All I would be able to do was try and manoeuvre the aircraft to be in the right place at the right time. We would also have to fly at very low altitude, perhaps at 100 feet or less, to try to get the shots that he wanted. This was no easy matter as the Canberra PR7 was a heavy old beast and it did not have powered flying controls. So this would be a very physical mission. And of course all of our low-level cameras were pilot operated too; once we had found *Kiev*, Fred could do little except watch. To cap it all, the Intelligence staff had no real idea of where *Kiev* or her escorts were, the last sighting having been the previous day with *Kiev* and a mighty Kara cruiser and a Krivak escort heading in Malta's direction. It was suggested that we search to the south of Malta, toward the Libyan and Tunisian coasts, where *Kiev* may seek some shelter from the gale that we could still hear blowing outside. Seeking shelter from the gale sounded like a very good idea to me.

There was then some discussion about the wind and the difficulties that it would present during take-off and landing. I was glad that aspect got a mention. I wasn't particularly uncomfortable about taking off in such a strong crosswind; we could sit at the end of the runway with the engines running at high power for as long as necessary, listening to read-outs of the crosswind component from air traffic control. I could then release the brakes during a lull and go for it. Landing though, might be a different matter, and I said so.

It was then announced that the long-disused airfield at Hal Far would be reopened for us for landing. It had a 6,000 foot runway, the minimum safe length for a Canberra, but crucially it pointed virtually straight into the prevailing wind. While it was 1,500 feet shorter than Luqa's runway and it began virtually at the cliff face, it should not be a problem. Runway sweepers, crash crews, an ambulance and air traffic controllers would also be despatched from Luqa, just as soon as the decision was made for us to launch. I was a little taken aback by all this; Hal Far had been disused for years, clearly our mission was considered to be of the highest importance. It also seemed that all eventualities had been carefully considered and each one had been covered. But no pressure was exerted on us whatsoever. That was the way of this particular Flight Commander; he was a good man to work for.

As we drove back across the airfield I reflected a little on what had been said. It was quite an accolade to have been selected for this mission, after all, XIII Squadron had upwards of a dozen operational crews available that day. Fred and I had been crewed together since we arrived on XIII Squadron nearly three years earlier, in August 1975. Fred was on his fourth flying tour and his second on Canberras. I was on my second tour and had close to 1,500 flying hours on Canberras. We also were pretty competent as a constituted crew, and had a deserved reputation for being able to get the job done and come back with the goods – usually. But I also figured that there was something that had been left unsaid during our briefing. Since the withdrawal of the Nimrod squadron from Malta, XIII Squadron was the only RAF source of real intelligence in the Mediterranean, and we too would be withdrawn to the UK within six months as part of the UK's final withdrawal from Malta. Was the presence of *Kiev* today seen as a last opportunity for XIII, and the RAF in Malta, to once again prove our worth?

Fred and I were quiet on the journey back to the squadron. As we crossed the main runway the wind had not abated. It was clear that the go/no-go decision would be ours. If we were prepared to go, my Flight Commander was sufficiently confident in our ability to authorize the sortie. A glance at Fred, and a nod from him, was all that was needed. The mission was on.

*   *   *

The aircraft chosen for the task was WT530; and it was fitted with a 12-inch F95 low-level camera on the starboard side, and 4-inch F95 on the port, both mounted in the forward camera bay. We would not be using any of our many other cameras on this sortie. There was very little else to cover in the preflight briefing except a reminder to include the codeword 'X-Ray' when we returned to Luqa if we felt that we had photography that merited immediate exploitation. My Flight Commander then signed the authorization sheet and I signed afterwards as aircraft captain. A few minutes later Fred and I strapped into the aircraft and then a towing vehicle arrived – the wind was too strong for us to attempt to taxy.

We were towed to the end of Runway 24 with the aircraft control locks fitted to prevent any movement of the aircraft controls in the frequent gusts of wind. Even the engine intake blanks were fitted, to prevent any 'debris' being blown into the engine intakes. Malta had a bit of a reputation for 'debris'. We were positioned well to the left of the runway centreline, not pointing down the runway, but at an angle of 30 degrees into wind. The control locks and blanks were then removed and we started the engines. Once the after start checks had been completed, our groundcrew moved to one side of the runway to watch and to wait. I checked in with air traffic control and we were cleared to 'take-off at your discretion'. I accelerated the engines to the maximum continuous RPM of 7,600 and then held the aircraft on the brakes. We were then given a continuous read-out of the crosswind component from the Visual Control Room on top of the air traffic control tower. I could also see that we had something of an audience on the balcony of the XIII Squadron HQ outside the first floor Operations Room.

When the crosswind component dropped momentarily below 30 knots I released the brakes, applied full power, and with a big boot of left rudder the aircraft slowly turned onto the centreline and off we went, lumbering up the gentle incline of Runway 24. Slow accelerations on take-off were a feature of the Canberra PR7. At 48,000lb all-up-weight, the PR7 was a heavy old beast, even without wing-tip fuel tanks fitted. Thankfully, as it was March, the outside temperature was quite moderate, on hot days take-offs concentrated the mind. The take-off was surprisingly uneventful and so we began our search.

*   *   *

Fred, as was normal for him on low-level sorties, had unstrapped from his ejection seat and come forward. Some navigators preferred to sit on the fold down rumbold seat, alongside the pilot on the right, but Fred much preferred to crawl down the narrow, claustrophobic tunnel to lie flat and look out of the Perspex nose of the twenty-five year old Canberra PR7. A navigators' lot on Canberras was all about mastering claustrophobia; if Fred had remained in his ejection seat, he had a bulkhead to look at directly in front of him and only two tiny windows through which he could occasionally snatch fleeting glimpses of the outside world as it moved swiftly past. Above his head was the frangible hatch through which his ejection seat would travel if he had to use it in earnest. If he had remained strapped into his ejection seat, Fred would have been no help to me on this sortie; I needed another pair of eyes, not that I ever had to ask Fred to come up front. Of course if we had a problem he would have to look sharp reversing down the tunnel feet first, so that he could then get up, turn around, and move to the rear of the cockpit behind my ejection seat. Then turn around once more, before quickly strapping into the double harness of the Canberra's elderly Martin Baker ejection seat. We often practiced doing just that; you never knew when you might have to opt for a Martin Baker let-down.

We flew on, varying our height between 250 and 2,000 feet, both of us scanning as far as we could see, but to no avail. It was blowing quite a gale outside, and had been all morning. The sea was running very high, with deep rolling waves and white surf being lifted and thrown across the wave tops by the gusting wind. I shivered inwardly at the thought of having to eject in such conditions. Despite being in the relatively warm environment of the Mediterranean there would be little chance of survival for long, even if we could board our tiny single-man dinghies. With the wind as it was, boarding our dinghies would be a very big 'if'. There were no search and rescue helicopters based in Malta. The nearest were in Italy, but we were a lot closer to Libya.

I reflected again, as I had done many times that morning, on the decision to launch us. Our mission must have been considered to be very important, although in the end the final decision to take-off had been mine. And if anything went seriously wrong, the final responsibility would also be mine. I was the aircraft captain. Aircraft captaincy could sometimes be a lonely place.

We simply must find her. Visibility was good, but it quickly reduced to only a few hundred yards in the frequent squalls which passed by. Could we have missed her? We were in the area that the intelligence staffs had suggested, but there was no sign of her at all. Could the intelligence have been wrong? It wouldn't have been the first time. We pressed on.

Nor would she be on her own; she should also have her faithful escorts, a Kara and a Krivak. How could all three of them hide from us? But there was not a sign. In fact we hadn't seen a single ship since our take-off. Perhaps our maritime brothers were a little wiser than we had been, venturing so far from land on a day such as this. If our quarry had any sense she would have sought shelter from the fierce north-westerly gale in one of the nearby bays in Tunisia or Libya. We continued our search as I hauled the heavy PR7 around the sky, looking far and wide, to see if we could spot a silhouette against the skyline that might give us a clue as to where our target might be.

*   *   *

Finally, with about thirty minutes of fuel remaining Fred suggested that we swing toward the east of Malta, and then head north-west between Malta and Sicily before calling it a day. I agreed. While this was not the area suggested by Intelligence it would be our last throw of the dice.

We could tell by looking at the sea that it was still blowing a gale, the conditions outside looked very bad. Thank goodness I wasn't a sailor – even the hardiest of sailors would have been uncomfortable on a day like today.

Soon we were within twenty-five miles of Malta. We were on the point of giving up when we spotted something ahead. Was it our quarry?

As we got closer, it was apparent that it was not, but it was definitely a warship – and it was Soviet. It was also struggling, not making any headway at all, simply pointing into wind and maintaining steerage. It was a Soviet destroyer, of the Krivak class, and we knew that she was one of *Kiev*'s escorts. She was pointing north-west, so, after taking a few photographs, we headed in the same direction. The trail was getting warm. Then we found the Kara class cruiser, and she too was making very little headway. The Kara was a magnificent looking vessel with so much firepower crammed into her 580 feet. Capable of well over 30 knots, even she was struggling, with the high seas often swamping her low stern and helicopter deck. But the trail was now getting hot, we had to be close.

A few miles further on, even closer to Malta, we found her. We learnt later that RAF air traffic controllers at Luqa could see *Kiev* on their radar and had done so since long before we had taken off. She was virtually on the centre-line of the approach to Runway 24, about twenty miles out. Of course they had no idea what the vessel was, nor did they know the precise nature of our mission until after we were airborne. Only when we began to fly around *Kiev* itself did they realize that the blip on their radar screen was the target that had been eluding us for so long.

Kiev was an amazing sight. Over 900 feet long with a displacement of 42,000 tons, she was the pride of the Soviet Navy and was a credit to her designer. She was also very heavily armed. No doubt conditions below decks would have been cramped for the majority of her crew of 1,612. Conditions below deck on that day must have been grim indeed, as even the might of *Kiev* was being dwarfed by the enormous waves crashing over her.

We had no time to lose and immediately set about taking as many photographs as we could. We had very little fuel left and we needed to have some reserve in case it took us a while to get down. We concentrated on the stern but also made numerous low runs alongside and over her deck. The Soviets totally ignored us, they had their hands full. With luck our 12-inch F95 camera should produce some good quality close-up shots, but all I could do was try and put our aircraft in the right place, I couldn't point the camera, and we wouldn't know anything of our results until after landing when the film negative was eventually rolled out on one of our large light tables. The flying was exhilarating but it was also tiring, and we had little time to enjoy the thrill of the very low passes that we made, sometimes even below deck level. Fred said nothing throughout, nor did he need to.

In no time at all we had used up all of our film and we headed back to Malta, by now only two or three minutes flying time away. I was confident that we would have the 'goods' so included the crucial word 'X-Ray' in our recovery radio call. That would ensure that our skilled team of 'photogs' and photographic interpreters would meet the aircraft on landing at Hal Far and get the film exploited within minutes.

As we approached Luqa and Hal Far, the wind if anything was even stronger than before and we were told to go immediately to Hal Far. I very much looked forward to this and approached Hal Far from over the sea at 250 feet and 420 knots. We flashed over the cliffs and then over the runway before I broke to the left and upwards, closing the throttles, selecting air-brakes out, and also opening our large flare (bomb) bay to reduce our speed. Fred was by now back safely strapped into his ejection seat. I turned finals at 1,000 feet and began a descending turn onto the final approach rolling out at about 300 feet with the speed now reducing toward 110 knots. That's when I realized that we had a problem, a big problem. We couldn't land.

*   *   *

For most of the time that we had been airborne we had been flying at speeds of between 300 and 350 knots and visibility through both the canopy and through the Perspex nose had been good. But as soon as we slowed down to approach speed for landing, I had to raise the nose of the aircraft to maintain the correct approach path. We were also heading directly into sun, toward the cliff, with the threshold of the short runway starting just beyond the cliff face. While there was no crosswind problem, I simply couldn't see anything. The lower part of the canopy was completely encrusted with salt; it was totally opaque. At higher speeds this had gone unnoticed. I overshot, and Fred scrambled back into the nose to see if he could talk me down onto the runway. I hadn't asked him too, he just came forward. Fred was not short of guts. But the lower part of the Perspex nose-cone was just as bad. I tried a couple more approaches at higher speeds but it was hopeless. In order to see the runway I had to fly so fast that I couldn't put the aircraft on the ground. Fred wisely crawled back out of the nose and strapped himself into his ejection seat. I overshot and explained my problem to air traffic control. What were we going to do now?

We had no choice but to return to Luqa and make an approach to Runway 24 to assess the conditions. We were given frequent read-outs of the crosswind as we tried a couple of approaches. The wind direction was still unchanged and the mean wind speed was still about 30 knots with regular higher gusts. And with the wind from the right, it came over the high hangar which had contributed to the Vulcan disaster in 1975.

The crosswind landing technique in the Canberra was to fly the aircraft with the nose pointing into wind, and just before touchdown as the aircraft was flared, rudder was applied to swing the nose so that at touchdown the aircraft would be pointing down the runway.

After trying one approach I gave thanks to English Electric, the aircraft designers and builders, all those years earlier in the late 1940s. To cope with severe icing conditions that were expected during high-level flying, a small

Direct Vision panel had been installed within the pilot's canopy. This was about 6 inches in diameter and about 20° to the left of the centre of the canopy. And it was electrically heated. The heating element was designed to keep the window clear of ice. But, luckily for us, it had also kept this tiny window free from salt. On my next approach I pointed the nose of the aircraft to the right into wind, and could then glimpse the runway through the small window. As I overshot I told air traffic control that I would be landing from my next approach and, from the moment I began the finals turn, my Flight Commander's reassuring voice could be heard giving crosswind readings. Remarkably, they were all within the aircraft's crosswind limits!

Just before touchdown, I flared the aircraft and then with a huge boot full of left rudder, the aircraft yawed to the left. It began to swing but it seemed to take forever! And then there was a great gust of wind! The port main wheel touched down but try as I might I could not get the starboard wheel onto the ground. I applied full aileron to the right but the wing stayed in the air as we sped down the runway. I couldn't brake, not until both wheels were firmly on the ground. And then the gust of wind dropped, and the starboard main wheel slowly sank onto the ground. We were safely down. We had been airborne for nearly two and a half hours.

*   *   *

A few minutes later, we met my Flight Commander in the Operations Room. He was grinning broadly and so were we. I never did ask him about the coincidence of the wind dropping to within limits as we turned finals on our final circuit. A short while later we all crowded round the light table to see the results of our efforts. The interpreters were going through each roll of film very quickly to see if we had any shots of the mystery gate on *Kiev's* stern. There were some pictures of the gate but none with it out of the water. I was bitterly disappointed.

Ah well, we had tried our best, but even as that thought had barely entered my head, there was a cry of 'bloody hell' from the senior intelligence analyst. I looked over his shoulder to see what had caught his attention. He was looking at a close-up picture not of the stern but of *Kiev's* bow. And it was completely clear of the water with almost the first hundred feet of the keel of the ship visible. We had flown rather low to get that particular photograph. There was great excitement but I only realized afterwards, when it was explained, how important that one photograph was. Armed with such a photograph a naval architect could determine so much about this brand new class of warship, things like displacement, maximum speed etc. The picture was thought to be so important that even before we left the squadron to go for that much looked forward to beer in the Mess; it was being referred to as possibly the intelligence scoop of the year. It wasn't; it turned out to be the intelligence scoop of the decade.

So our elderly Canberra PR7, long since relegated from NATO's all important Central Region to the southern flank, could still produce the goods. And

XIII Squadron and the RAF, so soon to withdraw from the Mediterranean for the final time, were not quite done yet. And as for the mystery gate, it was very simple really, it was a retractable gate that could be opened and through which a towed sonar array could be launched. So it wasn't that special after all.

We didn't witness the sequel to this sortie later that day when the Air Commander Malta went to see the Commander British Forces Malta. Apparently he threw the photographs across the Admiral's desk saying, 'Take a look at these!'

The Admiral was astonished and exclaimed, 'Where on earth did you get these?'

'One of my Canberras took them this morning,' said the Air Commodore.

'Good grief, what height was he flying?'

'Don't ask stupid questions,' was the reply.

* * *

As Fred and I 'bowed out' from XIII Squadron six months later, we presented the squadron with a large framed photograph of that picture of *Kiev* with her bow out of the water. It was displayed in XIII Squadron's HQ until the squadron was disbanded in 2011 although very few knew the story behind the photograph. As for our faithful WT530, she returned to Malta with a crew of three on a training flight from RAF Wyton some two months after XIII Squadron's redeployment. On its return flight on Monday 7 December, the aircraft lost power on take-off and the pilot and navigator ejected. They both survived, albeit injured – the aircraft was destroyed. The second navigator, Pilot Officer Marshall, occupying the Rumbold seat died. The carriage of a third crew member on the rumbold seat was then banned. One of our other 'regular' aircraft was WH779 and in 2012 the front section of this aircraft went on display at Newark Air Museum.

* * *

I was expecting news of my next posting at any time. I was very much hoping that I would at last be posted to the Buccaneer, the aircraft that I had wanted to fly since the very beginning of my pilot training. This would of course mean a number of courses beforehand and it could be a year and a half before we would be settled on a new squadron and we would have a new home. When my posting was announced, not to Buccaneers but to the Central Flying School to become an instructor, I was slightly disappointed, but from a family perspective it would be a very good move. As it turned out it was very good for me professionally too. Fred would also become an instructor, a navigation instructor at RAF Finningley. He later completed a tour on 60 Squadron at RAF Wildenrath in Germany and we met up when we moved to Germany.

* * *

In the meantime there was another Exercise Shabaz in Pakistan to take part in and the squadron deployed once more to Masroor. This time we shared the base with a USAF F15 squadron from Bitburg in Germany. I celebrated my twenty-ninth birthday in Karachi. The sorties were similar to those I had flown the previous year.

On one sortie our target was Karachi Docks and we were to simulate an attack at high-level. As we approached we kept changing radio frequencies to see if we could pick up any of the fighters sent to intercept us. We stumbled across a PAF F6 (Mig 19) scrambled from Masroor to intercept a high-level target approaching from the west. That had to be us. The F6 was told to climb to 35,000 feet so we kept climbing higher still, eventually reaching 45,000 feet. The fighter was unable to climb above 37,000 feet because of a reheat problem and, as it only had guns, we were completely safe. I almost laughed out loud over the radio when the F6 called 'Fox 3', a guns-kill! He was 8,000 feet below us. Impossible!

The F6 pilot recognized us as an RAF Canberra from Masroor, his home base, and said that he would shoot us down for a second time when we started our descent to land.

'I don't think so,' I thought!

With that, I closed the throttles, put the airbrakes out, opened the flare bay, and descended in a very tight high speed spiral from 45,000 feet to 500 feet! The fighter had no chance of tracking us and every now and again I saw him flying at high speed in a very wide circle around us desperately trying to turn inside us and track us with his guns. Not a hope! Of course, if he had been armed with an air-to-air missile it would have been no contest, he would have shot us down long ago, but it was nevertheless great fun.

*   *   *

After a few difficult days in early June which saw Jackie admitted into St Catherine's Nursing Home, and then discharged the following day in a wheelchair, unable to walk because of a perforated disc, our daughter Hannah arrived on our fourth wedding anniversary, 8 June 1978. Within a few days Hannah became very ill. To begin with the RAF doctor at Luqa didn't consider the problem to be serious but over the weekend we became increasingly alarmed as Hannah had great difficulty breathing. Another doctor, a squadron leader who had been in Malta for less than forty-eight hours, confirmed that Hannah was very poorly. But he could not recommend admission to a Maltese hospital as the Maltese doctors were still on strike and the earliest that Hannah could be evacuated as a medical emergency would be in another five days. By then the outcome would be known. He said that we could give better care at home than could be given within the Medical Centre. The next few days were very difficult but thankfully Hannah responded well and made a full recovery. We had a lot to thank that doctor for and we would meet him again in very unusual circumstances; on the second occasion his judgement and rapid diagnosis would save Jackie's life.

*   *   *

Soon the focus was on the squadron's forthcoming move to the UK. A ceremonial parade at RAF Luqa was to be held to mark Her Majesty the Queen's Silver Jubilee during which we would fly a nine aircraft formation. The squadron would then redeploy to the UK on 4 October 1978 and I would leave XIII Squadron the following morning. My final trip to Villafranca and to Verona was on 9 August and later that month I spent a few days in Cyprus doing some survey work. During September I flew a number of formation sorties leading up to our memorable flypast over the final parade on 29 September.

*   *   *

The squadron departed en masse for RAF Wyton on the morning of the 4 October. The Boss's plan was to fly all the way in a formation of nine aircraft but he was overruled by our new HQ, 1 Group. Welcome to 1 Group! Instead we flew in separate formations of three aircraft, separated by a few minutes, so that we could then join up for a grand arrival at Wyton. So we would end up doing a nine-ship low-level flypast after our 4-hour transit flight. The weather did however intervene and there was very low cloud at Wyton which meant that we had to split up and fly individual instrument approaches. Welcome to Wyton and to UK weather! The VIP who welcomed XIII Squadron back to the UK after thirty-six year's continuous service overseas was the newly appointed Deputy Commander-in-Chief (C-in-C), Strike Command, Air Marshal Sir Alfred Ball, whom I had last met in Tehran.

*   *   *

So that was it, my tour was over and it had been the most amazing second tour that I could have wished to have had. In three years and five weeks I had flown 909 hours. I now had a total of 1,720 flying hours, most of which were in command. What would life have in store next? With the flying experience that I had gained, surely the instructor's course should be fairly straightforward. I was quite wrong!

Chapter 5

Back to School

Central Flying School, RAF Leeming, 1978–1979
RAF Leeming had expanded significantly since I had received my RAF wings in 1972 and it was now at its largest and busiest. It was still commanded by a group captain and the home of No. 3 Flying Training School (FTS) but it was no longer a basic flying training school; it now comprised of four separate flying squadrons each commanded by a squadron leader under the overall command of a wing commander chief instructor. The Royal Navy Elementary Flying Training Squadron was actually an RAF squadron and it operated the two-seat Bulldog light piston aircraft; the Multi-Engine Training Squadron flew the Jetstream twin-engined aircraft, and the Refresher Flying Squadron operated the Jet Provost Mark 5a. A fourth squadron was Standards Squadron which operated both the Bulldog and the Jet Provost. Also at Leeming was the Northumbrian University Air Squadron operating the Bulldog.

HQ Central Flying School (CFS), together with some of its sub-units was also based here. The Central Flying School was commanded by an air commodore and it comprised of Examining Wing, a Jet Provost Squadron which would soon divide into two, Training Squadron and a Bulldog Squadron. It also included the Vintage Pair display team of a Vampire T11 and a Meteor T7, very much the preserve of a select few of the most experienced CFS instructors. To support all the various flying squadrons, there were two separate ground schools, one for CFS and one for 3 FTS.

*   *   *

We moved into an RAF married quarter just outside the main area of the Station. After disembarkation leave, I joined No. 288 CFS Course which began on 4 December 1978. The course to become a Qualified Flying Instructor (QFI) would last for six months. Afterwards I could be posted to one of the two basic schools, at either Linton-on-Ouse or Cranwell, although there was a slim chance of staying at Leeming on the Refresher Flying Squadron. If that was possible, it would mean a single location for four years, which would suit Jackie and I very well.

There were twenty-seven officers on the course; some were destined to instruct on the Hawk, some on the Bulldog, whereas I was one of sixteen on the Jet Provost. During ground school there was a lot of emphasis on teaching

409 (Consett) Squadron, Air Training Corps at RAF Kinloss, Scotland, summer 1964. I am on the back row, third from the left. (*UK MOD*)

Graduation Parade at RAF Henlow, 24 June 1971. The Reviewing Officer is Air Vice-Marshal Michael Beetham, later Marshal of the Royal Air Force Sir Michael Beetham. (*Studio Five*)

Award of RAF Wings at RAF Leeming, August 1972.

Canberra B2 WK119 of 7 Squadron after take-off from RAF St Mawgan, 1973.

Canberra TT18 WJ721 of 7 Squadron, 1973. (*UK MOD*)

In front of Jet Provost Mk 5 at RAF Leeming, August 1972. (*UK MOD*)

RAF Guard of Honour, Leeds, 8 June 1974. (*Dorchester Ledbetter*)

No. 7 Squadron aircrew and Canberra TT18 at RAF St Mawgan, 1975. The under wing pylons show the winches with Rushton targets. I am standing on the aircraft, second from the left. (*UK MOD*)

Malta's strategically important Grand Harbour, circa 1918.

Canberra PR7 WH773 starting up on a wet day at Villafranca, May 1976. The engines were started using a cartridge within the nacelle at the front of the engine. (*UK MOD*)

XIII Squadron crews conducting earthquake survey planning at Villafranca, Italy, May 1976. I am fourth from the right. (AUTHOR)

Kiev and an RAF F4 Phantom, 27 January 1978. The Canberra crew were Paul McDonald, Tony Payne and Chris White. Note the forward twin 76mm gun and the rear surface-to-air missile (SA-N-3) tracking the Phantom. (*UK MOD*)

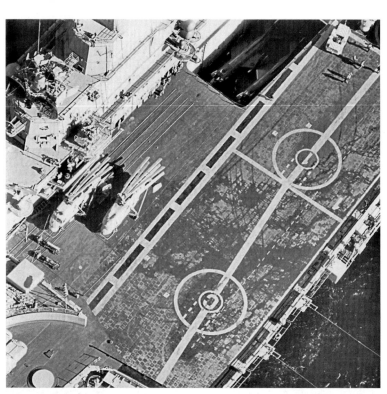

A glimpse of Forgers on *Kiev*'s lift, 27 January 1978. The Canberra crew were Paul McDonald, Tony Payne and Chris White. (*UK MOD*)

Heavy weather for a Kara Cruiser, 22 March 1978. The Canberra crew were Paul McDonald and Fred Stokes (*UK MOD*)

III Squadron aircrew and Canberra PR7 at RAF Luqa, Malta 1978. I am on the far left. (*UK MOD*)

iev head-on, 22 March 1978. The Canberra crew were Paul McDonald and Fred Stokes. (*UK MOD*)

Kiev in very heavy seas, 22 March 1978. The Canberra crew were Paul McDonald and Fred Stokes. (*UK MOD*)

Kiev bows out, 22 March 1978. The Canberra crew were Paul McDonald and Fred Stokes. (*UK MOD*)

A young Flying Officer Eric Androvardi, 1986. (*UK MOD*)

Before the Wall came down: changing the Guard at the Tomb of the Unknown Soldier, East Berlin.

Officers' Mess at RAF Linton-on-Ouse, 28 November 1944. Note the air raid shelters on The Green and the bomb craters in the foreground from left to right; the last bomb in the string hit No. 5, which became our home in 1992. The building behind the Officers' Mess at the top left was the original HQ of 4 Group when commanded by 'Bomber' Harris.

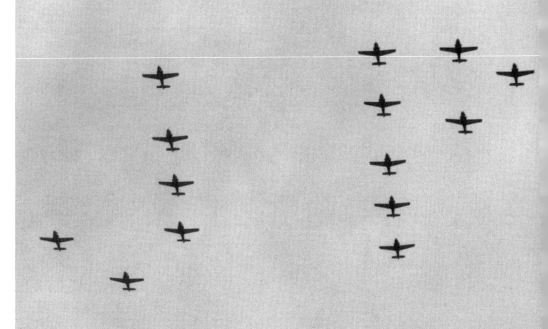

Rehearsal Flypast of the Jet Provost Farewell, 18 May 1993, led by Mark Heaton. I am flying in line abreast on Mark. Dave 'Cutty' Cuthbertson was leading the 'J'. (*UK MOD*)

Air Vice-Marshal Chris Coville and crews prior to his 4-ship farewell flypasts of the four No. 1 Flying Training School airfields, 12 August 1994. I am second from the right. (*UK MOD*)

Meeting Her Majesty the Queen during her visit to the Royal College of Defence Studies (RCDS), 1995.

His Royal Highness Crown Prince Hassan of Jordan and the RCDS Middle East Tour Group outside the Royal Palace in Amman, October 1995. The Crown Prince is third from the right and Air Marshal Sir Timothy Garden is third from the left; I am in the second row, second from the left.

'Free Kuwait': Kuwait Air Force Mirage, Skyhawk and F18 aircraft fly past the Kuwait Towers, Kuwait City.

The VIP tent at a Kuwait Armed Forces officers' graduation, Kuwait Military College, 1998. I am seated in the second row, fourth from the right.

First course of Kuwait Air Force student pilots and staff, Ali Al-Salem Air Base, Kuwait 2001. I am in the second row, second from the left.

both in the classroom, teaching a group, and one-on-one in the way that a flying instructor would brief his student.

My first trip in the Jet Provost 3a was on 14 December and my first flying test was the Progress Check. I failed it. I was devastated. Had I learnt nothing in the five years since I had last been on a training course? It was almost as if the 1,720 flying hours that I now had under my belt didn't mean a thing. Would I ever be able to get over the nerves that always seemed to affect me when I was on a course and under test? The answer to that was yes I would, but not yet. After a day or two I re-flew and passed the test and moved on to the more challenging part of the course, learning how to teach in the air.

There's a bit of an art in being able to fly and teach at the same time. But it hadn't just been my pride that had been affected by my early test failure; my confidence had been damaged too. I was also desperately keen to secure the one possible place on the Refresher Squadron so that I could stay and instruct at Leeming. If I failed the course we would most definitely have to move house once more; even if I passed, staying at Leeming might not be considered a good option if I was thought to be marginal. So I soldiered on, trying to get to grips with teaching in the air.

I tended to fly with different instructors and looking back this wasn't good for me, I needed better continuity. The key airborne test was the Basic Handling Test and I flew this on 2 April 1979. I failed. This was another major blow. It was a deserved 'fail' and I had no gripes with the testing officer. This was just as well, as we ended up as colleagues on the Tucano Simulator some thirty years later; his name was Ken Jones. I was placed on review, allocated to a specific instructor for continuity, and given a remedial package of sorties before attempting the test once more. If I couldn't overcome 'testitus', I did not have much of a future in the instructional world where tests and check rides were very much part of the routine.

My new instructor was Bob Radley, and we got on well from the start. I responded well to his manner and to his guidance. He was a natural instructor, eventually becoming an A1 which is the very highest category of instructor. There are four instructor categories: B2 (an instructor on probation), B1 (a competent pilot and instructor), A2 (an above the average pilot and instructor), and A1 (an exceptional pilot and instructor). Whatever Bob did, it worked and I passed my second attempt at the test on 23 April. Now I moved onto the Jet Provost Mark 5a and the more advanced teaching exercises which included low-level navigation and formation flying. I relaxed more and began to do rather better.

* * *

A few weeks later, on 22 May, Jackie and I were on our own driving slowly north up the A1. It had been a truly wretched morning and we reflected on the upsetting events that had taken place in a magistrate's court near Ripon.

The day had begun quite well but we had little idea how it would end. Jackie had been summoned to appear as a witness for the prosecution in a case against another driver who had run into the back of our car, and written it off, in January. From the very moment when the police arrived after the accident, they had reassured us that we had done nothing wrong and they had expressed complete confidence in securing a conviction for dangerous driving against the driver who had hit us while we were stationary at another accident which had occurred in fog. But for placing Hannah's carrycot on the left, rather than the right of our estate car, she would almost certainly have been killed. As I had not actually witnessed the second accident, I was not called to give evidence.

The court case had proven traumatic. I sat in the public gallery with no inkling of what was about to unfold. The prosecuting solicitor was inept in his questioning and his cross examination of the other driver was cursory; he seemed totally unprepared. The defence solicitor knew his business and did not challenge anything that Jackie said in the witness box. But he then went on to suggest that I had abandoned my car and my family in the outside lane of the very busy A1 and had gone off somewhere to make a phone call. There was no reference to the earlier accident, the fact the road was blocked, and that I was in a nearby service station telephoning the police. When I had left my car, it had been completely hemmed in, but drivers behind us manoeuvred onto the grass, and unbeknown to Jackie, left our car with her and the children on board as the back marker. The defence solicitor referred to the fog, which had actually lifted at the time of the second collision. The defendant said clearly, and with conviction, that there had been no lights of any description switched on in my car at the time of the accident. He went unchallenged.

I was furious but could say nothing. The magistrates still found him guilty of the lesser charge of careless driving. Dangerous driving would have been much nearer the mark, and perjury too, but at least it was a guilty verdict. I challenged the prosecuting solicitor afterwards explaining that after the accident I had been unable to switch off any of my car's headlights or fog lights; they were completely inoperative. He simply said, 'Oh, I didn't know that.'

Jackie and I were drained, frustrated, and upset when we left the court. Rather than spend the rest of the day in Ripon as planned, we decided to go home. We had suffered enough traumas that day; but we were wrong, very, very wrong.

*   *   *

About thirty minutes later, as we approached RAF Leeming and were about to turn right off the A1 into Gatenby Lane, I saw a Gnat climbing toward us having completed a touch and go (or roller) landing. While Gnats from Valley often visited Leeming, this one was a little unusual in that it was painted completely red; it was one of the Red Arrows aircraft soon to be replaced by the Hawk.

'Oh, look,' I said, 'there's a Gnat, it's a Red Arrows' Gnat.'

Not surprisingly, Jackie didn't react, still dwelling on her awful experience of the morning. Worse was to come. About halfway down Gatenby Lane there is a left turn, at 'Cow-shit Corner' as we called it. It was there that I heard a couple of bangs; the farmer must have been out with his shotgun again no doubt. A few seconds later Jackie cried out in horror, 'My God, it's going in!'

This was followed quickly by, 'No it's not.'

After a very short pause she then exclaimed, 'Yes, it is!'

* * *

When we talked later, she explained what had prompted her seemingly contradictory words. She had glanced out of the left passenger window and saw an ejection seat flying horizontally past; the pilot was still in the seat, hence her first statement. As she looked ahead once more, she thought to herself 'don't be silly, that sort of thing doesn't happen in real life'; hence her second statement. She then turned around to see an aircraft hit the ground a few yards behind us and explode in flames! That accounted for her final statement.

I had seen nothing of this at all. I stopped the car, got out and looked behind. I had trouble taking in the scene in front of me. Thick black smoke and flames were rising from the burning wreck of the aircraft in a wheat field about eighty yards behind our car. About fifty yards behind us, between us and the aircraft, lay the motionless figure of the pilot lying on the grass verge with his parachute draped over the hedge. I immediately sensed that he hadn't made it, he was much too close to the wreck and there had probably been insufficient time for his parachute to deploy properly. By now Jackie was also out of the car, so I told her to stay where she was, I didn't want her to get any closer. There was no one else around, no other cars, nothing, so I ran down the road toward the pilot, and yes, I put the hazard lights on first! Why I simply didn't reverse the car I don't know, but I sprinted for all that I was worth.

As I ran, I wondered how close the aircraft must have come to us. It could only have missed our car by the very narrowest of margins. As I got closer I kept thinking 'what are you going to do, it's obvious he hasn't made it?'

I could now see the pilot more closely. Even though he was still wearing his oxygen mask, and his clear visor was down over his eyes, I could see blood behind the visor. And then he moved. Very slowly, but he moved. He then pulled up his visor and released his oxygen mask. I stopped alongside him.

'Hello Mike,' I said.

'Hello Paul,' he replied.

Those words seem totally incongruous now. But what else do you say when you bump into someone that you know?

When I asked if he was in pain he said that his back was hurting; I told him not to try and move. It turned out that he had severe compression fractures of the spine. His facial cuts were largely superficial, caused by the miniature detonating chord used to shatter the canopy to allow the ejection seat to burst through. By now of course I had realized that the two bangs that I had heard earlier were the sounds of two ejection seats, and that there was another pilot somewhere nearby.

'Were you first out or second?' I asked.

'I was first,' said Mike.

'Oh dear,' I thought, 'so where was the second pilot?'

I looked over the hedge toward the wreckage only a few yards away and blazing furiously. If Mike had ejected first then the second guy was between me and the wreckage, or worse: he may have landed in the fireball. They had been very low when they ejected, and there was no sign of the other pilot.

I was then distracted by the sound of an approaching helicopter, a Puma. It had been coming in to land when the crew heard a brief Mayday call, and they saw the ejection and crash. It came toward me hovering low over the wheat field and I tried to indicate by hand signals that I was with a casualty and needed some help.

As I turned back, I got the shock of my life. Right in front of me on the other side of the hedge, the other pilot stood up. He seemed quite startled too! He had been lying in the field, stunned. We looked at each other for a second or two, then he calmly walked across toward the approaching helicopter, clambered aboard and it flew off!

So I was still on my own with Mike, still unsure of what to do next. Another car arrived and I told the driver to stop any traffic heading toward us and then, thankfully, the RAF ambulance arrived. Thank goodness, I thought. But to my dismay there was no doctor, only a young nurse and she was unsure about what to do and said so. She looked close to tears but said that the RAF doctor was on his way. I told her just to treat Mike's face. The crash crews then arrived and drove into the field to put out the fire.

Other people began to arrive too, including a squadron leader. He said that we should lift Mike onto a stretcher. I said no, we should leave Mike where he was until the RAF doctor arrived. He didn't agree and said that he played rugby and knew all about back injuries and we should pick Mike up and put him on the stretcher. But by now I was in my 'stroppy' frame of mind, and said as firmly as I could that as the doctor would be arrive at any minute, Mike must not be moved. I didn't know much about rugby but I knew what ejection seats could do. The squadron leader backed off. The doctor arrived soon afterwards and took charge, so I wondered off back to our car where Jackie had watched the scene unfold.

When we arrived home a few minutes later, I had a large brandy as I was still pretty hyped up. Jackie calmly set about making tea for the children. Later I asked her about her 'calmness', which had surprised me, but I think that her calmness had been forced, more apparent than real. Her answer surprised me even more.

'Paul,' she said, 'you are an RAF pilot. We have two small children. RAF pilots sometimes get killed. Don't you think that I have had to think about that, consider what I would have to do if it was you?'

I felt a rather small. It was alright for me. Apart from trying to make 'provision' for my family, had I really given much serious thought to the 'what if' scenario?

* * *

A few days later we were back in court, both of us as witnesses this time to give evidence to the RAF Board of Inquiry. This was a far more pleasant experience and it was interesting to see the thorough and painstaking way in which the board went about its business. The Board President was a wing commander; a few years later as an air commodore, he would be appointed as the Central Flying School Commandant. With me, the Board focused on why I associated the two bangs with a shotgun rather than the aircraft I had just seen.

'But you are an RAF pilot, within a mile of your base, and a few seconds earlier you had just seen a fast-jet get airborne. Why did you associate the two bangs with a shotgun rather than the aircraft?'

My instant response, without thinking, was, 'Because there was no engine noise.'

The Board President paused then and said, 'Really?'

And of course there had been no engine noise at the time of ejection, the engine had already flamed-out, although the Board were not certain of that at the time.

I was also quite scathing about how long it had taken the crash crews to arrive. I was then shown the transcripts of all the radio messages between air traffic control and the crash crews, all of which were timed. The fire crews had been at the site of the crash five or six minutes from the crash alarm which was pretty good going considering its location off the airfield. For me, and not for the last time, time had stood still.

The questioning of Jackie was equally thoughtful and when they asked her to describe what she had seen they focused on one particular comment she had made, 'And then the aircraft hit the ground and caught fire.'

'The aircraft hit the ground,' they asked, 'and THEN it caught fire?'

Jackie was certain that that had been the sequence, which suggested no fire before impact. This again was correct as the subsequent technical investigation would reveal.

I found the experience of seeing how a board carefully took their evidence before gently probing witnesses very reassuring. That experience would stay with me throughout my career. In 2005, my last task as a serving officer was as President of a Board of Inquiry investigating the circumstances surrounding a sudden death and I tried hard to be just as painstaking and thoughtful.

Incidentally, both Gnat pilots returned to full flying duties although it was to take Mike about six months. He struck quite a pose at the RAF Leeming Summer Ball in 1979 in his mess kit but wearing a steel brace around his back and supporting his neck!

* * *

Now flying regularly with Bob Radley, I was beginning to enjoy the course and was much more at home with the more advanced aspects, especially low-level navigation. It was soon confirmed that I would be staying at Leeming on graduation to instruct on the Refresher Flying Squadron. I was delighted.

The last two low-level sorties that I flew involved a night-stop at RAF Wyton, now the home of XIII Squadron, and I flew there with Bob on 15 May. During the evening we talked about the course and how I'd found it. He happened to mention that I was still on review and that I was still being closely monitored. I was dumbfounded. As far as I had been aware, review was the process that followed a failed test and that process should end once the test had been passed. Not only had I passed the test but my subsequent sorties had been significantly better than the course minimum standard. And I said so, to which Bob had to agree because most of the subsequent sorties had been assessed by him. But, as he was neither my Flight Commander nor my Squadron Commander, he was not in a position to make a decision.

The sortie home went well and Bob disappeared soon afterwards; he came back a few minutes later to tell me that I was no longer on review.

* * *

My final test ten days later went well and I again flew in the aerobatics competition but, just like in 1972, I didn't win!

At my final interview, to my surprise, I was placed sixth out of twenty-seven in ground school. My Squadron Commander was spot on when he referred to my tendency to be under-confident and to suffer from 'testitus' but, again to my surprise, I had been assessed as high average in the air and finished sixth on the Jet Provost Course. I expressed my appreciation for Bob Radley's efforts on my behalf but being the only one out of sixteen to have been on review, and therefore the weakest, and having been on review until ten days before my final test, how could I end up high average and sixth, I asked? My Squadron Commander couldn't really answer that. Twelve years later, I bumped into him at RAF Scampton when I began a refresher course prior to taking command of the Flying Training Wing at RAF Linton-on-Ouse.

'Hello Sir,' he said.

I smiled and said how nice it was to see him again, and it was. In an amusing sequel, at the end of my Linton tour in 1994, a signal was read out from RAF Scampton at my dining out night. It was from my former Squadron Commander from 1979, and it formally removed me from 'review'.

Refresher Flying Squadron No. 3 FTS, RAF Leeming, 1979–1983

Originally the School of Refresher Flying based at RAF Manby in Lincoln-shire, it was renamed the Refresher Flying Squadron when it was absorbed within No. 3 Flying Training School in 1973. I joined the squadron on 25 June and immediately went into Standards Squadron for two weeks to learn how to adapt the basic teaching learnt on my instructor's course to meet the needs of a very different type of student: refresher students were all qualified pilots.

The squadron ran the Short Jet Refresher Course lasting eight weeks, two weeks ground school and six weeks flying, during which the students completed thirty-five flying hours at quite an intensive rate. Our students came from the widest range of backgrounds and had either been filling staff appointments and were now moving back into a flying job, or they were cross-rolling, changing perhaps from a heavy aircraft or helicopters, to fast-jets. Some were from overseas. Their ranks varied from pilot officer, through wing commander and group captain, to air vice-marshal. I soon realized that I could learn a lot from the students, many of whom were fast-jet pilots with vast experience, destined to command fast-jet squadrons and front-line stations.

My new squadron was also housed in what had been 3 Squadron during my basic course and our former student's crewroom was now the refresher crewroom. The coffee bar, lovingly built by my course using stone from a quarry in Wensleydale, was still there and looked as good as new. My first Flight Commander was Eric Constable; twenty-nine years later I would bump into Eric in the Officers' Mess bar at Linton. It was to prove a fortuitous meeting.

*   *   *

Toward the end of the year, with me still a B2 Qualified Flying Instructor and the most junior instructor on the squadron, my Squadron Commander Squadron Leader Dick Woodhead, announced that the Central Flying School was looking for two new pilots for the Vintage Pair Display Team for the 1980 and 1981 seasons. For the first time, the Refresher Flying Squadron had been asked to put forward four volunteers. This was apparently quite a break-through, as the Vintage Pair had always been the preserve of the Central Flying School since the team formed in 1971.

The team had a manager and four pilots, two for each aircraft and each year one pilot from each was replaced. I didn't take a great deal of notice as the last thing that I wanted to be doing with a young family was working at weekends. But I certainly did take notice when the Boss named the 'volunteers' that had already been put forward. My name was fourth on the list! I was gobsmacked!

After the meeting I went to see him to explain that, while I was honoured to have been considered, working at weekends for two years wasn't exactly what I was looking for given the age of our children. He said that he quite understood but asked that I think about it very seriously over the weekend as it could be a great opportunity. He then said, 'By the way, you are the only one who is being put forward as a potential Meteor pilot. The other three are being put forward for the Vampire.'

I was gobsmacked yet again!

*   *   *

The Vampire was a single-engined jet, fitted with ejection seats, and many pilots possessed the skill to fly it. The Meteor was twin-engined and it did not have ejection seats; flying it on one engine was a skill that many had not been able to master, and they had paid the ultimate price. The Meteor saw service in the RAF in huge numbers between 1944 and the late 1960s. But it is sobering to recount that the RAF lost 890 Meteors in accidents, 145 in 1953 alone. A total of 450 pilots lost their lives. Given how few aircraft the RAF now has, it is difficult to imagine such a loss rate through accidents.

*   *   *

There were a number of potential candidates for the Vampire from within the Central Flying School but none with 'previous Meteor or extensive Canberra experience'. The criteria had been set because of the Meteor's fearsome asymmetric reputation. When the Vintage Pair had been formed in 1971, its pilots came from within the confines of Examining Wing and many examiners had previous Meteor experience. Canberra pilots began to be considered when Examining Wing ran out of former Meteor pilots. For the 1980 season, the Central Flying School did not have any experienced Canberra pilots which is where I came in. From 1981, the rules on previous experience were relaxed even further and both pilots who were later killed had no Canberra or previous Meteor experience.

After a weekend to think about joining the team, and the impact that it would have on my family, I went back to see Dick Woodhead to try and find out exactly what my commitment would be and what flexibility he would be able to offer during the normal working week. At a meeting with Dick and the previous season's team leader, it was explained that the display season ran from early May to mid-September. At the beginning of the first season, I would go to every display sitting in the back seat of the Meteor until I, along with the new Vampire pilot, were given display clearance in our own right. After that, I would be away every other weekend. This was a very significant commitment and something of my reluctance must have been evident as, without prompting, Dick Woodhead offered to match the days away with the Vintage Pair with days off from work the following week. I agreed to this and my name was therefore put forward and was accepted.

*   *   *

In early February 1980 I went to RAF Marham, now the home of the Canberras of 231 Operational Conversion Unit, to spend three days practicing asymmetric flying in preparation for my Meteor conversion. I flew all of my sorties with the unit's flight commander, with whom I had served on XIII Squadron. It was gratifying to read that, after three hours on the Canberra some eighteen months after my last flight, I had 'coped extremely ably with the entire spectrum of Canberra engine emergencies'. Later that month I flew with my Chief Instructor and was re-categorized to B1 on the Jet Provost. I was now officially 'a competent pilot and instructor'.

In March I flew with Squadron Leader Bruce McDonald who would be the senior Meteor pilot for the 1980 season; he would be responsible for my conversion to the Meteor and for my work-up to formal display clearance. We practiced parts of the Vintage Pair display routine using Jet Provosts. Bruce was a grandfather, but his age certainly didn't show when he was at the controls. He was also well known within the RAF fast-jet world and had been a fighter pilot for most of his life. He was an A1 instructor from Examining Wing and regularly visited RAF fast-jet squadrons examining pilots on aircraft such as the Lightning, Phantom and the Hawk. He was one of that very rare breed of gifted aviators who was able to fly each aircraft type in exactly the way that they had been designed to fly. He would always tell me that whenever I flew the Meteor with him, he could immediately recognize my Canberra background, but that didn't bother me in the slightest.

Later that month I flew with the team manager practicing formation aerobatics in the Jet Provost; this was something not normally allowed, but it was authorized as some limited formation aerobatics were part of the Team's display. The Vampire and the Meteor were finally brought out of the hangar during April so that the crews could regain currency and start practicing for the coming season.

Flight Lieutenant Dave Lee, an experienced A2 instructor from Training Squadron was the senior Vampire pilot, and the new Vampire pilot was Flight Lieutenant John Halstead, another A1 examiner from Examining Wing. We also had four RAF engineers, all volunteers, and they would often be at the display location to meet us on arrival. After we had received public display clearance, two of the groundcrew would sometimes fly with us, to or from displays, often being on board during the displays themselves.

Our aircraft were immaculate and both represented types which had flown as trainers during the 1950s and 1960s. They were very popular on the display circuit and signed photographs of the aircraft and memorabilia, including Vintage Pair beer mats, were highly sought after. And, of course, we had to look the part when appearing in public: we wore yellow roll-neck shirts, light grey flying suits, black jackets, and yellow flying helmets. And, of course, I had to wear the Central Flying School badge on my flying suit despite not being a 'fully paid-up' member. I suggested that I could wear it on my elbow, or on another part of my flying suit, but was overruled. A pelican was central to the very ornate badge which was referred to by some as 'chicken in the basket'. I contented myself with comments like 'Do you know why the pelican is the mascot? It's because it has a bloody big mouth and can't fly!'

In fact, the pelican can fly incredibly well and I was to watch and admire many of their manoeuvres years later at Key West, and off the coast of California.

Because of their age, the aircraft were limited to 2½ G which meant that the display routine had to be very carefully planned and flown. Unusually, and like the Red Arrows, the Vintage Pair arrived at the display from crowd rear, behind the crowd line, flying in Line Abreast with the Meteor on the left. Once in front of the crowd, we pulled up before splitting left and right to complete a series of individual opposition low passes in front of the crowd, including an opposition turn through 360 degrees. After that, the Meteor would close up in Line Astern on the Vampire for a Barrel Roll from right to left in front of the crowd. After crossing in front of the crowd once more and turning obliquely away, the Meteor would move into Echelon Starboard as the aircraft climbed. The Vampire, closely followed by the Meteor, would then perform a Canadian Break, a roll to the left inverted through 270 degrees, before separate and final flypasts in front of the crowd. It was a graceful and eye-pleasing display which lasted about fifteen minutes and it showed both aircraft at their best.

*   *   *

My conversion onto the Meteor began on 21 April 1980. A major limitation was that the aircraft was only cleared to fly for seventy-five hours each year. This had to be split between two pilots and included all displays, transits and practices, as well as conversion flying. This was a very low number of hours for any pilot when compared to a 'normal' month's worth of flying of about thirty hours. My conversion consisted of two twenty minute dual sorties, a solo of twenty minutes, and then a forty minute Instrument Rating Test. That was it. Then it was the practice display routine sitting behind Bruce and picking up everything that I could.

The Meteor T7 was a delightful aircraft and I very much enjoyed flying it. It was very robust, and fast too, and its old engines with centrifugal compressors were extremely responsive, unlike most jet engines which were then in service, which had axial flow compressors. The latter tended to be rather slow to accelerate from idle to mid-power. But the Meteor had two vices: performance on one engine could be tricky and also it was essential to select the airbrakes in before lowering the undercarriage. If they were not, this resulted in what was known as 'the phantom dive'; a rapid loss of control as the fin stalled, and there was little chance of recovery if in the circuit. This characteristic gave birth to a generation of aircraft pre-landing checks which all began with 'airbrakes in', before going on to 'undercarriage down'.

For our first displays in May we operated from Coventry Airport, a good central location. We all travelled to the early displays as John and I built up experience. We displayed at Cosford, Gloucester, Biggin Hill, Newcastle-upon-Tyne, Long Marston and Henlow, before John and I were awarded Public Display Clearance. Our first 'solo' display was at Greenham Common on 29 May. Looking at my flying logbook for the summer of 1980 brings back lots of memories – Greenham Common, Duxford, Nottingham, Sunderland, York, Hatfield, Kenley, Strathallan, Lee-on-Solent, Bournemouth, Odiham, St Helens, Tyneside, Wyton, Lyneham, Abingdon, Duxford again, Coltishall, Biggin Hill again, Old Warden, Alconbury, Coventry, Mildenhall, Leicester and Roundhay Park in Leeds.

For many practices and displays we would offer the other seat in one or both aircraft to other instructors at Leeming so they too could experience a low-level flying display; they could often help out with navigation. On 29 July, the new Squadron Commander of the Refresher Flying Squadron, Squadron Leader Alan Rayment, flew with me during a display over the Town Moor at Newcastle-upon-Tyne. Alan was a former refresher instructor and I had met him soon after arriving at Leeming. Twelve years later, we would work together again at Linton-on-Ouse and twenty-eight years later we would be colleagues in the Tucano Flight Simulator.

* * *

In early July there were rehearsals for a visit on 4 July by Her Majesty Queen Elizabeth, the Queen Mother. She was Commandant-in-Chief of the Central Flying School and was very popular, always attending the reunions each year. This was a special year as she would celebrate her eightieth birthday, and His Royal Highness Prince Andrew was also at RAF Leeming under-going pilot training.

The rehearsal was quite amusing with various people co-opted to play the roles of the senior guests. A female squadron leader played the part of Her Majesty who would of course be met on her arrival by her grandson, Prince Andrew. For the rehearsal Prince Andrew apparently insisted that he play the role of one of the Air Officers, while his own instructor was to play the part of Prince Andrew. Everyone was given appropriate name badges of the person they were pretending to be. The scene was set for some fun, and potential chaos. On the day of the rehearsal, just as 'the Queen Mother' was about to arrive, apparently Prince Andrew told his instructor that as he was taking Prince Andrew's part, he must greet 'Her Majesty' in the same way that he, Prince Andrew, would the following day. He must give 'the Queen Mother' a big kiss and a hug and say 'Hello Granny'. I am not sure how the female squadron leader coped with that!

During the rehearsal a selection of aircraft and their crews, and other station personnel, had been assembled to be introduced, but many people, including me, found it difficult to keep a straight face when confronted by Prince Andrew's instructor wearing a large badge saying 'Prince Andrew' when, standing next to him, was the real thing.

*   *   *

Of all the displays that year, and perhaps the most memorable of all, was the weekend at the Strathallan Air Museum near Perth in Scotland. The museum had a grass airstrip and the Vintage Pair, operating from Edinburgh Airport, had always been popular participants, closing the show on both days. A Bulldog was used to ferry the team between Edinburgh and Strathallan. Traditionally, but unofficially, the show was closed after the team's display with a four-ship flypast comprising the Vampire, the Meteor, Strathallan's privately-owned Hurricane, and a Spitfire from the Battle of Britain Memorial Flight based at RAF Coningsby. This was regarded by many as the highlight of Strathallan's show but, in RAF terms, it was unauthorized. But we all agreed that we would do it, it would be a memorable experience, although this one proved to be more memorable than any flown previously. But Coningsby 'let the cat out of the bag' by sending a signal to Leeming saying 'I assume the rules for this year's flypast are the same as last year?'

The Commandant passed the signal to Bruce McDonald adding 'What *were* the rules for last year?'

Whatever explanation Bruce gave must have worked as we were soon off to Strathallan.

*   *   *

On the day, 12 July 1980, it turned out a little more complicated than we had thought and if the Commandant had been aware of how events would unfold, he would probably have had a fit!

The display briefing at Strathallan was straightforward. The Hurricane pilot (Duncan Simpson) said that because of a problem with his engine's propeller (he could not vary the pitch) he could not fly any faster than 180 knots so he needed to try and keep on the inside of all turns. After some discussion, we agreed that the Vampire would be at the front flying at 180 knots, and I would fly in line astern using a small amount of flap to make the Meteor a little easier to handle. The Hurricane would fly on the left and the Spitfire on the right. It would be my job to brief the Spitfire pilot at

Edinburgh when he arrived from Coningsby. As the briefing came to an end, there was an interruption from the rear of the tent, 'Excuse me, but would you mind if I tagged along at the back?'

The individual was a civilian, and we didn't know him from Adam! Was he some private pilot who thought he could join us in his Cessna?

'In what?' one of us asked.

'In the Mosquito parked outside.'

It was very rare to see a Second World War Mosquito on the display circuit and this particular aircraft, parked outside on the grass, was owned by British Aerospace. The quietly spoken civilian was their Chief Test Pilot, George Aird. I had seen George Aird once before; well, I had seen a photograph of him, thousands of people had, although few would have known him. During the 1960s he had ejected from a Lightning on a test flight from Hatfield in Hertfordshire. A photograph of him was subsequently shown on the front cover of a Sunday magazine. It shows a farmer on a tractor looking over his shoulder as a Lightning is descending vertically into a field. George is seen exiting horizontally from his aircraft having ejected only just in time. It was a remarkable photograph. And now George wanted to 'tag along' at the back of our formation!

A flypast of five such aircraft would be a sight to see! From an RAF perspective it wouldn't be particularly legal, but then neither would our four-ship flypast have been either. As long as we briefed it carefully, it would be perfectly safe, just unauthorized. So, we agreed. The Mosquito would fly in line astern immediately behind me. All that remained for us to do was to fly back to Edinburgh, and brief the Spitfire pilot. That wouldn't be a problem would it? Not unless the Spitfire was being flown by RAF Coningsby's Station Commander.

Back at Edinburgh, I couldn't believe my eyes when the Spitfire pilot climbed out of the cockpit: a group captain, RAF Coningsby's Station Commander! Our 'old plan' would have been difficult enough to brief; how on earth would he react to the new one? And he was late!

I rushed across to brief him about the 'four-ship'; he was a little worried as he was late. But he seemed happy enough about the 'four-ship' and was anxious to get airborne as soon as possible. Nothing ventured, I thought.

'There's just one small thing, Sir,' I said.

'What's that?' he replied.

'It won't affect you in anyway but, during the flypast, you may notice a Mosquito flying in line astern on me.'

He looked absolutely shell-shocked. So I pressed on, 'As I say, it won't have any effect on you. But you'd better get going now Sir, otherwise you might be late for your slot.'

And with that he climbed back into his Spitfire, and was off without another word. The formation of these five aircraft over Strathallan on Saturday 12 July 1980 went without a hitch. And nothing was ever said when we got back to Leeming. For over thirty years I regretted never having had a photograph of such a formation, five historic aircraft never to be seen again, flying together. And then on 6 January 2011, I received an email from our son Matthew, living in Los Angeles, saying simply 'Look familiar?' Attached was a splendid photograph taken that day by Derek Ferguson, of Handforth in Cheshire. It is a photograph that I will always treasure.

*   *   *

One of our final displays during 1980 was at Biggin Hill in Kent, for the Battle of Britain weekend. It was here that I had undergone my RAF selection in 1970.

We flew to RAF Marham on the 20 September to refuel and then displayed at RAF Coltishall before heading for Biggin Hill. The plan was to display at Biggin the following day, before again crossing the Thames Estuary to refuel at RAF Wattisham, and then head home.

Biggin Hill, probably the most well known Battle of Britain fighter station, was a very popular air show and it attracted many participants, especially historic aircraft from the Second World War. Two in particular, both American, were the B17 Flying Fortress *Sally B* (used in the film *Memphis Belle*) and a smaller twin-engine bomber, an A26 Invader. In 1979 I had watched the Biggin Hill air show on television. The B17 had been unable to raise its undercarriage after take-off, but the pilot completed his display, which included at one point descending out of sight of the crowd into the valley at the end of Biggin's runway and then reappearing at the very last second. The crowd loved it, and it certainly looked impressive; even Raymond Baxter the television presenter waxed lyrical about it, but many pilots must have thought such a manoeuvre ill-advised; the pilot may well have been at the very limits of the aircraft's capability, and his own; 1979 was his last season flying the B17.

During 1980 he reappeared on the display circuit flying the A26 Invader. Earlier in the year I had seen him arrive at Bournemouth. He came in very low and fast, breaking over the runway threshold at about 30 feet into a very tight 360-degree turn to line up with the runway at a very late stage. Throughout the turn the A26 remained at very low altitude, not much more than 100 feet. I have to admit that it looked good, but when the aircraft landed, first on the nose wheel and then bouncing heavily, I realized that this pilot was not all that he made himself out to be. And then came that fateful day, 21 September 1980.

There was, as always, a Pilot's Briefing for all participants before the air show to cover the weather, the display programme and any safety features. On that particular day the westerly runway was in use and as it is quite short, the Vintage Pair had no choice but to take off into wind. As Biggin Hill did not have any taxiways, in order to make our programmed display time, we would need to taxi down the runway while the aircraft ahead of us in the programme was displaying above us. The aircraft that would follow us in the programme was the A26. We therefore asked during the briefing whether the captain of the aircraft ahead of us would be comfortable with us taxing down the runway during his routine. He said, 'I have no problem with that at all. My name is not …'

With that, the A26 pilot, who was sitting further back, leapt to his feet and there was an angry outburst from him. Things calmed down, and later we taxied down the runway without incident and took off into our routine which went well. When we landed at Wattisham we were met by our groundcrew with the words 'Oh, we're glad it wasn't you then!'

An aircraft had crashed during the air show not long after we had departed. It was the A26, and the pilot and his engineer had been killed. What was worse, much worse, was that they had taken five passengers with them; all on board had perished, including two USAF servicemen along for the ride, and one young air cadet. They had had no chance whatsoever. The A26 had flown across the airfield very low and fast and then pulled up into a barrel roll which the pilot planned to complete by dropping into the valley at the end of the runway to again disappear out of sight of the crowd before pulling up once more. Except that he got it very badly wrong and plunged into the ground. Thankfully the crowd did not see the impact, just a pall of black smoke rising in the distance. The air show carried on.

There are, of course, risks involved in all display flying; within the RAF these are usually mitigated by careful selection of the pilots, and very close supervision during the various practices at different heights until eventually the pilot is given public display clearance. Apart from the Red Arrows, who fly for three years, most other RAF display pilots only fly for one display season and I have always thought that to be a good idea. After a year, you begin to think that you are good at it and there is a risk of overconfidence. I have always thought that many display pilots perform for their colleagues in the Pilot's Tent at air shows, not for the general public. The RAF has had its share of accidents at displays and during work-ups, but it always seemed to me that in those days the rules for civilian pilots were a little too lax and not sufficiently enforced. There were many civilian pilots that I met during the 1980 and 1981 display seasons who subsequently wrote themselves off.

* * *

Soon afterwards, the Refresher Flying Squadron was subjected to its annual visit from the 'Trappers', Examining Wing. Each year they would examine all of the instructors and fly with a selection of students to assess how the squadron as a whole was performing. I was delighted to be assessed as above the average although I was still a B1 category instructor.

* * *

And then there was the day that Ronald Reagan was elected as President of the USA, 4 November 1980. It would be a very memorable day for many people; it would be especially memorable for me.

Andy Walton and I, together with two of our refresher students, planned a total of three trips which included an overnight stop at the Royal Naval Air Station Yeovilton, in Somerset. As Sword Formation, we would head west into Wensleydale where we would split up before completing separate low-level navigation sorties, rejoining in North Wales to head to RAF Valley. The second sortie would follow a similar profile to Yeovilton. We would return to Leeming the following day. I suppose that is more or less what we did but it didn't go entirely according to plan.

The flight to Valley was uneventful and so was the majority of the sortie to Yeovilton. As we closed on Andy (Sword 1) climbing to 2,000 feet to head towards Yeovilton, I took control for the last few minutes of the sortie. I joined in echelon port, on the left and slightly behind Sword 1.

It was late afternoon, already gloomy with a dark overcast sky. I hadn't actually seen Yeovilton as I was concentrating entirely on flying in formation. Andy was talking to Yeovilton Approach and, when he was visual with Yeovilton, he called for us to change radio frequency to Yeovilton Tower. The radio in the Jet Provost is on the left hand side of the cockpit in front of the left hand pilot; I was sitting on the right. As my student began dialling the new frequency, the Amber Attention Getters illuminated, indicating that we had a problem.

Looking at the Central Warning Panel, I saw that we had a booster pump caption. The electrical fuel pump had failed and fuel was no longer being pumped into the engine. Not a major drama, as the fuel could still flow by gravity, usually. No sooner had the fault registered with me than the engine stopped; a flame-out. Now that was a little unusual!

I broke away from Andy to the left to clear his aircraft, climbing to gain as much height as possible. Without an engine, more height results in a better gliding range than more speed. We had no choice but to turn left away from the leader but by doing so, we were turning away from where I knew Yeovilton must be. As the flame-out had occurred while we were changing radio frequency there was also no one that we could immediately call for assistance, we couldn't even tell Andy about our problem.

I reversed the turn to head east and attempted a hot relight; the engine began to respond but then it wound down again. Over the next few minutes, I tried a couple of cold relights, but both failed. I asked my student to select the UHF distress frequency Guard (243.0) on the main radio. What we needed now was a steer, a magnetic bearing, to Yeovilton, which was the only airfield that we had any hope of reaching. But I did not know exactly where it was or how far away we were, I just knew it was somewhere to the east. I then transmitted a brief emergency call, we didn't have much time, 'Mayday,

Mayday, Mayday, Sword 2, Sword 2, Sword 2, Jet Provost aircraft, two on board, west of Yeovilton, engine failure, request a steer to Yeovilton.'

And then we waited for a reply. And we waited. And then we waited some more.

Nothing happened. No reply.

'That's all we need,' I thought, 'not only has the engine flamed out but the main radio has packed in too!'

I still couldn't see Yeovilton in the murk to the east with the dark clouds above and the sun already beginning to set behind us. I asked the student to select the separate emergency radio and again I made a desperate call asking for a steer to Yeovilton. This time we were answered by West Drayton, the Distress and Diversion agency based at the time in West London. They simply said, 'Sword 2, this is Drayton Centre on Guard, squawk emergency.'

Of course I complied, but I was very frustrated to be asked to squawk, to set the emergency code that would assist air traffic control in identifying which 'blip' on their radar screen was us. I didn't care about the squawk, nor did Drayton Centre need it. What we needed was a steer to Yeovilton and that is what I had asked for. Why couldn't they just have given me that? My radio transmission was all that they had needed in order to get a bearing on our transmission and give us our much needed steer.

Then, thankfully, I saw the airfield ahead of us. It was not a minute too soon. Even now as I looked at the airfield and considered our height, it was clear that our approach would be far from straightforward.

The normal forced landing pattern for the Jet Provost was to glide into the overhead of the airfield to reach a position known as High Key at 2,500 feet, before spiralling onto the final approach by turning through 180 degrees to reach Low Key at 1,500 feet, then executing another 180 degree turn onto finals. Except that we were too low, we couldn't make it into the overhead. At that point, West Drayton called us again saying, 'Mayday Sword 2, this is Drayton Centre, standby for Yeovilton Approach on this frequency.'

'Well,' I thought, 'that's helpful! Best we get on with this on our own.'

We were about two to three miles finals now and maybe around 1,500 feet. We were too high to fly a straight-in approach, and we were too low to make Low Key. I therefore executed a very tight 360 degree turn to the left, selecting take-off flap to tighten the turn. That should put us on short finals to the runway. About half way around the turn I blew the undercarriage down on the emergency air system as the hydraulic pump needed the engine to work properly. Now was not the time to see if there was sufficient residual hydraulic pressure to get the gear down on the normal system. And then there was another call from air traffic control, 'Mayday, Sword 2, this is Yeovilton Approach on Guard, how do you read?'

I really didn't have time for this chit-chat!

'Mayday, Sword 2, Finals gear down,' was my brief reply.

Yeovilton simply acknowledged my call.

As we completed the turn and rolled out on the centreline of the runway at about 300 feet exactly as I had hoped, disaster stared us in the face. Between us and the runway there was another aircraft about to land directly in front of us. It was a large RN four-engined passenger aircraft, a Heron. It must have been directly beneath us during our turn and, of course, it was on a different radio frequency to us. But surely they would have been listening out on the emergency UHF frequency as was normal practice for military aircraft? Even if they had not, surely air traffic control would have warned them that there was an aircraft on a 'Mayday' right behind them? Apparently the answer to both questions was no. By now, the 'niceties' of correct radio procedures were beyond me and I simply said, 'Get that bloke off finals, will you!'

What I then heard on the emergency frequency filled me with disbelief.

'Aircraft on finals overshot, overshoot, overshoot, I say again, aircraft on finals overshoot, overshoot, overshoot!'

As we were the only aircraft on the emergency frequency the call had to be for us. Someone on the ground didn't really have a clue about how very serious our predicament was. This was confirmed when the Heron continued its approach and landed in front of us. It then began braking hard, completely blocking the runway.

To add insult to injury, the runway controller in the red and white caravan next to the threshold of the runway fired a red very at us! A red very was only used by the caravan controller in a dire emergency. Well, this was certainly a dire emergency! The red very was a clear instruction for the aircraft on the final approach to overshoot; we were now the only aircraft on the final approach. Now I knew that someone on the ground didn't really understand what was going on. We were fast running out of options.

Yeovilton has two parallel taxiways. We were closer to the northern taxi-way and it began at almost the same point abeam the threshold. But there were three aircraft already on that taxiway preparing for take-off, so that was out. We were now down to 100 feet. The southern taxiway was further away and was inset from abeam the threshold of the runway. Well, it was either that or step over the side. But could we make it? It would be very, very tight.

I turned right then quickly reversed the turn. We made the taxiway with a few feet to spare. As we gradually slowed down on the taxiway, we overtook the Heron which was still slowing down on the main runway to our left; we had been very close behind. When we climbed out of our aircraft, no one came near us. There was no sign of the crash crews or the Search and Rescue helicopter which was on five minutes standby at Yeovilton to deal with such an eventuality.

So there we waited, standing next to our aircraft in the middle of a busy airfield with no one apparently taking a blind bit of notice! I actually began to feel slightly embarrassed 'alone and palely loitering'.

I'm not sure if I was as pale as I had been as an air cadet in 1966 but I was beginning to get rather cross. Andy, in Sword 1, landed a few minutes later and he waved to us as he came past on the runway. After a few minutes, a RN Land Rover came round the corner quite fast and braked to a sudden halt. The driver had no idea that we were there.

'Why have you stopped here Sir?' he said.

'We landed here.' I said.

'Oh,' he said.

By the time we were towed back across to the other side of the airfield the Heron had taken off. A pity, I would have liked to have had a word with the aircraft captain. Andy was pretty ecstatic about having witnessed the successful outcome; it had been a close run thing. I was quiet, but becoming unhappy that things seemed to have gone so terribly wrong on the ground. Everything that I had assumed would happen, expected to happen with air traffic control had not. Why was that? Was it not absolutely clear that we were in real trouble and were desperate for help? A 'Mayday' call is never made lightly and, for a single engined aircraft, it means that ejection may be imminent and it is a demand for immediate help. It seemed to me at the time that I had received no help whatsoever and I wanted to know why.

So I set off for the air traffic control tower to speak personally to the controllers concerned. But the day shift had gone off duty, which may have been just as well. I simply asked for transcripts of all radio transmissions during the period.

We spent most of the evening in the bar where we were obviously the subject of some discussion amongst the naval officers as word of what had occurred began to get around. But no one said anything directly to us. I stayed much too long in the bar, and probably had far too many beers, but I knew I wouldn't be going anywhere first thing the next morning. I got that wrong as well, as very first thing I was asked to go and see 'Wings', the Fleet Air Arm's senior aviator on the base, their equivalent of Officer Commanding Flying Wing.

I'm not sure what impression I gave; I was pretty non-committal about what had occurred as I wanted to study the transcript. But I think that I probably looked a bit 'shabby', as it was very much the morning after the night before. Perhaps the most important point that came out was how long the events of the previous day had actually taken. I had experienced once before how time can seem to stand still when you are under pressure and this was another example. The radio transcript showed less than three minutes had elapsed between my first Mayday call, and landing. I began to consider the actions and reactions of others in a slightly new light.

* * *

Over the next few days we were able to put all the pieces together. My first Mayday call was in fact heard by both Yeovilton Approach and Drayton Centre. But, because I had not addressed it to Yeovilton, the procedure was that Drayton Centre must take precedence in replying, and they did, giving me a steer (as I had requested) to Yeovilton of 090 degrees. However, Drayton Centre did not use Yeovilton's forward radio relay when they transmitted, and, because of our low height, we didn't hear their reply; there had been nothing wrong with my main radio after all.

Yeovilton Approach had heard Drayton Centre's reply and assumed that I had heard it too so they were required to maintain radio silence on the emergency frequency until invited to take over by Drayton Centre.

Meanwhile, upstairs from Yeovilton Approach, in the Visual Control Room all was fairly quiet with the local controller oblivious to the drama about to land in his lap. He was not listening on the emergency frequency (there was no requirement at the time for him to do so) and was not aware of what was going on a few miles from the airfield. Andy was orbiting in the overhead talking to the local controller and trying to raise me on the radio. The local controller advised him that he could see another Jet Provost to the west. Andy quickly responded by saying that he thought that the other Jet Provost (us) appeared to be positioning for a forced landing; he had quickly realized that something was amiss. There was no response from the local controller to his call.

By now things were happening very quickly. Drayton Centre's call for us to squawk emergency was entirely logical if I had heard their first message, but I had not. Undoubtedly the approach room should have advised the local controller about what was going on; the approach controller or the supervisor should also have told the talkdown controller, sitting a few seats away, who would have been talking to the Heron. By the time that Yeovilton Approach was in a position to talk to me I was already turning hard for the final approach and well below 1,000 feet. Following my late call, the approach controller only realized at the last minute that we were about to be baulked by the Heron, so he then transmitted on all frequencies an urgent message for the aircraft on finals, meaning the Heron, to overshoot. The Heron pilot chose to ignore the call. We, of course, heard the call on the emergency frequency and, as it was not addressed to anyone in particular, I assumed that it was for us. But as we had run out of options, we had to ignore it.

The individual in the runway caravan could simply see a dangerous situation developing with the Heron about to land and a Jet Provost that wasn't on the local frequency appearing out of the murk and attempting to land as well. So, he correctly fired a red Very.

While some mistakes were undoubtedly made, all of this happened in less than three minutes, so it was no surprise that one or two people found themselves well 'behind the drag curve'. But I did feel a little sorry for the crew of the Search and Rescue helicopter and the Crash Crews, all on standby, but who were never alerted and missed out on all of the excitement.

*   *   *

Within a few days of returning to Leeming, I was back in Standards Squadron for some intensive flying and ground training. I was hoping to become an Instrument Rating Examiner, which involved a detailed oral examination covering instruments and meteorology as well as a flying test with an examiner from Examining Wing. On 18 November 1980, I passed the test. Maybe I had at last turned a corner. Undoubtedly the sortie was rather better than the worst ever instrument rating test that my Gnat examiner had ever seen in 1973! Not long afterwards Al Rayment appointed me as one of the squadron's two deputy flight commanders.

*   *   *

On 24 March 1981, the London Gazette announced that I had been awarded the Queen's Commendation for Valuable Service in the Air for gallantry during the incident at Yeovilton. There was a flurry of publicity, mostly local thankfully, but also a radio interview with Radio London over the telephone and a television interview with Tyne Tees Television. I also received a number of congratulatory letters including one from the Under Secretary of State for Defence, and one from the Chief of the Air Staff, Air Chief Marshal Sir Michael Beetham; he had been the reviewing officer when I had been commissioned ten years earlier. All of the publicity was handled by the Station Press Liaison Officer, Flight Lieutenant Roger Lane. Roger also instructed on the Refresher Flying School and he handled things very well on my behalf. I hope that I was able to do a good job for him two years later in what would be my first official duty as a squadron leader. I was presented with the commendation by the Station Commander and I also received an oak leaf which was mounted on RAF blue material and worn beneath my pilot's brevet. It was to be quite lonely there for the next fourteen years!

*   *   *

On 6 April 1981, the Meteor had its first air test of the year, which I flew with Bruce, and practices began at the end of the month with Ian Gristwood, this year's new Meteor pilot, in the back seat. Ian was a former Lightning pilot and went by the nickname of 'Weed' as he was a heavy smoker, not that that was unusual in those days. Some years later he died of a heart attack whilst serving in Oman; he was forty-two.

The practices all went well and the Commandant CFS flew with me on 13 May to give us formal display clearance. The following day we were off to Biggin Hill for the first air show of the season. Our schedule for 1981 was again busy: Biggin Hill, Long Marston, Dunstable, Henlow, Blackpool, Manchester, Sunderland, Isle of Wight, Lee-on-Solent, Portland, Bournemouth, Filey, Coningsby, Old Warden, Teesside, Leicester, Halfpenny Green, Leeds, Marham, Wyton, Jersey, Leuchars and Finningley.

Throughout our displays up and down the country the Vampire, flown by John Halstead, led the formation and he did most of the flight planning work.

He and I worked well together; he was a totally committed aviator and put in far more hours than I did. I still got my one or two days off every week following a display but John rarely took much of the time off that he was due. As an examiner on the Bulldog (he was also an examiner on the Jet Provost), he would often visit a University Air Squadron on our 'free' weekend, resulting in three consecutive working weekends. I admired his dedication. He was one of that rare breed, an A1 instructor.

On 16 June whilst heading back to Leeming I was diverted to RAF Dishforth because of an aircraft crash. Later, when Leeming had re-opened, I taxied past the wreckage of a Jet Provost Mark 5 on the grass. It had no wheels, one of the wings had come off, and it was in a very sorry state, a complete write-off. But the canopy was open and the ejection seats were in place, so it looked as though the crew may have been able to walk away. Indeed they had, neither had been hurt.

After some leave it was the final part of the display season and I began a new role as a flight commander. The display at Teeside Airport, now Durham Tees Valley, on 22 August was one of the few watched from the ground by Jackie and the children. Our last displays of 1981 were scheduled for the Battle of Britain Open Days at RAF Leuchars in Scotland and RAF Finningley in South Yorkshire with Bruce McDonald flying the Vampire. We flew directly to Leuchars to display on arrival. Given the distance, this was a little tight for the Meteor and we would need to land immediately. During our display routine, the airfield was ours so there was little likelihood of anything getting in our way. Or was there?

The flight to Leuchars went according to plan and we went straight into our display routine. The display was, I think, the very best that I had flown throughout my time on the team which seemed fitting as this was my penultimate display and my last day on the team. We then broke into the circuit to position for landing.

Two things then happened coincidentally: I got a nose wheel 'red' indication; the nose wheel was unsafe having perhaps failed to lock down; and Bruce burst a tyre on landing! He came to a halt about halfway down the only runway, effectively blocking it. Oops!

Air traffic control told me to overshoot and I then totally spoilt their day by telling them about my problem. The controller told me to hold off until the runway could be cleared and that this might take some time. He then said, 'Vintage 2, Leuchars Tower. What is your endurance?'

'Leuchars Tower, Vintage 2,' I replied, 'five minutes.'

'Roger, Vintage 2,' came the reply, 'understand that you have five minutes before you need to divert.'

'Vintage 2, negative,' I said, 'I have five minutes to dry tanks.'

My reply was met with a very brief 'Roger.'

Then there was a loud and long silence!

The Vampire was about halfway down the runway, slightly to the right of the centreline and it couldn't be moved until the wheel had been changed; it was also surrounded by crash crews and a flurry of engineering personnel. The display programme had come to a grinding halt. So with few alternatives opening up, I asked air traffic control to clear everyone off the runway so that I could land on the left hand side of the runway. The display director clearly realized that there was no alternative. The runway was duly cleared and I landed alongside the Vampire without any problem. My nose wheel was locked down; thankfully, it was only an indication problem.

A few days later, the Station Commander of RAF Leuchars, Group Captain Mike Graydon, later Air Chief Marshal Sir Michael Graydon, wrote rather a nice letter to the Commandant about his concerns that the 'McDonald twins' might have come home to roost! I was quite affronted, as Bruce was at least twenty years my senior! The Vampire was eventually towed clear of the runway but too late for us to make our slot at Finningley. So I flew back to Leeming on my own to refuel and then on to Finningley; my final display of my two years with the Vintage Pair was on my own.

* * *

It had been a great experience to have flown with the Team for two seasons and I had enjoyed every minute. In total I had flown just over seventy-one hours on the Meteor, a very low figure considering the number of displays. I counted myself to have been very lucky to have been selected; in the fifteen years that the Vintage Pair aircraft displayed, I was to be the only member of the team not to have come from the Central Flying School. The Vintage Pair continued for another five years delighting crowds across the country with their graceful synchronized flying until tragedy struck at Mildenhall on 25 May 1986 when they collided during their display. The Vampire crew ejected and survived. With no ejection seats, the Meteor crew had no chance and both the pilot and one of the team's engineers died.

The sole surviving Meteor T7 continued on the display circuit for two more years until one of the aircraft's 'vices' resulted in yet another tragedy. During a display at Coventry Airport on 30 May 1988, the airbrakes were not selected in before the undercarriage was lowered. This resulted in what was know as 'the phantom dive' as the rudder stalled. Another pilot lost his life.

* * *

In September 1981, Al Rayment appointed me as his deputy and in December I went back into Standards Squadron for an intensive work-up covering both flying and groundschool. I re-categorized to A2 on 10 December; I was now officially an above the average pilot and instructor.

Rumours had been rife for some time that the squadron would be downsized in the New Year as our task was reduced. Although we continued to fly the Jet Provost Mark 5a for currency, most of our instructional sorties were now conducted on the slower and much older Jet Provost Mark 3a. But I still relished the job, especially the additional responsibilities as Deputy Squadron Commander. I was also the only junior officer at Leeming at the time to be appointed as a duty senior supervisor, responsible for flying supervision on the station. Also, whenever Al Rayment was away, I supervised Mike Wherrett, the 1982 Jet Provost aerobatic pilot who was one of the refresher instructors. Al was keen that I consider re-categorizing to A1, but my eyes were firmly focused on a fast-jet future.

*   *   *

During the summer of 1982, Jackie was taken ill while we were on holiday in Norfolk. Luckily we were within a few minutes of RAF Coltishall, so we drove to their Medical Centre. The Senior Medical Officer arranged for Jackie to be admitted to Norfolk and Norwich hospital that day. I said that I would take her but would pick up her overnight things on the way. The doctor's mood changed instantly. 'You don't understand lad,' he said, 'you either take her there now, directly, or it's an ambulance and a blue light. I think that your wife may need an immediate operation.'

He was right. Thankfully, the operation was a success and Jackie fully recovered. She had been very lucky, lucky that RAF Coltishall had been so close and lucky that the RAF doctor who saw her so quickly was spot on in his diagnosis. The doctor was the same chap who had so correctly diagnosed Hannah's life-threatening condition six years earlier in Malta.

*   *   *

My tour at Leeming had been tremendous and I was lucky to have served with a great bunch of instructors and also beneath two very good squadron commanders, Dick Woodhead and Alan Rayment. I had also flown with dozens of 'students' and I had learnt a great deal from them. There was Jerry Yates, a very gifted pilot on his way to command a Buccaneer Squadron; sadly he would be killed in a Hawker Hunter accident; John Houlton whom I would meet again at the Central Flying School in 1991 and who would be on the staff of the Tucano Simulator when I arrived there in 2008. There was Sam Atcherley-Key, a nephew of the famous Atcherley twins of Second World War fame. Sam was a true RAF character with a wonderful sense of humour and as I was his instructor he insisted on calling me 'Father' throughout his course; he would be at Linton when I arrived there in 1992. Keith Holland taught me and so many others about 'the art of low-level navigation' but sadly he would die in a Harrier accident whilst in command of 4 Squadron in Germany. And there was Mike Smith, dear Mike, who became a stalwart of 14 Squadron at Bruggen.

And, of course, during one year of my tour, 1982, a lot of our instructional flying was taking place whilst the UK was at war thousands of miles away on some remote islands in the South Atlantic, the Falkland Islands. We could only stand and watch.

*   *   *

Some of my fondest memories of those days are about the 'spoofs' for which the Refresher Flying Squadron was renowned. While the squadron was very professional and the instructors took their jobs seriously, we all had an eye open for any opportunity for a laugh, especially if the weather precluded the possibility of flying.

Our operations room looked out across the car park to the buildings occupied by the Northumbrian University Air Squadron and their operations desk was usually occupied by their duty authorizer. On one occasion, a refresher instructor purporting to be a telephone engineer called the duty authorizer explaining that he needed some help in rectifying a fault on the other telephone line on the operations desk. He then proceeded to take his unsuspecting prey, step by step, through the process of dismantling the telephone piece by piece. When the telephone was reduced entirely to its component parts, our 'engineer' hung up!

On another occasion during a very cold winter, ground school was contacted and directed to turn off all of the radiators in their building because of a leak in the central heating system. They duly complied. As they were housed within the HQ Central Flying School complex, which included the Commandant's office, it was not just the course members who spent most that day in their greatcoats.

Over the years, I had almost perfected the art of impersonating the station tannoy, which was forever springing into life announcing something or other. All I needed was a metal dustbin and a long rolled-up map. One day, while the Station Commander was in our crewroom, I wondered into the room next door, closed the door, and a few minutes later announced, 'Standby for broadcast, standby for broadcast. There will be a station stand-down today from 1500 hours. I say again, there will be a station stand-down today from 1500 hours.'

But someone must have given the game away; the door opened with a crash and the Station Commander attacked me with a chair!

Nor were our own staff safe from 'spoofs'. One newly-arrived instructor, fresh out of Standards, was immediately put under pressure by being told that he was already late and he was rushed into a briefing where three others awaited, his flight commander and two refresher students. It was to be the first formation sortie for the students. Our newcomer was a former transport pilot and, while he was perfectly competent in formation, it was one of his least practiced skills. His protests that he had not had a chance to read his student's training folder were brushed aside and within a few minutes he found himself 'demonstrating' the close formation references to his 'new' student. When he handed over control to his student, he then witnessed some of the most immaculate close formation that he had ever seen, with the pair of aircraft manoeuvring hard up to 4G in close formation and banking up to 90 degrees. He realized that he had been well and truly 'had'! When he got back to the squadron, he quickly checked his student's folder to find that he had been trying to teach close formation to a former member of the Red Arrows!

We also had a small device for the initiation of new course members and few could resist having a go. At first sight, it looked simple; it was a small metal instrument with a tube to blow through; this was connected internally to an outlet which somehow rotated a small metal windmill. But there were also two other metal tubes pointing in the direction of whoever was blowing the instrument. It was very easy to demonstrate but whenever any un-suspecting visitor had a go, they were covered in talcum powder which had a particularly delicate fragrance.

We also had a unicycle which usually came out at the end of the day, perhaps after a beer. Few could master the unicycle. In fact, as I recall, only one: the very popular Roger Lane, whose posting from the Refresher Flying Squadron was coincident with mine.

*   *   *

Toward the end of the year it was confirmed that I would be posted early in 1983, and it would be a fast-jet cross over to the Tornado GR1 strike/attack aircraft being introduced into service. This would mean leaving home for about eighteen months and travelling to various stations to undergo courses.

At the end of the summer of 1982, I became the standards instructor standardizing all refresher instructors. Although my tenure was fairly short, I did have a 100 per cent success rate in preparing instructors for their various recategorizations.

My penultimate sortie, on 23 February 1983, was with our own Commander-in-Chief, Air Marshal Sir Michael Beavis and I flew my final sortie the following day. I had flown a total of 1,073 hours while on the Refresher Flying Squadron. My next stop was a return match with No. 4 Flying Training School at RAF Valley, to once again undergo Advanced Flying Training, this time on the Hawk. The last time that I had gone to Valley I had a total of 152 flying hours under my belt; this time I had 2,907. All being well, I hoped that I would do rather better.

Chapter 6

Fast-Jets at Last

No. 4 Flying Training School, RAF Valley, 1983

My four courses would be at Valley, Chivenor in Devon, which was expected to be the most demanding course of all, then Cottesmore and finally Honington near Bury St Edmunds in Suffolk. I would commute at weekends. And after that, where would I go next? The Tornado GR1 force was in its infancy and only three squadrons were expected to be based in the UK, with the majority, eight squadrons, being based in Germany. So RAF Germany would be our most likely destination.

The ground school at Valley began on 14 March. 'Alcatraz', or the Officers' Mess, had changed little during the last ten years. Roger Lane was also there undergoing the CFS Hawk course and he would become an instructor at Valley on graduation. Roger was good company during my short stay at Valley. My first flight was on 23 March and I went solo five days later after three hours flying.

On Thursday 7 April I received a bizarre telephone call from the Acting Station Commander at Leeming. There had been a tannoy for me from operations and as I rushed to the telephone in the crewroom I couldn't help but wonder 'what has he found out?'

'I'm ringing about your letter,' he said.

'But I haven't written to you, Sir,' I replied.

'Stop messing about,' he said, 'you know what I mean! It's about a letter that you have received.'

'I'm sorry Sir, but I have no idea what you are talking about.'

He sounded very confused and said, 'Right, forget this conversation ever happened!'

And then he hung up. I was none the wiser but intrigued. The following day I got a lift back to Leeming in a Hawk and called in at the Officers' Mess to collect my mail before going home to the house that we had bought the previous year in Bedale. There was a letter, a blue letter, announcing that I had been selected for promotion to squadron leader with effect from 1 July 1983. While this was very good news, I was slightly concerned that my fast-jet training would be terminated and I might be sent back to take command of a Jet Provost squadron.

I contacted my Desk Officer, Squadron Leader Rocky Goodall; he would become a major influence on my career in the years ahead. He confirmed that

I was still destined for Tornados but, because I had no fast-jet experience, I would need to spend about eighteen months on one squadron before moving to another to fill an executive appointment as a squadron leader. The good thing was that, because of my promotion, the gaps between my courses would be shortened to get me onto the frontline as quickly as possible. My most likely destination would be RAF Laarbruch in Germany, which was to be the first Germany base to re-equip with the Tornado, replacing the existing Buccaneers, the type that I had wanted to fly for so long but which was now gradually being withdrawn.

One of my colleagues on the course was a RN lieutenant who was cross-rolling from helicopters to the Sea Harrier. One evening we were chatting about our earlier training and I ended up telling him about my first experience with the Senior Service when I was Orderly Officer at RAF Church Fenton in 1971 and had ended up 'arresting' three RN officers. I suppose that I should have noticed that he became rather quiet. At the end of my tale he said, 'So, it was you, you bastard! Do you realize how deeply in the "dwang" we were?'

He had been one of the 'Church Fenton Three'; I bought him a beer.

I thoroughly enjoyed flying the Hawk at Valley and the course of twenty-six flying hours went very well. My Final Handling Test was on 19 April. I then had a two week break before reporting to 151 Squadron of No. 2 Tactical Weapons Unit at RAF Chivenor in Devon as a member of No. 29 Course. The course began on 4 May and it was here where I would learn something about basic weaponry and tactics.

151 Squadron No. 2 Tactical Weapons Unit, RAF Chivenor, 1983

RAF Chivenor was a delightful station on the coast of Devon just north of Barnstaple. After a week in ground school I flew my first trip on 10 May. Again I loved the flying and the course moved on very quickly into areas that were very new to me.

There was a lot of emphasis on tactical formation both as a pair and as a four-ship at low-level, which was flown at 420 knots. The attack runs from the initial point to the target were often flown as a coordinated pairs attack to ensure that both aircraft would be through the target area as quickly as possible. We simulated either using the BL755 cluster bomb, which meant that it was possible for the second aircraft to overfly the target about ten seconds after the first, or 1,000lb retard bombs, which demanded a minimum of thirty seconds between aircraft over the target to avoid being 'taken out' by the blast from the first aircraft's bombs.

We were introduced to cine weave, which involved following and filming another aircraft using a camera looking through the gun sight as the aircraft ahead performed various manoeuvres. We then moved onto lay-down (level) bombing, dive bombing, and strafe using a 20mm gun fitted in a gun pack underneath the aircraft.

The gunsight was very basic and extremely accurate flying was required to achieve good results. Very precise heights and speeds had to be flown, and we were taught various phrases to use in the event that you were not as accurate as you had hoped: 'If you're high, go on by,' before, that is, pressing the 'pickle' button, and 'If you're low let it go!'

The wind had to be taken into account by aiming off, left or right, depending on the wind speed and direction. It was all great fun even if I did sometimes miss the target widely. Sometimes I felt that the safest place to be within Pembrey Weapons Range in South Wales, was actually sitting on the target itself!

We also covered air-to-air gunnery against a sleeve target towed by another Hawk and I personally found this event to be the most demanding; the target was usually very safe when I was firing at it! Then we moved onto air combat, which I loved. I think that I relished the idea of a former Canberra pilot 'holding his own' against fast-jet instructors. Perhaps I was also trying to prove a point, that I merited a place as a fast-jet fighter pilot. It was during air combat that I was usually at my most aggressive and I worked hard to achieve 'kills' against all of the staff against whom I flew; I did not like being beaten. But the staff were a good bunch and I found them all helpful. One was Dick Cole, a former instructor from the Central Flying School whom I had known at Leeming. While we only flew one trip together we would end up as colleagues some twenty-six years later.

I very much looked forward to the final phase of the course, the Simulated Attack Profile Phase. This involved planning and leading a pair of aircraft to Pembrey for a first-run attack, and then academic weaponry, before heading off at low-level to attack two targets. Throughout the sortie, a third aircraft acted as the 'bounce', trying to intercept us and claim a kill. 'Bring it on' was my attitude and I couldn't wait.

*   *   *

On the morning of Friday 24 June rumours began to circulate about an accident involving a Hawk from RAF Valley. It was soon confirmed that one of their Hawks had crashed into the Isle of Man and both the instructor and the student had been killed. The instructor was Roger Lane.

This was tragic news. The circumstances surrounding the accident were especially sad. Roger had successfully graduated from the Central Flying Squadron Hawk Squadron and had joined another squadron at Valley. But he had immediately been loaned to yet another squadron, which was temporarily short of instructors. It was also the day of RAF Valley's Summer Ball and Roger's wife, Chris, had set off by train from North Yorkshire to Bangor, where Roger had planned to pick her up. Roger was killed while Chris was en route. His colleagues knew that Chris was on her way but, as no one at Valley had actually met her before, there was a desperate search to find someone who knew her. Early that afternoon one of the instructors still on the

Refresher Flying Squadron at Leeming was flown to Valley and taken to the railway station to meet Chris. Of course, as soon as Chris got out of the carriage she knew the worst. Roger was thirty-five years old and had two young daughters.

I was contacted by Roger's Squadron Commander the following week; there was to be a service funeral for Roger at RAF Leeming. It was normal on such occasions for the Squadron Commander of the deceased to make a valedictory address, but as he didn't actually know Roger, he asked if I was prepared to do it on his behalf. I quickly agreed. While I had little idea what this would involve, it was the very least that I could do.

Initially, the funeral was going to be held in the small Anglican Church at RAF Leeming but this was quickly changed when it became known just how many people planned to attend. Roger had been very well known within the RAF and he and Chris had many friends. The funeral was switched to one of the large hangars, after which Roger would be buried with full military honours in the churchyard in Leeming village. The chaplain had originally suggested that after the interment the family might like to return to the small church hall to have a cup of tea, but Chris, who had a much better idea of 'the score', said that everyone would be invited back to the Officers' Mess afterwards where she would put on a barrel of beer in memory of Roger.

The funeral took place on 5 July. It was my first 'duty' as a squadron leader. It was a very moving service, and I found it very hard to get through the valedictory address. I spoke briefly about the facts of Roger's RAF service career before offering a more personal tribute. Whenever Roger ever bumped into one of his friends his greeting was invariably the same, 'Hello mate!'

And he always meant it. I had to stop partway through to compose myself. I could sense that the emotion that I felt was shared by everyone in the congregation; there was not a sound within that huge hangar. I finished with extracts from two poems: one from Bunyan's *To the Fallen* and the other from Christina Rossetti's *Remember*:

> Yet if you should forget me for a while
> And afterwards remember, do not grieve:
> For if the darkness and corruption leave
> A vestige of the thoughts that I once had
> Better by far you should forget and smile
> Than that you should remember and be sad.

The interment in the graveyard in Leeming village soon followed and I was one of the pall-bearers. Roger of course had the last laugh as when we gently lowered him into his grave, part of the turf at the side of the grave began to give way and one of the other pall-bearers began to gently slide into the grave with Roger. That brought a smile to many of our faces, including to Chris.

There was then a volley of shots from the escort, which made the hair on the back of my neck stand up; the Last Post was played and then there was a flypast by a solitary Hawk from Roger's squadron at Valley. It was all quite magnificent but very moving.

When we arrived back at the Mess all the service guests turned right on arrival and headed for the bar, whereas the family turned left and went to an anteroom for a cup of tea. Within a few minutes one or two family members joined us in the bar. Within half an hour the anteroom was empty and the whole family were in the bar saying farewell to Roger in the RAF's traditional manner. Chris had indeed judged things right. It was the most fitting of farewells to a popular 'mate' who had been so very well known throughout the RAF.

I would have liked to have stayed on but I had to fly back to Chivenor the same day. We climbed to about 35,000 feet and set course to the south-west. Although there was very little cloud about, it was a very hazy day and we soon lost sight of the ground; it was like that for most of the trip to Chivenor. Except for a few minutes when far away to the west the sun picked out a small area of the ground, an island. It was the Isle of Man.

*   *   *

Back at Chivenor, there was little time to be too reflective as we entered the final and busiest part of the course, the attack phase. Again I loved it. I was very comfortable at low-level, even at the higher speeds flown in the Hawk, so I was able to concentrate on the challenge of leading a tactical pair and fighting our way to the target and then back home. Very few of the 'bounce' aircraft ever achieved a 'kill' against me but I regularly chalked one up for the good guys.

On the way to the target it was important to try and evade the fighter; in order to fight on equal terms with the bounce, we would have to simulate jettisoning our bombs. This would mean that the fighter had in effect 'won', as he would have stopped the bomber from putting bombs on target. If the bounce did get right behind you, in your six o'clock, there were few options left. One final option before leading the fighter away from your mates in the rest of the formation – referred to as 'heading off to die like a man' – was to try and manoeuvre so that the fighter was exactly in your six o'clock before employing the tactic known as 'knickers'! This involved dropping a 1,000lb retard bomb in the fighter's face. With luck, the ensuing explosion would either take out the fighter altogether, or put him off his game so much that you might be able to make good your escape. Thankfully, I never had to try out this tactic for real. In our more 'PC world' these days, this tactic is now referred to as 'bomb in face.'

On Friday 29 July, I made the long journey by train to Northallerton where I was met by Jackie. When I arrived, Jackie looked slightly relieved. She said simply, 'It wasn't you then.'

Three Hawks from the two Tactical Weapons Units had been lost that day. One from our sister unit at RAF Brawdy in South Wales had crashed killing the solo student, and two from Chivenor had been involved in a mid-air collision over Devon, although all four pilots had ejected safely.

*   *   *

The last few weeks of the course was very busy but I loved it and the final sorties went very well. Jackie and the children also joined me and we rented a bungalow in the lovely village of Georgeham. My last sortie was on 22 August after fifty-nine flying hours on the course. I was pleased that it had gone so well, especially as I knew that there would be many who would look at me in the future as a squadron leader totally new to the fast-jet world, and wonder if I could 'cut the mustard'. While academic weaponry had been new, and it would take me some time to master this art, I loved fast-jet flying and especially the low-level attack and air combat sorties. My Squadron Commander commented that despite having cross-rolled at a relatively late stage, I 'had shown a true flair for fast-jet operations and had completely justified my cross-over training'. With the course complete, we could now relax and enjoy the last two weeks of our holiday in Devon.

Tornado Tri-National Training Establishment, RAF Cottesmore, 1983–1984
Cottesmore was now the home of the Tri-National Tornado Training Establishment (TTTE) and manned by the RAF, the Luftwaffe and the Italian Air Force. Since the completion of Rutland Water, the area had changed dramatically and no longer would it be a challenge to find the airfield. Rutland Water is the largest reservoir in England, but it came at a price paid by many local people with about four miles of the valley near Empingham being flooded. Now there is only one village with Hambleton in its name, when there had been three. To the south, the few houses of Normanton and its former hall (now a hotel) avoided flooding, although the church, with its semi-circular portico and tower almost did not. It was saved through a project which raised the floor level and protected the lower part of the building with a pier of stones, and it now stands out into the reservoir from the south shore.

*   *   *

My course began on 10 October 1983, straight into the inevitable ground school which was interspersed with simulator trips. One of the simulator instructors was Squadron Leader Dickie Lees, my former Flight Commander from officer training and from my Canberra course at Cottesmore ten years earlier. Perhaps he was fated to ensure that whatever I was taught stayed taught!

The Tornado was one complicated aircraft! At the time, it was estimated that each engine cost £1 million and each aircraft over £20 million. The flying control system was computer controlled using the CSAS (Control Stabilization Augmentation System) which meant that moving the control column did not directly move the control surfaces; it merely sent an electronic signal to the computer which then moved the control surfaces. It had an inertial navigation system and many of the systems, including weapon aiming, were computerized. What was completely new for me was the head-up display, which was a system that displayed information from the aircraft's instruments and computers directly onto the canopy in front of the pilot. We referred to this as 'the green writing' and it allowed us to take in information while looking outside, without having to look down into the cockpit.

The Tornado also had a very good ground mapping radar used for navigation and targeting while one of its key features was the terrain following radar. This meant that the aircraft could be flown on autopilot at low-level in cloud or at night. This was quite a revolutionary system and we would spend the next few years clearing the system to fly lower and lower. The autopilot system was very good but it also contained one or two 'traps for the unwary' which I would soon discover.

The tactics employed by the RAF for potential use against the Warsaw Pact relied on low-level flying, so the focus of our training would be toward low flying and weapon delivery from low altitudes. We would in time progress onto operational low flying at 100 feet, at speeds of 480 knots or more. Egress from the target would be faster. The aircraft could exceed Mach One, and we all experienced doing so, but it was only cleared above Mach One if it was 'clean', not carrying any external stores such as fuel tanks or weapons.

*   *   *

There was much discussion about the Tornado Command Ejection system. By selecting the system to 'both', whichever of the two crew initiated ejection, the other crew member was automatically ejected. In those early days, some pilots who came to the Tornado from a single-seat background seemed to be slightly less willing, to begin with, for their navigators to have control over whether the pilot was ejected or not, whereas those of us more used to flying with navigators were a little more sanguine.

One reason for the lively debate was because of the first RAF loss of a Tornado just two weeks before my course began. The aircraft had suffered a total electrics failure at medium level at night over Norfolk. As such a failure leads to the electronically controlled engines accelerating to destruction the crew were quickly faced with a double engine failure too, so ejection was their only option. Even with no intercom, the crew were able to shout to one another as they had a few minutes in hand and they agreed to eject, not that they had any choice. The aircraft came down close to Sandringham and the navigator was found safe and well soon afterwards. As I recall, it took a very long time before it was confirmed that the pilot had not ejected; he was still in the wreckage. It was thought that he must have become incapacitated when the navigator ejected and had been unable to eject himself. This was quite tragic; if the Command Eject had been set to 'both' then the pilot would have been ejected and he almost certainly would have survived.

A year later, a Tornado crew suffered a very near miss with another aircraft when flying at low-level in Southern Germany. The pilot had to take immediate and quite violent avoiding action to avoid hitting the other aircraft. The navigator sensed that the pilot had lost control and immediately ejected. As the Command Ejection system was set to 'both' the pilot was ejected too. So the debate continued. I made up my mind fairly early and I always insisted that the switch be selected to 'both'.

* * *

My course consisted of six pilots and six navigators, a mixture of RAF, Luftwaffe and Italian officers. Backgrounds and ages varied, and as I was the senior officer on the course, I was the course leader and 'labelled' the SBO – Senior British Officer – which was quite amusing, as the last time that I had come across the term was in the Second World War film *The Great Escape*. I was crewed with a first tour Luftwaffe navigator.

The pace of the course was slower than that of an RAF course but I didn't mind that, there was a lot to learn about this amazing swing-wing aircraft. The wings had three positions: fully swept for high speed was 67 degrees; 45 degrees was for normal low-level flying, and 25 degrees was for take-off and landing. The wings did not swing automatically; the pilot used a lever on the left hand side of the cockpit next to the throttles. Approaches with the wings in other than 25 degrees were practiced regularly.

* * *

My first sortie was on the 2 December 1983. I flew eight sorties with various instructors covering general handling, instrument flying and some formation flying before my first flight as captain on 20 December. For that sortie I flew with a staff navigator, a German Navy korvetten capitan (lieutenant commander); it didn't take me long before I learnt a sharp and valuable lesson in crew cooperation.

The sortie was meant to last about two hours and involved some low-level flying, medium level handling, and circuits back at Cottesmore. Over a long straight leg at about 500 feet over the sea off Norfolk, I engaged the autopilot, although I didn't mention to the navigator that I had done so. Shortly before turning to coast in, I disconnected the autopilot and began a planned climb to medium level.

During the climb the aircraft began to try to do its own thing, much to my concern. The nose began to rise, gently at first, despite my best efforts to stop it doing so. Then suddenly the nose dropped sharply. That woke my back-seater up! He asked me what was happening and I said that I didn't know. Then it happened again, but this time even more violently. It happened three or four times altogether and we were both convinced that we had a flying control problem associated with the flying control system. So I selected the most degraded mode of the system, called Mechanical Mode, which gave more of a direct input to the flying controls, relying less on the computer. Flying in this mode was not particularly straightforward. It always reminded me of the 'nodding dog' that you sometimes see on the ledge in some car rear windows. That's how the aircraft felt, gently nodding, flyable but not particularly comfortable.

We declared an emergency, a PAN call, and came back to Cottesmore to land from a straight-in approach. After detailed discussion with the staff it became abundantly clear that the problem had been entirely self-induced. I hadn't disconnected the autopilot properly so had actually been fighting against the autopilot during the climb. My major error though, and it was a very basic one, was not telling my navigator that I had used the autopilot. If I had, he would immediately have told me to use the Stick Force Cut-out, a paddle switch on the front of the control column, which would immediately have disconnected all autopilot signals and would have solved the problem in an instant. I learnt a valuable lesson; it wouldn't be my last.

The course ended on 10 February 1984. After a week's leave, I set off for my final course on 45 (Reserve) Squadron, the Tornado Weapons Conversion Unit at RAF Honington in Suffolk. By now it had also been confirmed that I would be posted to 20 Squadron at RAF Laarbruch in West Germany.

45 Squadron Tornado Weapons Conversion Unit (TWCU), RAF Honington, 1983–1984

Our course of twelve RAF students began at the TWCU on 20 February and I flew my first sortie on 29 February. The course concentrated entirely on the applied aspects of using the Tornado, including low-level tactics, use of the terrain following radar, air combat manoeuvring, and there was a lot of emphasis on air-to-ground bombing. At that stage, strafe, using the 27mm internally mounted Mauser cannon had not been cleared for use.

We used four weapons ranges, all on the east coast: Wainfleet and Holbeach, in the Wash, and Donna Nook and Cowden on the east coast further north. We practiced lay-down bombing, shallow dive bombing, and loft bombing. The latter involved pulling up from low-level at high speed about four miles short of the target, 'tossing' the bomb at the target during the climb, and then rolling almost inverted and pulling hard to get back to low-level and exiting from the target as quickly as possible in the direction from which we had come.

The computer technology for weapon aiming was state of the art, with the imagery being shown on the head-up display. The terrain following radar was also a magic bit of kit, although over the UK we were only allowed to practice using it in relatively good weather conditions. It was nevertheless a remarkable feeling to be flying at low-level at night on autopilot and watching the aircraft climbing and descending entirely on its own as it passed over high ground, or climbing to clear pylons before descending once it was clear of them.

One of the staff navigators was Al Vincent; we had last flown together on 7 Squadron and he also had been in the Guard of Honour at our wedding. It would be another fifteen years before we met again in Kuwait of all places; by then he would be a group captain. I took up squash once more playing with one of the navigators on the course, John Sheen. Married with a young son, John was a great character and an experienced former Buccaneer navigator. He was posted to 617 (Dambusters) Squadron based at RAF Marham. Sadly he died along with his pilot when their aircraft failed to return from a night sortie over the North Sea in December 1985.

The course ended on 10 May, and ten days later I flew to Germany to join 20 (Designate) Squadron at RAF Laarbruch. It would be August before Jackie and the children would be able to join me.

20 Squadron, RAF Laarbruch, 1984–1985

RAF Laarbruch was one of four operational flying stations within RAF Germany which formed part of No. 2 Allied Tactical Air Force. The three near the Dutch border between the Rhine to the east and the Mass to the west, Laarbruch, Bruggen and Wildenrath, were referred to as 'the clutch'; the fourth was RAF Gutersloh, further east and closer to the Inner German Border, which separated West and East Germany.

RAF Laarbruch had four flying squadrons. II Squadron was equipped with the Jaguar in the attack/recce role and 15 and 16 Squadrons had been the first RAF squadrons in Germany to re-equip with the Tornado GR1. No. 16 Squadron was commanded by Wing Commander Rocky Goodall, my former desk officer. No. 20 Squadron (Designate) was in the process of forming when I arrived. It was called 'designate' because 20 Squadron was still fully operational at RAF Bruggen flying Jaguars and would remain so until the formal hand-over of the Squadron Standard on 29 June 1984. No. 20 Squadron's motto was *'Facta no Verba'* – Deeds not Words.

* * *

I joined a number of other officers living in the Mess all waiting for married quarters to become available. The station was a scene of frantic activity as the new aircraft were introduced, and regular alert exercises were very much the order of the day. In fact they would be the order of the day for the next five years; the pace was rapid and intense and there would be no slackening whatsoever.

Unlike RAF airfields in the UK, Laarbruch was well camouflaged, having been built in a forest. Only the runways and parallel taxiways were in the open, and the station facilities blended well with the surrounding country-side. Each squadron had its own set of hardened aircraft shelters which were small individual hangars, each designed for a single aircraft, and these were made of reinforced concrete with huge steel doors. Narrow taxiways wound their way through the woods from each site, before joining the main taxiway. However, 20 Squadron's site was still under construction with new Mark III shelters, purpose built for the Tornado. These were larger than the Mark I shelters used by our sister squadrons. It would be a few weeks before we moved into the new site, in fact when I arrived, 20 Squadron only had one aircraft and five aircrew officers. This was no bad thing as I felt much less like the 'new boy' as most of the crews arrived after me.

Each Tornado squadron was established for thirteen aircraft and eighteen crews, with twelve of the aircraft being strike aircraft, while one was a trainer with dual flying controls, although it was fully strike/attack capable. The eighteen crews included a wing commander as squadron commander, and five aircrew squadron leaders filling executive appointments. These five included a Qualified Flying Instructor, a Qualified Weapons Instructor, a Navigation Instructor and two others. In addition, there was a squadron leader Senior Engineering Officer and a flight lieutenant Junior Engineering Officer. There was also an Army major as Ground Liaison Officer and a flight lieutenant or flying officer Squadron Intelligence Officer. Add to that about eighty groundcrew and the total complement was about 120 personnel.

Over the next few weeks increasing numbers of aircraft, aircrew and groundcrew began to arrive, but for a few weeks flying opportunities were a little 'thin'. Jackie and I were allocated a married quarter in the town of Goch, about twenty-five minutes north, and we moved there during August 1984, eighteen months after I had embarked on cross-over training.

Goch was just south of the Reichswald, a huge area of forest to the north-west toward the Dutch town of Nijmegen. This area had seen very fierce fighting during the Second World War and within the forest there was a large Commonwealth War Graves Cemetery. Like all of them, it was beautifully kept and so tranquil. It was very sobering to wander around the graves, with this particular one being the final resting place of many RAF crews. To see their names and their ages was incredibly moving with so many of them being in their teens or early twenties. There was one highly decorated squadron leader buried there at the age of twenty-three.

* * *

I soon had my arrival interview with the Station Commander, Group Captain David Cousins later Air Chief Marshal Sir David Cousins. At the appointed time, two of us were waiting for interview, hats in hand. We could then walk smartly in, salute and give the 'Staish' a good listening too. About five minutes after the due time, the Group Captain came out of his office apologizing profusely. We stood up and tried to put our hats on, but that proved difficult as he grabbed my colleague's hand in a long handshake and put his other hand on my shoulder as he ushered us into his office, still apologizing for being late. Before we knew it we were sitting in comfortable chairs still holding our hats and being served coffee by him!

He said that he had been very busy as His Royal Highness Prince Charles was due to visit the station the following week and he had been trying to put together a presentation for him. He then suddenly stopped in mid-sentence and said, 'That gives me an idea. Would you mind if I practiced my presentation on you? And I really would appreciate it if you would tell me straight if there is anything that I could do to improve it.'

He then went on to give us one of the most succinct and interesting briefings that I had ever heard, with lots of slides to illustrate the role of the station. At the end he asked for our opinion and we both said that there was little that could be done to improve the presentation. He then asked if there were enough slides, or if any of them were superfluous. My colleague mentioned that he had used two slides to demonstrate the work of the Royal Engineers in rapid runway repair after bomb damage. David Cousins exclaimed, 'You're absolutely right! I only used one slide for every other aspect of station life. I will take that one out. Thank you very much.'

He then took his seat for the rest of the 'interview'. Turning to me, he said, 'You used to fly the Meat Box with the Vintage Pair, didn't you? That must have been fun?'

The term 'Meat Box' was RAF humour to describe the Meteor, given the huge numbers of losses, in much the same way that the RAF ambulance was usually referred to as the 'Meat Wagon'.

The interview lasted only a few more minutes and covered fairly routine stuff, but when we left, Group Captain Cousins had both of us well on board. His whole manner and personality had touched me in such a way that if he ever ordered me to jump, I would simply have said 'how high?'

Over the next few months I began to realize that he did not need to practice public speaking on anyone, he was a natural. What he had done was to put us both at ease completely and by doing so he had given us a great insight into the work of the station. He had also, in a very short time, earned our loyalty. I have no doubt that he had planned the interview and that the reason he was slightly late was that he was reviewing our files immediately before inviting us in. Group Captain Cousins certainly knew how to get the support of his officers and it was something that I would try to emulate in the years ahead.

*   *   *

As the squadron's manning increased so did the pace of work as each squadron worked toward being evaluated and declared to NATO as a fully operational 'strike' squadron. The training was constant with each squadron running a series of Operation Days, or Op Days; these were small exercises lasting a single day, which were evaluated by the squadron itself. Op Days had little impact on the rest of the station but they would often involve us being called in at 0400 hours in the morning. Then there would be a MINIVAL, a mini evaluation, which would be similar to an Op Day, but it would last about three days and the evaluation would be carried out by one of our sister squadrons. After a series of MINIVALS, the whole station would be subject to a MAXEVAL, a maximum evaluation, lasting four days and nights during which the station would be evaluated by RAF staff from other stations.

All of these were designed to lead us toward a full TACEVAL, tactical evaluation, which involved NATO staffs conducting the evaluation. All of these exercises involved no-notice call-outs, often in the middle of the night, so the sound of sirens even within Goch was a regular event. The first to embark on this programme was 15 Squadron, followed by 16 Squadron and then 20 Squadron. The whole regime revolved around intense training, exercising and evaluation. Little wonder that Friday evening 'Happy Hours' were well frequented and lengthy affairs. We worked very hard, and we played hard too. For those of us who were Goch residents, a bus (often referred to as the 'Drunk's Bus' by our long-suffering wives) would collect us from the Mess at 1830 hours on a Friday evening to bring us home.

*   *   *

The aircrew on 20 Squadron were an interesting mix of experience and inexperience. I was crewed with Bob Ankerson, although I probably only flew about a quarter of my sorties with him. He was one of the last RAF aircrew to be taken prisoner by the Iraqis during Gulf War I after his aircraft was lost. There were two officers whom I had known previously: Bill Eaton had been a navigator on XIII Squadron in Malta, and Bill Ramsay had been a Central Flying School instructor at Leeming. One of the first tourist pilots on 20 Squadron would be awarded the Distinguished Flying Cross for gallantry during Gulf War I. Later he would also eject from a Tornado. Stan Bowles was a young, keen, and enthusiastic first tour navigator who had been on my course at Honington.

Some of the navigators had major problems with air sickness and I couldn't help but admire the way they were able to say 'going off intercom for a minute' and then a little while later 'back with you'. In the intervening time they had been forced to use a sick bag. How they were able to then carry on with their task was beyond me. One in particular was Neil Anderson, an experienced ex-Nimrod navigator who was prone to air sickness, which he was determined to overcome, yet he was still able to perform to the very highest of standards and had a growing reputation on the squadron. He was promoted at the end of his tour on 20 Squadron and joined 27 Squadron in the UK as a flight commander. Both Stan and Neil were killed in separate accidents over the North Sea within three days of one another during August 1990. They were both married; Neil had three young children.

*   *   *

Much of our flying and ground training during the first few months concentrated on training for our strike role and it wasn't until autumn before we began to fly regularly as attack pairs and four-ships. The pace didn't slacken during winter as the station was totally geared up to deal with the worst of the German winters. It was often colder than the UK and there was more snow too, but much less of the snow, freeze, thaw, snow, freeze, thaw regime that we so often experienced in the UK.

*   *   *

In the New Year I found out that I would move to a squadron at Bruggen to fill an executive tour after only a year with 20 Squadron. Professionally this was good news, but this would mean another house move: house number seven within ten years. It would also result in another change of schools for the children.

In my new role I would be required to be a Tornado Qualified Flying Instructor, so I began my conversion to the rear seat of the Tornado in February 1985. During these sorties, another Tornado instructor would occupy the front seat of the trainer, with me in the back. The conversion would not only cover flying the aircraft from the rear seat, but also being able to operate all the navigation equipment including the radar. Bombing was an important part of the conversion course. If I was expecting a formal 'course' I was very much mistaken. It consisted of three trips, two of which were on 19 February, with the final one the following day! These were hard rules!

After my first trip I seriously began to question whether I would ever cope in the back seat. I flew with one of 20 Squadron's flight commanders who was a Weapons Instructor and as such rear-seat qualified. He suggested that I lower the ejection seat as low as possible so that I could get the best possible view of the radar. And off we went. I found the radar immensely difficult to interpret and within fifteen minutes of getting airborne I felt distinctly unwell. For the rest of the trip I concentrated on flying the aircraft, but I was not at my best and felt like death. Even blasts of 100 per cent oxygen didn't help. I flew my second trip later that day in the same aircraft with the same instructor in the front; this time I lasted about twenty minutes before I felt ill, but thankfully I wasn't sick.

This was awful, I thought, I had never been sick in an aircraft but it looked as though I had now met my match. And I couldn't believe how hard it was to get a very clear picture on the radar. My opinion of Tornado navigators went up a hundred fold.

The following day I flew my third trip, this time with the Squadron Training Officer who was a Tornado Qualified Flying Instructor. As we walked toward the aircraft, the same one as I had flown the day before, I explained about the difficulty I had had the previous day.

'Where did you have your ejection seat set?' he asked.

'As low as possible,' I replied, 'so that I could get the best view possible of the radar.'

'Well,' he said. 'If you're anything like me you'll feel sick after about twenty minutes!'

He then went on, 'You need to have the seat set as high as possible so you can concentrate on looking outside!'

When I explained about my trouble making any sense of the radar, he told me to get strapped in and then he would look at the radar settings. As he looked over my shoulder at the very poor, dark, and indistinct picture he said, 'Try this.'

And with that he flicked up a switch. Suddenly what had been blurred and indistinct became crystal clear! The switch was labelled 'Hi Lo Intensity' and it had been at the 'Lo' setting for night flying! No wonder I hadn't been able to make anything out in the bright sunlight. My third trip went extremely well, I felt fine and had no trouble using the radar. My opinion of navigators reverted to the one I had previously held, which was of course still very high!

A few days later I was checked out as rear-seat qualified, and over my last three months on the squadron I built up a few more hours in the back seat before being certified as 'Competent to Instruct' by the Central Flying School Agent for the Tornado on 30 May 1985. By then it had been confirmed that I would be posted to 14 Squadron at RAF Bruggen.

* * *

There was still a major hurdle for me to get over before I left 20 Squadron and Laarbruch. It was traditional on posting to be dined-out of the Officers' Mess and while I had attended many of these functions before, I had never been required to speak. However, my Squadron Commander was very traditional about such matters and he insisted that no senior officer from his squadron would ever be dined-out without speaking, so I had better prepare myself. This was likely to be an ordeal.

After the Loyal Toast at such events the 'game was on' and banter and barracking from the assembled officers was the 'norm'. Woe betide the speaker who could not give as good as he got. Group Captain Cousins was an absolute master at such affairs, he always seemed to be at ease and spoke with great confidence and humour. His ability to respond to the quips from the other diners was renowned. How on earth would I cope with the banter? And what should I say?

On the night in question, I was particularly cautious with the wine. I was on the top table next to the Station Commander and, as I was the senior guest, I had to reply to his speech of farewell on behalf of all the other guests being dined-out. As the time for speeches rapidly approached I was surprised to see that Group Captain Cousins seemed nervous, glancing at his notes before he had to stand up. This was quite a revelation; clearly the art of good speaking was more about being prepared than about flair, or being naturally confident. Then it was my turn.

I stumbled through the normal words of thanks on behalf of the guests. As I did so, I took out from my pocket a large white handkerchief and began tying a knot in each corner. Actually, I had cheated and had tied two knots already, just in case my nerves got the better of me. Then I stood on my chair and put the knotted handkerchief on my head. That brought a bit of a hush in the dining room as this was unheard of behaviour in an Officers' Mess dining room.

I then launched into an abridged version of how Moses led his people out of the land of the Pharaoh to the Promised Land. Except that I had changed all of the character's names; I used the names of people from 20 Squadron and from the station, including both the Squadron Commander ('Moses') and the Station Commander ('The Almighty'). And it was all in the purest Geordie accent that I could muster! It ended with a reference to 20 Squadron's motto, *'Facta non Verba'*, with the 'Almighty' declaring to 'Moses' that he needed 'Deeds not Words' to get the waters of the Red Sea to part. There was no 'banter' or interruptions at all during the speech, just laughter as everyone realized that I was sending up virtually every senior officer who was attending the dinner. It went down a storm. I was very well hosted in the bar afterwards. My Boss was especially pleased that one of 'his' had delivered so well in front of the rest of the station.

*   *   *

A few days later, I had my final interview with Group Captain Cousins. If anything, this made a far greater impression on me than my arrival interview. Shortly before, an incident had occurred on another squadron while they had been practicing operational low flying at 100 feet above the ground. After one sortie, branches of a tree had been found sticking into one of the under-wing fuel tanks of one aircraft. Most of us knew about the incident and there had been some rumours that an attempt had been made to deal with the incident 'in house'. That had failed and the Station Commander had initiated a Unit Inquiry.

The Group Captain was very candid during my interview, trying to impress upon me the role that the squadron's executives (the squadron leaders) had in advising their Squadron Commander appropriately and how important it might be to say 'No, you must not, you cannot do that'. I took his advice. In saying farewell, he also mentioned that I would find my new Station Commander at Bruggen to have a very different approach to his. He was not wrong!

My final sortie with 20 Squadron was on 5 June 1984 and my short tour came to an end on 7 June. That just left my final 'Happy Hour', after which I headed off with the other Goch officers on the 'Drunk's Bus' at 1830 hours. Our kitchen faced the main road and Jackie happened to be there when she saw the bus stop outside the house. This was unusual, as normally it dropped everyone at the end of the road.

'That's nice of them,' she thought. 'They've brought Paul right up to our door.'

I duly clambered out of the bus and walked up our footpath. And to Jackie's horror, so did everyone else! All the passengers followed me up the garden path and into our living room. This was the 'social' equivalent of a TACEVAL, a no-notice arrival, usually on a Friday evening, of crews various, demanding beer and bacon and eggs!

Chapter 7

I Spread My Wings and Keep My Promise

14 Squadron, RAF Bruggen, 1985

On 10 June 1985 I arrived at RAF Bruggen as the Training Officer on 14 (Designate) Squadron. At the time 14 Squadron was still fully operational as a Jaguar squadron and would remain so for a further six months, until we were declared operational in the strike role.

Bruggen was south of Laarbruch, a few miles east of the Dutch town of Roermond and like Laarbruch, built within a forest. The western boundary was the border between West Germany and the Netherlands. The station adjoined the German village of Elmpt and the nearest German town was Monchengladbach about thirty minutes drive to the east. The single runway, orientated east/west, had two parallel taxiways of the same length. Most of the infrastructure was to the north of the runway and there were four separate sites of hardened aircraft shelters, one in each corner of the airfield. To the north were 31 Squadron and 17 Squadron (west and east respectively), and 14 Squadron (Jaguars) was in the south-eastern corner. We would be accommodated temporarily in the south-western corner adjoining the Quick Reaction Alert site until the last Jaguars departed. The Bruggen Wing would then expand with 9 Squadron arriving from the UK. This would make the Bruggen Wing, with fifty-two Tornado GR1 aircraft, an incredibly formidable force. All of the shelters at Bruggen were of the Mark I type, much smaller than the Mark IIIs of 20 Squadron at Laarbruch. I would realize just how much smaller at the end of the year.

Commanded by a wing commander pilot, the Squadron was established for seven other senior officers, six squadron leaders and one major. The Deputy Squadron Commander was known as the Executive Officer (Exec) and there were two flight commanders, a weapons leader and a training officer. There were also the senior and junior engineering officers, the ground liaison officer and the intelligence officer. Over the coming months, we soon built up to a full strength of eighteen crews, with a lot of *ab-initio* pilots and navigators. I was crewed with a former Vulcan navigator, Bob Wright; Bob had been the navigator radar on Black Buck, the Vulcan which bombed Stanley airfield during the Falklands War in 1982.

During my arrival interview with the Station Commander it was soon evident that he was indeed a very different character from Laarbruch's Station Commander. At the appointed time, I entered his office, saluted, gave him a 'good listening to', saluted, and left. Not a lot of warmth there then!

I lived in the Mess for a few weeks until we were allocated a married quarter on camp; this made living there very secure. At the time the IRA posed a very real threat and it was a threat which expressed itself: a number of servicemen had been murdered on the European mainland, including two in Roermond. An IRA explosives cache was found not far from Bruggen and car searches on camp were routine. The NAAFI shop had been evacuated on a number of occasions, and our son Matthew can still recall seeing the RAF police conducting searches of our gardens, and being taught at school how to check the wheel arches of the family car for car bombs. It was at Bruggen that he began his fourth primary school in three years; he was not yet nine years old. That was the price that service children had to pay.

* * *

During the summer of 1985 we rented part of a farmhouse in France near the town of Royan on the northern side of the Gironde Estuary. The other half of the farmhouse was occupied by the elderly owners. They could speak no English and our French, even with a phrase book, was very poor. On our final evening we joined them, and some of their friends of a similar age, for 'aperitifs'. All communication was largely by gestures and smiles, until that is, the atlas was produced. It was opened at a map of England and they wanted us to show them where we had come from. There was silence as I turned the pages to a map of Germany and when I pointed to where we lived there was an audible gasp and '*Allemande! Vous etes Allemande?*'

Oops! All of the group were of an age to have experienced occupation and the atmosphere changed immediately, becoming icy cold. We were clearly being looked at in a completely new light. Trying desperately to recover the situation, I burst into my best schoolboy French, '*Non, non! Je suis Anglais. Je suis un aviator, un aviator Anglais. Je suis L'Armee de L'Air!*'

In an instant the atmosphere changed again, and I was grasped warmly, we both were, with kisses on both cheeks amidst comments of, '*Ah! Vous etes un aviator Anglais de L'Armee de L'Air! L'Armee de L'Occupation!*'

For them, we were part of the forces so justifiably occupying the country that they still perceived as their enemy. Those few minutes of misunderstanding and then clarity were both revealing and moving. If they remembered that the RAF had flattened much of Royan in 1944, they were far too polite to make any mention of it.

* * *

Soon, 14 Squadron was at full strength. Every pilot and navigator underwent a short familiarization course and I checked out each pilot in the dual-controlled trainer in separate sorties by day and by night. Then there were formation checks and regular routine checks on pilots and navigators alike. In a very short period I had flown with every pilot and navigator on the squadron.

Each annual Qualified Flying Instructor check that I flew followed a similar pattern involving simulating an engine failure soon after take-off, followed by a heavyweight radar approach, medium level general handing, including aerobatics, and recoveries from unusual positions.

Unlike the UK Tornados at the time, the RAF Germany aircraft were fitted with a Spin Prevention Incidence Limiting System (SPILS), so all pilots had to be familiarized with what this system could offer. Providing that the aircraft was flown within certain configuration and angle of attack limits, SPILS ensured that the aircraft would not 'depart' or 'flick' into a spin; it would continue to fly, even if the pilot was demanding something that the aircraft was not capable of producing. It was an amazing system, although it had some limitations as I would experience during practice air-to-air combat later in my tour.

The instructor check sortie would always include a swept-wing approach, simulating that the aircraft's wings were stuck fully swept back at 67 degrees. The approach speed was very fast at about 250 knots and touch-down would be at about 225 knots. This was always a challenging approach as the nose of the aircraft had to be held high in the air at a very high angle of attack, or Alpha, of 16 degrees. On touchdown the nose of the aircraft could only be raised to 17 Alpha to avoid scraping the tail. During the approach the front-seat pilot could only just see the runway, the navigator or rear-seat instructor could not. For practice the approach would end with an overshoot. For real, the hook would be lowered to engage the Remote Hydraulic Arrestor Gear, a cable stretched across, and a few inches above, the runway. Once the aircraft's hook engaged the arrestor cable, the aircraft would be brought to a very rapid standstill. The arrestor cable could also be used in the event of a high speed abort during take-off, or if the aircraft suffered a brake, hydraulic or nose wheel steering failure.

I would resort to using the hook on half a dozen occasions over the next few years. It was always an incredible experience. The hook would be lowered during the latter part of the final approach and you would work hard to touch down as close to the runway threshold as possible. As you crossed over the arrestor cable nothing would happen, so you would immediately have doubts. Had the hook bounced over the cable? Of course it hadn't, the cable was running out beneath and behind the aircraft. Then there would be the most incredible sensation as you were brought to a sudden halt from about 150 knots within a matter of a few yards. A great system!

The instructor check sortie would always conclude with three or four visual circuits, some were normal and some were flown simulating failures of an engine, flaps, or part of the flying control system. The latter usually involved an approach and landing in mechanical mode, the 'nodding dog' type of approach that I had so unnecessarily flown during my course at Cottesmore.

One or two of the squadron's crews didn't stay long; they were moved onto other squadrons to spread the experience. During my tour, I flew with nearly forty-five pilots and navigators who served on 14 Squadron, as well as a number who served on our sister squadrons. No less than six would eject at some stage during their flying careers, two of them twice, and sadly, eight would be killed.

* * *

The work up to strike status throughout 1985 was intense and on 1 November the formal parade to mark the hand-over of the Squadron Standard took place. The squadron motto, emblazed on the standard, is unique in the RAF, as it is in Arabic. In English it read 'I spread my wings and keep my promise' and is an extract from the Koran; it was suggested by His Highness the Emir Abdullah of Transjordan in 1916 where the squadron was based at the time. In 1985, the squadron was equipped with an aircraft that could indeed spread its wings, and five years later it would keep its promise by being part of the first RAF Tornado GR1 squadron to deploy to the Gulf following Saddam Hussein's invasion of Kuwait.

* * *

During the 1970s and 1980s the whole ethos of RAF strike/attack operations from RAF Germany was ultra low-level flying with our pre-planned targets being largely in East Germany. It was always assumed that it wouldn't take long before our targets would be invading Warsaw Pact forces on West German soil. In our strike role we operated as single aircraft; in our attack role we operated as pairs for mutual support, or multiples of pairs, flying in line abreast about one to two miles apart with each pair following about two miles behind. Some packages could involve as many as twenty-four Tornados. During training sorties, other Tornados would often act as the 'bounce', an enemy fighter, attempting to intercept and achieve missile or guns 'kills' against the formation. Often, unplanned fights would occur with RAF air defence fighters from Wildenrath or other 'roving' NATO aircraft; we were happy to have a go at anyone.

Unlike my Recce Canberra days, when we simply flew as low as we could and hoped for the best, we could at least defend ourselves in the GR1 as it carried a pair of AIM 9L Sidewinder air-to-air missiles for self-defence and a 27mm Mauser cannon. We also had an electronic counter measures pod, called Skyshadow, which could be programmed to jam enemy air or ground radars trying to acquire or lock on to us. We also carried a Boz pod to dispense flares that would hopefully fool a heat-seeking missile, or to dispense 'chaff' to create radar clutter. As well as two or sometimes three external fuel tanks, we also had our air-to-ground weapons.

For our strike role, what we would have carried was obvious. For our attack role, we could carry up to eight 1,000lb bombs, or BL755 cluster bombs, or a weapon known as JP233. This was a huge weapon which combined runway penetration ordnance and minelets which would be dropped at the same time. The idea was to crater enemy runways and taxiways, while the minelets would slow down any attempt at runway repair. We were confident that our tactics would work but their very high-risk nature would be demonstrated during Gulf War I. Flying straight and level across a well-defended airfield to deliver JP233 at high speed and low-level, especially at night and bad weather, would certainly concentrate the mind.

For training we carried practice bombs: 3kg retard bombs for level bombing, called laydown, and for dive-bombing, and 28lb free-fall bombs for loft, or toss, bombing. Our most frequently used weapons range on the continent was Nordhorn in Northern Germany, but we also regularly used Vliehors on the Dutch coast, especially for loft bombing. There were other ranges too, and we often flew High-Low-High sorties to one of the UK ranges before returning to Bruggen. Sometimes we would land in the UK to refuel. All the weapons ranges could 'score' our bombs accurately. Prior to the Tornado, any bomb which got within fifty feet of the target would be scored as a direct hit. But the accuracy of the Tornado weapons system was staggering, so all the range scoring systems were upgraded so that a direct hit would only be credited if the bomb impacted within ten feet of the target. Even so, a fully operational crew could often score four direct hits out of four.

*   *   *

With the squadron declared operational in the strike role following a TACEVAL, we were soon scheduled for Quick Reaction Alert. This duty lasted for twenty-four hours and involved sleeping fully kitted in a hardened and specially guarded facility. The duty came round once every seven to ten days throughout the year. It began at about 1600 hours and it was the one duty during which you hoped that you definitely would NOT fly. There was little likelihood of it being a return mission.

Bruggen was a very secure base, and the Quick Reaction Alert compound was doubly secure and extremely well guarded night and day by live-armed RAF policemen. It was like a mini Fort Knox and on arrival you would take over your strike-armed aircraft from the off-going crew. Before being scheduled for the duty, many hours had to be spent studying the targets and the routes for ingress and egress. Whenever a new crew was rostered the 'hooter' would sound at some stage, usually in the middle of the night, and everyone had to react at great speed. The fully armed alert aircraft had to be airborne within fifteen minutes of the 'hooter'. No matter what your intellect told you, no matter that there had been no East/West crisis a couple of hours earlier when you went to bed, when that so-distinctive alarm sounded you could never be sure that it was just another practice. You ran for your aircraft just as fast as you could. You, your navigator, and your groundcrew would be met on arrival at the shelter by armed policemen who would carefully verify identities before you could gain access to the aircraft, and then it was the most rapid starting procedure imaginable.

Once in the aircraft you would immediately connect to the telebrief and check-in with the Command Operations Centre, and then you would hear those chilling words, 'Standby for the Force Commander's code words'.

By now the auxiliary power unit would be running and the shelter doors would be on the verge of opening. Everyone would be very, very tense. And then, 'Stand down'.

On the way back to the accommodation to hopefully grab a few hours sleep, the ease of tension was visible, although everyone said, 'of course, I knew it was only a practice'. In truth, you never, ever were sure. Within ten days you would be back for a repeat performance. It never got any less tense, it never became routine.

*   *   *

In November 1985 I was programmed for a night familiarization sortie with one of our more promising first tour pilots, he had not flown at night in Germany before, although he had flown at night in the UK. I had flown with him previously by day and looked forward to this sortie as fairly routine. Maybe I was just a little too relaxed. We started the engines normally within the shelter and then the front-seat pilot slowly taxied forward. There was the slightest of judders as we cleared the shelter. We stopped, and then the groundcrew indicated that we should shut-down; we had hit the left-hand door.

When we got out, to our horror, the end of the port wing was badly damaged, with the wing-tip housing and one of the navigation lights having been removed by the solid steel door handle of the left-hand door. What a disaster!

The front-seat pilot was mortified. While he had been in control of the aircraft (the Tornado could not be taxied safely from the rear seat as the view ahead is obscured), I was the aircraft captain and the responsibility for what had happened was mine. As we slowly walked back to the 'Hard', the squadron's bombproof operations facility, I knew that what would follow would be serious. I was not wrong.

There would have to be an investigation and it was likely to be a very public 'lesson learned'. For me, only six months into my executive tour, it could not have come at a worse time, and I knew it would reinforce in some the prejudice that existed towards pilots like me who had cross-rolled to fast-jets at a relatively late stage. I wasn't at all certain whether I would be able to remain in post, and the impact that a posting back to the UK would have on me and my family didn't bare thinking about.

A Unit Inquiry was convened and it commenced the same evening with the Officer Commanding Operations Wing, a wing commander, as President. He asked to see me first. My initial response would be crucial in deciding how the inquiry would progress. While there were some mitigating factors, if I raised these they would not in any way change the fact that the responsibility for what had occurred rested with me. It could also be seen as an attempt to wriggle out of my responsibility. So I determined to 'take it on the chin' and made my views clear to the Board President; this made his job relatively simple.

About a week later, the front-seat pilot and I were interviewed separately by our Boss; the front-seater was given a Verbal Warning, the minimum administrative action that could be taken against an officer, while I received the next one up, a Written Warning. For a senior officer this was a serious administrative warning and it would only remain on my file for the remainder of my time with 14 Squadron. While that would be for another three years it could have been a lot worse; at least I was still on the squadron. Over the next few months I also had to live with a lot of 'banter' from the guys. In some ways, that was harder to take.

Like so many incidents, what had occurred was not down to a single act. The expression 'being nibbled to death by ducks' is probably apt. There were probably a dozen individuals who played a part and any one of us could have broken the chain. Most accidents and incidents are like that, they are very rarely down to a single action or omission, but usually the result of a chain of events which many people have the opportunity to influence or to break. I learnt a harsh and salutary lesson and it certainly put me 'on the back foot' on the squadron. But at least I and others were able to learn from my mistake. In the years ahead, others would be unable to learn from theirs.

The damage to the aircraft amounted to over £100,000 and the aircraft was out of service for weeks. So I got away quite lightly: damage to my pride and to my reputation and my proportion of the cost of a couple of crates of beer that we delivered to the engineers who repaired the aircraft. I completed that particular pilot's night check a few weeks later in January 1986 and, as expected, it went extremely well.

* * *

We had a civilian driver on 14 Squadron, by the name of Alf. He was in his late fifties and drove the squadron mini-bus; it was often Alf's welcoming face that we saw on our return from a sortie. Alf was English and he had married a German girl when he had been in the RAF many years earlier. We all knew him as 'Mind yer head, Sir!', as that was invariably what he said every time anyone got in or out of his mini-bus. As he was a civilian, whenever we were on exercise he had to go on leave for security reasons. On one occasion after he returned I asked him where he had been.

'Oh,' he said, 'we went to visit my wife's parents.'

'Where do they live?' I asked.

'Colditz,' Alf replied.

That left me completely lost for words. While Colditz Castle had many fascinating tales to tell, both the castle and the adjoining village were in EAST Germany!

*   *   *

By early 1986, we were well established in our new accommodation in the south-eastern corner of the airfield. We referred to different parts of our site as the 'hard', the 'soft', and the hardened aircraft shelter site.

The 'hard' was the hardened, filtered facility which included the operations room, planning and intelligence rooms, briefing rooms, as well as the squadron's offices. It was actually called a Pilot's Briefing Facility, or PBF, having been designed and built with the single-seat Jaguar in mind. However, the navigator's union insisted on referring to the building as the 'hard', although most pilots continued to refer to it, with a smile, as the PBF. Within the building was an area of showers and changing rooms so that during exercises and operations we could be de-contaminated, and change from our nuclear, biological and chemical warfare suits before entering the fully-filtered 'clean' area of the inner sanctum.

For real, we would wear a piece of equipment called an AR5, an aircrew respirator, which was a rubber head cover with an attached visor that fitted beneath our flying helmets, and was connected to filtered breathing equipment which gave complete protection from chemical or biological agents. At least it said so on the label. But it was a very claustrophobic and uncomfortable piece of kit, especially when we had to jump into a swimming pool from the high board during one of our regular visits to North Luffenham.

The 'soft' was the name given to our normal peacetime accommodation, two long single-storey buildings, one each for the groundcrew and the aircrew. The aircrew building had a crewroom, a history room for all of the squadron's memorabilia, a 'quiet room', and the main briefing room.

We also had one hardened shelter for each aircraft. While they all looked the same from a distance, two of them were simply steel frames with a weatherproof cover.

*   *   *

As a parting gesture, the departing Jaguar Squadron Commander presented us with a mascot. His name was Flying Officer Eric Androvardi, named after a Second World War predecessor on 14 Squadron. Eric was a young and, at the time, quite small, Burmese Rock Python and he was absolutely useless at marching! He was placed in the tender care of a young first-tourist navigator who had the challenging job of trying to wean Eric from his staple diet of live food, but thankfully he was successful. To begin with Eric lived in a large glass container in the squadron quiet room. Eric grew rapidly and he became a well known character, especially when we had visitors. They were rarely warned about our mascot and the look on visitor's faces when they were having coffee in the crewroom when in slithered Eric, was something to behold. But he was also capable of giving us all a bit of a turn.

I had a deputy, who was also a Tornado flying instructor. One day he had gone into the quiet room to talk to a couple of guys who were working there. He stood at the door with his right arm on the chest-high filing cabinet on his right, with his hand hanging over the front of the cabinet. After a few minutes he noticed that he no longer seemed to have eye contact with the chap he was talking too; he was still looking in his direction but seemed to be focusing to his lower right. My deputy leant forward to look. Eric had quietly wondered across the room and had climbed vertically up the front of the filing cabinet. He was now a few inches from my deputy's right hand and Eric's forked tongue was moving quickly fore and back, gently 'tasting' the tips of my unsuspecting deputy's fingers! He moved in a flash!

*   *   *

The squadron had its own football team which played against other squadrons throughout RAF Germany. Whilst playing at Laarbruch, one of our first-tourist pilots broke his leg. The ambulance duly arrived and he was carried on board on a stretcher. Before the ambulance had gone more than a few yards, it was stopped by the rest of the team who promptly opened the back doors and carried our injured player back out of the ambulance. They put him back on board after they had taken the team photograph.

*   *   *

Life on the squadron involved a constant stream of Op Days, MINIVALS, and MAXEVALS leading up to the long awaited TACEVAL, following which the station would be declared to NATO as both Strike and Attack capable. We also practiced what was known as Option Alpha, which involved a mass launch simulating attacks against various Soviet airfields in East Germany. These were spectacular missions to watch depart or to be involved in; on one I was number nineteen of twenty-four aircraft in a single formation.

Despite the intensity of the work, we still had an eye for an opportunity for a laugh or a 'wind-up'. On one occasion, our intelligence officer got dressed up in the Boss's flying suit to greet a new batch of first tourist crews. As I recall, the Boss became a rather aggressive and rude cleaner for a few hours. The new crews did wonder what they had got themselves into. On another, when refuelling at RAF Honington I met some crews destined for 14 Squadron and warned them off about the squadron's training officer who 'was a right b*****d and would give them a hard time during their familiarization sorties!

Also early in 1986, it was announced that one of our pilots, Dave Snow, had been selected as RAF Germany's Tornado display pilot for the coming season. Bob Wright would be his navigator, so I was re-crewed with a first tourist navigator, Jeremy Payne. Dave's display work-up began in March, and to start with he flew exclusively with the Boss in the dual-control trainer; I had nothing to do with the sequence of low-level aerobatics that Dave would eventually be cleared to fly, or so I thought, until the Boss announced that he was going on leave during Dave's work-up. As the Exec was a navigator, the Boss decided that I was to take over as the Display Supervisor until he returned from leave.

'I've cleared Dave at 5,000 feet,' he said. 'You will need to fly with him and clear him at each new height as he works down to 500 feet. Once you clear him at 500 feet, he can then fly with his navigator.'

I paused to take this in. The Boss continued, 'And you will need to do this in the aircraft specifically allocated for the displays.'

The aircraft allocated for the displays was, of course, a strike aircraft, not our dual-controlled trainer. So, I would be flying in the back seat of an aircraft which had no flying controls in the back, supervising Dave who would be hurtling around at very high speed doing low-level aerobatics! Wow! This was a little different from supervising low-level aerobatics from the control tower, which I had done at Leeming. In fact I thoroughly enjoyed the experience, and Dave proved to be a very good display pilot at air shows throughout mainland Europe.

* * *

In May 1986, we began a ten day detachment to the Italian base at Decimomannu in Sardinia. This would be an annual event, an Armament Practice Camp, so that we could practice intensive air-to-ground weaponry at the nearby Capo Di Frasca Range. We lived on base in a barrack block allocated for RAF use. Over the years, various squadrons had converted two of the ground floor rooms into a makeshift bar which had a paved patio outside. It was extremely basic but had its own sign and was renowned throughout the RAF fast-jet world as 'The Pig & Tape' – tape as in tapeworm! Many an evening was to be spent here talking tactics and ways to improve our weaponry. You could always spot a group of RAF aircrew in civilian clothes – they were the ones who only seemed able to talk whilst using their hands!

The nearest town was Cagliari, although it was certainly not renowned as a tourist destination in those days. It was at Decci that I had my first 'go' at strafe, air-to-ground gunnery using the Tornado's 27mm Mauser cannon. The scoring system on the range was very accurate and every bullet could be counted if it went through the rectangular target.

* * *

In October, I was seconded to the NATO TACEVAL Team as a member of the evaluation staff. We arrived unannounced at the Luftwaffe Base at Hopsten in Northern Germany. The Base faced a four day evaluation with every aspect of their operations tested. They were subject to intruders, bomb threats, air raids and the like, and I spent my time assessing one of the resident Luftwaffe F4F Phantom squadrons, flying in the rear seat of one of their aircraft.

On one mission their target was a bridge. In order to achieve an assessment of 'Excellent', all four aircraft had to 'hit' the target. During the attack, one of the aircraft called a 'miss' and went back for a re-attack. This would automatically drop their assessment to 'Satisfactory'. After landing, we crowded into the debrief room to view the cine film of each aircraft's attack. The debrief was over quickly, too quickly, and all three crews claimed 'hits' on the bridge during their first run attacks. But then I asked for one film to be viewed again, which quietened things down a bit. I pointed out that the bridge on that particular film was a different bridge! So that dropped the assessment to 'Marginal', much to the crew's disappointment.

It was hard rules in those days; they needed to be, as we were practicing for war. I also knew that it would be just as tough for us when we were subject to our own TACEVAL. I enjoyed flying the Phantom and the Luftwaffe crews were extremely capable, but the aircraft wasn't a patch on the Tornado. In fairness though, the F4 used 1960s technology but it was a very powerful machine. The experience was also invaluable when I got back to Bruggen where we continued to exercise hard.

*   *   *

Once 9 Squadron arrived from RAF Honington, the Bruggen Wing was complete. Our new Station Commander thought it would be a good idea to have the wing lined up on the main runway for a series of photographs. The wing flying standards instructor, who went by the title of STANEVAL (F), standards and evaluation flying, was landed with the job. This was my former Canberra instructor from 1973, Mike Dineen, who was now also a squadron leader. The day in question was cold and damp, and Mike received little sympathy or understanding as he tried to assemble the massed aircrew, all feeling decidedly stroppy. It must have been like herding cats!

The photographer was a well known Fleet Street photographer, the late Terry Fincher, and at one stage when he was high up at the top of a huge gantry called a 'cherry picker' he announced that at long last everyone was in the right place. He then looked more closely at the aircrew to find that all the officers behind the station executives were nicely lined up as ordered, except they were all wearing their flying helmets back to front. However, the final photographs taken by Terry were magnificent. The sight of 'the Bruggen 40' and their crews could only be described as awesome. That one photograph dramatically captured something of the meaning of the Cold War.

*   *   *

The attack runs, or initial point to target runs, that we planned were basically similar to those that I had used on the Canberra and the Hawk. The Tornado's radar and its computer also allowed us to attack a target very accurately even if we couldn't see it; this was especially important at night, if the weather was poor, or if the target was well hidden. During the planning stage, we would select up to three features called offsets. These were features that we definitely could find either visually or on radar and they would be between the initial point and the target. The position of the offset would be calculated and the details entered on the aircraft computer. This would then give us a very precise range and bearing of the target from each offset. During the attack run, the navigator would work the offset on his radar and this would constantly update the position of the target. The pilot could also 'work' the offset visually. The target symbol on the pilot's head-up display would also then be updated automatically. The attack run could be flown manually, or on automatic pilot using the terrain following radar.

If the sortie was to be flown by a formation of aircraft, or at night, or in bad weather, the route would be planned using a system known as parallel track, which kept all the aircraft safely apart but close enough to allow minimum separation over the target.

One of my favourite sorties was acting as the 'bounce' aircraft, the 'fighter' trying to intercept and achieve a kill against a formation on an attack mission. My new navigator, Jeremy, was also very good at this; he was very aware tactically and superb at picking out other aircraft amidst the ground clutter on his radar screen.

*   *   *

In mid-January 1987, the squadron went back to Decimomannu, but not for weaponry, for ACMI (Air Combat Mission Instrumentation). This was the very stuff of *Top Gun*. The external fuel tanks were removed and a special pod was fitted. Without the fuel tanks our duration was obviously much less, but we could fly faster and we could manoeuvre the aircraft more aggressively. We operated in a range over the sea to the west of Sardinia practicing air-to-air combat against each other and against other types of aircraft. The pods transmitted data to a ground station so that the whole combat could be watched and recorded. Every time we pressed the 'fire' button a missile would be shown leaving the aircraft and the computer would determine whether the missile being simulated had been fired within prescribed parameters. If the 'shot' resulted in a 'kill' then a coffin would appear around the target aircraft. The 'killed' aircraft then had to exit the range.

I loved this type of flying and Jeremy once again proved his worth. He was one of the best navigators at being able to maintain situational awareness and we usually did well. While the tactical application of what we practiced was limited (we were bombers with a limited self-defence capability, not fighters), it certainly improved the fighting skills of our crews and the handling skills of our pilots.

On 15 January I flew back to Bruggen which was in the depths of a German winter. Given the station's tactical nuclear role, it was essential that the runways were kept useable, but the snow was so bad we were unable to land and were diverted to the Luftwaffe base at Hopsten. Within a few hours we were able to try again and this time we were successful, although by then it was already dark. It was a very eerie feeling, and one that I have never experienced since, taxying back into the floodlit HAS site across a carpet of snow in blizzard conditions.

* * *

After a break in order to complete a four week residential staff course at the RAF Staff College at Bracknell, it was back to Bruggen and into the station's long-awaited TACEVAL which began on 30 March 1987. At dawn on Day One, we were scrambled in mass formations simulating our Option Alpha attack against Soviet airfields. The launch must have been quite a sight. All the aircraft remained in their shelters until the last possible moment and then taxied out to the runway without stopping, taking off under radio silence in a pre-determined order. A green light from a cupola buried near the threshold of the runway was the sole air traffic signal.

The Boss led the first formation of eight aircraft and I followed about five minutes later leading a six-ship. After take-off we swung around to the north before heading east to cross the Rhine at Wesel at 500 feet. Each formation took off in a thirty second stream until we dropped down to 250 feet as we crossed the Rhine; at that point we moved into our tactical card formation. Wesel is not far from RAF Laarbruch and, as I approached, I heard the distinctive sound on the distress frequency of an emergency locator beacon. These would start transmitting immediately on ejection. However, it would also transmit if a crew member forgot to disconnect the attachment between the life jacket and the dinghy when climbing out of an aircraft. This was a regular occurrence and I assumed that a Laarbruch crew had done just that. I was quite wrong!

Our mission was successful and about an hour later, having dropped our bombs at Nordhorn Range, we began our recovery to Bruggen. The German controller manning Clutch Radar then told us that our crew, whose aircraft had crashed, were safe! What!

As we approached Bruggen I think that a number of us thought that the TACEVAL would be stopped, so we could look forward to an early stack! Wrong again! We were told to taxy directly to another squadron's site and to standby for re-tasking. Despite the loss of an aircraft, with the crew thankfully on their way to hospital, the TACEVAL continued without interruption. Our aircraft was refuelled and rearmed very quickly, new maps and computer tape were sent out to us, the mission having been planned by another crew while we had been airborne, and we were soon off once more as a member of a completely different formation. The pace set on that first day continued for the next four days and it was only at the end of the exercise that the story of our crashed aircraft was told. It was a great tale, thankfully with a happy ending, although the navigator, for reasons that became obvious kept a straight face.

As the crew were both able to give statements, the Board of Inquiry could quickly focus on the likely problem. The board's task should also be made easier as the Tornado was fitted with an accident data recorder and a cockpit voice recorder and both were recovered undamaged. The board began their work by listening to the tape which would have recorded every word said between pilot and navigator, and any radio transmissions. Having pressed 'play' they could then compare what was being said against the detailed timeline of events that they had received from air traffic control. Or so they thought, except that they couldn't hear anything. There was no conversation between the crew, nothing at all. Even though they knew from the timeline that the aircraft was taxying, nothing was said between pilot and navigator. The aircraft got airborne and flew toward the Rhine, still with no 'chat' whatsoever. Only as the aircraft reached the Rhine did the tape pick up the very first, and last, words from the crew.

'Oh, shit!' said the pilot.

This was followed instantly by the unmistakeable sound of a double ejection!

They were very lucky. While at 480 knots accelerating to close up with their leader, and just before they descended to 250 feet, a technical failure occurred in the all-flying tailplane, one side of which went to full scale deflection. The aircraft immediately departed controlled flight into a rapid and totally uncontrollable roll. The instant decision to initiate command ejection was only just in time.

What happened next was the subject of a very amusing article written by the pilot for the station magazine. He had been unhurt and he went off to look for his back-seater. When he found him, the navigator was not in good spirits. He had broken his arm on ejection and then had become entangled in the top of quite a tall but rather thin tree. One of the smaller branches had gone through his lower lip and into the top of his mouth. And there he was, completely stuck.

He was not best pleased, less so when he realized that his pilot thought the spectacle was highly amusing. The pilot of course had no idea of the extent of his navigator's injuries. The navigator's predicament didn't get any easier, as first a civilian helicopter, and then a USAF CH53 helicopter arrived on the scene. The CH53, a huge helicopter also known as the Jolly Green Giant, hovered above the navigator. The CH53 is also well known for the enormous downdraught that it produces. The navigator only had the most precarious of holds on his tree, which apparently began to sway with increasing severity.

At least he had the presence of mind to wrap his anti-G hose around the tree trunk and re-attach it to his equipment just in case he couldn't hold onto the tree with his one good arm. His trials were not yet over however, as the local German Fire Brigade, complete with a very short ladder arrived. The navigator's concern deepened when he heard a distinctive and quite unmistakeable sound, that of a chainsaw. However, all ended well and he soon found himself in the RAF Hospital at Wegberg. He soon returned to full flying duties.

*   *   *

The TACEVAL went very well and Bruggen received a good assessment. Within two days, my bags were packed once more and I joined the TACEVAL Team for another evaluation, this time at the Luftwaffe Base at Pferdsfeld in Southern Germany. It was another F4 Phantom Base and I flew a number of sorties in the back seat as part of the assessment. It was clear from early on though that the exercise was not going as well as expected and at the debrief, the Base Commander was not at all pleased when he was told the base had been awarded a 'Marginal' assessment.

All the base officers were assembled in a huge briefing room and then the TACEVAL team arrived to take our places at the front. The Base Commander then entered, everyone leapt to their feet with much clicking of heals as he made his way to the platform. There then followed a vitriolic tirade aimed at the TACEVAL Team with much banging of fists on the podium! It was reminiscent of an earlier era! He then ordered the TACEVAL Team off his base! That bit was almost laughable. We left of course, but it had been a fair exercise and the assessment was fair; it stood. Accurate assessments were vital if deficiencies were to be addressed. If they were not, the unit would pay a high price in the lives of its personnel if they had to do any of this 'for real'.

*   *   *

May 1987 found us back at Decimomannu. By now strafe was a regular feature of our armament practice camps and, since our aircraft had been fitted with a laser for range finding, accuracy had improved dramatically. The Tornado Mauser cannon only had a very limited number of rounds and it was fired in very short bursts of six or seven rounds at a time, a fraction of a second, but the range could identify every single hit. With practice, scores of 40 per cent or 50 per cent soon became the 'norm', whereas 10 per cent would have been good on earlier generation aircraft.

On one sortie, after carrying out four or five separate attacks, I came in for what I knew must be my last attack. When I pressed the fire button, there was a single shot; only one round had been left in the magazine. The range controller's call was immensely satisfying, 'Crusader 1, one hit.'

One hundred per cent! After that detachment I was awarded the 'Top Gun' trophy for best gunnery. This was quite a 'coup' for a Tornado flying instructor. We were not meant to be any good at weaponry! Soon afterwards the Boss wrote that I was 'one of the better formation leaders on the Bruggen Wing'. Such praise had been hard-earned but it was well-timed, coming only a few weeks before the annual 'Trappers' visit during which I was rated above the average.

* * *

My deputy had been promoted, and he moved across to 31 Squadron as the Training Officer along with one of our first tour navigators. On 27 July their aircraft suffered a double hydraulic failure while flying at low-level just south of the North Yorkshire Moors and they both ejected safely.

In September, I lead two aircraft to RAF Akrotiri in Cyprus, refuelling at the Italian base at Gioia Del Colle en route. It was a great weekend and we resolved to buy a 'gopping' present for display in one of the squadron's display cabinets on our return. There was always a bit of a competition amongst the crews to see who could return from detachment with something truly 'gopping'. We did rather well and returned with a plate with an enamelled photograph in the centre of the four of us crammed together in a photo booth!

The normal formation for such transits was loose trail, but on the way back, the other pilot, 'AB', gradually closed up until he was flying line abreast. He and his navigator, Al Grieve, had removed their flying helmets and were wearing multi-coloured short umbrellas mounted on their heads!

* * *

On 4 October the squadron detached to North America for six weeks. At Goose Bay in Labrador we practiced low flying at 100 feet and use of the terrain following radar by day and night down to lower heights than we had previously experienced, regardless of the weather. This was work-up training for the much talked about Exercise Red Flag which was another three weeks operating in the Nevada Desert from Nellis Air Force Base near Las Vegas. Jeremy and I would fly together throughout. For most of us this would be the ultimate in flying, short of actually going to war. No one anticipated that many of the same crews would go to war soon afterwards.

Goose Bay is a Canadian Air Force Base, which, during the summer can be reached by air or by sea; during the winter it can sometimes be reached only by air as the sea is invariably frozen. There are roads on the base and to the adjoining town, Happy Valley; after that there are just hundreds and hundreds of miles of coniferous forests and lakes. The accommodation blocks were linked together with a long series of heated tunnels as during the winter it was often too cold to venture outside for long.

This part of Northern Canada was very well known for the vast herds of caribou which wondered everywhere. It was weird coming across their tracks which were easily visible from the air and you could then follow them for hundreds of miles until the herd was found. One of our first briefings was from the Canadian Flight Safety Officer, who talked about mandatory restrictions in relation to these amazing and very hardy animals. The environmental lobby was very strong and expressed major concerns about the impact of low flying aircraft on the caribou, and in particular on their breeding habits. Twelve caribou had been fitted with radio transmitters and their location and movements were monitored by satellite.

Each morning when we began mission planning we would find the positions of these caribou marked on our maps, six in red and six in blue. Those marked in red had to be avoided by a minimum of five miles, whereas those marked in blue could be over flown and in fact we were encouraged to do so. We listened carefully to all of this, wondering whether this was a 'wind-up' by the Canadians at our expense. But no, it was for real. The survey lasted for about four years and it must have been quite expensive, but then it was quietly forgotten. And the reason it was forgotten? It was apparent that those caribou which we overflew were breeding far more successfully than those which we had so carefully avoided! We put this down to the fact that they were probably fast asleep until we overflew them, and when we had woken them up they looked around to decide what they should do.

The flying in Canada was amazing. There was something quite unreal about flying at low-level covering hundreds of miles without seeing anything that was man-made. The flying at 100 feet and at 480 knots or more was also very exhilarating, but it was also very warm work as we had to be dressed for arctic survival with multi-layers of clothing. That area of Canada is very sparsely populated, there was nothing except coniferous forests and lakes as far as the eye can see. With the trees gradually diminishing in height further north, it was difficult to judge one's height visually and it was very easy to inadvertently fly significantly lower than 100 feet, careful use of the radar altimeter was essential.

The night terrain following radar training certainly concentrated our minds. The weather was not brilliant and with no surrounding towns, villages or lighting of any description, it was very, very dark. On my first night mission with the terrain following radar, and the aircraft being flown by the autopilot, we began to climb up one side of a ridge, which was the first in a series of ridges and valleys which crossed our track at right angles. Then we went into cloud! The aircraft continue to gently climb toward the crest of the ridge and then it began to descend down the other side, still in cloud. Our minds were concentrated a little more. Then we broke clear of the cloud as the aircraft descended into the valley before pulling up toward the next ridge line and entering cloud once more. And so it went on, up and down, in and out of cloud, in pitch darkness, with a constant commentary from Jeremy describing what he could see in plan-view on his ground mapping radar, while I described what I could see on the E-scope which gave an elevation-view of the terrain ahead. I don't think that either Jeremy or I flew another sortie which involved the same degree of prolonged concentration. But it certainly gave us a lot of confidence in one another and in the capability of our kit.

Toward the end of our detachment the Boss invited a number of the base officers and their wives for drinks in the RAF bar on the ground floor of our accommodation block as a way of saying 'thank you' for looking after us so well. Flying had finished at about midday and we all arrived back at our accommodation block together. The Boss headed straight for his room, which was on the ground floor, having first reminded us all to be in the bar before 1700 hours to meet our guests.

We all headed upstairs, to the large crewroom for a quick beer. Someone produced a video of a film not long released, so we all grabbed a few cans and settled down to watch it. It was *Top Gun*. Well, that was it for the afternoon, beer followed beer, pilots sat next to their navigators, and the whole squadron, minus the Boss, sat riveted during the highs and lows of the film, despite some of the totally unrealistic air combat scenes. When Maverick's navigator, Goose, was killed, emotions ran high with one or two crews sitting with their arms around one another's shoulders. The film finished at about 1645 hours. Then the Boss looked in having found no one in the bar. What he saw was not a pretty sight. His squadron was well and truly wasted. He gave us five minutes to shower and change and be on parade! We all made it too, and it was a great party.

* * *

On 19 October we left Goose Bay heading south-west. En route, my No. 2 suffered a hydraulic failure, so we diverted to Bagotville to see him safely on the ground before continuing on our way.

Our first stop was at the USAF Base at Griffiths, in New York State, where we refuelled. Then we were off once more for Offutt in Nebraska, but via Niagara Falls to take in the amazing spectacle. We stayed overnight in Nebraska before flying to Nellis, just to the north-east of Las Vegas. The three long transit sorties brought home the sheer vastness of the North American continent. Once we saw the size of Nellis Air Force Base and the hundreds of military aircraft lined up, we realized just how small the RAF was in comparison to its very much bigger, if rather younger, brother. We were to take part in Red Flag 1/88, even though this particular exercise took place in November 1987.

The aim was for us to practice our wartime tactics against a range of military targets within a huge area due north of Vegas. Many of the targets were covered by video cameras and all could accurately record the results of our attacks. There were surface-to-air missile systems deployed which could track us and try to achieve a 'lock' and a simulated kill. Also based at Nellis was the USAF's Aggressor Squadron which operated F5 fighters painted in Soviet colours and these would try and intercept our packages of aircraft.

RAF F4 Phantoms from 19 and 92 Squadrons, based at RAF Wildenrath, were also taking part in the same exercise.

In the middle of the desert where we would be operating was Area 51, a top secret USAF facility, which we were to go nowhere near. Long after the exercise I showed our son Matthew one of the maps that I had used during Red Flag; it had Area 51 marked and showed an airfield in the middle of it. Years later, after he had settled in Los Angeles he mentioned Area 51 and its 'top secret' airfield to some of his work colleagues who all reacted as if he was 'shooting a line'. They all said that there was no such place or airfield and that it was just a figment of Hollywood's imagination. Then along came Google Earth and they realized, not for the last time, that Matthew knew what he was talking about.

We were divided into two teams: one flew the morning sortie having planned it the previous day, and the other flew the afternoon mission having planned it in the morning. The flying was brilliant, the best that I have ever taken part in, then or since. The weather was good and we were able to practice all of the tactics that we would need to use for real. Jeremy once again proved his worth as a very capable 'fighter-gator' with very good tactical awareness and great planning skills.

On one sortie Jeremy kept encouraging me to fly even lower and I was always happy to oblige. As we came around one hill we were suddenly confronted by a B52, a huge USAF eight-engined bomber, coming our way at about 300–400 feet. I had no time to take avoiding action and all I could do was fly underneath him. It went quite dark for a fraction of a second and both Jeremy and I ducked! It turned out afterwards that the B52 should have exited the area much earlier, but he had flown all the way from Hawaii and was slightly behind his timeline!

As we taxied back toward dispersal, Jeremy mentioned that he had something of a confession to make. He had taken his camera with him, hence his encouraging noises for me to fly even lower. That was against all the rules; if the USAF had known he would probably have been arrested, his camera confiscated and we both would have been sent home. I wish that he had told me, as I'm sure I could have arranged for him to get some better pictures. But there was worse to come, he had dropped the lens cap in the cockpit!

A loose article in the cockpit is a serious issue. It had to be found, otherwise the offending item could eventually gravitate to a place which could cause a control malfunction. The aircraft had to be declared unserviceable, and even the ejection seats had to be removed until the item was found. Jeremy was hugely embarrassed and apologetic, but it caused an awful amount of work for our hard-pressed groundcrew. Jeremy was therefore 'invited' to assist the groundcrew by cleaning and polishing the aircraft radome. He happily obliged. And as for the photographs, they were fantastic!

As if participating in Red Flag was not a prize enough, we were also housed in the Embassy Suites complex in nearby Las Vegas, just one street away from the famous Strip. Life in Las Vegas was fun. The hotel was very comfortable and the casinos were doing their very best to attract customers. All sorts of offers of very cheap meals were advertised to try and persuade people to cross their doors and hopefully go into their casinos. 'Surf & Turf' for $3 or $4 was not unusual. But they hadn't really counted on a typical RAF detachment. We were very happy to eat and drink for Queen and country, but then went nowhere near the casinos! I think that the hotel profits took a notable dive during our detachment.

The Commander-in-Chief RAF Germany, Air Marshal Sir Anthony Skingsley (later Air Chief Marshal), came out to visit for a few days and it was my job to take him flying. The US authorities were very helpful and because of his VIP status we were given clearance to fly a single aircraft down the Grand Canyon; normally this was strictly off-limits. Taking a Tornado down the Grand Canyon was another unique experience but, unlike Jeremy, Sir Anthony didn't bring his camera! He seemed to enjoy the flight, although at one stage he did say 'I think that is low enough Paul.'

*   *   *

The final day of Red Flag involved only one mission and the Boss decided that it would be made up of the best performing crews from both teams. Jeremy and I were to lead the final mission and the Boss would fly one of the aircraft 'down the back'. On the penultimate afternoon, Jeremy and I planned the final mission. The weather forecast was very good, so our main effort was on a 'good weather plan' rather than spending hours planning a 'bad weather option'. Throughout Red Flag all of the crews had spent hours planning both good and bad weather options, only to find that it was another nice sunny day in the desert. We did plan a poor weather option but it was very simple. But meteorological forecasters don't always get it right. I should have known.

The next morning when we all assembled it was a lovely day and we crewed in as planned after a short briefing. I started our aircraft's auxiliary power unit as normal. This is a small jet engine fitted toward the rear of the aircraft which is started first; it is then used to start the engines. Soon afterwards, our groundcrew moved toward the rear of the aircraft as there seemed to be something going on behind us. Within seconds there was feverish activity nearby. We heard on the radio that an aircraft was on fire, so Jeremy and I strained our heads to see which one, in case it was one of the aircraft from our formation. Then one of our groundcrew came back and invited us in no uncertain terms to get out of our aircraft, quickly. It was our aircraft that was on fire! We exited pretty sharpish!

I then ran down the line of aircraft to find our No. 2 and tell him that he now had the lead. When I got there I tried and failed to pass the message by hand signals; he seemed to be incredibly slow on the uptake. He just kept giving me 'thumbs down'! I then realized that he was unserviceable too! So off I went on another sprint to finally give the 'lead' to our No. 3, who was one of our first tour pilots. That woke him up! But it was a good 'good weather plan', even if I say so myself, and as I had also said at the briefing 'the bad weather option will not be a player today'. Famous last words!

Jeremy and I then headed back to the operations facility to watch the attacks on the targets. For the best training value, we, unlike some participants, only selected targets that were covered by video cameras. The main operations room began to fill up, which was unusual with so many aircraft due to be airborne. We kept looking at the screen which was still switched off. Eventually, I asked one of the technicians to switch it on, and he said that it was on already! The grey screen was because of the fog and low cloud!

And why was the briefing room now so full? All the other missions, 'except for the crazy Brit all-weather Tornado guys' had been cancelled because of the bad weather! Jeremy and I looked at one another and cringed. Of course all went well, as all of our crews had practiced flying in poor weather on autopilot during our operational low flying in Canada. However, the extremes of some of the mountains and deep valleys in Nevada on that day in November 1987 must have demanded total concentration.

*   *   *

Back home, Jackie and I had to face the difficult decision about the children's secondary education. Matthew was eleven years old in November and he had already attended five different schools, Hannah had attended four. They needed stable secondary education; if we remained in Germany, boarding was the only option, as service schools only covered education up to the age of thirteen. Even with a posting back to the UK we came to the reluctant decision that boarding school was still the best option. Matthew and Hannah weren't particularly fazed about the prospect as many of their friends boarded and often talked about it. While the RAF offered an allowance, it in no way covered the very high fees involved.

A critical factor in all of this was my next posting: where would it be and, perhaps more critically, when? My appointment, along with the other squadron leaders on 14 Squadron, had originally been for three years, and as we had all arrived virtually at the same time, a spread of postings had to be arranged to avoid everyone being replaced all at once. The Exec and one of the flight commanders were posted early; the Boss and the other flight commander were to be posted by April 1988, and I, along with the weapons leader would be extended until the autumn. I would also take over as the Exec, coincident with the arrival of the new Boss.

*   *   *

After a short break following Red Flag, routine training began once more. On 1 December, I flew a 1v1 (one versus one) air combat sortie in a training area to the east of Bruggen. For these sorties, which I loved, we operated above 5,000 feet, practicing pure air-to-air combat, trying to achieve a missile kill, a

Fox 2, or a gun's kill, a Fox 3, against the other aircraft. We did not have the capability to fire a head-on shot, a Fox 1. I was flying with Jeremy, who was now both a four-ship leader and an air combat leader; these were unusual qualifications for a first-tourist navigator. The other aircraft was flown by the Boss and the outgoing Exec. The Boss was a very capable aviator and weaponeer and I relished the prospect of flying against him.

To commence the fight both aircraft would fly line abreast about 800 yards apart. The leader would then call 'Outwards call for combat go'. Each aircraft would then turn 90 degrees away from the other and run out for about seven or eight miles. The leader would then call 'Inwards turn'. As soon as one navigator picked up the opponent on radar, he would call 'Contact', and then once one crew saw the other aircraft the call would be 'Visual'. From that moment the game was on, it became a pure flying exercise, often using maximum G, with both crew straining against the high G forces despite the constantly inflating then deflating anti-g suits, as you tried your hardest to keep the other aircraft in view and manoeuvre into a position to claim a kill.

The Boss was very good, but we were well matched, and after we had crossed one another three or four times neither one of us had gained any significant advantage. This simply encouraged me to try even harder and I pulled up into the vertical with full reheat, then it was full back-stick, full taileron and rudder to attempt a sharp low speed turn. In most fast-jets of that time, such control inputs would guarantee that the aircraft would 'depart', in other words enter a spin. A spin in a fast-jet normally only had one outcome, and because the rate of descent in a spin could be so high, a minimum abandonment height of 10,000 feet was stipulated. But as our Tornados were fitted with SPILS, Spin Prevention Incidence Limiting System, this prevented the aircraft from spinning. The clever SPILS computer ensured that the aircraft would perform the best possible manoeuvre to match, or sometimes despite, the pilot's demands. It was a great system. Except that at the worst possible moment, when I had all the controls at maximum deflection, in other words with full pro-spin control, and with very little speed and very high power, the SPILS failed!

According to our bible, the Tornado Aircrew Manual, in the event of a SPILS failure the system would gradually fade out over a period of about eight seconds. This was more than enough time for me to centralize the controls before use of the system was lost altogether. It didn't quite work out that way.

At the time I was looking behind us when the 'lyre bird', the audio warning, sounded. The attention getters were flashing red, which was serious (they only flashed red for a fire, oxygen failure or SPILS failure; all other lesser emergencies were accompanied by amber attention getters). I looked at the central warning panel and saw the red SPILS caption; even so, I was not unduly alarmed. But within a fraction of a second, long before I could central-ize the controls, the aircraft departed from controlled flight. It entered a very rapid uncontrollable roll which normally preceded a fully developed spin.

There was a startled exclamation from Jeremy as I centralized the controls. Then luckily the roll stopped and I was able to recover the aircraft. The Boss, manoeuvring hard to try and get behind me, saw what happened. He could see that our aircraft had departed and, as we were at 10,000 feet, he already had his thumb poised on the transmit button to order us to eject. Luckily we recovered before he transmitted.

I reset the SPILS and was all for getting on with the fight but the Boss wisely made the call of 'knock it off'. As we headed home a couple of things occurred to me which I began to worry about. First the Accident Data Recorder (ADR) would have to be 'pulled' to analyse what had happened. This would show whether I had exceeded any of the aircraft's limits during the fight; if I had, maybe that had caused or contributed to the SPILS failure. Had I? I wasn't sure, but I was well aware that I had been flying the aircraft hard, very close to the limits. There was one other thing, perhaps even worse: the Cockpit Voice Recorder (CVR). Every word said on the radio and every word spoken on the intercom between Jeremy and I would have been recorded. Every one of my utterances would be there for everyone to hear, and I think that I had said rather a lot of unflattering things about our 'opponents'. My language may well have verged on the 'colourful' too. The tape recording would have to be pulled too, and listened to, by the Boss.

During the debrief, the Boss mentioned that the ADR would have to be pulled. He was concerned about how much Alpha (angle of attack) I had been pulling when the SPILS failed. The angle of attack is the angle between the wing and the airflow, and by pulling the maximum Alpha you can achieve the best possible turning performance. Alpha was measured and shown in units, with the limit in the configuration that we were in being 21. I told the Boss that I would have been very close to the limit but I had not intentionally, or knowingly, exceeded it. Then it was a matter of waiting.

A couple of hours later the engineers reported that the Alpha at the point of SPILS failure was 20.9! Well judged? Or was I lucky? Now it remained to be seen how the Boss would react when he played back the CVR.

Later that afternoon he came into my office, walked up to my desk, placed something in front of me and walked out again without saying a word. It was the one and only copy of the tape from the CVR. Had he listened to it? I have no idea. I destroyed it; it was never mentioned again.

Following this incident, there was a flurry of activity amongst the engineers at Bruggen and in the UK to determine why the aircraft had departed from controlled flight so quickly after the first indication of SPILS failure. The Aircrew Manual said that in the event of a fault the SPILS would fade out over a period of quite a few seconds, about eight seconds I think. The manufacturers reported back in due course. Yes, it would take eight seconds or so to fade out completely, but the rate at which the 'fade out' occurred would be logarithmic not linear, i.e. the rate of failure would not be in a straight line, but in a steep curve. In the event of SPILS failure during anything like the manoeuvre that I had been performing, effective control of the aircraft would be lost in less than a second! Perhaps it would have been helpful to know that beforehand.

The incident resulted in a rapid amendment to the Aircrew Manual and a warning being issued to all Tornado operators. This was the second time in my career in which one of my incidents resulted in such an amendment; the first was following my Yeovilton incident in 1980. The 'flame-out' that I experienced then had been caused by an imbalance of fuel between the wing fuel tanks which led to cavitation, too much air, in the fuel collector tank.

*   *   *

In February 1988, about half of the squadron deployed to Decimomannu for air combat practice in support of 4 Squadron, a Harrier squadron based at RAF Gutersloh. The aim was for each squadron to practice dissimilar air combat.

Hannah gave me one of her toys to take with me: Snoopy fully decked out with goggles, scarf and leather helmet, and I was under strict instructions that he must fly in a Tornado. The opportunity came over the weekend during the middle of the detachment when I lead two other aircraft to Naples. The other two pilots were Mike Smith and Steve Wright; both were very capable and experienced pilots.

We left Decimomannu late Friday afternoon and flew across the Mediterranean at low-level. My navigator for this sortie, Terry Mitchell, took a series of photographs commemorating Snoopy's adventure. Over the Mediterranean, one photograph shows Mike Smith, looking behind him to the rear cockpit which is empty, the second shows Mike's navigator looking at an empty front cockpit! The third shows both cockpits empty, apart from Snoopy! Thank goodness for autopilots. It was a memorable weekend made more so by the hospitality of Bruggen's former accounts officer, a bachelor who had just arrived on posting to the NATO HQ in Naples. I often think back to that weekend. Within a year I would be the only surviving pilot.

The final day of our Decci detachment was to involve air combat between the RAF and the USAF, with two Harriers and two Tornados being pitted against two F15 Eagles – a 2+2v2. This would be a challenge as the F15 was a very capable fighter with very good air-to-air radar and it could take a head-on missile shot, a Fox 1, from about fifteen miles. We had little chance to counter such a shot and needed to try and get in close, within visual range, to have any chance of success. But at least the Tornado had two sets of eyes and two brains, so we talked about tactics with the Harrier pilots well into the evening. The best that we could come up with was what we referred to as 'the F15 wall'. We would run in at the F15s in line abreast, about two miles between each of our aircraft but with all our aircraft at different heights. At about twenty miles we would perform what is called a 'shackle', during which we would swop places with the aircraft next to us, but also change heights significantly. This hopefully would confuse the F15 pilots, who would be trying to interpret their radar picture, and maybe it might delay them from taking a Fox 1; this might give us a slim chance of getting in close.

The next morning dawned dull and grey with lots of layered cloud. It soon became clear that all our talk about tactics would mean little: one Harrier went 'u/s' and so did one Tornado. Both F15s were serviceable. My aircraft was fine and the remaining Harrier was flown by 4 Squadron's Exec. We took off as planned and immediately entered cloud. We were hoping that the cloud tops would not be too high as our aircraft performed better the lower we were; the F15s were very capable at both high and low-level. We eventually cleared cloud at 25,000 feet! This had the makings of being an embarrassing disaster.

The agreement was that if one aircraft was 'killed' that aircraft had to exit the range. Once clear of the range the 'coffin' was removed and the aircraft was free to rejoin the fight as a 'new' aircraft. The fight would formally come to an end if both aircraft on the same side ended up as 'coffin kills' at the same time.

The F15s were waiting for us, and with the cloud tops at 25,000 feet we would have to fight above 30,000 feet. Neither I, nor the Harrier pilot, had ever practiced combat so high and we realized that we had little chance. What we didn't know was that because of the weather, all subsequent take-offs had been cancelled, and all the RAF and USAF crews were crowded into the Ops facility to watch the ensuing combat unfold.

We started at about twenty-five miles from the F15s, and performed our shackle as briefed. It did delay the F15s taking their first shot, but they both fired claiming Fox 1s. We manoeuvred hard to defeat the missiles but one hit, one missed. I was a 'coffin kill' so exited the range at high speed, in 67-degree wing and with full reheat. I then headed back into the fight again at very high speed, approaching Mach 1. Meanwhile, the Harrier was fighting very hard and with some success. Both F15s had made the mistake of manoeuvring close, rather than one of them running out to gain some separation, while the other one kept the Harrier busy. They were both concentrating hard on the Harrier and were oblivious to my rapid approach. I took a Fox 2 shot and was rewarded with a kill. The other F15 was so put off by what had happened to his colleague that the Harrier pilot was able to get behind him, and he too took a shot, and claimed the other F15! Both F15s were 'coffin kills'; the fight was over. In the Ops facility there was consternation, with a cry of disbelief from one of the USAF controllers, 'Both Eagles are dead!'

At that point we both announced that we were so short of fuel we had to head home, delighted with the outcome, and thankfully with no fuel left for a rematch.

*   *   *

During March my next appointment was confirmed: I would go to the Department of Air Warfare at the RAF College Cranwell, as the Central Region Specialist. Apart from knowing that the job involved some form of lecturing, I knew little else about the post.

*   *   *

Planning was well underway for yet another detachment to Goose Bay and Steve Wright, now one of the squadron's weapons' instructors, did a lot of the preparatory work. Steve was due to be posted to another Bruggen squadron in September. However, it was announced that Steve would move early, before our Goose Bay detachment, because his new squadron was short of four-ship leaders. I argued against this, saying that their shortage was because of the reluctance on that particular squadron to appoint navigators as four-ship leaders. I was also very conscious of the challenge that the new Boss would face, not to mention the new Exec (me!), and didn't want to lose such an experienced pilot any earlier than had been planned. But the move was already a 'done deal' apparently, and Steve moved on.

*   *   *

The new Boss, Wing Commander Vaughan Morris, arrived toward the end of April. We got on well from the start and he made my role very clear. Vaughan was a navigator and had been involved with Tornado since the aircraft's introduction into service. He had very high standards. As far as he was concerned, the Exec was first amongst equals. It was my job, behind closed doors, to tell the Boss exactly what I thought, even if I thought he was wrong about something; in fact, especially if I thought he was wrong. When the door was open I would do exactly what he said, offering total support. I was more than happy with this and we worked extremely well together for the remainder of my tour. In fact, over the next six months I felt that I was at last able to realize my full potential and this would have a very positive impact on my attitude and on my future.

The next role that Vaughan asked me to fill was a little more challenging. He felt that he needed to be seen as being approachable by all of his crews; he did not want to appear as either distant, or as a 'hard man', even though he had incredibly high standards and did not shy away from taking very tough decisions. He wanted me to be the hard man. That came as a bit of a shock to me, and to everyone else too, as for three years I had been the approachable training officer, the good listener who flew with everyone. Now I had to change my spots a little.

Friday afternoons were traditionally reserved for ground training with lectures in the Squadron Briefing Room. This was normally followed by a squadron meeting, and then we would head off to 'Happy Hour', led by the Boss. I would have a pre-meeting with the Boss during which we would review 'parish notices' which I would cover at the end of the afternoon. The

Boss would also give me points that he wanted me to specifically cover, sometimes this would include a 'mass bollocking', or a firm directive about something or other. But I had to deliver the 'bollockings', not the Boss. Vaughan therefore retained his image as the approachable 'nice' Boss who was nevertheless firmly in control of a fully operational squadron. The boys thought the world of him, and I learnt quite a lot from him then, and later, about man management. Vaughan Morris went on to become an air-vice marshal before taking early retirement.

*   *   *

Within a couple of weeks of taking over, Vaughan took the squadron to Goose Bay for two weeks of intense Operational Low Flying (OLF) and Terrain Following Radar (TFR) training. Nearly all of the crews were very experienced at this stage with the majority having completed similar training the previous November. That Vaughan was able to lead the squadron from the front during this detachment spoke loudly for him as an individual, and as leader in the air and on the ground. He would face many challenges during his tour, but was never found wanting. A team from the British Forces Broadcasting Service accompanied us, interviewing groundcrew and aircrew alike, and they put together a very good feature, including some amazing air-to-air footage which was shown on British Forces TV not long after our return to Bruggen. Sadly, one of the Boss's first challenges came all too soon.

On 10 May, as the detachment was coming to an end, the Boss called us all into the briefing room to give us the grim news that Steve Wright and his navigator had both been killed in a crash in Germany earlier that morning. Both were married with young children. The squadron returned to Bruggen in sombre mood. There was a service funeral for Steve at RAF Bruggen, and he was buried with full military honours in the cemetery at the Joint HQ at Rheindahlen, on 17 May 1988. He was laid to rest with his first daughter who had died at birth a few years earlier.

*   *   *

The squadron was now facing a growing problem – Eric. He had long out-grown his fish tank home and needed something bigger and better. So I had a word with the Squadron Warrant Officer, Gus Bathoon, who simply said, 'Leave it to me, sir.'

A few days later I walked into the large open area used as the Squadron History Room and came to a sudden stop. Eric was in his new home and it was perfect. It was a tall double-glazed structure in a steel frame. It was about eight feet tall, six feet wide and about three feet deep. Inside there was a floor, a small tree trunk, some rocks and stones, and some foliage. Eric looked completely at home. Except that I recognized the structure, and I knew exactly where it had come from. I rang Gus and asked him to come straight away. When he arrived I said, 'Did you get permission to use this?'

'Not exactly sir,' he said, 'but if they want it back, they can come and get it.'

I said no more. A few days later, Bruggen's third Station Commander during my tour came to fly with us. This was Group Captain Rocky Goodall, the same chap who posted me to Tornados in 1983. When he walked into the History Room, he came to a sudden standstill with a look of recognition on his face. He knew exactly where Eric's new home had come from. He then looked thoughtful for a few seconds before he shook his head and walked away. Nothing was ever said. Eric's new home was one of the RAF Police picket posts from the Special Storage Area. How on earth it had been removed from there I've no idea, I never asked. And the RAF Police never did come to ask for it back.

* * *

Every Monday the Station Commander held his weekly Execs meeting, attended by all squadron commanders. I only ever attended if the Boss was on leave. Group Captain Goodall had a remarkable 'knack' of finding out what was going on, and he always seemed to take great delight in doing so before the squadron commander concerned. So whenever I was due to attend his meetings, I always made a point of coming to the squadron first, to find out if anything had occurred over the weekend. At one meeting, I was sitting comfortably in the knowledge that I had a complete grip of things on the squadron. The meeting was quite short and very routine, with nothing significant until Rocky asked each of us in turn whether we had anything to add. He ended with the Officer Commanding Administrative Wing who said, 'There was just the one incident over the weekend, sir.'

We all perked up at that. He went on, 'Yes sir, on Saturday evening Flight Lieutenant 'AB' was stopped whilst driving on camp.'

Rocky smiled and fixed me to my seat with a piercing stare; 'AB' was one of our first tour pilots. What on earth had he done, I thought? And why didn't I know about this? I sincerely hoped that he had not been stopped for drink driving.

'So what was the problem?' asked Rocky.

'He wasn't wearing his seat belt,' was the reply.

We all looked a bit perplexed at this, especially the Station Commander.

'He was stopped by the RAF Police for not wearing his seatbelt?' he said.

Everyone clearly had the same thought: why bring such a trivial matter to the attention of the Station Commander? The Officer Commanding Administrative Wing then went on, with just the hint of a smile, 'Yes, sir, he wasn't wearing a seat belt, but what he was wearing, was a black lace bra and pants, a suspender belt and black nylon stockings!'

Station Execs ended in uproar. As for 'AB', he had been on his way to a 'Vicars and Tarts' party. I assume he was going as a tart.

* * *

On 24 June the squadron went back to Decimomannu for our annual armament practice camp. Lots of intensive air to ground bombing was practiced, including steep dive attacks using 1,000lb bombs. Vaughan Morris was very keen that we all thought 'outside the box' to constantly challenge and adapt our techniques and procedures to suit changing circumstances. Up until then, we had concentrated solely on low-level attacks, but Vaughan wanted us to consider and practice other options too. Looking back I wonder whether he was psychic, somehow anticipating what our crews might be called upon to do in the not too distant future. We still practiced all of our low-level attacks, but again he pressed us to consider variations. Loft bombing, running in low and fast and tossing the bombs at the target from about four miles away, was a well known technique which we practiced often, but there were inherent inaccuracies. On the plus side it meant staying well clear of the target so there was less likelihood of being hit by anti-aircraft fire. 'Mini Loft' had been developed, pulling up at eleven seconds from the target. Accuracy was significantly better but you were much closer to any target defences. We therefore developed and practiced 'Midi Loft', which captured the best of both techniques, involving pulling up at about twenty seconds.

On 1 July I had my 'swansong', which was a weekend of training flights taking two aircraft from Decimomannu to and from Villafranca. It was a great weekend, we enjoyed sitting on the wide piazza opposite the wonderful Roman amphitheatre in Verona; we also travelled by train to Venice. On the Sunday evening as we walked into the centre of Verona for a final meal we passed long queues of people waiting patiently for the gates to open to the amphitheatre where there was to be a performance of Verdi's *Aida*. One of our number remarked that we could have gone there but for the long queue, best we go for a beer. We all agreed.

A couple of hours later as we came back, there was no queue, but the opera hadn't started so we wandered across to find that a handful of seats were still available. Why not, we thought? The seats weren't the best, but that didn't matter; it was a truly amazing spectacle and we sat enthralled throughout the performance which didn't finish until the early hours of the morning. All in all, it was a very memorable and enjoyable 'swansong', and a great final detachment with a squadron that I felt very much part of. On 5 July 1988, about halfway back from Sardinia to Bruggen, high up above France, I logged my 1,000th flying hour on the Tornado.

*   *   *

Two other crews had a similarly enjoyable trip to Italy some months later. They enjoyed themselves so much that as they headed back to their hotel they thought it only right that they should send a postcard of thanks to the Boss. So they penned an appropriate message offering thanks for the loan of £40 million worth of Her Majesty's aircraft for a lovely weekend in Italy, and saying how wonderful they thought the Boss was for allowing them to do that sort of thing. They posted the card in the certain knowledge that there was no chance of it ever making it back through the Italian postal system. But, of course, it did!

It wouldn't have been so bad if they had actually sent it to the Squadron Boss, Vaughan Morris, but no. Even if they had sent it to Bruggen's Station Commander Rocky Goodall, he would probably have seen the funny side too. But alas they had not. They had sent it to THE BOSS, Her Majesty Queen Elizabeth! The postcard was intercepted by some humourless civil servant who duly forwarded it to the Commander-in-Chief RAF Germany, last seen in the back seat with me flying down the Grand Canyon.

Vaughan Morris was duly invited to put on his very best uniform and pop across to the Joint HQ at Rheindahlen for a 'chat without coffee', with the Commander-in-Chief. He duly marched in, saluted, and stood rigidly to attention while the Commander-in-Chief delivered his bollocking, at the end of which he said, 'Have you got anything that you wish to say?'

'I'm not sure if now is the appropriate time to ask Sir,' said Vaughan, 'but did the postcard to Mrs Thatcher get through?'

The crews had sent two cards, not one; one to Her Majesty and the other to the British Prime Minister, Margaret Thatcher. Apparently the Commander-in-Chief couldn't keep a straight face.

*   *   *

That summer, our last one in Germany, we had a week's family holiday at RAF Gatow. We thought that this would be an interesting trip as the Cold War was still at its height, and we intended to drive through East Germany to get to RAF Gatow. Neither of us had ever visited Berlin. It turned out to be a fascinating experience, which provided all of us with some vivid memories.

There were strict rules covering our travel, and what we could, and could not do whilst in East Germany and in East Berlin. We had to carry a detailed travel order, which was in English, French and Russian, and headed for a crossing point on the inner German border for a briefing; this crossing point was at Helmstedt, and was known as Checkpoint Alpha. I had known about Checkpoint Charlie since watching spy films as a youngster, but hadn't realized that Checkpoint Alpha was the British checkpoint to enter East Germany; Checkpoint Bravo was the point at which you entered West Berlin from East Germany, with Checkpoint Charlie being the checkpoint to East Berlin.

The briefings were fascinating and I had never seen Matthew and Hannah so attentive. We were told that when a British couple visited East Berlin and went to a restaurant, they were shown to a table marked 'reserved', even though they had not booked a table. During the meal the lady felt something fall into her napkin and when she looked she saw that it was a microphone. She said nothing, but folded the napkin and put it in her handbag. Having left the restaurant, she was mugged, and her handbag was stolen. As the thieves made their getaway, the handbag was discarded. When she retrieved it, the only item missing was the microphone. The children were totally enthralled by this and, for us, it was to have an amusing sequel. We were also advised to be very cautious when we were in East Berlin, as it had been known for civilians to hide in car boots to try and make their escape to the West.

In the event of our car breaking down in East Germany, or if we were stopped by East German police, we were to stay in the car with doors locked and show a card asking that they contact a Soviet officer. This was because East Germany was not recognized by the UK.

RAF Gatow was quite beautiful, having being built as a showpiece Luft-waffe airbase before the Second World War. As a member of the 'Occupying Powers' I was allowed to enter East Berlin with my family providing I wore No. 1 uniform and we did not stay overnight. The East German police and border guards could not impede us in any way.

We visited East Berlin on two occasions, once during the day and once in the evening. At Checkpoint Charlie I showed no form of identity card, but Jackie and the children were required to hold their passports up against the closed windows of the locked car for the guards to check. The guard then indicated when to turn the page, but the guard was only to be shown the first two pages. Matthew and Hannah thought that all of this was magic.

The famous Unter den Linden was very striking, but once into the side streets the city was very tired, and many buildings still bore the scars of the Battle for Berlin. Everything was significantly cheaper than in the West but often the quality of things like clothing was poor. Many shops were reminiscent of UK shops in the 1950s and toy shops featured mostly wooden toys etc. The very centre of the city was fascinating, with the Berlin Wall as a stark reminder of exactly where we were and what that wall stood for. Not that we needed any reminding, as there were Soviet soldiers on guard at various locations.

We visited two separate restaurants without booking either in advance. On both occasions we were shown to 'reserved' tables in the far corners of virtually empty restaurants. That certainly got Matthew and Hannah's attention and, throughout the meals, they did their very best to slide down their chairs to peer underneath the table searching for hidden microphones. Not that the East German Secret Police, the Stasi, would have learnt much from us except 'What's that?' and 'I'm not eating that!' I'm glad that Matthew and Hannah saw something of the Cold War that ended so long ago, and only now features in history books or old movies. They both remember that visit very well.

*   *   *

During 1988, a major change of crews began to take place; this was very much a feature of RAF aircrew lives and it was unusual to serve on the same squadron twice. Unusually, two of our new squadron leaders had been promoted from within 14 Squadron, which was very rare; they were the 1986 Display Crew, Dave Snow and Bob Wright, my first navigator on 14 Squadron. A new bachelor crew arrived straight from training, Kieran Duffy and Norman Dent; we referred to them as the YTS (Youth Training Scheme) crew because they looked so young, but they were both very competent. In my job as Exec I flew a little less with the new crews, leaving much of that work to a new deputy, the very capable Martin Townsend-Smith.

*   *   *

As my posting drew ever closer, the rate at which I flew eased off slightly, although I still had many enjoyable trips to come. One of the sorties that I flew with one of the squadron's most capable and experienced navigators could so very easily have been my last. He was a good friend and we had been programmed for a very routine sortie. Like me, he had flown many sorties with inexperienced crew members, so we were both looking forward to flying together once more. Perhaps we both should have heard the warning bells ringing!

We were very relaxed as we walked to our aircraft. It was located in the shelter known as the 'rub', the one with the waterproof fabric over a steel frame designed to look exactly the same as one of our shelters. From the air it was virtually identical, it was only on the ground that one or two limitations became clear. In winter it was freezing, but more importantly, it did not have an annex for the ground power unit that we used for start up, it was kept inside the 'rub'. There was just enough room underneath the port wing, which meant that the normal after start procedure of selecting flaps to take-off before leaving the shelter could not be carried out. As the flaps are re-checked during the challenge and response pre take-off checks that was not necessarily a problem, normally.

The flaps, on the trailing edge of the wings, are used to provide increased lift during take-off; they are normally selected fully down for landing. The Tornado also had slats (manoeuvre flaps) on the leading edge of the wings and these automatically operated when flap was selected, to further increase lift. They could also be selected on their own to increase turn performance.

We taxied out in a fairly relaxed frame of mind as the sortie was very straightforward; it was also good to be flying together once again. My back-seater read out the pre take-off checks and I made the appropriate responses. The aircraft was heavy; as well as two under wing fuel tanks on the inboard wing pylons, we were also carrying a third fuel tank under the fuselage alongside a carrier bomb light store which contained our practice bombs. The outboard wing pylons carried the Skyshadow electronic warfare pod and the Boz pod containing chaff and flares.

I ran up the engines on the runway threshold to full power, selected reheat, and as I released the brakes I moved the throttles forward to full reheat.

Despite our weight (close to thirty tons) we accelerated rapidly down the runway to rotate speed of about 165 knots. I raised the nose wheel and it slowly lifted off the runway, but as I eased the stick back further to rotate, the aircraft would not lift off. The nose just kept rotating, getting higher and higher as we continued to accelerate down the runway, the end of which was getting closer by the second. Something was very definitely wrong. Thankfully, something inside me instinctively said 'flap'. There was no time to check the flap gauge, or look at the flap selector, my left hand simply shot out and hit the lever. The aircraft leapt into the air, but by then we were a very long way down Bruggen's 8,000-foot-long runway. We cleared the trees. As we climbed away, nothing was said by either of us, but the enormity of what had almost happened hit me very hard.

We would not have got airborne without flap. The aircraft would just have kept going, accelerating faster and faster until it went off the end of the runway. We would have been faced with a very high speed abort, with little time to drop the hook to engage the arrestor cable near the upwind end of the runway. The barrier at the end of the runway would not have stopped the aircraft at that speed either. But the trees would. By then of course, my navigator would certainly have initiated the command ejection system. No doubt we would have 'got away with it', just, but what an ignominious end to my tour that would have been.

I had not selected the flaps to take-off during the pre take-off checks. I was the Deputy Squadron Commander, and a Tornado instructor. I had over 4,000 flying hours and more than 1,000 hours on Tornado. How could I have made such a stupid mistake?

All of these thoughts went through my mind as we climbed away from Bruggen, and I was thankful that a 'sixth sense' had got us out of trouble. Or had it? The nose of the aircraft had reared up very high. Could I have scraped the centreline fuel tank on the runway and put a hole in it? 'Ignominious' may not yet be over!

For the next few minutes I monitored the contents of the centreline tank very carefully until I was sure that it was OK. So far I hadn't admitted anything. While the error had been mine, my back-seater should have spotted my mistake, that's why those checks were challenge and response. The navigator challenged, the pilot responded, and the navigator checked the response. Like me, my back-seater had been a little too relaxed, assuming that he was in the safe hands of an 'experienced' operator. He needed to know what had so nearly occurred.

'Did you notice anything unusual after take-off?' I asked.

'Yes', he said, 'it was a bit steep.'

'Have you any idea why?' I asked.

'Flap?' he responded.

'Yes,' I said.

'Oh,' he said.

That said it all. The rest of the sortie was uneventful, but after landing, as I walked away from the aircraft I couldn't help but steal a long lingering glance at the centreline fuel tank to see if there were any tell-tale scrape marks. Thankfully there weren't. And that was the end of it. It shouldn't have been of course, if I had been the thorough professional that I thought I was I would have immediately reported what had occurred so that others might learn from my mistake. To my shame I said nothing, then. I only admitted what had occurred to the whole squadron some six months later, after my tour was over. On that occasion we had gathered in an Officers' Mess bar the evening before yet another service funeral to say farewell to one of 14's own.

*   *   *

A few weeks later, Mike Smith, asked me if aircrew and groundcrew names could be painted on each of our aircraft. I liked Mike a lot. He had red hair and was usually smiling. A keen cricketer, he had two sons about the same age as Matthew and Hannah, and he often included Matthew in the cricket lessons he gave to his two boys. Matthew remembers him well. During training Mike had ejected from an F4 Phantom. Later he flew Vulcans before being selected for the single-seat Jaguar. With the withdrawal of the Jaguar he moved onto Tornados and had been with '14' for most of my tour. We got on very well professionally and socially, and he was overdue promotion. Late on a Friday evening, toward the end of Happy Hour, he and I would often be found in the bar having deep and meaningful conversations, none of which we could remember the following day. In the bar, he had this particularly endearing way of looking you straight in the eye and saying with a huge grin, 'You're absolutely right!'

Mike's idea was to have the name of a crew, one pilot and one navigator, painted below the canopy of each aircraft; on the other side of the fuselage the names of two of our groundcrew would be painted. Lots of the crews thought that this was a good idea, and it would give them a firm link with a particular aircraft. But I was unconvinced. We had thirteen aircraft, but eighteen crews. Also, we had something like eighty groundcrew. Mike suggested that it would be a matter of time served on the squadron; as an experienced crew was posted out the next crew on the list would be featured on an aircraft. It would take little work to paint the names using a simple stencil. He also said that the groundcrew were very keen on the idea too and they would come up with their own process of selection. Apparently, before the Boss went on leave he had said that he didn't mind, but he would leave the decision to me. So I relented and told Mike to go ahead. As he was leaving the office I jokingly said, 'Oh Mike, just make sure that the first aircraft to be done has my name and Jeremy's name on it!'

Mike laughed as he left the room.

A couple of weeks later there was a tannoy from squadron ops saying, 'Exec, go to HAS 27'. This normally meant that there was a problem. When I got there I found Mike and Jeremy both grinning broadly, standing next to one of our aircraft (tail letter BM) with my name and Jeremy's neatly painted below the canopy. Photographs were duly taken, but I remarked that as both Jeremy and I were leaving the squadron within days, hadn't this been a waste of effort? Mike explained that BM was to be towed across the airfield that afternoon for lengthy servicing, during which it would be completely re-sprayed. Another crew's names would then be added. It was a very nice gesture from Mike even though BM was 'ours' for only half a day.

A few years later Jeremy sent me a book as a Christmas present called *Tornado* by Ian Black, which Jeremy nicely inscribed and signed it off 'From your favourite Rear'. The book featured various Tornado pictures high-lighting squadron badges and what was referred to as 'nose art', cartoons drawn on some aircraft during Gulf War I. In the middle of the book there was a photograph of BM showing our names. What was remarkable was that BM only existed with our names on it for a matter of hours; it was a touching legacy of my time on 14 Squadron and a lasting memory of the charming and friendly man that was Mike Smith. There was one other personal legacy of my time on 14: the affectionate and regular reference to 'Bonny Lad'.

*   *   *

My final sortie was on 23 September 1988; we would leave Bruggen a week later for a very different life at Cranwell. I had flown 772 hours on 14 Squadron, and another seven hours in Luftwaffe F4 Phantoms. It was particu-larly satisfying to have been assessed by Vaughan Morris as 'well above the average' as a Tornado pilot. It had been a brilliant tour, and the last six months as the Exec working for Vaughan had made a great deal of difference to my outlook. But the pace of life and work over the previous five years had been frantic, and both Jackie and I were looking forward to a slightly quieter lifestyle.

I wasn't completely through with the Tornado as I had a General War Appointment, valid until 30 September 1990 to return to the squadron in the event of increased tension. With such an appointment I could also return to 14 Squadron every six months or so for refresher flying and I very much hoped to be able to do that. I looked forward to maintaining the link with '14', although none of us dreamt – even in our worst nightmares – what the next few years would mean in terms of continual losses and far too many service funerals.

I had been very privileged to serve with such people but I also knew that I had been very lucky. Between 1979 when the first RAF Tornado squadron formed, and when I left 14 Squadron in 1988, the RAF had lost eighteen Tornado GR1 aircraft; by the end of 1990 the number had risen to twenty-seven and when the Tornado GR1 was finally replaced by the Tornado GR4 in 1999, a total of forty-nine Tornado GR1s, along with many of their crews, had been lost on operations or in training accidents. When people remark that the Cold War was won by the West without suffering casualties I disagree.

*   *   *

It was traditional on leaving to present your squadron with something as a memento; these usually took the form of a picture or something similar to display in the squadron HQ. As a few of us were leaving at the same time, including 'my favourite rear', Jeremy, I suggested getting something different, perhaps something that would live on long after we had left. The others agreed, and we clubbed together and bought a range of plants and shrubs which were delivered to the squadron early one Saturday morning. We then set about, over a very long and very wet weekend and turned the lawn outside the squadron HQ into a garden set deep within the coniferous forest which surrounded RAF Bruggen. We hoped that this would be a more lasting gift to those who served there long after we had gone.

*   *   *

14 Squadron continued to serve at RAF Bruggen until 2001, when it re-deployed along with Eric Androvadi, by now an 18-foot-long squadron leader, to RAF Lossiemouth in Scotland. The squadron served with distinction in Gulf War I, the Balkans and Kosovo, in Gulf War II, and served regularly in Afghanistan. It also saw action in Libya, only three weeks before the squadron was stood down in April 2011. When RAF Bruggen had been closed in 2001, it had been the very last RAF airfield in Germany to close. The station was taken over by the British Army and it is now known as Javelin Barracks. I wonder if a small garden still exists, surrounded by hardened aircraft shelters in the south-eastern corner of a disused airfield that was once on the frontline facing the might of the Warsaw Pact?

*   *   *

As for the people that I served with, as so often happens, you drift apart sometimes never to meet again, although sometimes a name gets mentioned which brings back memories.

Two of the Tornado Station Commanders under whom I had served, David Cousins and Rocky Goodall, would become air marshals and both would be knighted. My Boss on 20 Squadron, and my first Boss on '14', would both be promoted to group captain, and both would command their own stations. Vaughan Morris was awarded a well deserved Air Force Cross (AFC) following Gulf War I and would go on to command RAF Honington; he reached the rank of air vice-marshal before he took early retirement. The squadron's first Exec would retire as a group captain. Hylton Price, the first OC A Flight, retired as a wing commander but sadly was killed while flying as a reservist from RAF St Athan in 2009. Another of the original flight commanders would be appointed MBE following Gulf War I, and retired as a wing commander, as did my successor as Exec.

A number of pilots left the RAF and joined airlines, with quite a few going to British Airways, including my deputy, Martin Townsend-Smith. I always listen carefully when I am flying with British Airways just in case the pilot is ex-'14'. I served briefly with another ex-'14' pilot, Mike Napier, in the Training Group at Innsworth in 1997, shortly before he left the RAF as a squadron leader to join British Airways. A few years later we would meet again when he flew into Kuwait; he also became Honorary Secretary of a very active 14 Squadron Association, doing very good work keeping old comrades in touch and keeping the spirit and memory of '14' very much alive.

'My favourite rear', Jeremy Payne, left the RAF and became an airline pilot flying in the Middle East before joining Ryanair! Well done Jeremy! Another of the pilots rose to the rank of air commodore, and five others became group captains. My first deputy, who ejected in 1986, ejected again in 1991 in Saudi Arabia a few days before Gulf War I began; after that he never regained a flying category, but he was promoted to wing commander, and he and I would meet again in Kuwait. Mike Smith and Al Grieve were killed on a routine training flight. I would bump into 'AB' of 'vicars & tarts' fame at Scampton in 1992 after he became an instructor, and he would go back to 14 Squadron as a flight commander.

Kieran Duffy and Norman Dent were killed in Saudi Arabia a few days before Gulf War I began. Max Collier, dear Max, who lived just a few doors away from us, was killed when his aircraft was lost, having successfully attacked an Iraqi airfield during Gulf War I. 'Wes', Richard 'Wes' Wesley, a cheerful first tour navigator and one of the squadron characters, also served in Gulf War I, only to die in tragic circumstances soon afterwards.

They were all a magnificent bunch of guys and I remember all of them with great fondness and pride.

Chapter 8

Trenchard Hall to Painted Hall

The Department of Air Warfare, RAF College Cranwell, 1988–1991
There was a lot to think about on the way back to the UK for my first ground appointment in seventeen years. My Tornado tours had gone very well. With a good staff tour I might be in the running for promotion, although it would probably be a good idea to try and get selected for advanced staff training. But I remained a realist: having cross-roled to fast-jets at a relatively late stage and having spent my first two years as a squadron leader either on courses or not filling an executive appointment, I was well behind the drag curve in the promotion stakes. I was also approaching my fortieth birthday and promotion was most unlikely before I was forty-two at the earliest. I also knew that I would not be a 'front-runner' for command of a frontline Tornado squadron, as I would be competing with officers four or five years younger.

However, I had long ago decided that I would like to command a flying training wing and it was in that a role that I felt that I could contribute most. I had listed Officer Commanding Flying Training Wing/Chief Instructor at Linton-on-Ouse, as my first choice on my last annual report. Rocky Goodall at Bruggen had said I was 'a first rate Tornado operational pilot' and 'an outstanding QFI' and he thought that I would make 'an ideal chief instructor or frontline squadron commander'. I was delighted to read such comments. While commanding a Tornado squadron might be seen by many as the ultimate goal, for me, and from every perspective, including family, a tour as a chief instructor seemed to be a better answer. A posting to Linton-on-Ouse, following promotion to wing commander, would be the icing on the cake. However, all of that was still a long way off. I needed to perform well in my new job, be selected for Staff College, be promoted, and then get selected for a command flying appointment! Best I focus on one step at a time.

Cranwell was an amalgamation of many different departments and, apart from attending a week-long flying supervisor's course in the early 1980s; I had never been based there. In 1988 it primarily comprised of the college for officer training, a flying training school, the Department of Specialist Ground Training, and the Department of Air Warfare, which was housed within Trenchard Hall.

I began my new job as the Central Region Specialist on 30 October 1988. The Department of Air Warfare was quite small having about thirty specialist personnel, mostly senior officers, and it was headed by a group captain. It was subdivided into branches, all of which had responsibility for running various courses dealing with a wide range of subjects including flying super-vision, weapons employment and tactics, and operational studies; it was also in the early stages of developing computerized war gaming. I joined the operational studies team of five, headed by a wing commander. I shared an office with another squadron leader, Maurice Flemings, who was the UK Specialist. I had met Maurice some years earlier at Leeming and he had come to Cranwell from F4 Phantoms at RAF Wildenrath.

The other two members of our team were lieutenant colonels, one from the British Army and one from the USAF. My task was to research and lecture on NATO and Warsaw Pact air tactics and capabilities, concentrating primarily on offensive roles. I had access to NATO's top secret air operation orders and for that I needed an even higher security clearance than that which I had previously had on strike squadrons in Germany! For many of the courses that we taught, I was normally one half of a 'dog & pony show' with my army colleague. We gave lectures to many courses, including the embryonic Air Warfare Commander's Course which succeeded the much longer Air War-fare Course; we also travelled widely to talk to various audiences, including the RAF Officers' Command Course at RAF Henlow and the equivalent RN course at Greenwich.

*   *   *

And then there came one of those truly awful coincidences, one of those horrid events which make you question whether there is such a thing as fate. And of course it just had to occur on a Friday, the thirteenth – Friday 13 January 1989.

Maurice and I were returning from RAF Neatishead in Norfolk where we had been invited to lecture to an audience of Neatishead's fighter controllers; we had stayed overnight at RAF Coltishall. As we headed home, we chatted about mutual acquaintances and one that we had in common was Mike Smith whom I had known well on 14 Squadron at Bruggen. As we were having this conversation, an awful combination of circumstances was unfolding in Northern Germany.

That evening there was an item on the TV News which referred to the loss earlier that day of an RAF Tornado from 14 Squadron. It was unusual for the squadron to be identified in this way, but as I had missed most of the news item, I was unsure if anyone had been hurt. However, the film footage showed the wreck of the aircraft upside down in a field. While the aircraft had been destroyed most of the fuselage seemed to be in one piece and the undercarriage was down. This led me to hope that the accident may have happened during an approach to land and that there may well have been time for the crew to eject. I very much hoped so. Despite my anxiety, I resolved to wait until the next news bulletin before telephoning anyone at Bruggen.

It was an anxious wait, but the news was grim. The aircraft had been lost following a mid-air collision with two Luftwaffe Alpha-jets in Northern Germany. One damaged Alpha-jet had made it back to its base; the pilot of the other had ejected and was seriously injured. The crew of the 14 Squadron Tornado had been killed. Jackie and I were distraught. My first reaction was to pick up the telephone and phone the Boss, Vaughan Morris. I was halfway through dialling when I stopped and replaced the receiver. It could have been him.

After a few minutes I called 14 Squadron's Ground Liaison Officer, Major Harry York, a charming man from The Queens' Regiment who always seemed to deal with 14's younger crews as if they were slightly unruly children in his care. He gave us the terrible news that the pilot was Mike Smith, and he had been flying with his regular navigator, Alan Grieve. We knew them both well. Mike lived with his wife and two boys in married quarters at Bruggen. Alan was also married and lived in the village of Elmpt, he had a young daughter. I had flown with both of them often: I had spent a memorable weekend in Naples with Mike (and with Steve Wright so tragically killed in 1988) and it was he who was featured in the framed photographs I had at home of Snoopy on his memorable first Tornado flight. I had also flown with Alan about a dozen times from his very first 'Fam 1' sortie when he had joined the squadron in 1985. A tall, gently spoken Scot with a lovely personality, we had also spent a memorable weekend in Cyprus.

*   *   *

On 20 January 1989, Jackie and I joined a number of former 14 Squadron crews and their wives and flew to RAF Bruggen for Mike's funeral. The small station Church of St Nicholas was packed. One of the pilots from 17 Squadron was a gifted organist and he played beautifully as we awaited the arrival of Mike's family. Once the organ music stopped, the church was absolutely still.

Then there was a most unusual sound, which seemed so out of place on an RAF station and in a church; it was the unmistakeable sound of heels being clicked together. And then six young Luftwaffe pilots, resplendent in their beautiful blue uniforms with the yellow lapel flashes, and all from the squadron involved in the accident, quick marched one at a time toward the coffin, halted, came to attention with another crisp click of heals, saluted, then about-turned and marched to the rear of the church. It was one the most poignant and emotional scenes that I have ever witnessed and many within the congregation, me included, struggled to retain some composure.

The service was terribly sad but it also had humour too, as something of Mike's sense of fun was referred to in the eulogy given by the squadron's first Exec. RAF Bruggen's Station Commander, Group Captain Rocky Goodall, recited *High Flight* by the young American, John Gillespie Magee, who was killed before the US entered the Second World War while serving as a pilot with the Royal Canadian Air Force:

Oh! I have slipped the surly bonds of Earth
And danced the skies on laughter-silvered wings;
Sunward I've climbed, and joined the tumbling mirth
Of sun-split clouds, – and done a hundred things
You have not dreamed of – wheeled and soared and swung
high in the sunlit silence. Hov'ring there,
I've chased the shouting wind along, and flung
My eager craft through footless halls of air ...
Up, up the long, delirious burning blue
I've topped the wind-swept heights with easy grace
Where never lark, or ever eagle flew –
And, while with silent, lifting mind I've trod
The high untrespassed sanctity of space,
Put out my hand, and touched the face of God.

Mike was buried in the British Military Cemetery at the Joint HQ at Rheindahlen, amongst many other fellow airmen, and others, and not far from Steve Wright. The interment ended with a volley of shots, the Last Post and Reveille, and a flypast by a Tornado of 14 Squadron. All of it so utterly heart wrenching. Afterwards we returned to the Officers' Mess at Bruggen to say farewell in the aircrew way, and it was in the bar where I had spent many a Happy Hour with Mike that I met his parents. Mike's father was serving at RAF Linton-on-Ouse as the Regional Commandant of the Air Cadets.

It was the Greek historian Herodotus who said, 'In peace the sons bury their fathers, but in war the fathers bury their sons.'

Mike had been buried by his father and he truly was a Cold War Warrior, a casualty of a war that we had never been called upon to fight.

* * *

A few days later, on 24 January, I travelled by train to Aberdeen and then to RAF Lossiemouth. Most of 14 Squadron flew in during the day to attend Al Grieve's funeral the following morning in Aberdeen.

That evening in the bar there were some toasts to absent friends, but most of us did not want to dwell on the circumstances which had brought us together. There would be enough time to reflect on that the following morning.

Soon there was a lot of banter of the type so unique to aircrew and to RAF aircrew in particular. One of the squadron execs, a pilot, who had arrived on the squadron just after I left, was absent, and the reason for his absence was the source of some amusement amongst one or two, but I stood stony faced, feeling very guilty. This particular pilot, a Tornado instructor like me, had tried to take-off without having first selected take-off flap. He was sufficiently concerned that he may have damaged his aircraft that he landed immediately to check. He clearly had far more integrity than I had all those months ago when I had done exactly the same but had said nothing. So I interrupted the banter and said, 'I did that.'

That shut people up. I also said that at least he had the guts to front-up to what he had done, unlike me. As the assembled crews took this in another voice chipped in with, 'So did I.'

It was one of 14 Squadron's most highly respected pilots and weapon's instructors. Earlier in his tour, he had done the same thing and he too had kept quiet. Everyone quietened down a little after that and hopefully reflected inwardly about integrity and the importance of admitting ones mistakes so that others could learn from them.

*   *   *

The following morning the crematorium was packed to overflowing. It was another terribly sad but beautiful service, and Vaughan Morris delivered a moving eulogy. Mike Napier recited *High Flight* and another pilot read a poem by Robbie Burns.

Most commanding officers hope to be able to complete their tours without having to cope with the aftermath of an accident. By now Vaughan had already had to deal with more than his share but the way he led '14' during those difficult days showed something of the character of the man. Yet more challenges were to come when he was selected to lead the first Tornado GR1 squadron to the Gulf following the invasion of Kuwait.

There was a lot to think about on the overnight sleeper from Aberdeen that night. There was the Naples weekend which I had shared with Steve and Mike; there was the Cyprus weekend with Alan and the 'gopping' plate complete with our photographs that we presented to the squadron. And there were many other flights that I had enjoyed with both of them. They were an extremely competent crew and if such an accident could occur to them, it could occur to anyone.

But it was mostly the so very cruel twists of fate that had combined and contributed to Mike and Al's death that I thought about most. I still do. The sortie that they were on was the culmination of a four day TACEVAL. On that morning the whole of the Bruggen Wing had been scrambled. Each aircraft was required to fly a very precise route at low-level, timed very carefully, to arrive at the Nordhorn weapons range in northern Germany, where each aircraft would drop a single practice bomb at one minute intervals. Each sortie was critical to the assessment of the wing as a whole and the timing had to be near perfect. Each mission was referred to as a 'line number', and aircraft were allocated to each 'line', which therefore dictated the route and the timing for each individual aircraft. A crew was then allocated to each aircraft. So it was not the crew who determined the route or even the timing, it was the aircraft to which they had been allocated.

When the 14 Squadron crews arrived to be authorized for their missions, Mike and Alan noticed that 'their' aircraft (tail letters BB), the one that had their names painted on the side, had been allocated to a different crew. They therefore asked to be switched to that aircraft. The authorizer agreed. Mike and Alan now had a different route with different timings that two hours later would take them directly into the path of a formation of Luftwaffe Alpha-jets operating in free airspace.

Was it fate? Or was it just a fluke, or a horrible coincidence? What if six months earlier I had not agreed to have crew names painted on the aircraft? It probably would have been done eventually, but maybe even a few weeks delay might have meant that Mike's and Alan's names would have been painted on a different aircraft. What if they had simply accepted the programme on that fateful Friday the thirteenth? There were so many ifs.

* * *

Back at Cranwell I found my job interesting and rewarding. My Boss was keen that I kept up-to-date with what was happening on the frontline, and he was more than happy if I stayed current as a pilot and also returned to Bruggen for refresher flying as part of my two year war appointment. It undoubtedly increased the credibility of the operational studies team if some of us were still operational.

I spoke to Vaughan and he agreed to my return for a week; my first visit was planned for September 1989. I was also accepted as a pilot with No. 9 Air Experience Flight which flew Chipmunks for air cadet air experience at RAF Finningley (now Robin Hood International Airport), in South Yorkshire. I had my first ever flight in a Chipmunk on 4 May 1989.

The Boss of the Chipmunk Flight immediately recognized my 14 Squadron badge as he had served on the squadron in the 1950s flying Hunters. Thankfully he was very patient; he needed to be! Finningley's main runway was being resurfaced at the time, so all take-off and landings were from the much narrower taxiway. I had never previously flown an aircraft with a tail wheel and I found taxiing and landing the Chipmunk to be quite a challenge. Once in the air I was fine, but I certainly revised my views about having regretted missing out on the Chipmunk course that most of my student contemporaries completed in 1971. If I had undergone that course, I might well have found that my career as an RAF pilot might never have got off the ground.

I went solo on my third trip and from then on tried to get up to Finningley for an afternoon's flying every two to three weeks. I managed to fly a total of forty hours before my last trip on 26 April 1990, and it was immensely satisfying to give some cadets their very first taste of RAF flying. I developed a great deal of respect for the Chipmunk Flight Commander, and for many others like him who did such a great job managing their various charges and offering so many boys and girls that all important first step. The task of a

Chipmunk flight commander was no sinecure. He had to have his finger firmly on the pulse as far as flying supervision was concerned. The Chipmunk could bite and many of the pilots, like me, flew irregularly and could easily become non-standard and a little too casual. The clear, but gentle, control and direction offered by the Officer Commanding No. 9 AEF, Flight Lieutenant Ron Pavely, was ideal. I have often thought since that these flight commanders were underrated.

* * *

During the summer holidays, Her Majesty the Queen and His Royal Highness Prince Phillip, the Duke of Edinburgh, paid a visit to Cranwell. For me it was a normal working day, but when I got home Jackie casually dropped it into the conversation that Hannah had given Her Majesty some flowers! Jackie and the children had been behind a roped barrier along with a number of other families as the Queen and Prince Phillip walked past. A lady nearby gave Hannah a bunch of flowers and told her to go and give them to the Queen. There was no way that Hannah would ever do such a thing! However, as Prince Phillip passed by, he saw Hannah and came straight across saying, 'Are those for Her Majesty?'

'Yes,' said Hannah.

With that the Duke of Edinburgh promptly lifted the rope above Hannah's head and said, 'You had better come through and give them to her then.'

And so she did! A few days later we were delighted to see some lovely photographs, one showing Matthew and Hannah with Prince Phillip, and the other showing Hannah giving the flowers to Her Majesty. These photographs have had pride of place in our hallway ever since.

* * *

In September I flew in the weekly 'trooper' to Germany and headed back to Bruggen for a week's worth of refresher flying. I completed two simulator sorties on Friday 8 September, and then a check flight with the Squadron Training Officer the following Monday. That afternoon I flew my Instrument Rating Test. The next day I flew a singleton low-level navigation sortie with my first navigator, Bob Wright, who was now a flight commander. My final trips were both on 14 September, and I flew as the No. 2 of an attack pair on a high-low sortie to the UK, before landing and refuelling at RAF Waddington; we then flew a low-high sortie back to Bruggen. My navigator was my successor as 14 Squadron's Exec, Squadron Leader Herm Harper. It was a very enjoyable week and I was very pleased that, despite the year away from Tornado, I was still capable of performing satisfactorily as a No. 2. I had flown nine hours and twenty minutes during my five sorties. It was also good to see 14 Squadron in such good shape.

On my return to Cranwell, I heard from my desk officer that my tour, nominally three years, might be foreshortened, as I was on the reserve list for

Staff College. A number of others who had been offered places had yet to make the decision to accept, or decline. At the time there were four options: each service ran its own Advanced Staff Course, the RN at Greenwich, the army at Camberley, and the RAF at Bracknell, and their courses ran from January until late November. The vast majority of RAF officers went to Bracknell, although there were always a couple of places on the RN and Army courses. The other option was to attend the Joint Services Defence College (JSDC), also at Greenwich, and it accepted students from all three services, as well as civilians from both the civil service and the police. This was by far my preferred option, especially as the course ran for only seven months. In November 1989 I was doubly pleased to hear that I had been selected for Staff College and, with the Bracknell course starting in January already full, I was to join No. 11 Course at JSDC at Greenwich. The course would last from April to November 1990, at the end of which I would receive a new posting.

We would almost certainly have to move home at the end of the course, but my prospects for the future were much improved. I therefore decided that the time was right for me to state my case to be considered, in due course, for the post of Chief Instructor and Officer Commanding Flying Training Wing at No. 1 Flying Training School, RAF Linton-on-Ouse. I duly put pen to paper, arguing that my instructional experience on both the Jet Provost and Tornado made me an ideal candidate. Also, given the fact that I had cross-roled to fast-jets at a relatively late stage, only six years earlier, I was very up-to-date concerning the challenges that students would face during fast-jet training and on the operational frontline. It was only in the final paragraph that I alluded to the 'minor' issue that I was actually at the wrong rank to be considered, and that I would need to be promoted to wing commander. I glossed over that bit. Well, I thought, what was the harm in asking? I got a brief letter of acknowledgement from the RAF Personnel Management Agency at Innsworth stating the obvious, that I needed to be promoted first, but at least my letter would stay on file.

*   *   *

In February 1990 I returned to 14 Squadron for another period of refresher flying. Following a couple of simulator sorties I flew a combined instructor check and Instrument Rating Test with the Training Officer on 28 February, before flying a low-level sortie with Herm later the same day. My final two sorties were on 1 March, a singleton sortie first, then a second sortie as the No. 2 of a pair with 'Cookie', Nigel Cookson. A first tourist, Cookie had developed into a very capable navigator; he would later become a flight commander on '14' and we would meet again in Kuwait. The pairs sortie included a first run attack into the weapons range at Nordhorn in Northern Germany, followed by level bombing. It was immensely satisfying to be credited with four consecutive 'direct hits', although I never did ask Cookie if he had 'fixed that for me' with the Range Safety Officer; I hoped not, but didn't ask. My four sorties totalled six hours twenty-five minutes. Although I didn't realize it at the time, that sortie during the afternoon of Thursday 1 March 1990, would be my last with 14 Squadron, and my last ever in a Tornado GR1.

As I returned to the UK I did wonder whether that would indeed be my final 'swansong', but it was very clear indeed that '14' was in very good hands. My short tour with the Department of Air Warfare (DAW) ended on 27 April 1990. As I headed south to London and the historic college at Greenwich on the following Sunday, I wondered how I would find the academic world of advanced staff training. Well, it came as something of a shock.

Joint Services Defence College (JSDC), Greenwich, 1990

The JSDC was a training academy for British military personnel from 1983 to 1997. The course covered crisis management, international issues, UK foreign and domestic policy, NATO, and joint operations in order to prepare officers for joint service staff work, and for key posts in operational commands. The aim was to improve students understanding of the other services and their capabilities, and it introduced pressures and constraints which were likely to bear on high-level defence decisions. The course was purely UK-based, there were no overseas students.

The Commandant was a major general and the senior directing staff were colonels and lieutenant colonels, or equivalent. Officers selected for the course had to have the potential to be promoted at least two ranks. Each course had sixty officers, seventeen from each service, plus nine from the civil service or the police.

* * *

The first challenge was coming to terms with a RN establishment. The Officers' Mess was the Wardroom, our rooms were cabins, and the communal bathrooms went by the glorious name of the heads. Visiting a nearby pub was going for a run ashore. Well, they were the Senior Service. As some RN 'wag' pointed out, the RN had traditions whereas the RAF only had habits.

The RN students were commanders, the army officers were all majors, destined to move to new posts as lieutenant colonels, while the RAF students were either squadron leaders or wing commanders. We also had two police superintendents on our course. Some of the backgrounds of my fellow officers were fascinating: there were three OBEs, five MBEs, and one MC (Military Cross) amongst the student body, which also included former ship's captains, a Polaris submarine skipper, Falklands veterans, an SAS officer, and many others who were destined for high rank. Some would also be 'pulled' early and sent to a war that was only just around the corner.

* * *

It was an honour to be able to study in such surroundings. The college was described by UNESCO as being the 'finest and most dramatically sited architectural and landscape ensemble in the British Isles'. Planned by Sir Christopher Wren and built between 1696 and 1712, it was built as a hospital for veteran and disabled seafarers on the instructions of Mary II, who had been inspired by the sight of wounded sailors returning from battle.

The buildings were split to provide an avenue and a riverside view from the Queen's House, and Greenwich Hill beyond, and this gave the hospital its distinctive look, with four main buildings, known as the Courts, and a Grand Square. Queen Mary Court houses the chapel, and King William Court is famous for its Painted Hall, which is where, on 5 January 1806, Lord Nelson's body was laid in state before being taken up the Thames to St Paul's Cathedral for a state funeral. The Painted Hall comprises a Lower Hall, originally intended for the seafarers, and the Upper Hall beyond, reserved for staff and officers. The Naval Hospital closed to pensioners in 1869 and it became a Naval College in 1973.

In 1990 we found it slightly amusing that here, in the centre of what the then local politicians referred to as, 'the Greenwich nuclear free zone', was JASON, the RN's Department of Nuclear Science and Technology research and training nuclear reactor, which had been commissioned in the King William building in 1962. Not exactly a nuclear-free Greenwich then! The reactor was finally dismantled in 1999.

We occupied much of the King Charles building. Our dining room was of course the Painted Hall, and to dine formally here was a real treat. But to sit in such a place early in the morning eating corn flakes verged on the surreal. A passageway known as the Chalk Walk, lead from the Painted Hall to the large bar and anteroom, and then on to our accommodation, or rather to our cabins. It was said that the Chalk Walk, with its white painted walls, was named because of the white chalk remains of so many clay pipes discarded there, which had been smoked by so many thousands of sailors who spent the last years of their lives in such surroundings during the 170 years that it served as a hospital.

*   *   *

While there was much to admire in our surroundings there was little time to settle in and enjoy the view. We were divided into three seminars for each of the three terms and each seminar was subdivided into two syndicates. On the very first day, syndicate discussions began with each of the ten officers taking it in turn to introduce themselves and describe something of their background. I was last, and as each individual spoke I listened with a growing sense of trepidation.

They all sounded so very interesting and they were all confident and eloquent. I felt neither. There was the officer from the Parachute Regiment who had served numerous tours in Northern Ireland, the cavalry officer who simply exuded knowledge. There was the RN Polaris captain who had commanded HMS *Perisher*, the school which selected RN submarine captains. Then there was the very quietly spoken officer who had been based at Hereford for most of his career. Then there was the bespectacled civil servant with the gentle manner, surely I would have his measure? But no, this very charming man was a Balliol graduate who had worked in Cheltenham ever since. He was not allowed to say anything about his job; Cheltenham is the home of the Government Communications HQ.

I must admit to being a little in awe of my colleagues and I began to feel like a fish out of water. When it came to my turn, I said my bit, and thought I'd try and inject a little bit of humour, given the interesting and often secret lives that my colleagues appeared to have been living.

'I'm afraid that if I tell you any more then I will have to kill you,' I said.

No one laughed, there were just one or two slightly bemused smiles, like those some people use when they feel a little sorry for someone. Except for the civil servant and a Royal Signals officer; their smiles seemed genuine. But the senior directing staff colonel didn't smile!

Over the next few days my sense of trepidation increased while my morale fell into my boots. Syndicate discussions came thick and fast, interspersed with lectures. We often had some fascinating speakers; Dennis Healey in particular went down very well. There was usually a lot of time allocated for questions, and it seemed as though the question, rather than the answer, and who was asking the question, was a matter of much interest to the staff. I began to dread the syndicate discussions which followed. In this type of forum I lacked confidence, yet my colleagues appeared to thrive on being able to discuss, to debate, and to question.

In my field, I was as knowledgeable as the next man, perhaps more than many, but as an operational RAF pilot I had been brought up in a very hard school which did not tolerate 'bullshit' or 'bull-shitters'. On an RAF squadron, or even in a Mess, such individuals were easy to spot and to deal with. If you didn't know what you were talking about, it was wise to keep your mouth well and truly shut until you were on firm ground. While I was interested in many of the subjects that were discussed, I tended too often to hold back until I felt I had something important or relevant to contribute. But by then it was often very difficult to get a word in edgeways. It was also clear that lines had already been drawn, with various officers having already asserted themselves from the very start. When they spoke, people listened, or when they interrupted, people deferred, while they themselves rarely gave ground if interrupted. On the other hand, I was that chap who stood at the bar for twenty minutes unable to attract the attention of a passing barman, while everyone else was being served. I felt ill at ease and totally out of my element. And it showed.

The colonel who ran our seminar, and moved between two syndicates, always seemed to be there whenever I, for whatever reason, was unable to contribute to the discussion. This did not bode well.

At the end of another frustrating session in syndicates I headed back for lunch. Walking with me was the Royal Signals officer from my syndicate. As we talked about the morning session, I mentioned some of my concerns. He recognized immediately where I was coming from, and was very understanding and supportive. He explained that the style of discussion was very familiar to all of his army colleagues who had been well trained in syndicate work during their earlier staff training. He went on to say that much, although not all, of what was said, especially by some of the syndicate members, was a bit 'thin'. Views might be well expressed but some didn't bear close examination.

He suggested that all I needed to do, and often, was to 'Press to Test', in other words to challenge, to question, and try to establish whether others actually held clear views and were knowledgeable about the subject under discussion. In other words I needed to get 'stroppy', just a bit. Now that shouldn't be difficult, I had been stroppy enough on different squadrons in the past, I just had to try it outside my normal comfort zone. The Royal Signals officer and I became good friends during the remainder of the course, often 'chewing the cud' as the course progressed, and we were joined by the gentlemanly civil servant, our man from GCHQ.

So, with a new found confidence, I got stuck in and began to rather enjoy myself, although one or two of my colleagues in the syndicate were taken aback by this sudden surprise attack from what had been a rather quiet flank.

* * *

The main college activities commenced at 1100 hours on Mondays, with the hours beforehand being for 'private research'; in other words we could travel back during the morning. To make up for the late start, the college midweek routine was busy, and evening work was essential. Normally we would finish at midday or early afternoon on a Friday, for more 'private research'.

Socially the course was very active and one or two of my colleagues freely admitted that they had saved up so that they could fully enjoy the course. An element amongst the RAF students also formed a most secret society – in common with our traditions (habits!). It was a formation drinking team know as the Red Barrels. The civilian senior directing staff, who did not share our sense of humour, appeared to take the existence of the Red Barrels as some sort of personal challenge, and he set about trying to uncover the identity of team members. Needless to say, he failed. Even now, some twenty years after the course ended there is still no clear certainty about the identity of all the members. If I told anyone, I would of course have to kill them afterwards.

* * *

Soon, the course 'war game' began, during which each syndicate had to plan and execute a full joint war-fighting operation. A few days beforehand I was approached by the RAF directing staff. Aware of my previous tour as the Central Region Specialist, they asked for advice on the capabilities and tactics of Soviet aircraft that were in the model for the war game. They welcomed my input, as some of their information was inaccurate and outdated, and this did wonders for my confidence.

For the war game, each student had to fill a particular appointment, but not one from within one's own service. Within our syndicate, the overall commander was a Parachute Regiment officer, the air commander was also an army officer, while the ground commander was from the RN; I was the deputy ground commander. An RAF officer was the naval commander.

It was a fascinating and detailed operation in which we had to plan all the elements of a joint operation involving two fictitious countries. A complex amphibious operation had to be planned and then a land and air campaign with naval support. Most of the day was spent in planning, coordinating, and then executing the operation. Once we pressed 'execute' we adjourned to the bar while the directing staff 'played' out the various actions and likely reactions by both sides. We were given the detailed results the following morning. That well known military maxim that 'no plan survives first contact with the enemy' could not have been more accurate, and each new day saw feverish activity as plans were revised, or in some cases completely rewritten.

By playing the role of another service, we all learnt a great deal. Mistakes were made, but some paid accidental dividends. I split our ground forces to advance on two roads which diverged. Apparently this was a huge tactical error. But coincidentally the 'enemy' sprang a surprise attack and were hit for six as they bumped into our much wider frontage. From that moment on, the 'enemy' was on the back foot, and we worked hard to keep them that way. I then suggested to our air commander that he leapfrog his batteries of surface-to-air missiles rather than moving the whole unit and this also helped keep enemy air at bay. The end result was a decisive win by our syndicate, which was also judged to be the best executed plan of the course. The champagne that was awarded to the winning team didn't go very far!

* * *

Each student was required to write a service paper on a defence related subject; this would be a key part of the end of course assessment. It would be assessed not only by our directing staff, but also by a specialist from the Department of History. Perhaps slightly foolishly I chose for my subject *The Royal Air Force Approaching the 21st Century – A Time for Change?* My challenge was that Options for Change, a Defence White Paper, was due to be published during the summer of 1990, and I needed to get my paper submitted before that occurred. So May and June saw me working hard and of course all my work was in longhand. My Royal Signals colleague stepped in to help, and as he had a word processor, he willingly typed my later drafts and the final version which I submitted before the summer break. While the staff thought that it was commendably early, I simply had to get it in before it was overtaken by events.

*   *   *

Throughout the course many of us had been practicing for the Army Battle Fitness Test, which the Commandant insisted that we all complete. So from early on in the course, I reminded myself how utterly useless I was at tennis, in the hope that it might improve my fitness. Once or twice each week I would also jog to Greenwich Park, to practice the route that would be used for the Battle Fitness Test. The test involved marching as a squad for one and a half miles in exactly fifteen minutes. After a one minute halt, we were then required to run the same route to achieve a best possible time. I measured the course carefully, largely for my benefit; the various lamp posts and park benches would then take on a completely new meaning come the day.

Whenever I went for a run, I just got on with it without making a song and dance about it, unlike the two Parachute Regiment officers on our course who always announced loudly in the corridors that they were off 'jock-strapping', in a vain attempt to persuade far more sensible colleagues to join them, and no doubt return feeling inadequate. When they returned they would always ensure that we were aware of their 'best time'. One day I came across one of them returning, but he was looking rather reflective. When I asked why, he explained that he had just seen our SAS colleague exercising in the park and what he had witnessed he found most depressing. He had spotted him gently jogging until he reached the bottom of some very steep concrete steps in the centre of the park. After a pause he ran up the steps very fast, before immediately turning round and running back down again at breakneck speed. Then he did the same again, except he did it backwards, and then he did it again on one leg and then the other. After that he quietly resumed his jogging. Individual training became a little quieter after that.

On the day of the test, a bomb scare precluded the use of Greenwich Park. This was good news indeed as there was no real alternative to the park. However, there was some suspicion that the threat may not necessarily have originated from the IRA! Our hopes of a reprieve were quickly dashed when it was announced that we would complete the test within the secure confines of the college grounds, on the cobblestone roads. Cobblestone roads! And where were my lamp posts and my park benches so essential to my success? The test was duly completed and passed by all, but any good that it may have done us was quickly undone by the bacon and eggs and champagne which followed in the Painted Hall.

*   *   *

The Summer Ball took place on 6 July and this was a glorious affair which also incorporated Beating Retreat. It was the most colourful ball that Jackie and I had ever attended. The variety of Mess Dress was amazing with so many army regiments represented: infantry, cavalry, gunners, engineers, all with so many wildly differing uniforms. It has been said, by a naval officer I think, that the only time that army officers are in uniform is when they are wearing civilian clothes. The ball began with champagne in the King William Colonnade. The Grand Buffet was in three beautifully decorated marquees and also in the Queen Mary anteroom. Later, everyone gathered outside in front of the marquees facing the Grand Square for Beating Retreat, which was conducted by the Central Band of the RAF, and The Queen's Colour Squadron of the RAF Regiment. They were both absolutely magnificent and everyone was impressed by their superb performance. The RAF has habits indeed!

*   *   *

Shortly afterwards, the RAF students had interviews with a wing commander from the Personnel Management Centre at RAF Innsworth to discuss our future appointments. His opening words should have warned me what was about to unfold.

'I was impressed by your letter about being considered for Chief Instructor at Linton,' he said.

Ah! What was coming next? I knew that I would be graduating as a squadron leader, so what did he have in mind?

He said that in order to strengthen my case to be considered for such an appointment, it would be best if I went to a staff appointment within the flying training world, perhaps within the Training Group at RAF Brampton, near Huntingdon. I was happy with that and said so. From my point of view it was a much more attractive prospect than working in the Ministry of Defence Main Building in Whitehall. He then went on to say that it would also be in my best interests if I went to a 'high profile' appointment. I think my face may well have lost a little colour at that point.

'We would like to propose you as the next Personal Staff Officer to the Air Officer Commanding (AOC) Training Group,' he said.

As I lost what little colour was left, I simply couldn't stop myself.

'Who? Me? A PSO? Are you serious?' I said.

And of course he was.

There are 'high profile' staff appointments and then there are PSO appointments; they don't come much higher than that for a squadron leader. I had always tried to maintain a low profile, being quite content to play 'the grey man' lest I be found out, but now it seemed I had been hoisted by my own petard, or in this case by my own letter. If I got the job, many places that the AOC went, I would go; every letter and every piece of staff work that went into or came out of his office would pass through my hands. Of course, if I did a decent job, I could not be better placed for a command flying appointment as the AOC had the right of veto over any such appointment within the Training Group. So, there was nothing much to say really. I would probably be invited for interview with the AOC, Air Vice-Marshal Mike Pilkington, during the imminent summer break.

*   *   *

The highlight of the course during the final term was for each syndicate to conduct a wide-ranging defence review. Senior officers from the MOD's central staffs would be invited to attend detailed presentations and discussions which would last a whole day. While we would all have roles to play, and many would have speaking parts, by far the greatest burden would fall on whoever was selected to 'lead' each syndicate. It came as a great relief when it was announced that our SAS colleague would lead our syndicate. He was very articulate, an excellent leader, and a very capable staff officer; we would be in good hands.

After that we all headed off on leave, the first four week period of summer leave that I had ever had during my RAF career. But, unknown to all of us, a man called Saddam was about to enter the world stage once more. The effect would be devastating for many of those involved, but there would also be some ripples felt in the academia that was Greenwich.

On 2 August 1990, Saddam Hussein invaded Kuwait. The first composite Tornado GR1 Squadron to be deployed to the Middle East in response to the invasion was formed from 14 and 17 Squadrons from RAF Bruggen, led by Vaughan Morris. It would be the first of many Tornado squadrons. A total of eleven aircraft and a number of their crews would not return.

*   *   *

Shortly before returning to Greenwich I was invited to HQ Support Command at Brampton, for an interview with Air Vice-Marshal Pilkington. He was a gentleman and I liked him immediately. He confirmed then and there that I had got the job, and I was to start on the Monday morning immediately following completion of my course in mid-November.

Back at JSDC I could relax while the majority of my colleagues were working hard to complete their service papers. The bad news was that because of what was going on in the Middle East our ranks had been thinned a little. Critically for our syndicate, our leader for the final presentation had already been recalled and no doubt was already in a sandy place. And from my purely selfish point of view, much worse was to come: I was selected to replace him as syndicate leader.

'And by the way Paul,' said the Directing Staff Colonel, 'your syndicate will be presenting to the Chief of the Defence Staff, General Sir Richard Vincent.'

I looked in vain for some sort of escape route. How about a recall to 14 Squadron? Apparently I wasn't needed. I could be an operations officer perhaps, or help with the planning? Alas not. Surely there was something that I could do? Apparently all I could do was to knuckle down and co-ordinate the writing and presentation of a strategic defence review for a day-long presentation to the head of the UK's Armed Forces. That's OK then.

*   *   *

On Tuesday 16 October 1990, the Royal Naval College hosted a guest night to celebrate the 185th Anniversary of the Battle of Trafalgar. To attend such an evening in the Painted Hall, the very place where Lord Nelson's body had been laid in state the night before his funeral, was an honour. Nelson's body had been transported back to England from Trafalgar in a barrel of brandy.

The principal guest was General Sir Richard Vincent. Also amongst the senior guests was a senior Russian naval officer, Vice Admiral V.N. Ponikar-ovsky. A former Soviet submarine captain on his first visit to the UK, he was asked what he thought of England. His reply, through an interpreter, was priceless – 'It's a lot nicer than through a periscope.'

*   *   *

My service paper was duly returned and it had received a good overall mark and positive comments from the RAF directing staff and a professor from within the Department of History and International Affairs. The Commandant though was more restrained, saying that he was 'disinclined to run this for publication' although it was 'an interesting paper – as far as it went.'

Almost before we knew it, the course came to an end, and even our presentation to General Vincent went extremely well. I was also well pleased to achieve a standard above the average for the course. There was a final guest night on 15 November 1990 to formally dine out our course, and the following day we all dispersed to our various new appointments. I suspect that some also headed off to an overdraft and a liver transplant too.

Headquarters Training Group, RAF Support Command, 1990–1991
In 1990, Support Command, with its HQ at Brampton, was a large organization commanded by Air Marshal Sir Michael Graydon, later Air Chief Marshal and Chief of the Air Staff. He had been the Station Commander at RAF Leuchars in 1981 during my last display with the Vintage Pair, and it was he who had referred to 'the McDonald twins coming home to roost' in a letter to the Commandant of the Central Flying School. He moved on to become Commander-in-Chief Strike Command six months into my tour, and was succeeded by the late Air Chief Marshal Sir John Thomson.

When I arrived in the HQ, the command incorporated three Group HQ in the same building, training, maintenance and administration, each with a two-star officer (air vice-marshal) in command.

My tour began on 19 November 1990. My uniforms had to be modified with epaulettes fitted to the shoulders and other attachments, which were necessary so that I could wear aiguillettes, an ornamental braided chord which was attached to my left shoulder whenever I was on formal duty with the AOC. I shared an office with the AOC's aide-de-camp (ADC), a flight lieutenant; our offices were next door to those of the Commander-in-Chief. A couple of doors down the corridor was a friend from Canberras at Cottesmore, and Tornados at Bruggen, Mike Dineen, now a wing commander and the Command Flight Safety Officer.

For the first two months of my tour, I lived in the Officers' Mess until we moved into a married quarter on base. I soon began to enjoy my job very much. It was fascinating and reassuring too, to see the way policies were determined and decisions made. It also gave me sight of intelligence summaries of what was going on in the Gulf at a fairly early stage. I did not have privileged access to intelligence, more perhaps just an early indication of what was happening. The AOC, Mike Pilkington, was excellent to work for, and his wife, Janet, was a delightful lady. I had heard horror stories in the past that some air officer's wives could make life very difficult for PSOs and ADCs. That was not my experience, then, or since.

The Training Group was a vast organization which included all aspects of airmen and officer training on the ground and in the air. While I had a good understanding of some aspects of pilot training, there was much that was new, and I had little time to get up to speed especially with the ground training of officers and airmen. How new became abundantly clear during the first of the AOC's weekly staff meetings which were held every Friday morning. I attended these meetings to take notes which I would then write up for the AOC's approval before distributing them throughout the HQ during the afternoon. The meetings included two air commodores and four or five group captains and others, and to begin with, it was a struggle to understand what they were talking about. I even struggled to decode some of the acronyms that were used.

For most of my career, group captains had been fairly distant figures. At Brampton, if I was to do my job properly I needed to get to know them better. Luckily, the two air commodores could not have been more helpful and they did much to help me ease my way into my new job. One was Air Commodore Engineering Training, in charge of all aspects of ground training for both officers and airmen. Air Commodore Flying Training (ACFT) was the capable and very well regarded Air Commodore Chris Coville, a former Lightning, F4 Phantom and Tornado F3 pilot. In a break with previous practice, he was the first ACFT to be appointed who was not a flying instructor, and he was a breath of fresh air. With Mike Pilkington as AOC, and Chris Coville as his Deputy, the RAF flying training system was in good hands.

For the first couple of meetings I was not at all up to speed with what was going on. The AOC was very patient, often correcting or adding to my notes, and he was never in any way critical. But I realized that I had to do something to get on top of this part of my job, and I had to do it quickly. What I needed was a cunning plan.

So, after each meeting, I wandered off down the various corridors to have a chat with one or more of the attendees and I often asked for clarification, or a more detailed explanation of various topics that had been covered. Some, like the air commodores, were happy to clarify what had been said, which was exactly what I wanted. One or two of the group captains though saw this as the perfect opportunity to influence what went into the notes of the meeting. In other words, they could suggest to a gullible PSO what they had meant to say, rather than what they had actually said! Only once was I taken in and later the AOC looked slightly bemused when he read my notes. Normally I stood near his desk as he read them and made minor amendments. On this occasion he read one section, looked slightly quizzical, and then he looked up, and peered questioningly at me over the top of his half-moon spectacles. After a few seconds he smiled slightly and nodded saying, 'OK.'

He then passed the notes back to me for final printing and distribution.

After that I made a point of spending some time each week visiting the various group captains and their staffs and soon I had established a good working rapport. They soon realized that I was not completely gullible. On one occasion, when I was in someone's office, in walked the AOC saying, 'Ah, here you are!'

Overall though, I think that he was very happy with the approach that I adopted.

*   *   *

As mid-January approached it was fairly clear that things in the Middle East were coming to a head. Then, on 13 January 1991, exactly two years after the loss of Mike Smith and Alan Grieve in Germany, a Tornado GR1 of 14 Squadron was lost in an accident in Saudi Arabia. The crew, Kieran Duffy and Norman Dent, were both killed. I attended Kieran's funeral at Kidderminster later that month.

Gulf War I began with a prolonged air war on 16 January. As expected, the RAF Tornado force, which specialized in airfield attacks, were employed against some of the most heavily defended targets. Iraqi airfields were very different to those in East Germany which had been our intended targets in the 1980s: they were huge, often having three or four runways with many taxiways, some parallel, some oblique, many of which could also be used as runways. Each mission against a single airfield would involve eight or twelve Tornados in a coordinated attack, usually at night, and every mission involved air-to-air refuelling on the way to and from the target.

Once in Iraqi airspace, the aircraft had to be flown at extremely low altitudes. And of course, the Iraqis knew that their airfields would be targeted, and they had defended them accordingly. There was no avoiding the anti-aircraft defences and surface-to-air missile engagement zones: in order for the Tornados to deliver their specialist runway denial weapon, the JP233, each aircraft had to fly directly over the target airfield with the wings level. What went through the minds of so many crews as they approached their target with such heavy and obvious anti-aircraft fire, is unimaginable.

Aircraft and crew losses were inevitable and were not long in coming. On 17 January 1991, shortly after an attack on an Iraqi airfield, the aircraft being flown by the Officer Commanding 27 Squadron was seen to crash. His predecessor had been killed in a Tornado accident the previous August. Over Iraq, his navigator was Max Collier, a former 14 Squadron navigator; they both died instantly. I later attended a memorial service for Max at RAF Marham. Max and his family had lived a few doors from us at Bruggen.

Some crews were lucky; they were taken prisoner, although their treatment at the hands of the Iraqi secret police was appalling. A number who had been severely beaten were paraded on television for the world to see and to judge.

A few days into the air war, after it had become clear that Iraqi aircraft posed no real threat to coalition ground forces, the RAF's Tornados were switched to medium level attacks using laser guided bombs. The loss rate reduced, although questions have long been asked whether the RAF's tactics could have been adjusted a day or two earlier. One RAF pilot who had successfully ejected and was captured (sadly his navigator had been killed when they were hit), was taken to the airfield that he had actually been attacking! He said later when I met him, that he was treated courteously by the Iraqi commander who had been trained in the UK. The Iraqi colonel had then apologized for what was about to occur next, as he was handed over to the secret police.

My first Tornado navigator from 20 Squadron at RAF Laarbruch, Bob Ankerson, was taken prisoner during the latter days of the war, which thankfully came to an end after only a very short ground war. The ground had been 'well prepared' by a highly successful air campaign. The RAF had lost a total of eleven Tornado GR1s. I would hear perhaps the most valid comment about RAF Tornado operations during Gulf War I when I was in Kuwait some years later, and it came from an American four-star general. Back at Brampton, from the safety of my office, I watched and read about what was going on with an increasing sense of frustration. For twenty years I had trained for, and trained others, to do the job that was now unfolding. But there was nothing that I could do to help.

*   *   *

On some occasions I would be required to listen in to telephone conversations so that I could readily access files and pass them quickly to the AOC, even during the phone call itself. I also saw all mail that went into, and out of his office too. Most of the staff in the HQ were aware of this and some would often call in to see me 'for a chat', while their real intention was to find out what was going on by glancing at the papers that were in one of three trays adjacent to my desk. One particular group captain was particularly blatant about doing this, and invariably looked at the trays constantly, whilst trying to conduct a slightly stilted conversation with me. My counter was to stand up and, with a straight face and no interruption in conversation, slowly and deliberately turn each of the trays around so that he would have to learn to read upside down.

Being able to see the AOC's mail first also had some other advantages too. Whenever he was away, even if only for a day, I would go through the mail deciding what needed to be dealt with in his absence, what could wait until the following morning, and what I needed to take with me to brief him when he returned home. One morning the six-monthly RAF officer promotion list arrived. Such lists were always submitted early to air officers before the individuals themselves had been notified of their selection. I sat down with a cup of coffee to go through the lists to see if there was anyone that I knew. On page one, about halfway down there was a name I recognized. It was mine! I had been selected for promotion to the substantive rank of wing commander with effect from 1 July 1991.

Of course I was delighted, but this would inevitably mean another posting and another house move; we had only been in our current house for six weeks. That evening I telephoned the AOC to brief him on the day's events in the office. I assumed that he must have known, that he had been forewarned that his own staff officer was about to be promoted. But he had not. While he was obviously pleased for me, I think that he was also a little irritated that he would have to 'break-in' another PSO when he had barely got me house-trained.

*   *   *

In due course, I was contacted by my desk officer at the RAF Personnel Management Agency at Innsworth. He confirmed that I was being considered for a command flying appointment. Before asking my views, he went on to say that the next position as a Tornado GR1 squadron commander would not be coming up for about eighteen months; the squadron concerned would be 617 (Dambusters) Squadron based at RAF Marham. I paused for thought, but not for long. My reasons for asking in writing for a flying training command appointment a year and a half earlier remained unchanged. While command of a squadron such as 617 Squadron would be considered by many to be the ultimate, there was no guarantee at this stage that I would be selected. I asked if I could be considered for a Chief Instructor appointment, especially if one was coming up earlier. He agreed to look at it. After that, it was a matter of being patient. No doubt Air Vice-Marshal Pilkington's views would be sought in due course; that would be a telephone call that I would most definitely not be asked to listen into.

*   *   *

The Red Arrows, based at RAF Scampton in Lincolnshire, were also part of the Training Group. Each year the team, with three new members, would commence training for the new display season almost as soon as the previous one ended. This would culminate in an intensive period of training, normally at RAF Akrotiri in Cyprus, where the team could make the most of the good weather to perfect their display. Towards the end of their detachment, the AOC would fly out to Cyprus to see the final practices before granting public display clearance. In April 1991 I accompanied Air-Vice Marshal Pilkington to Cyprus.

This was a tremendous opportunity for me to gain a unique insight into what went on behind the scenes with the Red Arrows. I had often seen their displays, but now I was able to attend their briefings for each practice and also sit in on their all-important and detailed debriefing sessions too. Every practice and display was recorded, as was every word spoken on the radio, so that all aspects of each practice could be dissected, analyzed and discussed. While most RAF pilots fully recognized the skill and ability of the Reds, in their red flying suits they were also often subject to much 'banter'. But quite often 'banter' masks admiration, and what I was to see in Cyprus and what went into their performance, day in and day out, was hugely impressive. They were totally professional perfectionists and I couldn't help being impressed. Nor did they 'pull their punches' during debriefs either; each individual said it how it was as they learnt from one another and moved on.

The highlight, and perhaps one of the highlights of my flying career, was when I flew in the back seat of the leader's aircraft during a display practice over the Mediterranean, off the south coast of Cyprus on 24 April 1991. It was a fantastic sortie; I simply cannot describe it in any other way, and my view on the Royal Air Force Aerobatic Team, the Red Arrows matured that day, and has remained unchanged ever since. They are still the very best display team in the world.

*   *   *

On 4 June I received a letter from an air marshal in the MOD saying that my JSDC service paper, *The RAF Approaching the 21st Century – A Time for Change?*, had won the annual RAF essay competition and I had been awarded the Gordon Shephard Memorial Prize. What was even more satisfying was the letter of congratulations from the Commandant of JSDC. He was the chap who had been disinclined to run it for publication because it didn't go far enough. He now thought it 'an excellent paper' that was 'rated highly at Greenwich', and that he had been 'sure it would be a strong contender for the laurels'. He apparently now held up my example as a template of the high standards that JSDC expected from their students! He went on to say that he knew that I would be modest about my achievement and the well-deserved accolades that would follow, but that I was to enjoy the limelight and the loot. The so-called loot amounted to about £60, as I recall. More importantly, despite him having worked so closely with RAF aircrew at Greenwich, not to mention the Red Barrels, had he learnt nothing? The most important criteria essential to being a respected and credible fast-jet pilot, was that you had to be, or more importantly, you had to appear to be, rubbish at staff work!

Luckily for me, my secret was safe; when my article was published in November 1991 in the RAF magazine *Air Clues*, the editorial team screwed up my name, and credited a Squadron Leader A.T. McDonald with the piece. My reputation therefore went unsullied for a while longer!

*   *   *

I soon became aware that things were beginning to move, as far as my next posting was concerned, and I was aware that my desk officer had been in touch with the AOC. Also, the next Station Commander at RAF Linton-on-Ouse had been confirmed. It would be Group Captain Tom Eeles who was serving just down the corridor from me as Group Captain Flying Training; he would take over command during January 1992.

I was soon told that my appointment as Chief Instructor was likely, but I was to say nothing until everything was confirmed. This led to an amusing thirty minutes at a Happy Hour one Friday evening when I ended up at the bar with the ADC and Tom Eeles. The ADC knew that I would be the next Chief Instructor at Linton, so did I, and so did Tom. But I was under instructions not to say anything to anyone. Tom also knew, but he wasn't sure if I knew. This resulted in a rather stilted conversation as we both avoided talking about the one subject that we both wanted to talk about: Linton! Eventually, as no one else was within earshot, an exasperated ADC said, 'Oh, for God's sake you two, you both know; why can't you just acknowledge it and have a beer!'

So we did!

Within a few days, details of my appointment were confirmed. I would be detached to CFS, now at RAF Scampton, at the end of October, to complete refresher training on the Jet Provost and renew my instructor qualification. Then I would learn to fly and teach on the Bulldog, a single engine piston aircraft, which I hadn't previously flown. My tour at No. 1 Flying Training School, RAF Linton-on-Ouse, would commence on 16 March 1992.

*   *   *

Pilot training in the RAF was about to go through a period of significant change, and the affect that this would have on many individuals already in the training system would last for years. The collapse of the Warsaw Pact heralded major changes in defence policy and, not surprisingly, there was a huge outcry from politicians, and the public alike, for a 'peace dividend'. Options for Change, published in 1990, heralded major cuts throughout the Armed Forces. The impact on the RAF was very significant as frontline squadrons were axed. With squadrons being disbanded, training units would close, but there was a hope that the changes and the drawdown's could be managed over a period of time. The RAF now had too many young officers in the long training pipeline and there would be insufficient cockpits for them to move onto. What to do about that was a key question.

One option was to simply make them redundant as they were commissioned, or while they were still undergoing training. That would probably have been the 'business' solution. I think that many within the HQ, including the AOC, thought that this would result in the RAF being labelled as a 'bad employer'. These young men and women had been recruited in good faith to meet a requirement, and even though that requirement had now changed, it was thought that a better solution could be found by managing the reduction in the training throughput. At the time no one could imagine how difficult that would be, and how long and painful the process of holds and backlogs would become. It was inevitable that there would be an impact on the number of flying training schools that we had, especially on the three basic flying training schools at Cranwell, Church Fenton and Linton-on-Ouse. Two of the basic flying training schools would close.

*   *   *

Regular guest nights were a feature in the splendid Brampton Park Officers' Mess. Normally the AOC would attend and I would be on duty until he left. Probably my most important role was to carry a spare copy of his speech, as it was normal practice for one of the more junior officers attending to 'lift' the AOC's speech notes if at all possible. Mike Pilkington was always considerate; he usually left at about midnight and this allowed his staff to relax. I learnt quite a lesson fairly early on. After the AOC had left, I relaxed all the way until about 0330 hours! Despite the rather staid environment of a HQ Mess, Mess 'rugby' was soon underway, lead as always by Chris Coville. Later, as I 'floated' my way gently home across the sports fields I suddenly came to my senses realizing that because it was a HQ Mess, guest nights were held on Thursday nights! In just over three hours I needed to be up, and then into the outer office by 0730 hours!

I made it, but felt grim, and probably looked once more like that 'knight at arms . . . palely loitering'. At 0735 hours an incredibly bright and cheerful Air Commodore Coville bounced into my office full of the joys of spring. I did my best to look and act professionally but I felt like death warmed up, and he knew it. Once he had gone, I flung the office window open and took some long, deep breaths. The AOC gave me rather a funny look when he came in!

*   *   *

As I came to the end of my very short tour as a PSO, I couldn't help but reflect on how much I had actually enjoyed it. I had been at the very heart of the HQ which would determine how flying training would develop over the next few years, and I had been greatly reassured by what I had seen. I had also been able to work with my next station commander for nearly a year and we had got on well. Also, I had got to know well – and admired – two of the key players on the flying training scene: the AOC, Air Vice-Marshal Pilkington, and although he didn't know it at the time, his successor, Air Commodore Coville.

But, as I cleared my desk and prepared to handover to my successor there were indications that all was not well at Linton. One or two examples of a lack of professionalism and flying indiscipline had come to light. This was worrying. In the meantime though, I had almost five months of refresher flying to look forward to, and I couldn't wait.

Central Flying School (CFS), RAF Scampton, 1991–1992

My refresher flying began on 29 October. As it was over three years since my last flying tour, I was allocated thirty-five hours flying on the Jet Provost before moving on to practicing basic teaching skills. While I had covered these on my original CFS course twelve years earlier, the type of instruction at a basic school was very different to that on my Refresher Flying Squadron tour. I had previously 'refreshed' qualified pilots; I had not taught student pilots to fly. I was also aware that there had been raised eyebrows from some of the more 'traditional' basic instructors at the news of my appointment, because I had not in their eyes 'served my time' as a basic instructor. While at Scampton, I would also complete a short elementary course on the Bulldog, a type new to me, but one which was a key part of No. 1 Flying Training School.

But before even arriving at Scampton I again heard some troubling rumours. These came from staff of the Flying Supervisor's Course which was run from my old department at Cranwell. This course was another crossroads within the RAF aircrew fraternity, with junior and senior officers spending a week discussing supervision issues and analyzing past accidents. Experiences were shared, and it was often here that issues might be mentioned that had been kept quiet at unit level. This wasn't about 'whistle-blowing', as the staff on the course would not react formally to anything that they had heard in the confidential surrounds that were essential to the success of the course.

One senior officer regularly gave a presentation to the course about a fatal accident in which he had been involved as a supervisor, and it was clear to all, that reliving the experience affected him deeply. That he was willing to share his experience for the benefit of a new generation of flying supervisors spoke loudly for his profound sense of responsibility.

It was with that same sense of responsibility that one of the staff told me about examples of flying indiscipline at Linton. He wasn't suggesting formal action but he felt that I needed to be aware. Apparently one chap at Linton, having recently received his 'blue letter' advising him of his impending promotion, celebrated by performing aerobatics at low-level over a disused airfield. Illegal low-level aerobatics was one thing, but to have performed them with a student sitting alongside was something else.

*   *   *

It was also good to meet old friends at Scampton: the Station Commander had been a wing commander at Leeming when I had been there; he had also flown in the back seat of the Meteor with me on a display weekend at Bournemouth. My first Boss at Leeming, Dick Woodhead, was also at Scampton as one of the examiners on Examining Wing, and so was Peter Howlett. Peter had been one of the crew when I famously broke my demijohn of sherry on landing at Luqa on our way back from Cyprus when I was on 7 Squadron. Peter had moved on to XIII Squadron, and on our arrival, he and his wife Andrea invited Jackie and I to stay with them until we found somewhere to live. Also at Scampton was 'AB' of 'vicars & tarts' fame at Bruggen. He was now a refresher instructor and we would fly together on a number of occasions. He would soon become a flight commander on 14 Squadron. And in command of ground school, was my former Central Flying School squadron commander from the time that I had struggled so much during my instructor course.

*   *   *

After a few days in ground school, I flew my first sortie on 4 November. Over the next eight days I flew seventeen sorties. It was then decided to end my thirty-five hour refresher course early and move on to the teaching phase. The 'patter' covered those delightful exercises such as Effects of Controls, Straight and Level 1 and Descending 2. While they were all very important, I did thank my lucky stars that my first instructional tour had been as a refresher instructor, rather than a basic instructor.

Over the next sixteen days I flew twenty-three sorties, and I flew my 'check ride' with the Station Commander on 13 December. This went well, and I was awarded the typical category for a returning instructor of 'Competent to Instruct'. But, I very much wanted to reconfirm the A2 category that I had earned in 1981. That, however, could wait until after Christmas.

On the 8 January 1992, I was back in the air once more, and the following day I passed my A2. After three instrument flying sorties, I then passed the Instrument Rating Examiner's Test. I was in good shape for my new job which was still two months away.

Over the next few weeks I 'filled my boots' with as much flying on the Bulldog as I could, as it was important that I was credible on this aircraft as well. I also flew a couple of sorties in the Tucano which would be introduced gradually at Linton shortly after I arrived. I passed my Instrument Rating Test in the Bulldog on 20 February and was awarded a 'Competent to Instruct' category the following day.

*   *   *

One of the more important sorties that I flew at Scampton was not part of the course at all. I was asked by the staff if I would fly with a foreign exchange officer who was due to be posted to Linton as an instructor. They were at a loss as to whether to allow him to graduate so they thought 'why not get his next Boss to make the decision?' Initially I thought that this sounded a bit of a 'cop-out', but it wasn't; the staff had the interests of the officer very much at heart.

I took to this quiet and reserved man immediately. He had a very good sense of humour just waiting to come out, but I soon recognized the staff's concerns, as his briefing and teaching skills were basic and perhaps not good enough to merit graduation in normal circumstances. However, for him to be sent back home would have been a huge blow. Nevertheless, he was a very good pilot and was capable of very accurate flying. While he sometimes stumbled with the 'patter' in the air, his flying was largely unaffected. He could still teach by demonstration and by example and all being well, the 'patter' would develop in time. So I said yes, I was happy for him to join the Linton instructional staff and I never regretted that decision. He went on to become a very popular and highly regarded instructor at Linton.

* * *

My course came to an end on 25 February; I had flown just short of fifty hours on the Jet Provost and twenty-three hours on the Bulldog, and I was pleased with how it had gone. Now it was a matter of moving home for the tenth time in eighteen years. Jackie and I were also invited to Linton for a dinner party and to stay overnight in the home of the current Chief Instructor. It was a great opportunity to meet, in a social setting, the squadron commanders who would be working for me within a few weeks. But there did seem to be rather a lot of them. In fact there were nine squadrons within Flying Training Wing. This might well be a challenge I thought, and it was; but it was one that I relished.

Chapter 9

Centre of Excellence

No. 1 Flying Training School, RAF Linton-on-Ouse, 1992–1994
Linton-on-Ouse has always enjoyed a reputation as a happy station, a nice place to live and something of a jewel within the RAF's flying training system, a system that is still the envy of many. Only eight miles north of the beautiful city of York, it is off the beaten track and many who have travelled through the Vale of York would have been oblivious to the station's location. The River Ure meanders toward Linton to become the Ouse just to the west of the airfield, before it curves south for York and on to the Humber estuary.

With the airfield blending in so well with the surrounding farmland it was often the river which provided a beacon for generations of student pilots trying to find their way home. And during the 1940s, it was the river, so easy to follow from the Humber, which guided countless Whitleys, Halifaxes and Lancasters back from their perilous journeys. No doubt the Ouse also helped a number of Junkers and Heinkels to find Linton too.

The station motto says it all: *A Flumine Impugnamus* – From the mighty river we strike. Linton had been built between 1936 and 1938, which saw the construction of some fifty new airfields in response to German rearmament. The station opened on 13 May 1937 and was considered to be the premier airfield of 4 Group which had its HQ for a time in huts behind the Officers' Mess. The Air Officer Commanding was Air Commodore A.T. Harris; long before he became 'Bomber' Harris and Commander-in-Chief Bomber Command.

Linton's Whitleys were on operations on the very first night of the war. In 1941 the new Halifax four-engined bomber arrived, and soon afterwards, on 10 May, the Luftwaffe attacked Linton and a number of airmen were killed, including the Station Commander of less than forty-eight hours, Group Captain Frederick Garraway. He is buried in Newton-on-Ouse. Sadly his son, also a pilot, would be killed in 1944 on operations from Breighton in the East Riding.

In 1992 we moved into the former Station Commander's house and found that it still bore the scars of the 1941 raid. One side of the house had been hit and rebuilt, but it continued to suffer from subsidence. A 1944 aerial photograph shows a line of bomb craters marching inextricably from Linton village across the fields, and the final bomb hit our house.

When the faithful Whitleys of 58 Squadron moved out in April 1942, they had flown 200 raids for the loss of forty-nine aircraft. Group Captain Leonard

Cheshire VC, DSO, DFC, served at Linton on both 102 and 35 Squadrons and later commanded 76 Squadron. On his 103rd mission of the war, he was the official British observer of the nuclear bombing of Nagasaki. Many assumed that it was this event which 'emptied him', but as he kept pointing out, it was the war as a whole that did that. He left the RAF in 1946, and went on to set up Cheshire Homes, charitable homes for the disabled. He is known by many, more for his charitable work, than for his remarkable contribution during the Second World War. He maintained his links to the service that he had loved, and to which he had given so much, and officially opened the No. 1 Flying Training School ground school. The main briefing facility which has seated so many thousands of student pilots and their instructors is called Cheshire Hall. Leonard Cheshire died in 1992.

During the summer of 2008, I was in my garden when I heard a sound that I recognized immediately, so distinctive to anyone with an interest in aviation. It was the sound of a Merlin engine, but not just one. I soon found myself running down our drive to catch sight of what I knew was heading in my direction. It was a Lancaster approaching very low from the north, and as it got closer it pulled up and turned, flying directly over the lane in which we live. It was from RAF Coningsby and it had been completing a flypast at a Cheshire Home in a nearby village to mark the 60th Anniversary of the foundation of Cheshire Homes. I was glad that the RAF had remembered Leonard Cheshire.

*   *   *

In June 1943 Linton-on-Ouse was transferred to the RCAF as part of 6 Group, and it became the home of 408 and 426 Squadrons. On 17 August 1043, 426 Squadron flew its first raid and lost two aircraft, including that of its Squadron Commander. The Canadian Group HQ was at Allerton Park Castle, on the north side of the A59 just before it crosses over the A1 (M). Driving past there on a gloomy, wet winter's day, one can so easily understand why many Canadian airmen referred to their HQ as 'Castle Dismal'.

Beningborough Hall, the former home of the Countess of Chesterfield, was taken over as a Sergeant's Mess Annex and many Canadian crews lived there. Apparently the Countess was not best pleased to be moved into the gatehouse! After her death in 1957 the Hall and its extensive gardens were given to the National Trust. During our time at Linton, Jackie acted as a National Trust volunteer guide at Beningborough. Built in 1716 on the site of an Elizabethan manor, the Hall is very imposing, set in lovely grounds south of Newton-on-Ouse and next to the river. It has a beautiful walled garden and the house itself boasts an impressive cantilever staircase, the latter was cordoned off lest it be damaged and one day Jackie was approached by an elderly Canadian who said that he had lived there during the war. He asked why the staircase was cordoned off. When Jackie explained he expressed surprise as he and his friends used to ride their motorcycles up and down the stairs!

It always intrigued me that the pub favoured by many of the Canadians was the Alice Hawthorn in Nun Monkton, which was on the opposite side of the river. How did they get to it? The only bridges across the river were the Aldwark tollbridge many miles upstream, and another on the outskirts of York many miles south; neither could be considered for an evening's stroll to 'the local'. The answer had been provided by a Yorkshire entrepreneur who ferried the aircrew across the river from Beningborough in his rowing boat. The outward journey was three pence (in old money), the return journey being six pence!

There are a number of touching short stories about the people who lived at Linton and at Beningborough to be seen in a first floor room above the National Trust shop in the stable block. Still more are on view, along with many photographs and exhibits, in the first class Memorial Room at Linton, so well looked after by Alan Mawby, a retired wing commander. Former wartime personnel and their families still visit Linton, often arriving un-announced at the Guardroom. Many remark that much of the station remains as it was in the 1940s.

The last mission flown from Linton was on 25 April 1945, and the RCAF squadrons departed soon afterwards. A total of 339 aircraft had failed to return during operations from Linton; this was the second highest loss for a Bomber Command airfield. Of these, 72 were Whitleys, 26 were Lancasters, and 191 were Halifaxes. Each Whitley had a crew of five; the Halifax and the Lancaster each had a crew of seven.

After the War, Linton became a transport base, then a fighter station, before being transferred to Flying Training Command in preparation for the arrival of No. 1 Flying Training School, in October 1957. No. 1 FTS, the world's oldest flying training school, has been at Linton ever since.

*   *   *

My first day at Linton was 15 March 1992. The station comprised of three wings: Administrative Wing, Operations Wing, and Flying Training Wing. Also based at Linton was a RN commander who filled the role of the Senior Naval Officer (SNO); he had responsibility for the officer development of the RN officers attending courses at Linton.

Within the Flying Training Wing's HQ, there was a Deputy Chief Instructor (DCI), a Training Wing Planner, an RAF corporal as Training Wing Secretary, and a clerk typist. My first deputy was the able and experienced Squadron Leader Roy Turgoose. The Training Wing Plan's post was traditionally filled by Linton's only navigator, and for the majority of my tour this was Flight Lieutenant Dave Taylor. The wing comprised of nine squadrons, six of which were flying squadrons. There were three basic squadrons and a standards squadron operating the Jet Provost, and a basic ground school and the General Service Training Squadron; then there was the Royal Navy Elementary Flying Training Squadron (RNEFTS) operating the Bulldog, a RN ground school, and finally Bulldog Standards Squadron.

In total, the wing had about eighty permanent staff and up to 120 student pilots at any one time. The 1 FTS weekly 'Execs' meeting tended to be a very crowded affair. Over the next year, as the Jet Provosts and Bulldogs were joined by the Tucano and the Firefly, 1 FTS built up to over 100 aircraft. RAF Church Fenton was added to our two existing relief landing grounds of Topcliffe and Dishforth, and the Tucano Flight Simulators were also brought in from Church Fenton and Cranwell. The simulators would eventually total four, with an instructional staff which increased to twelve. It was good to work with Alan Rayment again, my former Squadron Commander, in a new role commanding the Tucano Simulator. One of Linton's first simulator instructors was Richard Kimberley, and I would work with both Richard and Alan sixteen years later. During my tour, both ground schools were combined and absorbed the General Service Training Squadron and the Tucano Flight Simulator to become one enlarged Ground Training Squadron.

*   *   *

As 1 FTS moved toward becoming the sole basic flying training school, I was very conscious of my responsibility and also of the history of such a distinguished school. Formed at Netheravon in Wiltshire on 29 July 1919, 1 FTS was the world's very first flying training school. The first Commanding Officer was Wing Commander Playfair, and the Playfair Trophy continues to be awarded to a student from each graduating course. In those early days, the instructors were a versatile lot: in the transport strike of 1921, detachments of aircraft were sent to Bristol to help with mail deliveries. While some officers worked on the railways one even became a driver on the Great Western Railway!

In 1924 the arrival of the RN and the Royal Marines marked the beginning of a link with the 'dark blue' that has continued ever since. No. 1 FTS was based at numerous locations before its final move took place on 28 September 1957, and Linton became the 'spiritual' home of 1 FTS for generations of RN and RAF pilots. The 1 FTS Unit crest is unusual: it consists of crossed Naval and Military Swords, enfiladed by a winged crown, and it was designed to be representative of the three Services. The badge and motto, *Terra Marique ad Caelum* – By Land and Sea to the Sky – commemorates the close links between 1 FTS and the RN.

*   *   *

The RN has always been an important feature of life at Linton. Whatever criteria were used to select Fleet Air Arm pilots, it was spot on. Their students were invariably charismatic and keen, all very much individuals, but totally focused on the need for naval aviation and for the route that they had chosen.

In 1992, RN staff and students made up almost a third of 1 FTS and they always made their presence felt, professionally, and socially. Their contribution extended to every aspect of station life and their annual celebration of Taranto Night was something not to be missed. It was based around a traditional guest night, but before dinner everyone was invited to the front of the Mess to witness a re-enactment of the Battle of Taranto. It was in the heavily defended Gulf of Taranto that the Fleet Air Arm, in their slow, obsolescent Swordfish bi-planes, successfully attacked the might of the Italian Battle Fleet. Even though Germany had been on the other side at the time, the German Navy students were also involved in the re-enactment, and the event was always spectacular, with fireworks and explosions, mostly at the right time. On one occasion one of the rockets fell over just before it ignited. It then set off at great speed, about two feet off the ground, heading directly across The Green, straight at my front door! There was a deathly hush as everyone realized the unintended target. When it fizzled out a few feet from the door there was great applause.

A year later, in the anteroom, just before another Taranto re-enactment, I found myself talking to two young German Navy student pilots. When I joined them there had been the typical Prussian clicking of heals to which I had said, 'Oh, please don't do that, it makes me very nervous.'

They had some difficulty trying to relax and smile, while also trying to be upright and proper as befits young German officers talking to their Wing Commander. They had a little more difficulty when I went on, 'Now you two, your lot have had a go at my house on two previous occasions, I trust that tonight will not be the third?'

They looked quite bewildered; they said that they knew about the previous year's slight problem with the rocket but didn't know about any other occasion.

'Last year was the second attempt,' I explained, 'the first was in 1941. I sincerely hope that tonight will not be your third?'

I left them at that point; their faces were a picture.

*   *   *

My first task on arrival was to spend the first few days being 'standardized' in the ways of 1 FTS. My first sortie on 17 March was with that most capable of instructors, Brian Russell. Five years later, a few weeks before I left for Kuwait, it would be Brian, by then the Central Flying School Tucano Examiner, who would award me my A2 category on the Tucano. Thirteen years later, in 2010, he would join the staff of the Tucano Simulator. My second trip was with another vastly experienced and highly respected instructor, Rod Leigh. Something of an oracle in the instructional world, Rod would also be on the staff of the Tucano Simulator when I joined Thales in 2008.

I also had to be 'standardized' on the Bulldog at Topcliffe, and one of the sorties that I flew was with Dave Lee, the senior Vampire pilot during my first season with the Vintage Pair.

As well as being the 'spiritual' home of 1 FTS, Linton was also one of the RAF's better known and popular crossroads; this beautiful part of North Yorkshire was also the area that so many chose for retirement.

Wing HQ was on the first floor, on the side of No. 3 Hangar directly above 2 Squadron. While space was cramped, it was an ideal position overlooking the airfield, and close to all of the squadrons. It also meant that I, and the HQ staff, could be seen every day; we were not distant from the people that we were working with and flying with every day. For a student to fly with the Chief Instructor could be a worrying event and I always thought it important to try and take the edge of the formality that so often existed; being seen around the workplace dressed as they were in a flying suit was part of that process. This would become increasingly important as my tour at Linton progressed, and the stark realities of cuts to the RAF began to strike home.

The students at Linton were a great bunch, although it would take me a while to become familiar with the names and faces of each course member already in residence. It was easier as each new course arrived and I talked to them on their first day. Interestingly, most students wanted to know the answers to the same three questions that had been doing the rounds in 1972: What is the 'chop' rate? Who is the instructor to avoid at all costs? Who is the 'natural pilot'?

I did my best to answer, although I tended to avoid Question Two in case the answer was 'the CI'. The reality was of course that I was often the instructor that they did want to avoid, as it was often down to me to fly a student's very last sortie, a Senior Supervisor's Check or, as student's called it, the 'chop ride'. In early 1992, the 'chop' rate was relatively low at about 5–8 per cent as students from a Basic Flying Training Squadron (BFTS) could be streamed to fast-jet, rotary, or multi-engine training. Only those without sufficient pilot aptitude would be 'chopped', and some of these could be re-streamed to other branches including navigator, or at least they could at the beginning of my tour. However, factors far beyond our control were about to intervene and this would see suspension rates rising to an appalling 40 per cent. But that was still to come.

What was irrepressible was the spirit of the students. That spirit was the same that I could recall from the early 1970s and it is still the same now. Shortly before I arrived an incident had occurred which was just one example of that spirit. At the time the Boss of 2 Squadron was Squadron Leader Craig Goodwin, a New Zealander, whose family had a sheep farm in New Zealand. One Monday morning he arrived to find that all of the furniture from his office had been removed, the floor had been 'turfed' and two sheep were quietly grazing there. There was little doubt that the culprits were students from 3 Squadron as there had always been great rivalry between the two squadrons. After a few weeks 'to let the dust settle' the students of 2 Squadron exacted their revenge.

In those days the exterior of the squadron buildings had changed little from their Second World War days. All of the external doors opened outwards. One Monday morning, the 3 Squadron Duty Student arrived early to unlock the Squadron HQ only to find that every single door had been bricked up, very professionally too, and the mortar had set. There was no way in.

Rumour had it that the culprits were all from 2 Squadron's senior course, 118 Course, which was an unusual course in that it only had six students, three of whom were female. It was also thought that it had been the girls who were the main instigators of the revenge attack. Perhaps I should ask one of them. One was Keren Cavaciuti, and in June 1992 I flew with her on her Final Handling Test. She was an extremely able pilot. Later having completed her Hawk course at Valley she was 'creamed off' and returned to Linton as a Tucano instructor while I was still in post. After a very successful tour as an instructor, she was posted to the single-seat Jaguar ground attack aircraft, the only female pilot ever to serve on a Jaguar squadron. As Keren Watkins, and a mother of four, she returned to Linton in 2006 as an instructor, and she is now the very highly respected Central Flying School Examiner on the Tucano, working just down the corridor from the Tucano Simulator. Another of 118 Course also now serving at Linton is Helen Gardiner. After successful tours as a Tornado F3 fighter pilot, she returned to Linton as a squadron commander.

*   *   *

Air Vice-Marshal Mike Pilkington paid his last visit to RAF Church Fenton on 20 May as the station wound down prior to becoming one of Linton's relief landing grounds. He and I flew a sortie in a Jet Provost; it was the only time that we ever flew together, and it was good to see that he had not lost any of his skills as a pilot despite many years filling staff and command appointments. He would retire from the RAF within a few weeks and he would be succeeded by his deputy, Chris Coville.

The following day I flew to RNAS Culdrose with Linton's Senior Naval Officer, Commander Barry Kirby, to see the next stage of flying training for the majority of RN graduates from 1 FTS. Only one or two would remain at Linton to fly the Jet Provost or Tucano, and go on to the Hawk and finally the Sea Harrier. This was my first opportunity to fly the Gazelle helicopter. Little did I know that within six years I would be examining Kuwaiti Gazelle instructors for re-categorization!

On 29 May I flew in a four ship flypast at a funeral in the nearby village of Newton-on-Ouse. I had never met George Broadbent; he was already terminally ill when I arrived at Linton. He had been a long-serving instructor on Standards Squadron and was one of the most experienced Jet Provost instructors in the RAF. Like many others, I had assumed that the reference to him as 'Sir George' was because of his long-standing reputation on the Jet Provost and throughout the instructional world. But no, he was actually Squadron Leader Sir George Walter Broadbent, 4th Baronet. I joined his colleagues to fly a four ship in 'finger 4' formation as Sir George was laid to rest; I flew as No. 3. Overhead the cemetery which overlooks the River Ouse to the west, I pulled up, and turned left to disappear to the south leaving the other three aircraft to fly onwards to the west in 'missing man' formation. A few seconds later I came back, low over the cemetery but with the engine at flight idle in a final, almost silent, salute from 1 FTS to Sir George.

* * *

The delivery of Tucanos to Linton was now in full swing and I began my conversion in June while continuing to instruct on the Jet Provost and the Bulldog. We also began to lose some of our Jet Provosts; most went into storage at RAF Shawbury and one or two went to more interesting locations. We delivered four Jet Provost Mark 5s to RAF Halton on 12 June, for RAF apprentices to use for training. Halton of course only had a grass airfield. We received approval to land on the grass, which must have been fairly unusual for a jet aircraft.

* * *

Life for the instructors, and especially for the students, was about to undergo some fundamental changes which would have far-reaching consequences. The RNEFTS had been planned to disband for some time to make way for the contractorised Joint Elementary Flying Training Squadron (JEFTS) which was to be formed as part of 1 FTS at Topcliffe. The Bulldog would be replaced by a civilian registered aircraft to be operated in accordance with both the civilian Air Navigation Order and Military Flying Regulations. This would prove to be a challenge. The instructors would primarily be civilian, although a small number of service instructors would be retained. Once JEFTS was up and running, RAF and RN students would complete their elementary flying training on the new type. RNEFTS would disband on 1 July 1993.

By far the biggest change was as a result of Options for Change and the significant downsizing of the RAF which followed. Front line squadrons were being disbanded, and it was already clear that there were far too many student pilots in the training pipeline. There were simply insufficient cockpits.

The first thing to occur was that the multi-engined Operational Conversion Units (OCUs) closed to all *ab-initio* pilots. This would normally amount to 30–40 per cent of our output. Soon afterwards, the helicopter OCUs closed to all *ab-initio* pilots too; they normally took about 10 per cent of our output. So, almost overnight, 40–50 per cent of our throughput had nowhere to go. We were directed that only students who reached fast-jet entry standards at Linton could graduate. Those who did not meet that standard, even though they had sufficient pilot aptitude for other types, would have to be suspended with little chance of a transfer to any other branch within the RAF. The prospect of our suspension rates rising to 40 per cent or more was horrendous.

What made matters more difficult was that 1 FTS had been, up until that point, a very traditional BFTS with its instructors being drawn from fast-jets, helicopters and multi-engine aircraft. The instructors would now have to recommend for suspension students who were actually better than they themselves had been at the same stage of training. I was in that position; in 1973 I had not been up to the standard required to continue on to fast-jets, but luckily there had been another option open for me. Now those options were gone.

There were other issues too which would be immensely difficult to manage. The fast-jet front line could not absorb the output of trainees either, and progressively, gaps and holds would occur throughout the training pipeline. For many young fast-jet pilots this would mean an additional two or three years 'holding' in the training system or in 'backlog' before they would reach an operational squadron. All in all, these issues would become a nightmare for the RAF and a personal disaster for many young men and women who had their hearts set on an RAF career.

*   *   *

Flying indiscipline was something that I came across very rarely indeed. When it did occur it had to be firmly 'nipped in the bud'. One junior instructor thought it acceptable to 'beat up' Linton whilst flying solo on a Friday afternoon before he was detached to another station for six months. The individual concerned had been very keen to go on the detachment but still thought it acceptable to breach everything that he stood for as an instructor and bid farewell in his own way. He was not sufficiently qualified to authorize his own training sorties; they normally had to be authorized by his squadron or flight commander. On this particular day, with both his squadron or flight commander elsewhere, he persuaded a slightly naive deputy flight commander to authorize him for a solo training sortie. A few minutes before his expected return, all of the students from his squadron walked outside to await his arrival. Therefore, what he was about to do was premeditated, and he had told one or more students. He flew across the airfield low and fast, pulled up into the vertical and performed a stall turn before landing. I didn't actually see his arrival but my deputy had, and he was not at all happy!

The impact that such flying could have on our students could be significant. What he had done could not be allowed to stand. Having established the facts I asked to see him and his Squadron Commander. I grounded him and cancelled the detachment that he had looked forward to for so long; I could no longer trust him as a representative of 1 FTS at another unit. A few days later I issued him with a written warning. For an officer to be issued with such a warning was a very serious matter; I should know, I had received one at Bruggen. But it was one step short of the ultimate sanction, an Adverse Report under Queen's Regulations which would stay on his record permanently. A written warning was an opportunity for him to turn things around; it would also be destroyed when he eventually left Linton. When I interviewed him I expressed the hope that he would take heed, and work to regain my confidence and that of his Squadron Commander. His reaction was positive, and he knuckled down over the next year and went on to eventually become a Deputy Flight Commander. I hoped that he had genuinely learnt the lesson; sadly he had not.

*   *   *

I qualified as an instructor on the Tucano on 21 August. The newly appointed Air Officer Commanding, Air Vice-Marshal Chris Coville visited Linton on 25 August and I flew two sorties with him. In mid-September I paid another visit to the Fleet Air Arm with Barry Kirby, this time to RNAS Yeovilton. This visit, in a Jet Provost Mark 5, was a little less dramatic than my last one in 1980 and I landed with a working engine, and also on the runway. Whilst there, I flew two sorties with the RN, one in a Gazelle and one in a Sea King.

During early September preparations were underway for the annual Battle of Britain Parade through York, and a flypast at York Minster. The parade was led by Squadron Leader Craig Goodwin and I led the flypast over the Minster. A nice touch by Craig was to march the whole parade, complete with the Band, around the married quarters at Linton for the benefit of the families before heading off to York. He was posted soon afterwards, but not before I arranged to take over his very elderly service bicycle. Within a few weeks, that bike would take on a life and character all of its own.

The new squadron commander for 2 Squadron was Squadron Leader Rod Wren, a former 1 FTS instructor who had spent some months running the Ground Training Squadron. One Friday afternoon, I came out of Wing HQ to head for Happy Hour. I looked for my bike in vain. The bicycle shed outside Wing HQ was empty. Surely no one would 'borrow' the CI's bike? Within a minute or two, Rod came out from his office. He was smiling nervously and said that he was confident that the bike would be returned 'within a few days'.

'Ah,' I said, 'I'm going back into my office for five minutes. Just make sure that when I get back there is a bicycle for me to get to Happy Hour.'

When I got back, Rod was wearing an even bigger smile and presented me with a temporary bicycle. It was more like a mountain bike, with very wide handlebars, but I could hardly refuse it. It was quite tricky riding to the Mess, especially with my briefcase held by one hand on top of the handlebars. It was even more difficult trying to get home after Happy Hour!

A week later I was chairing the weekly Wing Execs meeting. As the progress of every student was discussed, these meetings could easily last for a couple of hours and the Wing HQ staff fielded all calls to avoid the meeting being interrupted. It came as some surprise to everyone, except perhaps to Rod, when there was a loud knock on the door halfway through the meeting.

The door slowly opened and in came two students from 2 Squadron. They were dressed in the white jackets used by stewards in the Officers' Mess and they carried a large pot of tea and a dozen cups and saucers. They then brought in my bicycle. It was unbelievable, and it was met with laughter from everyone. It had been completely repainted and rather well, if not completely to my taste. If I was being generous, I could describe the colours as red, white and blue, except that the red was a little pinkish while the blue verged on the turquoise. But it was very striking. A well fitted piece of plywood was inset within the bicycle frame, and on each side it bore the 1 FTS crest and the letters 'CI 1 FTS'. The pink carnation attached to the front handlebars was also rather sweet.

So I now had a new mode of transport and there was no way that I could not be seen to use it. During formal functions in the Officers' Mess, the Station Execs' service vehicles would be lined up in the named reserved car parking spaces opposite the front door. There would be the Station Commander's car complete with his flag on the front, then the cars of the Officer Commanding Operations Wing, the Officer Commanding Administrative Wing, the Senior Medical Officer, the Contract Manager and what was that in the gap in the middle? That was the CI's bike of course!

In some ways the bicycle was exactly what was needed at that time. Life was very tense for many of our students and the bicycle perhaps showed a lighter side, that perhaps the CI didn't take himself too seriously, or at least not all of the time. Soon everyone on the station began to react positively to the sight of me on my bike and invariably it brought a smile to their faces and a wave of recognition. After one Happy Hour, I came out of the Mess to find an empty space where I had left my bike. But it hadn't gone far; it was gently swinging from one of the hanging baskets above the front entrance. After Dining-in nights, the bicycle would invariably find its way into the bar where students would have wheel-changing competitions. And then it was kidnapped. It disappeared after another Happy Hour and by Monday morning there was still no sign of it. In the mail that morning there was a ransom note. Letters had been cut from newspapers to read, 'Deliver two crates of beer behind Station HQ by 1200 hours on Thursday or your bike gets it.'

Suspecting that the culprit came from one of the basic courses, I summoned OC Ground Training Squadron, Squadron Leader Dave Lewis. If anyone had his finger on the pulse, it was Dave. I simply told him to find the bike.

Within twenty-four hours, Dave reported back. The bike had been 'kidnapped' by the Naval Staff Officer who worked for Barry Kirby. The bike was in the Naval Staff Officer's garage, and while both he and his wife were out at work, it was secretly removed and then hidden in my locked garage. I then enlisted the support of our daughter, Hannah, who completed a much more professional ransom note in colour – 'Either the bike is returned unharmed by 1200 hours on Thursday or you get it.'

I wish that I had been in the Naval Staff Officer's office the next morning when his mail arrived. Apparently he exited at great speed and headed home only to find his garage completely empty! He was left to fret for a few hours and duly paid the penalty in Black Sheep ale at the next Happy Hour.

*   *   *

Such light hearted incidents were a welcome feature of life at Linton, but they could not completely take the edge of the realities of flying training at the time. With the students spending ten months at Linton, the staff got to know each course member very well and it became increasingly difficult to recommend so many for suspension, especially when it was abundantly clear that a year earlier, or a few years later, they would have made the grade and gone on to earn their RAF wings.

It was my job to suspend. If it became clear that a student was not progressing sufficiently well to achieve fast-jet entry standard, then an internal squadron process was initiated to ensure that the student received continuity of instruction; usually there would be also be a change of instructor. The process would usually begin if a student failed a flying test. The student would be placed on Review in order to highlight the problem and the staff would try and rectify any weaknesses. Review was a process with which I was very familiar from my own pilot training and from my instructor course in 1979. The process would often culminate in a Senior Supervisor's Check. This could be flown with me, my deputy, or with one of the squadron commanders, but not the student's own squadron commander. If the student did not achieve the standard necessary then he was recommended for suspension from training and his flight commander would start the lengthy process that was necessary to terminate the individual's flying career. This was never an easy undertaking, but the process was designed to ensure that the student had been given every opportunity to reach the standard required.

The suspension paperwork would review the student's career to date, and then give a detailed account of the flying completed on the course. All aspects would be covered, including strengths as well as weaknesses. Once the flight commander had completed his task, the squadron commander would then review the report adding his own comments and recommendation. It would then come to me and I would interview the student. I would read the complete report out and the student would then be given a copy for him, or her, to consider before returning it later with any comments that they wished to make.

These interviews were always difficult, and sometimes emotional. The report would go to the Station Commander for his comments before being forwarded to the Training Group HQ. Once there, it would be reviewed by a range of staff officers until it reached the Air Officer Commanding who would confirm, or not, the suspension. Sadly, during my time in post I completed many dozens of such interviews. In only one case, was my recommendation for suspension overruled and the student was reinstated. He was suspended for a second and final time a few weeks later.

*   *   *

At the end of the summer the JEFTS contract was awarded. The new company would commence work in January 1993 and take over all elementary flying training on 1 July 1993. While we recognized that this would be a challenge, our aim was to make JEFTS a success and try to arrange as seamless a transfer as possible from the existing training arrangements. We also realized that trying to 'marry' the civilian flying rules with military flying regulations, as the new squadron would be under military command and control, would be a challenge.

Civilian registered aircraft were not allowed to fly within 500 feet of anything on the ground so low flying and navigation at 250 feet was out. This had been an important part of the RNEFTS syllabus as it was one of the few areas within their syllabus where a student's capacity could be looked at closely. At the speed at which the Bulldog flew, as well as its successor the T67 Slingsby Firefly, navigation at 500 feet was relatively simple. The RN in particular needed to identify as early as possible which students had the capacity for potential single-seat fast-jet flying on the Sea Harrier, and low flying and low-level navigation had been an ideal vehicle to make that assessment.

I was under remit, and so was Linton's Station Commander, to make JEFTS a success, but rumour had it that the winning company's bid was less than half of that made by the nearest rival. If that was true, I sincerely hoped that the RAF had got itself a bargain. In January 1993 the new manager arrived, and over the next few months we held many meetings to try and ensure that the transfer from RNEFTS to JEFTS would be as smooth as possible. And it seemed as if we were making progress. I did have some concerns about the rate at which aircraft were being delivered, and even the planned rate began to fall behind schedule. I flew my first trip in the Firefly on 4 March, and qualified as an instructor on 6 May. It seemed a fine aircraft.

In anticipation of the new and enlarged task at Topcliffe, and following the retirement of Roy Turgoose, I split the Flying Training Wing into two parts, each headed by a Deputy Chief Instructor: DCI (Basic) was Squadron Leader Mark Heaton at Linton, and DCI (Elementary) was Lieutenant Commander David Bomby, based permanently at Topcliffe.

*   *   *

One of the more unusual tasks that we were given in May 1993 was in support of Tornado F3s from RAF Leeming, who were about to be deployed to Italy in support of ongoing operations in the Balkans; we were to act as relatively slow speed targets for the F3s to intercept, and escort to an airfield. This was practiced at low-level in the Pennines to the west of Leeming, and the difference in speeds made this quite a challenge for the Tornados which operated in pairs against a single Tucano. While they could have taken a 'shot' relatively easily, that is what they had to avoid doing.

The F3s had to intercept us, and then control us in such a way that we would have little choice but to go in the direction that they wanted, and land at their base. This was great fun and I often took great pleasure in trying to break away when one Tornado had overtaken us because of its much higher speed, while the other was not quite in a position to 'cover' us from the rear. These sorties took place on and off throughout the summer and they were very valuable for the Tornado crews who would be faced with slow-moving aircraft in the Balkans.

*   *   *

During the months leading up to the retirement of the Jet Provost, we had been planning how to mark the event. Shortly before leaving the RAF one of the standards instructors liaised with Coalport, who produced an excellent limited edition of plates showing a Jet Provost overhead Linton. On the reverse of the plates were the unit badges of all the RAF flying schools which had operated the Jet Provost. With my Linton callsign as 02, No. 2/5000 had to be the one for me!

Throughout May we also practised some slightly unusual formation flying for the formal date set for the retirement of the Jet Provost, 20 May 1993. The Guest of Honour would be Air Vice-Marshal Coville. We planned to fly a formation over the airfield in the shape of the letters 'J' and 'P'. Mark Heaton was nominated as the overall formation leader and would lead the 'P' with me flying alongside him in line abreast. The squadron commander of Standards Squadron, Dave 'Cutty' Cuthbertson, would lead the 'J'.

All of the rehearsals went well and the plan was to arrive over the saluting dais from the north-west. A number of photographs were taken during the rehearsals, which was just as well as 20 May was a grey day and the forecast was for a gradually reducing cloud base with an increasing likelihood of rain. While the forecast was marginal, it looked as if the very poor weather would hold off until about midday, so we all got airborne and formed up as we headed north-west. Timing had to be to the second, and, as we turned for the final time to commence our run, all looked good. Then the cloud began to lower.

So we had to descend. In descending we began to accelerate, which we could not afford to do, otherwise we would have been much too early. We did not have enough time to turn around nor could such an unwieldy formation jink very much to the left or right to lose time. All Mark Heaton could do was to very gently throttle back, but this had to be done so carefully as speed changes tended to cascade back down the formation making it very difficult to hang on. It was harder for the formation alongside us and especially for those aircraft flying in line astern. We got lower and lower. Something had to give. And it did. It was Cutty. He simply said that he could no longer stay with us and he descended even lower to accelerate and make his formation more manageable before diverging away from us to the west. What a disaster I thought, but Cutty had no choice if he was to safely retain the integrity of his formation.

I could see all of this unfold as I was on the port side of Mark as the 'J' began to move away. If we continued Air Vice-Marshal Coville would be over flown by a 'P' only, which would have been awful. We were within seconds of calling the whole thing off when Cutty called that he was coming back in but he needed the formation leader to give him another ten knots. There he was, just skirting below low stratus cloud to the west moving closer and ever closer toward us. But we were also getting closer and closer to the airfield. Would the formation be back together before we reached the airfield boundary? Thankfully the weather helped. On the ground it had begun to rain heavily and the visibility was much reduced. Most people had sought shelter, but Air Vice-Marshal Coville and the Station Commander remained to take the salute, albeit with umbrellas raised.

The 'JP' arrived exactly on time, in perfect formation, albeit significantly lower than planned. This had been a huge test of the character and professionalism of both Cutty and Mark but neither had been found wanting. With no photographs on the day, it was left to one of the Officers' Mess Honorary Members, Norman Appleton, to recreate the event in an excellent oil painting which captured the atmosphere of the day and the low threatening grey cloud as a backdrop to a very good piece of formation flying. Well done, Mark Heaton and Cutty Cuthbertson and to all of those instructors who hung on so well 'down the back'! The first day cover commemorating the farewell to the Jet Provost and signed by all of the instructors flying in the formation was also a great memento of the day.

* * *

Three weeks later, on 8 June, Air Vice-Marshal Coville was back at Linton on a beautiful bright blue day, this time for the Annual Formal Inspection of the station, and we were able to show him that the introduction of Tucano was complete with a first class series of formation flypasts of Tucanos in 'Diamond 9' formation.

* * *

On 17 June, Lieutenant Commander Jock Gunning, AFC, paraded RNEFTS for the final time. The squadron's disbandment included a flypast by a single Bulldog flown by Mike Wherrett with me in the other seat. Mike and I had been colleagues on the Refresher Flying Squadron at Leeming and he had been the Jet Provost aerobatic pilot in 1982.

Final preparations were well in hand for JEFTS to take over the elementary task and indications were that this was on track. There had been no significant problems during the six month work up period, although there were some concerns about the rate of aircraft delivery. JEFTS formally took over on 1 July 1993.

At midday on the first day I received a call from Jock, who was the Duty Senior Supervisor, advising me that JEFTS no longer recognized his authority at Topcliffe. I suggested that there must have been a misunderstanding, but there was not. Nor was anyone from JEFTS willing to speak to me on the telephone. What to do?

There had been no hint that this would be an issue; quite the reverse in fact, the role of Duty Senior Supervisors both military and civilian was one area of operations where I thought that we had complete agreement. The Station Commander, Tom Eeles, was on leave and Air Vice-Marshal Coville was away, so I spoke to his deputy who sounded sympathetic. When he asked what action I intended, I said that unless the JEFTS was prepared to accept 1 FTS's authority over its operations, I had little choice but to cease flying at Topcliffe until the matter could be resolved. I asked if he would approve of such a decision.

'I would not wish to interfere with the decisions of the man on the spot,' was his answer.

I therefore directed Jock to close RAF Topcliffe. The matter was resolved following a meeting at Linton. However, such a crisis on Day One of the contract did not bode well.

*   *   *

The months ahead saw increasing difficulties. Problems ranged from the sublime to the ridiculous.

The civilian instructors were offered Officers' Mess membership as it was assumed that some would wish to attend the formal graduation ceremonies of their own students, to which families and friends were invited. These functions took the form of a formal silver-service luncheon followed by speeches, the announcement of prize winners, and photographs. These were good occasions and the 'formality' added something that was enjoyed and remembered. When it was mentioned that to attend such ceremonies, the JEFTS staff would need to wear a jacket and tie the response was that only the local manager had been provided with a company jacket. This was therefore 'swopped' around so that one, and only one, of the company's instructors could attend each graduation.

There were also issues concerning the manning of air traffic control at Topcliffe which was a JEFTS responsibility.

Increasingly, because of insufficient aircraft, JEFTS began to fall behind the task which would have a serious and knock-on impact on the flying training pipeline for both the RAF and the RN. This was referred to as falling behind 'the line' – the line being the rate at which sorties had to be achieved to make a fixed course graduation date.

As the situation gradually worsened the RAF was asked if RAF Topcliffe could be opened at weekends so that JEFTS could try and catch up on the task. I discussed this with Tom Eeles and with staff at the Training Group HQ. The contract was very clear on this point: weekend flying was specifically excluded as it would involve significant costs which would fall to the RAF. Air Traffic Control approach services would need to be provided from Linton, fire and medical cover would also have to be laid on, and there would be an impact on catering and transport. If JEFTS had fallen behind the task because of prolonged adverse weather then we may have been able to get approval for weekend flying. But the situation was different. The Training Group directed that JEFTS be advised that RAF Topcliffe would not be opened at weekends. We were accused of being 'inflexible' and of putting obstacles in the way of the JEFTS.

The Station Commander was required to submit a report after the contract had been running for six months. The report included inputs from the Officer Commanding Operations Wing who had serious concerns about operations at Topcliffe. The problems that we had been experiencing were well known within the Training Group and the HQ staff eagerly awaited the report which they asked to be delivered by hand; they would then pass it on to Air Vice-Marshal Coville.

In giving substance to what we had been saying for months, we also wanted to make it clear how hard we had been working to negotiate our way through a minefield in our determination to make JEFTS a success. The end result had to be balanced and objective. Both the Commander-in-Chief and Air Vice-Marshal Coville were fully supportive of our efforts, although we were aware that by the time the report arrived on Air Vice-Marshal Coville's desk it would have been 'staffed' throughout his HQ. The completed report was to be delivered to RAF Wyton by air during a training sortie and it was then meant to be taken to the Training Group Air Staff at nearby RAF Brampton.

Squadron Leader 'Cutty' Cuthbertson duly delivered the JEFTS report and he was back at Linton shortly after midday on the day in question. I gave the matter little thought until I got a call from the Air Staff during the afternoon saying that they hadn't received the report. I telephoned Cutty to see if there had been a problem.

'No,' he said. 'I handed it over this morning.'

'But I've just had a call from Air Staff,' I said. 'They haven't got it. Who did you give it to?'

'I gave it to the AOC,' said Cutty.

'You did WHAT!' I exclaimed. 'Didn't you realize that it had to go to the Air Staff first?'

'Sir,' said Cutty, 'I didn't have a choice. When I got out of the aircraft at Wyton, Air Vice-Marshal Coville was there to meet me and he asked for the report there and then.'

So Chris Coville had pre-empted the manoeuvres of his own staff and took the report home. The following Monday, his staff were probably faced with a number of questions.

During the months that followed things began to get a little easier with JEFTS. For my part, I genuinely tried to be as flexible as possible in order to make the introduction of JEFTS a success. I had no 'axe to grind' and was not in any way against the principle of contractorisation. But there was one aspect on which I would not compromise; and that was the safe supervision of flying training within 1 FTS. Nevertheless, I would be accused of 'micro management' by some who were well remote from our operations.

*   *   *

One part of the course enjoyed by staff and students alike didn't involve flying at all. This was the Leadership and Survival Training undertaken by each course near Otterburn in Northumberland. This lasted about four days and covered such things as map-reading by day and night, building survival shelters, and constructing ground to air signals to effect a 'rescue' by helicopter. Whenever possible a 22 Squadron Search and Rescue Sea King helicopter would fly in to winch our 'survivors' aboard. This was good training for their crews as well as for our students. The night exercise was always great fun with the students trying to cover a set route without being intercepted and caught by the staff armed with thunder flashes and flares. Often British Army units would also try to capture our young 'evaders'.

The staff stayed in a farmhouse high up in the Cheviot Hills. I never met the sheep farmer but his wife, Mary, was well known and loved by everyone for the most amazing breakfasts that really could last the day.

After one exercise, Terry Stone, our civilian manager who ran Engineering and Supply Wing, came to see me. All engineering and supply functions at Linton had been contractorised since the late 1980s and Terry was the Manager for Airwork Services Ltd. Terry was popular and highly regarded and a key senior executive on the station. About a year after I left Linton, I met Terry again at Buckingham Palace. He was being appointed as a MBE, an award that he had been recommended for by Linton's Station Commander, Tom Eeles.

I got on very well with Terry, but on this particular morning he was very serious as he came into my office and closed the door behind him; this was most unusual. He then also closed the connecting door into my deputy's office, so I knew that all was not well. He explained that the Safety Equipment Section had been going through all of the equipment that the latest course of students had been using during their Land Survival Training (LST). In one of the dinghy packs they had found some small self-sealing packets containing a green/brown tobacco-like substance. I looked on in horror as he took one of the packets out of his pocket and passed it across to me.

'What do you think it is?' I asked.

'I have no idea,' said Terry. 'What do you think it is?'

'I have no idea either,' I said.

Terry went on to say that a lot of this substance had been found but only within one dinghy pack. He also said that all of the staff within the Safety Equipment Section were aware of the discovery.

Terry left me with a few of the packets and I set off to see our resident RAF Police Sergeant to identify the substance. I explained the circumstances and handed over one of the bags.

'What do you think it is?' he asked.

'I have no idea,' I said. 'What do you think it is?'

'I have no idea either,' he said.

He said that we had no choice but to seek specialist help by informing HQ Provost and Security Services based at RAF Newton in Nottinghamshire. I told him to do that and left with one packet to go and spoil Tom Eeles' day. The impact of an RAF Police investigation into possible drug use at an RAF flying training school would be disastrous and long lasting. When I got into Tom's office, and explained the situation, his face noticeably lost colour. I then passed one of the packets across to him.

'What do you think it is?' he asked.

'I have no idea,' I said. 'What do you think it is?'

'I have no idea either,' Tom said.

The following day rumours were rife on the station that something pretty serious was going on and that 'the Feds' had been called in. By midday the police had arrived and I eagerly awaited their decision on what was in the bags. The police personnel were unable to identify the substance so it was left to the expert to determine the nature of this 'controlled substance'. The expert was the drug dog, a delightful Springer Spaniel. The bag was hidden in a room and then the dog was sent in. After a while she came out again, the police packed everything up and got ready to leave.

'But what is it?' I asked.

'We have no idea,' was the reply. 'But it is definitely not a controlled substance; otherwise the dog would have found it. She didn't, so we are off!'

'But, what do you think it is?' I pleaded.

'We've no idea,' was the reply.

With that they left the station, leaving me with a number of self-sealing bags with a green/brown tobacco-like substance inside.

That afternoon the twelve members of the course concerned were assembled in one of Ground Training Squadron's classrooms. They all sprang to attention as I arrived. They looked very worried. There were eleven RAF officers and one RN officer. I explained what had been found and then held up one of the bags so that they all could see. I then asked if anyone recognized the substance. There were eleven looks of concern, and eleven rapid shakes of the head. There was one look of mild recognition. It came from the young RN officer.

'I think that it may be mine Sir,' she said.

'Really,' I said, 'and what exactly is it?'

'It's herbal tea Sir!'

*   *   *

One morning after night flying, the Senior Air Traffic Control Officer at Linton asked for an urgent meeting. The previous night, controllers had become alarmed when they were controlling one of the solo students. On the radar screen, they saw another aircraft closing on the solo student who was in Linton's radar pattern flying under their direction. The solo student was unable to see the other aircraft; the suspicion being that it was flying without lights. The other aircraft got closer and closer until, in the controller's opinion, it was flying in close formation on the solo student. The solo student still could not see the other aircraft.

After a few minutes the other aircraft turned away and it was continually tracked by another controller. Eventually, this mystery aircraft called up for a recovery to Linton. The call sign indicated that it was a Linton Jet Provost being flown by an instructor, and it was the aircraft designated to stay airborne as the weather check aircraft, in other words the crew were to watch for any deterioration in the weather while solo students were airborne. What had occurred was inexcusable and unpardonable. Night close formation flying was something only practiced on operational squadrons after careful training. It was not something that could ever be sanctioned at Linton. For an instructor to switch off his aircraft's external lights and then to close on an unsuspecting solo student was beyond belief.

It took very little time to identify the crew concerned, two instructors from the same squadron. The aircraft captain was a young flying officer, a first tourist instructor with very limited experience. Sitting alongside him was his Deputy Flight Commander, the very same instructor whom I had warned nearly a year earlier. In normal circumstances, the Deputy Flight Commander, as the senior instructor, would have been the aircraft captain, but on this occasion he was not current to fly at night; he therefore had to fly with another instructor in order to regain night currency and the weather check aircraft was ideal for this purpose.

The squadron commander concerned quickly established the facts but there was little that the crew could say to excuse what they had done. They refused to admit whose idea it had been, simply saying that they had decided that the solo student had been doing something that he shouldn't; they had therefore decided to switch their lights off and close up to have a look. Horrendous!

In fact the student concerned had been doing exactly what he had been told to do by air traffic control. How to deal with this took some thought. The responsibility for the action undoubtedly lay with the aircraft captain even though he was the junior instructor. But whose idea had it been? There was no way of being certain without an admission, but one was not forthcoming. However, the more senior instructor was a deputy flight commander; he was not simply a passenger. He could have stopped such an act instantly. At the very least he had been complicit in what was potentially an extremely dangerous situation. I advised the Station Commander of what I intended and he concurred.

I decided to give the aircraft captain a formal written warning and would ensure that for the remainder of his tour he would be very closely monitored and supervised. But the deputy flight commander had lost my trust and I was no longer prepared to accept him as a member of my staff. I submitted an adverse report under Queen's Regulations and directed that he leave the station with immediate effect pending formal posting to a new appointment.

Training Group staff said that I couldn't deal with the deputy flight commander more severely than the aircraft captain but I disagreed. The Air Officer Commanding, however, supported the report and further directed the permanent removal of the individual's instructor qualification. I believed at the time, and still do, that the measures taken were both necessary and fair. The first tourist pilot went on to complete a satisfactory tour but he later had a troubled career and left the RAF. The other pilot continued flying in other roles. Unfortunately he was killed in an aircraft accident some years later.

*   *   *

Tom Eeles and I enjoyed a very good working relationship. It had been fortunate that we had been able to get to know one another during my ten months at Brampton and this had paid dividends at Linton. Within the first few days of arriving, Tom and I ended up in the bar and we were both regulars at Happy Hour. Many of the other Mess members were surprised to see us so often having a beer and a laugh together as this was not the sort of relationship that they had witnessed previously. Occasionally, we would also 'call' on one another and walk the mile or so down to the nearby village of Newton-on-Ouse for a pint or two on our own in the Dawnay Arms, a very pleasant and popular former eighteenth century coaching inn on the bank of the River Ouse.

In those days Newton was also very well known for the annual 'Newton Feast' which was a grand affair held on the Green opposite the Dawnay Arms, and on either side of the beautiful and aptly named Cherrytree Avenue. An ox would be barbequed on the Green and stalls would be set on

e and Jackie at the Summer Ball at RAF Luqa, Malta 1976.

Provost 5a from the Refresher ing Squadron, RAF Leeming, 81. (*Alan Rayment*)

Jet Provost 5a from th
Refresher Flying
Squadron, RAF
Leeming, 1981. Teessi
is in the distance.
(*Alan Rayment*)

Meteor Mk 7 WF791
of the Vintage Pair.
(*Mike Hall*)

The Vintage Pair.
(*Mike Hall*)

The Vintage Pair over the White Horse, North Yorkshire Moors 1980. (*UK MOD*)

The Strathallan 5-ship, 12 July 1980. (*Derek Ferguson*)

Me with Jackie, Matthew and Hannah, shortly before displayi[ng] the Vintage Pair at Teesside Air Show, 22 August 1981.

Tornado GR1 of 20 Squadron RAF Laarbruch over Northern Germany, 1985. (*UK MOD*)

very capable warrior: Mike Smith flying Tornado GR1 'BK' of 14 Squadron 1988. (*UK MOD*)

ɔ. 14 Squadron officers, including Eric, 1986. I am standing in the centre, ninth from the right, next
Eric. Jeremy Payne is standing and is sixth from the right. (*UK MOD*)

One of each: The Bruggen Squadrons, 1986, GR1s of 9, 14, 17 and 31 Squadrons. (*UK MOD*)

Winged Warriors: 'The Bruggen Wing 40', 1986. (*The Fincherfiles / Photographers International*)

'Can you go a little lower?' Red Flag, November 1987; crew: Paul McDonald and Jeremy Payne. (*Jeremy Payne*)

Turning toward the Initial Point during Red Flag, November 1987; crew: Paul McDonald and Jeremy Payne. (*Jeremy Payne*)

Over a ridge during Red Flag, November 1987; crew: Paul McDonald and Jeremy Payne.
(*Jeremy Payne*)

Happier Days, Tornado GR1 'B' of 14 Squadron over the Aegean Sea en route from Gioia del Colle to RAF Akrotiri, Cyprus, February 1986; crew: Mike Napier and Doug Steer.
(*Michael Napier; photo taken by the late Ian Grieve*)

Me and 'my favourite rear', Jeremy Payne, with 'BM' September 1988; all thanks to Mike Smith.

Flying with Red 1, Cyprus, 24 April 1991.

Provost Mk 3 display
craft of No. 1 Flying Training
ool, RAF Linton-on-Ouse
3. Note the White Rose of
rkshire emblem on the
gine intakes and the crest on
fins. (*UK MOD*)

hite Rose over Wensleydale':
Tucano of No. 1 Flying
Training School, RAF Linton-
on-Ouse. (*UK MOD*)

e Linton Wing 1992: sixteen
Provosts leading three of the
st Linton Tucanos, 1992.
K MOD)

Leading a Diamond Nine of Tucanos over the Battle of Britain Parade as it approaches the dais outside York Minster, 19 September 1993. (*UK MOD*)

ɔ. 1 Flying Training School 75th Anniversary Flypast crews, 17 July 1994. (*UK MOD*)

ading the 75th Anniversary Flypast over the International Air Day at RAF Church Fenton,
July 1994. (*UK MOD*)

Two generations,
RAF College Cranwell,
October 2002. (*Kamara Photo*

UK Senior National Representative,
HQ AIRNORTH, Ramstein 2002.

ack on blue: Tucano Mk 1 ZF491 of No. 1 Flying Training School, RAF Linton-on-Ouse.
offrey Lee, Planefocus Ltd)

good company; Tucanos in display livery with a Battle of Britain Memorial Flight Spitfire.
offrey Lee, Planefocus Ltd)

Me, Matthew and Dionne, following flights in a Vigilant ZH146 of 642 Volunteer Gliding Squadron at Linton, 16 April 2011. (*Matthew McDonald*)

A very special birthday: flying with Matthew in Vigilant ZH146 of 642 Volunteer Gliding Squadron 16 April 2011. Linton's Runway 21 is on the left. (*Matthew McDonald*)

either side of the road leading down past the Blacksmiths Arms which eventually led to Beningborough Hall.

A raft race would also be held from Linton Lock to Newton and entries would be submitted from lots of local organizations. There were normally half a dozen entries from Linton and the RN contingent could always be relied upon to come up with an unusual 'vessel'. There were always lifeguards and scuba-divers on hand just in case anyone got into difficulties. While there were lots of 'difficulties', these were rarely of a safety nature as crew members and friends attempted to sabotage one another's vessels midstream. They would then have to dock near the Dawnay Arms and sprint up and around a course amidst the many families enjoying the afternoon, before returning to their boats to cross the river for the final time. Then one of the crew members would scramble up the steep muddy bank to ring a bell at the top which marked the end of the race. The bank would become increasingly muddier on account of the chap at the top with the hose pipe directing a very powerful jet of water on the participants below.

The Newton Feast was a wonderful and memorable village event enjoyed by everyone. But then Risk Assessments were invented, and that sadly was the end of the raft race. The Feast continued for a few years afterwards, but as often happens in villages, it was 'the few' who did the work and once they moved on, or retired, there were insufficient to take their places. So the Newton Feast only lives on in the memories of those of us who were lucky enough to enjoy it.

Tom also continually encouraged me to upgrade my instructor category to A1. While this would be a good personal achievement, I didn't think that it would improve how I did my job; if anything the significant work-up to attempt recategorization would probably be quite a distraction, so I declined to take up his suggestion. Tom was an A1 instructor and a dedicated and talented aviator and was doing all that he could to 'fill his boots' with as much flying as he could get before the end of what was likely to be his final flying tour in the RAF. He was well on his way to achieving 6,000 flying hours, a remarkable achievement for a senior officer with a fast-jet background. Often I would be sitting in the office when the phone would ring and then there would be that cheery voice, 'Ah, CI' he would say. 'How about you and me getting airborne?'

This would usually occur on a Friday afternoon when the weather was pretty grim. Instructional flying would probably have ceased as little could be achieved. In other words, the weather would be perfect for Tom! Invariably we would be airborne in some horrid thick cloud and, while I was flying the aircraft, he would close the throttle and say, 'The engine's failed. What are you going to do about it?'

Even air traffic control would be slightly taken aback as a Tucano or Jet Provost came hurtling into the circuit from a radar forced landing approach in conditions that were well below the normal minima. Then they realized that the call sign was LOP 01 and they understood; it was 'the Staish'!

* * *

Tom didn't intend to do anything to mark the achievement of his 6,000 hours, but during the weeks leading up to it he must have mentioned it to me every other day. On the day in question, he got airborne in a Tucano for a solo sortie. There was no fanfare and as he wondered out to his aircraft he occasionally glanced over his shoulder. But there was nothing, no one around to mark the occasion. When he got back, things were a little different.

As he taxied clear of the runway he was met by all of the fire vehicles, which escorted his aircraft back to a lonely spot on Linton's wide dispersal. He spotted me, dressed as a fireman, manning one of the large powerful water jets mounted on top of one of the crash vehicles. Tom knew exactly what to expect! Once he was clear of the aircraft he was warmly congratulated by staff and students alike, all gathered at the rear of his aircraft. He was then escorted and left exposed in front of the aircraft where he was duly 'fired upon' by the fire tenders. A vehicle then arrived complete with a trailer on which a seat was firmly mounted high up. A very wet Station Commander was then liberally sprinkled with feathers! After that he was towed around his station before being deposited at his home. A video of the whole affair was taken by one of the students, but when Tom asked me for a copy I apologized and said that the student had totally screwed it up and it was completely blank. His reply was so very typical of Tom.

'Typical,' he said.

Of course the student hadn't screwed it up at all; I had plans for that video.

* * *

On 19 September 1993, I lead a 'Diamond 9' of Tucanos over the Battle of Britain Parade and Service at York Minster. Two days later there was a much smaller and very poignant and personal ceremony in Linton village at a small memorial in front of the village hall. The memorial had been erected in memory of the Canadian crews who were killed on operations flying from Linton during the Second World War. Each year some of the crews, accompanied by members of their families, would make the long journey to visit the places that had meant so much to them, and to remember friends, such very young friends, lost so long ago. That year was no exception, and a number of Canadians intended to take part in a very short service of remembrance. I planned to mark the occasion by a single aircraft flypast in a lone Jet Provost Mark 5, one of the very last at Linton, and this was my last sortie from Linton in a Jet Provost.

Accompanying me was Group Captain David Wardill. David was one of a rare breed of RAF engineering officers who had also completed an RAF pilot's course, flying aircraft ranging from the Hastings to the Gnat, on which he served as an instructor. He had previously commanded RAF Newton in Nottinghamshire, and when he retired from the RAF in 1991, he moved to Newton-on-Ouse. Like so many retired RAF pilots, David continued to 'give back' as a reservist by flying air cadets, and he flew with No. 11 AEF at RAF Leeming for the next ten years.

For our flypast on 21 September 1993, we approached the memorial from the east, from the direction of Newton-on-Ouse, flying down the main road. Having dived down, we reached close to 350 knots. As we approached Linton, I could see the group in front of the memorial; I closed the throttle so that the flypast was almost silent and as we cleared the village to the west I pulled up and climbed vertically before disappearing into cloud. Even though the flypast only involved one aircraft, it was I hope, an appropriate salute to the crews of 408 (Goose) Squadron and 426 (Thunderbird) Squadron, RCAF.

* * *

On 30 November I flew to RAF Aldergrove in Northern Ireland for an overnight stop and this proved to be one of the more unusual and fascinating trips that I had ever done. It also gave me a glimpse into a world, a very dangerous and demanding world, one that I had only seen during brief news bulletins. The suggestion for the trip came from the new Boss of 1 Squadron, Squadron Leader Mike Longstaff, who had served in Northern Ireland flying Puma helicopters with 230 Squadron. I had met him previously when he was a student on a refresher at Leeming.

I knew little about support helicopter operations and, as some of our students were now able to move down the rotary route once more, Mike suggested that a visit and night stop could be a good way for me to gain an insight into the world in which our rotary colleagues operated. I am sure he was not influenced in any way by the 230 Squadron Guest Night that was due to take place on the evening we arrived, and to which we had been invited.

We flew to Aldergrove in a Tucano so that while I gained some experience in a Puma, Mike could fly some of the helicopter pilots in the Tucano, a type new to many of them. On arrival, the Officer Commanding 230 Squadron took me off for a very thorough briefing about his squadron's role; this then developed into a detailed sortie brief. The plan was to get airborne during the afternoon and complete some general handling and low flying which would include pinpoint landing exercises in the nearby mountains. We would then land at the British Army base at Crossmaglen which was very much in the heart of what was considered at the time to be the 'bandit country' of South Armagh. After an hour or so we would return to RAF Aldergrove at night. For that sortie we would be wearing night vision goggles.

Most of the sortie preparation was fairly routine, not dissimilar to that which I had undertaken during my tours on Tornados. The weather was considered before outlining the plan and then there was the intelligence brief.

We then went to the Operations Room for the out brief with the Duty Authorizing Officer. He was a flight lieutenant and he briefed his Squadron Commander, which is an entirely normal aspect of RAF flying supervision. It was at that point that for me everything changed, and so did my perspective of what we were about to do.

'Now go and get your body armour, and the ammunition for your personal weapons,' said the Authorizing Officer.

That brought me out of the 'normal' mode into which I had lapsed.

What we were about to do contained significantly more risk than the training sorties which had filled my flying career up until that point. But for the crews of 230 Squadron and the other squadrons that operated in Northern Ireland, this was normal. As we clambered into our aircraft I was astounded by the size of the heavy machine gun mounted on the floor with its long belts of ammunition. The flight sergeant crewman in the rear cabin oozed competence. I did my best to wear a calm facade.

I thoroughly enjoyed trying to get to grips with the very different way that helicopters are flown. I found that trying to establish a hover, with one wheel touching a rocky ledge out of sight to one side, and only the calm voice of the crewman to act as a guide, was fascinating and very demanding.

Soon, we were off to Crossmaglen for an 'operational' approach and rapid landing, as attacks against helicopters by small arms fire were not infrequent. We were met by a British Army major and escorted quickly into their briefing facility where we were afforded VIP treatment.

I listened and watched fascinated, as one of the most interesting briefings that I had ever heard unfolded. In front of us was a huge scale model of a wide area of South Armagh, and we were then taken through a minute-by-minute account of a very complex attack by the Provisional IRA against a police patrol. The locations of the various vehicles and the routes that they followed were described, as was each of the IRA's fire points. How, and where, the British Army units and RAF helicopters responded was also covered. It was almost like a scene from a film made even more interesting, as I could recall some aspects of what had occurred from news bulletins a few weeks earlier. But this was very much the real thing, without any of the caveats that so often limited news bulletins. It was a privilege to be given such access and such an insight into what was happening on the ground in Northern Ireland on a day-to-day basis.

No sooner had the briefing ended and we crewed into our aircraft in the dark for our sortie back to Aldergrove wearing night vision goggles. The Squadron Guest Night was a tremendous way to round off what had been a very valuable visit. Within a few years Mike Longstaff would return to 1 FTS as Chief Instructor, and a few years after that he would command Linton.

*   *   *

Major decisions were being made throughout the UK's armed forces as a result of the strategic defence review stemming from Options for Change and the collapse of the USSR and the Warsaw Pact. A number of Defence Cost Studies were undertaken looking at every area of activity. Not surprisingly, these studies were about making savings. Reviewing how and why we do things is often worthwhile and there is often a good case for change, for efficiency as well as to save money. Whenever I asked the question 'why do we do things this way?' and got the response 'we've always done it this way', it was usually time for a close look.

There were significant improvements that could be made within flying training, but it also began to appear to many that the Defence Cost Study into flying training, and especially into pilot training, risked 'throwing the baby out with the bathwater'. Were there some 'closed minds' at work or what is sometimes referred to as 'situating the appreciation' rather than 'appreciating the situation'?

The AOC, Air Vice-Marshal Chris Coville, strongly supported by many HQ and Unit staff proposed an alternative to the Defence Cost Study into flying training; it was called Future Flying Training. This better solution afforded similar savings and it was accepted by the MOD. This resulted in 1 FTS becoming a Basic Fast-jet Flying Training School, with our throughput being destined primarily for advanced flying training on the Hawk at RAF Valley. Importantly, however, we would still have that all-important option to re-stream candidates to multi-engine or helicopter training midway through the course. We felt that this was an option that we must retain; many shared the view that to stream all pilots before they even got to Linton was too early for the majority and would probably lead to increased costs downstream.

* * *

We often hosted detachments of visiting aircraft, especially Harriers who came from RAF Wittering for the final part of their operational conversion course. Early in 1994 they were back again, and I arranged to have my first ever trip in a two-seat Harrier. I was looking forward to this immensely; even though it had been in service for over twenty years it was a remarkable aircraft and by far the most difficult for student pilots to master.

My chance for a flight came on 1 February 1994. We took off from Runway 22 accelerating rapidly down the runway. The view from the rear seat was much better than I had expected as it is mounted much higher than the front ejection seat. But what was that intrusive warbling noise? And what were those flashing red lights? Perhaps they were trying to draw our attention to the red caption on the Central Warning Panel which said 'FIRE'. Apparently our one and only engine was on fire!

The front seat pilot was totally unfazed by this, he simply turned downwind and within seconds we were back on the ground. So that was my one and only flight in a Harrier! And it had lasted a mere two minutes, although they had been quite a memorable two minutes. Entries in a RAF pilot's log book were rounded up or down to the nearest five minutes. So, in theory, my Harrier flight should be rounded down to zero! No way! I just had to have my one Harrier flight in my log book, so rounded up it had to be!

*   *   *

With so many students undergoing courses at Linton, the Mess was usually very full, and even at weekends it was a very active Mess and extremely well run. The two key players on the staff were the Deputy Mess Manager, Paul Medlicott, and the senior RAF chef, Bryan Griffiths. Both would stay at Linton long after they left the RAF.

The students were an incredibly responsible lot during the working week and I never had any worries about students 'hanging one on' the night before a flying day. Very occasionally one might end up a little worse for wear the next morning; if so he or she could play a 'once only' red card and advise his instructor accordingly. Nothing would be said on the understanding that the student concerned had learnt a lesson that would not be repeated. Heavy drinking the night before flying was not an issue that I ever had to deal with. However, for Happy Hour on Friday, students did tend to let their hair down and due allowances were made.

Even without Mess functions on a Friday or Saturday evening, the Mess would be full and lively. Early one Sunday morning I was outside the front of my garage opposite the Officers' Mess when I heard the fire alarm go off in the Mess. However, false alarms weren't that unusual. Nevertheless, the Mess would have to be evacuated until the Fire Section declared that all was well. Soon, dozens of students began to gather outside and I stopped what I was doing and looked across. There was something about the assembled group which caught my attention. When I realized what it was, I distinctly remember saying to myself, 'I didn't realize there were so many girls living in the Mess?'

Then it dawned on me and I turned away and went back into the garage muttering to myself 'stupid boy'!

*   *   *

On 15 March I lead two Tucanos on an overseas training flight to RAF Bruggen. The flights at medium level were very straightforward, but they demonstrated the amazing duration of the Tucano. Just prior to landing at Bruggen, we had sufficient fuel to overshoot and return to Linton, and then divert to Lossiemouth in the north of Scotland, all on one tank of fuel.

At Bruggen we visited 14 Squadron, now commanded by one of my staff college colleagues from my course at Greenwich. He had been a member of the Red Barrels! He mentioned that on a normal day he only had three or four aircraft available, so very different from six or seven years earlier. He was a little surprised to hear that at Linton the year before, 1 FTS had over a hundred aircraft of four different types. Of course the flying, and our roles, were so very different, but it again confirmed that my decision to ask for a Chief Instructor appointment had been the right one. It was also good to see that Eric, the Burmese Rock Python, was doing well, still living very comfortably in his lovely home. The RAF Police had not asked for his home back and he was still growing!

*   *   *

On 30 March we hosted a visit by the Chief of the Naval Staff, Admiral Sir Benjamin Bathurst, and he and I flew together in a Firefly. A few days later we hosted another much less formal visitor who arrived in his own privately owned Firefly. He was a fairly well known civilian aerobatic pilot who displayed at air shows throughout the country. Through one of the standards instructors, he had asked to visit Linton to see something of the training that took place. I was more than happy with such a request and he gave trips to a couple of RAF instructors in the Firefly; he also flew as a passenger in one of our Tucanos. Later that afternoon, as I looked out of my office window I was able to witness his departure. No sooner was he airborne than he rolled his aircraft upside down and flew inverted across the airfield at about thirty feet off the ground. I was not impressed!

I telephoned the Boss of Standards Squadron who was not at all surprised to receive my call. I said that the individual was no longer welcome at 1 FTS. The pilot did at least have the courtesy to telephone me later to apologize; he said that he had enjoyed his visit so much that he just wanted to offer a token of his appreciation. I explained what I thought of the example that he had offered our students who were very much in the formative months of their flying training. He apologized again. He then asked if, in the light of his apology, he would be welcome back at 1 FTS. I said no, although I thanked him for his call.

Part of his normal flying display was to complete a spin in front of the crowd, delaying his recovery until the very last second. It often resulted in a gasp of amazement from the many onlookers, and some incredulous looks from those who knew how close to the limits he was flying. A few years later, during an air show, his late spin recovery resulted in more than a gasp when he delayed his recovery by just a fraction. He crashed in front of the crowd and was killed instantly.

*   *   *

It was soon time to say farewell to Tom Eeles on his posting and this would be marked by a Dining-Out from the Officers' Mess. As I would make the farewell speech, I gained access to that most confidential document that travelled around with every aircrew officer and was always kept under lock and key. This was the Form 5000 series, and it contained every flying course report and every annual report covering aircrew flying ability and performance in fine detail. Being very much an ancient and experienced aviator, Tom's F5000 was a very thick document, but it also contained almost everything that I needed. There were of course many positive comments but also hidden here and there were one or two others which, with a little bit of poetic licence on my part, could raise some laughs.

At the time, the Officers' Mess kitchens were undergoing extensive refurbishment and temporary cooking facilities had been set up in portacabins at the rear of the Mess. The chefs, and all of the Mess staff, were very good at their jobs, but to serve a five course formal dinner for 140 people from such facilities would be a challenge.

Mike Fletcher, a former instructor of vast experience and, at the time, a lecturer in the Ground Training Squadron, offered to video the event and to capture not only what went on 'in front of house' in the dining room, but also what went on 'in back of house' in the portacabins and behind the bar. On the night he was very unobtrusive, and after some first-class editing, produced a fascinating insight into a dining-in night, capturing calmness, no hint of chaos, and a perfectly timed and superbly run dinner, served in the most difficult of circumstances. It showed many of the characters who worked behind the scenes who all helped ensure that it was not just 1 FTS which was 'a centre of excellence', but the Linton Officers' Mess as well.

The video also showed something of what was involved as a station bid farewell to a very popular Commanding Officer. In addition, the 'missing' video of Tom's 6,000th flying hour sortie had been appropriately edited by the late Mike Brooks to include a range of 'appropriate' sound effects.

As was usual, the dinner was presided over by the PMC, with Tom as the guest of honour. At the appropriate moment I duly highlighted some of the less well known aspects of Tom's flying career. I then referred to his 6,000 hours and the student who was meant to have made a video of the event but who had apparently 'screwed up'. Tom reacted in the same way that he had on the day with a loud, 'Typical!'

I responded by saying, 'Well, sir, that's what I told you at the time. Mr Vice, the video.'

With that, wooden screens at the end of the dining room, which had gone largely unnoticed until then, were removed to reveal four large televisions, which then burst into life with music and sound effects. The opening was a scene from the 1980s BBC series *Fighter Pilot* which showed Tom's previous aircraft, the Buccaneer, flying at ultra low-level with appropriate music. The pictures then merged to show a Tucano coming into land, but the sound effects were of an aircraft about to crash, then there was a thud as the Tucano touched down, followed by lots of clattering and banging as it taxied toward the dispersal area. As Tom climbed out of the aircraft there was lots of 'baaing' from the assembled throng. He then turned around and bent forward into the front cockpit to ensure that his ejection seat straps were tidy before vacating the aircraft. As he bent over, presenting his backside to the camera there was an inappropriate and extremely loud sound effect followed by the clink of bottles that Tom apparently had with him in the cockpit.

Once clear of the aircraft, he was toasted with champagne to the sound of much 'baaing'. He was then escorted to a clear area in front of one of the crash vehicles. Following the words 'ready, aim, fire', he was then very liberally soaked. The video showed him being covered with feathers, and then the words of the song made famous by Monty Python, *Always look on the bright side,* appeared and everyone picked up the song sheets on their tables and the whole dining room burst into song. It was a great occasion enjoyed by everyone, not least by Tom. It was a fitting farewell.

*   *   *

For my last six months, I served under a new Station Commander, Group Captain David Milne-Smith. He very much continued as Tom had left off and I was lucky to enjoy a good relationship with him. He was however, very much against smoking and, in a sign of things to come, he banned smoking throughout the Officers' Mess. This did cause some upset but it was not an issue on which he was prepared to compromise. He did agree however, that smokers could light up 'beyond the back door' to the main bar which opened onto a small courtyard. After one dining-in night, when everyone had moved into the bar from the dining room, some of the students produced a large model of a door, labelled 'The Back Door', complete with a door frame but nothing else. They set it up inside the bar but about ten feet short of the real door. They then promptly stepped through their door and lit up! Thankfully David saw the funny side of that. But the model was used just the once!

*   *   *

During May I was contacted by my desk officer about my next posting in November. The tour had passed incredibly quickly and, as my successor would need refresher training before arrival, he had already been nominated. I was offered two choices, both of which involved living and working in London. One was as a Press Officer in the MOD Main Building in Whitehall; that did not appeal to me in the slightest. The other post was as Directing Staff (Air) at the Royal College of Defence Studies (RCDS) in Belgrave Square. All I knew about RCDS was that their visits to stations were very high profile and usually involved their hosts in a lot of work. With nothing else on offer, I opted for RCDS.

*   *   *

Royal visitors to Yorkshire often landed at Linton where they would be met and escorted by the Lord Lieutenant, Sir Marcus Worsley and Lady Worsley; Sir Marcus is the brother of Her Royal Highness the Duchess of Kent. I rarely got involved in such visits, they were very much the Station Commander's territory, but during 1994 I met Sir Marcus on a couple of occasions when the

Station Commander was on leave. He and his wife would always arrive early, in a rather flash stretched 'limo', and they were usually accompanied by the same police inspector.

Sir Marcus was charming and he and Lady Worsley were very easy to talk too. On the second visit, some months after the first, I was taken to task by Sir Marcus about the somewhat fierce 'sleeping policeman' immediately in front of Linton's Main Gate designed to slow traffic down. Apparently, after their last visit, having picked up their Royal visitor, as they headed to Newton-on-Ouse, the exhaust fell off their 'limo'. Sir Marcus had not been best pleased. Later, the police inspector told me not to worry about it; he reckoned it was the car, not the ramp that had been the problem and had previously advised Sir Marcus not to buy it as he considered it to be a bit of a 'pup'.

*   *   *

Early in July we were tasked to deliver a Jet Provost Mark 5 from storage at RAF Shawbury to the new owner, who was operating from the former RAF airfield at Binbrook in Lincolnshire. As part of the contract the MOD had agreed to deliver the aircraft. The RAF has strict rules with regard to flying currency and no one within the RAF had flown a Jet Provost for about eight months. Also, Binbrook was disused, with no air traffic or crash and rescue services of any kind. So by our own HQ rules and regulations, no one was qualified to fly the aircraft and we couldn't land it at Binbrook. But the MOD had contracted to do exactly that! Left and right hands!

With the appropriate authorizations and exemptions, I agreed that we could do it, but I was unwilling to delegate such a responsibility to anyone else! So, on 6 July 1994, I flew solo the very final sortie to be undertaken by the RAF in a Jet Provost Mark 5A (XW336). It was a nice feeling.

*   *   *

On 17 July 1994 there was an International Air Day at RAF Church Fenton, and, as 1994 also marked the 75th Anniversary of the formation of 1 FTS, we assembled eighteen Tucanos for a formation flypast during the air show. The aircraft, all flown by 1 FTS instructors, represented the numbers '75'. It was a privilege to lead it.

*   *   *

Chris Coville came back to Linton on 11 August for a final 'flying' visit. His plan was to say overnight and return to the Training Group the following day. The Training Group had moved from RAF Brampton and now formed part of HQ Personnel and Training Command at Innsworth. With the Station Commander on leave, the AOC stayed with Jackie and I. Even working visits from an RAF two-star officer tended to have a high profile and they often involved some sort of semi-formal dinner in the Officers' Mess. While these were usually pleasant occasions, I wondered whether they were a bit 'same old, same old'. So when he arrived I suggested something a little different. As expected, Chris Coville was up for it. After a beer in the Mess at 1700 hours we adjourned home for an hour before we were picked up by a minibus full of junior instructors from Linton, and headed off for York. A beer in one of York's very many hostelries was then followed by a curry. Chris seemed to enjoy the change of venue very much; he never had any difficulty in establishing a great rapport with the young instructors. He was a man who had always led from the front. With that in mind, I then suggested something a little different for his departure and flight back to Gloucester the following day.

'What do you have in mind?' he asked.

'How about you lead a four ship of Tucanos?' I said. 'I'll fly as Number 4 "in the box" with squadron commanders on each wing.'

Needless to say, Chris Coville was more than up for it and we adjourned for an early night.

The next morning in Cheshire Hall he said farewell to the assembled officers and we presented him with a print of a 1 FTS Tucano. In saying farewell I remarked that I hoped that the next time that he visited Linton it would be as an Air Marshal and as the Commander-in-Chief. He did too!

Shortly before I left the office for the four ship, Jackie telephoned and asked me to pass on her thanks to Chris, who had very kindly left gifts in his bedroom for Matthew and Hannah, whom he had never met. In 2002, when Hannah was commissioned, her commissioning parchment was signed by the Air Member for Personnel, Air Marshal Sir Christopher Coville. In 2008, in celebration of the RAF's eightieth birthday, the RAF Club in Piccadilly hosted a formal dinner to which two junior officers from every RAF station were 'invited' as guests. Hannah, having recently returned from her second operational tour in Basrah in Iraq, was nominated as one of RAF Marham's representatives. She rang me from the club when she saw the seating plan, to see if there was anyone that I knew. As she read out the list of names of people on her table I stopped her and suggested that she thank Sir Christopher for the gift that he left for her fourteen years earlier.

The four ship on the morning of 12 August 1994 was magnificent. It was clear from the start that Chris had lost none of his very considerable flying ability (he was a former Lightning, Phantom and Tornado F3 pilot). All of us involved had to work extremely hard as he lead a very tight formation for a series of passes at RAF Church Fenton, RAF Dishforth, RAF Topcliffe, and finally at RAF Linton-on-Ouse. On the final pass at Linton, Chris, as formation leader called 'breaking, breaking, go' and with that the Numbers 2 and 3 broke left and right, as I flew straight on. He pulled up and climbed to the south-west heading back to Gloucester leaving Linton for the final time as Air Officer Commanding.

*   *   *

On 24 August I flew across to RAF Shawbury to collect another Jet Provost, this time a Mark 3 (XM378), again for delivery to Binbrook. So I was lucky enough to have the final RAF solo sortie in this venerable trainer which had served the RAF so well. On the way I took the opportunity to complete a flypast at Linton before landing at Binbrook.

By now Linton was operating the Tucano and Firefly only, but the days of the Firefly at Topcliffe were numbered. The RAF decided to concentrate all Tucano flying training, including instructor and navigator training, at Linton and at Topcliffe. To make room, JEFTS was required to move to RAF Barkston Heath near Cranwell and, as this was an RAF requirement, the RAF would need to pay for a substantial change to the existing contract. At Barkston, JEFTS would also take on responsibility for Army Air Corps elementary flying training, which would result in a further contract revision and an increase in the number of aircraft and instructors. The move took place in 1995 after I left Linton, and from all accounts JEFTS performed satisfactorily from then onwards.

Interestingly, in 2003 when the JEFTS contract was due for renewal, the RAF withdrew from the arrangement altogether, leaving the Army and the Navy to carry on. The RAF then undertook its own elementary flying training once more. I thought that this was 'a bit rich' as the concept of JEFTS had been an RAF idea in the first place.

*   *   *

In October I lead a pair of Tucanos to Villafranca, near Verona in Northern Italy. This was my 'swan song' as the Chief Instructor of 1 FTS and it marked the end of a fantastic tour. It also brought back many memories of Canberra detachments from Malta nearly twenty years earlier.

We flew back from Villafranca to RAF Finningley in a single sortie lasting three hours and twenty-five minutes. While nowhere near as physically robust as the Jet Provost, the Tucano was nevertheless a worthy successor, although it was difficult to teach students fuel awareness.

My final sortie at Linton was on 15 November 1994. I had flown 520 hours on nine types of aircraft. I then handed over my job and my bike to my successor, Steve Orwell, and prepared to swop the rural delights of North Yorkshire for life and work in London. Steve and I would work together in the Tucano simulator many years later. Working in London would prove to be another remarkable experience and one that was wholly unexpected.

Chapter 10

Belgrave Square

The Royal College of Defence Studies (RCDS), 1994–1996
In late November 1994 I left rural North Yorkshire for the urban sprawl that lay within the confines of the M25, for my first tour in London in twenty-three years. For a few weeks I lived in the Officers' Mess at RAF Uxbridge, West London, until we moved into a married quarter in January.

Uxbridge was one of the more famous RAF stations although it had never been an airfield. In 1936 it became the home of HQ 11 Group, Fighter Command, and it was perhaps the key HQ during that most crucial part of the UK's history, the Battle of Britain. During the battle, information about air threats first came to HQ Fighter Command at RAF Bentley Priory, before being allocated to the various group operations rooms, one of which was 11 Group under the command of that most able New Zealander, Air-Vice Marshal Keith Park. It was from the 11 Group HQ in Hillingdon House, and the nearby underground operations room that RAF fighter squadrons in the south-east had been coordinated and controlled. It was during a visit to 11 Group on 16 August 1940 that Winston Churchill made a statement, later repeated in the House of Commons, that was to become famous 'Never in the field of human conflict was so much owed by so many to so few.'

The 11 Group Operations Room, fully restored in the 1970s, was only a five minute walk from where we lived and we were privileged to enjoy a visit there during 1995. RAF Uxbridge closed on 31 March 2010, but the Operations Room and a museum have been preserved, and the Battle of Britain War Memorial above the bunker has also become a protected monument.

* * *

I began my new job on Monday 21 November 1994. While RCDS was only fourteen miles from my home, using the underground, the journey took an hour and a half. The train was empty when I set off and over the next two years I often compared the suburbs, and then the city, with the beautiful Vale of York. By the time I arrived at Hyde Park Corner there would be standing room only, and then only just, with rush hour in full swing. On that first day, as I turned into the architectural delight that was Belgrave Square, I got my first glimpse of the grand surroundings that would be my workplace for the next two years.

Previously, the Imperial Defence College, RCDS, owed its origins to Winston Churchill when he was Secretary of State for the Colonies in 1922. Its work in those days was chiefly concerned with the defence of the Empire, with students drawn from the UK, Australia, Canada, and New Zealand. The experience of the Second World War proved the benefit of such an institution, and there was unanimous support from the Commonwealth for the college to resume its work after the war. In 1946 the college reopened in Seaford House, with the course including members from the USA for the first time. It was renamed RCDS in 1970.

* * *

As I walked into the imposing entrance hall of Seaford House that first Monday morning I did wonder what exactly I was stepping into. Only a few days before I had been wearing a green flying suit and riding a rather ridiculous looking bicycle across an airfield. Now I was in a business suit complete with briefcase and umbrella, but thankfully without a bowler hat!

I was met by the outgoing Directing Staff (DS) Air, Wing Commander Martin Cocksedge, who was about to take over the role as DS (Coordinator). All five DS, one from each of the three services, a MOD civil servant, plus Coordinator, shared an office on the second floor.

When I got there, I noted with interest that there was a computer on each desk. What exactly was I meant to do with that? My only previous experience with a computer was during a Tornado sortie, when I might occasionally have said to my navigator 'Recycle the main computer!'

There seemed to be a marked lack of any capable airmen to assist, and I soon discovered that the lowest ranking servicemen within RCDS were the DS themselves. In fact there were only eight service personnel within the college, all the rest being civil servants on administrative duties. The Commandant was the extremely capable Air Marshal Sir Timothy Garden. There were four Senior Directing Staff, all of two-star rank, with one coming from each of the services and one from the Foreign Office.

The aim of RCDS was to prepare senior officers and officials of the UK and other countries, and future leaders from the private and public sectors, for high responsibilities by developing their analytical powers, knowledge of defence and international security, and strategic vision. Those officers undergoing training on the year-long course were referred to as members rather than students. Their minimum rank was colonel (group captain equivalent), and there were often brigadiers and major generals on the course. Many went on to reach very high rank.

* * *

This was another new world, and I felt as I had often done in the past, like a fish out of water. But it did look fascinating. Each member of the Senior Directing Staff had responsibility for various phases of the course and it was largely down to his subordinate DS to organize the various outside speakers on whom the college relied. The academic part of the day involved lectures from 0930 hours until 1230 hours, with those afternoons within the college spent mainly on discussion and research. Visits to industry, and academia, as well as to military establishments, featured heavily in the programme. There was also a week-long regional visit to different parts of the UK and visits to Europe, including to Brussels, and NATO HQ. The highlight of the one-year course was a four week overseas tour in October.

Each new DS was also required to complete the course as a member during his, or her, first year. While this was a great privilege and would lead to the award of the post nominal letters 'rcds', it meant that all of the routine work during a challenging first year had to be completed outside the academic parts of the college programme. I slowly began to appreciate the enormity of the task, but thankfully, I had the final three weeks of the 1994 course to get up to speed before the 1995 course began.

During the final part of Martin's handover, he added some other pieces of information which once again left me 'alone and palely loitering'. Each DS did all his own writing, hence the computer on each desk; these were quite old even by 1994 standards, using a DOS system, but they were light years ahead of my previous system – a pencil and a typist. I readily admit that, at the time, I had no idea what DOS meant! Next, the Commandant was heavily into Information Technology and was something of a computer 'whiz', and he expected all of his staff to get up to speed quickly. But Martin kept the very best piece of information until last: as the RAF was considered to be the most technically minded of the three services, DS (Air) was the IT specialist for the college and would be responsible for updating all college systems, and for the purchase and installation of a brand new IT suite for all the members. That would be me then! Wow!

* * *

Martin often picked me up at 0630 hours from Uxbridge Town Centre for the hour long drive down the A40 into London. On other days I would travel by tube. Early mornings became very much the normal and late finishes too. On most evenings I would be home at about 1900 hours but, with many evening activities in the college, often it was much later.

The 1995 course began in early January with eighty members. It was truly international with forty members from overseas countries. There were five from the Middle East including one from Israel, six from countries that I had spent my earlier years studying as potential targets – Russia, the Ukraine, Bulgaria, Romania, the Czech Republic, and Poland. The Romanian officer was a major general destined to become head of his country's armed forces. Europe was well represented too, and the Americas, with four from the USA. There were also members from Asia, the Far East, and Africa, with another major general from South Africa.

Invariably there would be representatives from various country's security services, and the 1995 course had one from MI5, one from the CIA, and one from the former KGB, now the Russian Foreign Intelligence Service. The first time that I wondered into the anteroom and found all three having coffee and in deep conversation was quite startling! But it was also very interesting to 'compare notes' with air force officers from the former Soviet Union and the Warsaw Pact. I think that some of our Tornado tactics would have worked rather well! It was particularly good to see Vaughan Morris, now a group captain, as a member of the 1995 course.

The very first phase, Science and Technology, was organized by my immediate boss, Air Vice-Marshal Peter Dodworth, so there was little hope of me easing into the academic routine slowly. The other major phase for which I had responsibility was called The Future and it was in the final term. Defence policy and the military were also covered during the course, and there would be three week-long visits to each of the services. Immediately prior to that, each DS pairing would give a detailed briefing about their respective service. However, the main focus of the course was not on military matters, but on wider aspects of economics, education, scientific developments, social issues and the like.

So, early January saw me trying to come to terms with a computer for the first time and also telephoning prospective speakers. Many had spoken to an RCDS audience in the past but some were invited for the very first time. One or two were understandably nervous and wanted advice about their audience and how to 'pitch' their presentations. And of course they sought that advice, including guidance on the content of their talks, from the DS who invited them in the first place. Little did they realize just how nervous I was in simply making the phone call!

I recall telephoning Lady Archer (Jeffery Archer's wife) out of the blue and inviting her to speak. She is a highly respected scientist, and former Cambridge University lecturer, specializing in solar power conversion. She specifically asked me for my views on the content of her lecture. My 'waffle' must have worked as she agreed to come, and she was so well received that she was invited back for the 1996 course. Another 'cold call' that I made was to Saltwood Castle, the home of the late Right Honourable Alan Clark MP. As well as being a well known politician he was the author of several books on military history, he was also well known for his flamboyance, wit, and irreverence, and in particular for his diary of political life under Margaret Thatcher. My 'waffle' clearly worked with him too, as he also featured in our programme.

I also contacted Sir Edward Heath, our former Prime Minister, and he also agreed to speak. One of the more pleasant aspects of my job was to meet each of the lecturers on arrival at the college, and show them round the Lecture Hall prior to their talk. Afterwards they would be hosted for lunch in the college restaurant. Ted Heath was particularly charming, and he did me the courtesy of writing to me personally afterwards.

Her Majesty The Queen visited the college during both the years that I was there, and for all of us, and especially the overseas members, this was a very special occasion. King Hussein of Jordan also attended during both years. There were many fascinating speakers and they offered insights into worlds that until then I had only ever seen on television. Ken Livingstone was very highly regarded and was an entertaining and interesting speaker.

*   *   *

During the spring we undertook a series of regional tours with members and DS split into eight groups, each visiting a separate region of the UK. I was with the group visiting the Midlands and we were based in Birmingham. These visits were not in any way defence related, they concentrated on looking at the regional infrastructure, local authorities, regional development agencies, industry, education, and hospitals. The most memorable aspect of the Midlands visit for me was undoubtedly the trip to a city that I had heard so much about but had never visited: Coventry, and in particular Coventry Cathedral.

Coventry has had three cathedrals: the first was St Mary's, a monastic building, of which only a few ruins remain; the second was St Michael's, a fourteenth century Gothic church, that remains a ruined shell after its bombing during the Second World War; the third is the new St Michael's Cathedral, built after the destruction of the former. The ruins of the old St Michael's had quite an impact on our group. Only the tower, spire, the outer wall, and the bronze effigy and tomb of its first bishop survived. The ruins remain hallowed ground and are listed. The spire rises to 300 feet and it is England's third tallest spire, after Salisbury and Norwich, and remains the tallest structure in the city.

The raid that destroyed so much of the city began on 14 November 1940, and it was the most severe to hit Coventry during the war. Code-named Operation Mondscheinsonate (*Moonlight Sonata*), it was carried out by 515 German bombers and lasted for over nine hours. To name such an operation after one of Beethoven's most popular sonatas was grotesque. The co-ordinated attacks were intended to destroy Coventry's industrial infra-structure, although it was clear that damage to residential areas would be considerable. Very early during the raid high explosive bombs knocked out the water supply, electricity network, and gas mains, and cratered the roads, making it difficult for fire engines to reach fires started by follow-up waves of bombers. At around 2000 hours, Coventry Cathedral was set on fire for the first time. The volunteer firefighters managed to put out the first fire, but other direct hits followed, and soon new fires in the Cathedral, accelerated by a firestorm, were out of control. Fires were started in nearly every street in the city centre and a direct hit on the fire brigade HQ disrupted the fire service's command and control, making it difficult to send firefighters to the most dangerous blazes first.

As the Germans had intended, the water mains were damaged by high explosives and there was not enough water available to tackle many of the fires. The raid reached its climax at around midnight, with the final all clear sounding at 0615 hours on the morning of 15 November. The raid destroyed or damaged about 60,000 buildings, and there was barely an undamaged building left in the city centre. It is known that 568 civilians were killed, although the precise death toll has never been established. The raid reached such a new level of destruction that Joseph Goebbels later used the term *Coventriert* ('Coventrated') when describing similar levels of destruction of other enemy towns. Certainly for me, as a former Tornado bomber pilot, the visit was one of great reflection, and fifteen years later, the only aspect of the regional tour that I can remember clearly is Coventry Cathedral.

*   *   *

In June the course was off to Europe with a few days spent visiting the British Army on exercise in the field; we then visited NATO HQ in Brussels. I thoroughly enjoyed the opportunity to drive a Challenger main battle tank at very high speed over rough terrain. The tank commander, a sergeant, encouraged me to drive even faster as we approached a significant water feature, saying that the higher the speed, the less chance there was of being soaked. Of course, he had had years of practice at 'seeing off' senior officers, and a significant proportion of the water feature ended up in my lap! But it was great fun. It was also fascinating to see how the staff of a fully equipped field hospital carried out their work, perhaps a precursor to what many of them would have to deal with a few years later at Camp Bastion in Helmand Province, Afghanistan.

There was also an opportunity for a historical visit during one afternoon, and about half of the college visited the site of the Battle of Waterloo. We had a very knowledgeable guide and it was fascinating to walk around Hougoumont Farm and La Haye Sainte. It was in the sandpit opposite here that the gallant 95th Rifles fought, the regiment portrayed so well by Bernard Cornwell in the *Sharpe* series of books. Almost 50,000 Allied and French soldiers lost their lives at Waterloo on that single day, 18 June 1815.

Our journey back to the UK was on board the Eurostar from Brussels to Waterloo Station, which was rather apt. I was sitting quietly thinking about the next major piece of planning that I had to get to grips with, our overseas tour scheduled for October. And it would take a lot of thinking about as my group would include our Commandant, Air Marshal Garden. Whilst dwelling on this there was a tap on my shoulder; it was the Commandant himself.

'Paul,' he said, 'could I have a word with you in private?'

As I followed him toward his seat a range of thoughts flashed through my mind. What on earth have I done now? Or what have I not done? What has he found out?

As we sat down, he said that he was delighted to tell me that the following day I would be appointed OBE in The Queen's Birthday Honours. I was lost for words.

*   *   *

By a complete coincidence, Jackie and I had tickets for the Trooping the Colour, Her Majesty the Queen's Birthday Parade, the very next day, Saturday 17 June 1995. We and a number of other RCDS members were lucky enough to have seats facing the parade not far from the saluting dais. To attend such a magnificent parade on such a day was very special indeed.

*   *   *

For the overseas tours which began in September, the college once again divided into eight groups and, as the tours commanded a very high profile in the host countries, a lot of effort went into the preparation and the programmes. Each group was led by an officer of at least two-star rank. The Commandant and the four two-star officers of RCDS were supplemented by three others who were 'imported' to join the college for the tours. Similarly, three additional DS of my rank were imported so that there would be one DS to support each group. The Commandant elected for the Middle East tour, and he made it clear to Martin Cocksedge that as there were two RAF wing commanders on RCDS's permanent staff, he wished one of them to be in his group. As Martin had two years seniority on me in the college he said, with a smile, 'That means you then!'

We would visit Israel, including Gaza and the West Bank, Jordan, Syria, and finally Egypt, spending about a week in each country. The members indicated their preferences and, as far as possible, these were accommodated, but the priority was always to try and balance nationalities and service within each group. No member could visit his own country. Our group totalled twelve and included members from the UK, Germany, Japan, Mexico, New Zealand and the United States, .

I was in regular touch with our Embassies in each of the countries to try and ensure that the in-country programmes achieved the right balance. Too often there were too many military or defence-related visits; what we needed was a fairly broad canvas. Two members of each group were nominated as country specialists and they gave a detailed presentation on each country before we left. On our return, each group was also required to make a presentation to the college on the region visited.

Tim Garden made it clear to all of the DS that while their roles leading up to, and during the tour, was one of organization and management, once the tour began we were to take a full part as a member of the college by being fully involved in all discussions. He was a very capable academic, having been awarded degrees from both Oxford and Cambridge Universities. When he left the RAF in 1996 he became Director of Chatham House before moving to university defence research. He said that following the high-powered presentations that would inevitably take place during our tour, he expected all the members of our group to be vigorous in their questioning of our hosts, whilst of course maintaining the courtesy for which RCDS members were renowned. I would need to be on top line from Day One. Perhaps missing the bus on the first day in Tel Aviv would not be a good start. But that is exactly what I did!

*   *   *

We flew to Tel Aviv on 16 September. The plan was to spend two nights in Tel Aviv, two nights in Tiberias near the Golan Heights and the Syrian border, and then four nights in Jerusalem. On the first morning everyone was in the hotel lobby in good time, and I had little to do while we waited for our coach. With ten minutes to go until it arrived I paid a quick visit to the cloakroom in the hotel lobby. I was back within two or three minutes to find the lobby empty! Thankfully, the coach returned within ten minutes and I was the recipient of lots of good humoured banter, and some apologies too, but not from the Commandant! Not the very best of starts then!

The next few days were very busy with briefings at the British Embassy, a meeting with the Head of the Israeli Defence Forces (IDF), further meetings at the National Defence College, and a visit to the Agricultural Research Organization. We paid a visit by air to the IDF's Hatzerin Air Base before travelling to Tiberias. Here we visited the Kibbutz Menara, which is in Upper Galilee adjacent to the Lebanese border and overlooking the Hula Valley. It had been established in 1943 by young immigrants from Germany and Poland, and Leon Uris visited here while researching his novel, *Exodus*. As Menara lies less than 100 metres from the Lebanese border, problems had often arisen during fighting between the two countries. Later we viewed the security zone and visited the city of Qiryat Shemona, a regular target for cross-border rocket fire from Lebanon. We also received briefings on water resources and their political implications in the Golan area; until then I hadn't realized just how much of a strategic issue water was in this part of the world.

On 20 September we travelled south to Jerusalem and visited the Yad Vashem Holocaust Museum, a very moving and remarkable monument.

The afternoon saw the highpoint of our visit to Israel, and the undoubted highlight of the whole tour, a private audience with Israel's Prime Minister Mr Yitzak Rabin. The meeting lasted over an hour and no subjects were 'off limits' during discussion. His deep voice, almost 'gravely', and his manner captured our complete attention, he simply oozed authority, and it was easy to see why he had commanded such loyalty throughout his army career; he had also commanded the Israeli Forces to stunning success during the Six Day War in 1967. He fielded all of our questions openly and well; even the very last question did not perturb him, 'What are you going to do about the illegal Israeli settlements on the West Bank?'

His reply was so very simple, 'Don't worry about those, I will deal with them.'

But of course he was unable to deal with them or very much else after our visit. He wrote to us to say how much he had enjoyed our meeting, and we received his letter a few days after he had been so cruelly assassinated by a Jewish extremist on 4 November 1995. What a waste. What a loss.

The following day we travelled to Gaza where we had briefings from the Commander of the Palestine Police Force and the Director of Operations of the UN Relief and Works Agency. We then toured refugee camps in the Gaza strip. As expected, these were very grim places indeed.

On 23 September we visited settlements in Bethlehem and Hebron and met a number of representatives of various Palestinian political factions. Bethlehem seemed chaotic with so many Christian religious 'variants' vying for position, or so it seemed to me.

In Hebron, a predominantly Arab town, the grave of a Jewish extremist, Baruch Goldstein, was a place of pilgrimage for Jewish extremists, with some proclaiming him a saint. In February 1994 he had entered the local mosque and opened fire on unarmed Palestinian worshipers, killing 29 and wounding 125. Goldstein was beaten to death by survivors. During riots which followed, the IDF killed nineteen Palestinians within the next forty-eight hours. We visited the mosque where the killings had taken place, and as we left, we were stopped by a Jewish teenager. He realized that we were some kind of official visitors although we were all in civilian dress. He grabbed hold of the Defence Attaché's arm and shouted loudly, 'You listen to me, all of you. I will kill every Arab here!'

The DA's response was something on the lines of, 'Oh do grow up!'

Later that day, we had lunch with a number of Palestinian officials, including representatives of the Palestine Liberation Organization (PLO), as well as Hamas. That was in the days when they were brothers in arms; it wouldn't take very many years before they were killing one another. I think all of us reflected on the divisions and the bitterness, so deep rooted, that kept people so far apart.

For me, I reflected on one other aspect too, which by comparison with what we had seen and heard, was rather trivial. The whole group had been keen and enthusiastic throughout this busy first week asking many penetrating questions. All course members were of course being assessed and, as the junior ranking officer within the group, it had been impossible for me to get my voice heard. Perhaps my chance would come during the next leg of the tour. Little did I realize that I would have yet another ignominious 'first day' and I would need urgent help from our Defence Attaché in Jordan.

*   *   *

Normally I have the constitution of a horse but the next morning I felt very poorly with an upset stomach. It was also a very busy morning with our group checking out and formal farewells to be completed before departing for the Allenby/King Hussein Bridge. This land crossing was normally closed and its opening for RCDS was because of the strong links between the college and King Hussein. Once across the bridge we were formally welcomed into Jordan and met the British DA. I felt like death, and looked it apparently, but it would be some hours before we would arrive in Amman. In Jordan we were due to spend five nights in Amman and two nights in Aqaba. Some members of our group expressed sympathy, but as I recall, our officer of the Royal Marines looked on slightly disdainfully at this officer of the junior service who couldn't quite 'hack' the pace.

At the Dead Sea Spa Hotel we were hosted by Jordanian Armed Forces officials. The fine cuisine was totally lost on me, although I made frequent use of the hotel's fine facilities. As we left, the DA came to my rescue and suggested that I accompany him in his vehicle rather than the less comfortable and slower coach. As we approached Amman my discomfort became acute and he diverted en route to his official residence. After the very briefest of introductions to his charming wife, as I was sprinting at the time, I made it to his bathroom, just. Later that evening we were hosted for supper by Her Majesty's Ambassador, but I was unable to enjoy his hospitality. However, what did brighten me up no end was the sight of our officer of the Royal Marines, who began to look increasingly pale as he also fell victim to whatever stomach ailment had laid me low. 'Oh what can ail thee knight at arms, alone and palely loitering'; yes, indeed.

Over the next few days we had the usual round of briefings and visits: to industry, an oil refinery and a potash factory, to the Jordanian War College and the 3rd Armoured Division. There was also time to take in something of Jordan's rich history. We visited Mount Nebo, the view from which provides a panorama of the Holy Land. According to both Jewish and Christian tradition, Moses was buried on Mount Nebo.

On our way south to Aqaba we stopped at the famous castle of Kerak, once an ancient Crusader stronghold situated on a hilltop about 3,000 feet above sea level, surrounded on three sides by a valley, and with a magnificent view of the Dead Sea. We later visited a cave where Bronze Age pottery was discovered in 1991. Speculation linked the finds with Abraham's nephew Lot, who, according to the Bible, moved to a cave in the hills above Zoar after the destruction of Sodom and Gomorrah.

Once in Aqaba, we visited the border and had a trip on the Red Sea in one of the Royal Jordanian Navy's gunboats. The trip to Petra via Wadi Rum was particularly memorable. Petra was established sometime around the sixth century BC as the capital city of the Nabataeans and it is very much a symbol of Jordan, as well as its most visited attraction, yet it remained unknown to the Western world until 1812. The BBC chose Petra as one of the forty places you have to see before you die, although I suspect that many will have to content themselves with a glimpse of it during the film *Indiana Jones and the Last Crusade*. Wadi Rum, with its impressive rock formations is very different and may be best known for its connection with T.E. Lawrence, who based his operations there during the Arab Revolt of 1917–18.

On 29 September we headed back to Amman for our last day in Jordan. It had been a very good visit and the Baqa Palestinian Refugee Camp made for an interesting comparison with the camps in Gaza.

Our trip was almost half over and so far, despite my 'late' start on Day One in Israel and my 'unfortunate' start to Day One in Jordan, it had gone remarkably well. The whole group was in good voice with all the members keen to lead in discussion. At very late notice, and in a change to our published programme, we were granted a private audience with King Hussein's younger brother, Jordan's then Crown Prince, His Royal Highness Prince Hassan. Would I have the opportunity to question such a key member of Jordan's Royal Family?

Much had been said about the hospitality of the Jordanian people in offering so much to Palestinians forced from the West Bank by Israel's occupation; we saw much evidence of this, especially at the Baqa Refugee Camp. Palestinians now made up almost 50 per cent of Jordan's population, but there had been a price for Jordan to pay, as a lot of PLO activity against Israel had originated from within Jordan's borders, which had sorely tested relationships between Jordan and Israel.

There had also been significant friction between Jordan and the PLO, and in September 1970, King Hussein moved to quash the militancy of Palestinian organizations and restore his monarchy's rule over the country. The violence which ensued resulted in the deaths of thousands of people, the vast majority Palestinian, and armed conflict lasted until July 1971 with the expulsion of the PLO and thousands of Palestinian fighters to Lebanon. Perhaps as Jordan's difficulties began to ease, Lebanon's were set to worsen. Nevertheless, large numbers of Palestinian refugees remained living – temporarily – in Jordan awaiting a peace settlement and a return to the West Bank.

As we sat in private audience with Crown Prince Hassan I thought about these aspects and wondered whether this was an aspect worthy of a bit of a challenge. In fact, as I looked around I would not get a better chance, as the Crown Prince decided when to take a question, and from whom. One merely had to indicate by gently raising one's hand and, once this had been acknowledged, there was no risk whatsoever of anyone else butting in. Soon, Crown

Prince Hassan nodded in my direction. Everyone else, including the Commandant, looked on with interest and some surprise.

'Your Royal Highness, before we came to Jordan we visited camps in Gaza. What we saw there, and in the occupied West Bank, many of us had seen before on television news items – poor conditions and housing, poverty and unemployment. And then we came to Jordan and to Baqa with its schools, and hospitals and industry. It was a town, with structure and order, not a camp, and it speaks so very loudly for the generosity of the Hashemite people. My question is this: when there is a lasting Middle East settlement, how will you persuade the Palestinian refugees living here to go back?'

I cannot for the life of me recall the detail of Crown Prince Hassan's answer but I did spot the beginnings of a smile on the Commandant's face.

*   *   *

We travelled to Syria by road on 1 October for a six night stay, five nights in Damascus and one night in Palmyra. As expected, the Syrians were much less open, but the visit nonetheless proved very interesting. After an initial round of briefings, including one from the UN and half a day visiting the main Damascus Souq, we headed off to Krak de Chevaliers. This was yet another Crusader castle, this one close to the border with Lebanon, and it is one of the most important preserved medieval military castles in the world. Having visited so many ruined castles in England over the years, it was good to be able to see such an old castle that was so structurally complete. We then headed east – far into the desert – to visit one of the most beautiful and magnificent of the Syrian historic sites, Palmyra. This ancient Arab town, which has now turned pink with age, used to be on the old Silk Road. It is called Tadmor by the Arabs and was referred to for the first time in writings in the second century BC. It is also mentioned in the Bible as a part of Solomon's territory, and became an important city in the Roman Empire.

We expected to be followed by the Syrian Intelligence Service (Shu'bat Al-Mukhabarat Al-'Askariyya) wherever we went and when in Damascus it was impossible to identify them. But on the long straight road to Palmyra, with no other vehicles around, it was impossible to miss the one car maintaining station behind us. And of course Palmyra only had one hotel! I followed normal RAF detachment rules: having checked in and dumped my bags, I headed straight for the bar! The bar was empty, or was it? At the far end, trying to remain inconspicuous behind a plant pot, were two Syrians in civilian clothes. Naturally, via the barman, I offered them a drink. They were mortified! The next member of our group to arrive was a member of his own country's security services. He pointed out the two Syrians and said that I should pretend not to have noticed them.

'I offered them a drink,' I said.

Now it was his turn to be mortified!

On our final full day in Syria we travelled to the largely destroyed and abandoned town of Quneitra, situated in south-western Syria in a high valley in the Golan Heights. It came under Israeli control on 10 June 1967, the last day of the Six Day War, and was almost completely destroyed before the Israeli final withdrawal seven years later. It now lies in the demilitarized zone between Syria and Israel, a short distance from the de facto border. Syria refused to rebuild the city and actively discourages resettlement in the area. Israel was heavily criticized by the UN for the city's destruction, while Israel has criticized Syria for not rebuilding Quneitra. It had been a city of 20,000 people. It remains a sad and desolate place, a bitter testimony.

*   *   *

The following day we flew to Cairo for the final part of our tour. We stayed six nights at the Forte Grand Pyramids Hotel at Giza. Our visits included the Saladin Military Museum, the Nasr Academy, and the Egyptian Museum. We also visited the Egyptian 2nd Field Army and the Suez Canal and Bar Lev Line, a chain of fortifications built by Israel along the eastern coast of the Suez Canal after it captured the Sinai Peninsula from Egypt during the 1967 war. The Bar Lev Line was designed to defend against any major Egyptian assault across the canal, and was expected to function as a 'graveyard for Egyptian troops'. The line cost around $300 million in 1973, and Israeli planners estimated it would take at least twenty-four hours, probably a full forty-eight hours, for the Egyptians to breach the sand wall and establish a bridge across the canal. In the event the Egyptians breached the Line in two hours.

The final cultural part of our visit to the Middle East was a wonderful sound and light show at the Pyramids. We returned to London on 13 October.

*   *   *

Tuesday 12 December 1995 was a very special day as Jackie, Matthew, Hannah and I set off by car for the journey into Central London. It was rather a nice feeling to enter the gates of Buckingham Palace in our ten-year old Opel for my investiture. On arrival we were split up, with Jackie, Matthew and Hannah being shown to the ballroom by one of the four Gentlemen Ushers to the Queen on duty that day. In the ballroom music was played by the Orchestra of the Blues and Royals.

Meanwhile, I was shown to one of a number of rooms set aside for recipients of various honours to wait being called. It was great to meet Terry Stone, Linton's civilian engineering manager, who was also to be honoured.

Her Majesty entered the ballroom attended by two Gurkha Orderly Officers, a tradition begun in 1876 by Queen Victoria. On duty on the dais were five members of The Queen's Body Guard of the Yeomen of the Guard, which was created in 1485 by King Henry VII after his victory at the Battle of Bosworth Field. This makes them the oldest military corps still existing in the

UK. The Queen was escorted by the Lord Chamberlain who announced the name of each recipient. They included Dames and Knights, Companions and Commanders, Officers and Members of the various orders: The Most Excellent Order of the British Empire, Knights Bachelor, The Most Honourable Order of the Bath, The Most Distinguished Order of Saint Michael and Saint George, The Royal Victorian Order, The Royal Victorian Medal, The Queen's Police Medal, and The Queen's Gallantry Medal. It was an honour to be in such company, and to enjoy a wonderful day that not even a grey overcast sky could dampen.

*   *   *

The 1996 course was another interesting mix of countries and personalities. From Australia came an air force officer who went on to become head of Australia's Armed Forces. From China came a charming army colonel. Having never previously been out of China and with the benefit of an English Language course immediately before travelling to London, he arrived complete with an English sense of humour. And, as in the previous year, we had a trio of spies too. One of the eight RAF officers on the course had flown with me in the Meteor during a display in Jersey, on 17 September 1981.

We also had a new Commandant with Air Marshal Garden taking early retirement, later to become Lord Garden of Hampstead and the Liberal Democrat defence spokesman in the House of Lords; it was in that capacity that I would meet him when he visited Kuwait. Sadly, Lord Garden died after a very short illness in 2007.

As I had completed the 1995 course and was now a RCDS graduate, the 1996 course was fairly straightforward. I was only required to attend those lectures that were in the phases that I had planned, although I could attend any others that I wished. Days were still long and I looked forward to the time when I would no longer have to commute in and out of London.

My previous annual report had been very good indeed and all the signs were that I would stand a good chance of promotion to group captain in 1997. As I would be forty-eight years old during that year, this would probably be my best, perhaps only, chance of being considered for command of a flying station if I was promoted. And I very much hoped that I would be considered for Linton-on-Ouse. So I began making moves to see if a posting back to the Training Group was on the cards at the end of the year.

*   *   *

In June 1996, Europe beckoned once more and we followed a similar trail as the previous year. This time I opted for a different cultural visit, to the site of the first Battle of Ypres, to Tyne Cot Cemetery, and to the Menin Gate.

There were three battles at Ypres, but it was the third, lasting from 21 July to the 6 November 1917, that was the largest and most costly in human suffering. It was also known as the Battle of Passchendaele and it resulted in nearly 500,000 casualties on all sides, with only a few miles of ground being won by the Allies. The town was all but obliterated by artillery fire.

The name 'Tyne Cot' is said to have come from the Northumberland Fusiliers who saw a resemblance between the German concrete pill boxes, which still stand in the middle of the cemetery, and typical Tyneside workers' cottages – Tyne Cots. The cemetery has 11,954 graves, 8,367 of which are unnamed. When King George V visited the cemetery in 1922 he said:

> We can truly say that the whole circuit of the Earth is girdled with the graves of our dead. In the course of my pilgrimage, I have many times asked myself whether there can be more potent advocates of peace upon Earth through the years to come, than this massed multitude of silent witnesses to the desolation of war.

There are two Victoria Cross holders buried there, a Canadian and an Australian. At another grave the personal message at the foot of the head-stone of Second Lieutenant Arthur Conway Young is much commented upon – 'Sacrificed to the fallacy that war can end war.'

The Menin Gate Memorial was opened in 1927 and it is inscribed with the names of many who fell at Ypres but who have no known grave. It includes the name of a relative of mine, Peter Boyle, who was killed while serving with the Durham Light Infantry. On completion of the Memorial it was discovered to be too small to contain all the names and many others were inscribed on the Tyne Cot memorial instead. A particular poignant phrase from Field Marshal Plumer's address at the unveiling was, 'He is not missing. He is here.'

The citizens of Ypres wanted to express their gratitude towards those who had given their lives for Belgium's freedom, and every evening at 2000 hours buglers from the local fire brigade close the road which passes under the Memorial to sound the Last Post. Except during the occupation by the Germans in the Second World War, this ceremony has been carried on un-interrupted since 2 July 1928. On the very evening that Polish forces liberated Ypres in 1944, the ceremony was resumed, despite the fact that heavy fighting was still taking place in other parts of the town. Our group, all in civilian clothes, attended this simple yet moving ceremony on the Sunday evening of our visit. There were townspeople and tourists there and everyone stood quietly behind the low rope which kept everyone off the road through the Gate. With a few minutes to go to the ceremony, our guide turned to face us – 'Serving officers may stand on the road on the other side of the rope. Please step over the rope.'

We all stepped over the rope; there were nearly fifty of us. And we got such looks, full of respect, from the many hundreds of people waiting quietly for the short evening ceremony. And then the local fire brigade played the Last Post.

This one short day had an impact on everyone, but by far the greatest impact of all occurred in our coach when our guide, a retired British Army officer who worked in Brussels, told us a simple story. I cannot remember his name and I hope that I can do justice to the tale that he told.

He explained that he visited many battlefield sites and cemeteries and had often visited Ypres and Tyne Cot. On one particular day he had parked some distance from the car park and walked into the cemetery on his own, wandering slowly around looking at the gravestones of so many, so many unnamed. There was one that he had noted which gave the name of a young soldier, but also said 'known as'. He had given a false name and age in order to enlist; he was fifteen years old when he died.

Our guide was alone in the cemetery. He heard a vehicle enter the car park and then lots of noise from the car park. He looked down the hill and saw that the vehicle was a school bus and the children, all about four or five years old, came rushing into the cemetery accompanied by two female teachers. He looked on in horror as the children began playing games around the gravestones, with some sitting in front of the headstones and having a picnic. Our guide looked on in complete anguish. His first reaction was to go and remonstrate with the young teachers but then he thought it best to quietly leave without being seen; he was angry and upset. As he tried to walk away he was spotted by one of the teachers who ran toward him. She apologized for disturbing him and he tried to brush her apology away, 'Do you think that this is right? That what the children are doing here is appropriate?'

The young Belgian teacher explained, 'Sir, I am very sorry. We always wait to try and make sure that the cemetery is empty before we come here.'

Our guide became slightly intrigued.

The teacher went on, 'All of these children have just begun school. They all come from the towns and villages near here. Every few months, the remains of yet another soldier are found near one of their homes, or in their gardens or in the fields. When they begin school we try so very hard to explain what happened here, why so many young men died here so close to where they live. It is so very difficult.'

Our guide became acutely embarrassed. But she had not finished, 'So every year, we bring each new intake of boys and girls here to meet the soldiers, so that they can talk to them. Sir, we bring them here to play with the soldiers.'

By the time that our guide had finished telling his tale to fifty very senior officers from across the world, none could maintain eye contact with him.

* * *

My posting to the RAF Training Group was soon confirmed, and on 25 November I would take over as Flying Training 2, the wing commander staff officer responsible for Hawk and Tucano flying training. I would also have staff responsibility for the Red Arrows. I had enjoyed working at RCDS, especially the visits. While living on the outskirts of London had many advantages and we had had a glimpse at the good things that city life could offer, the daily routine of leaving home at 0615 hours and then getting back so late in the evening, had been a real grind. I yearned to wear my flying suit once more.

When my posting had been approved, the Personnel Management Agency group captain commented that I was 'an ideal candidate, but I suspect that he won't be in the job for long.' I had scored well in the 1996 promotion board and he was optimistic about my chances in 1997. He was right about me not being at Innsworth for long, but not for the reason that he thought.

So rightly or wrongly, when my two-year appointment as Directing Staff (Air) at the most prestigious military college in the UK came to an end, I would go back to the world that I had known and felt sure that I would enjoy. But not quite yet; there was another overseas tour to organize, and this one had the makings of being an epic.

*   *   *

For the 1996 tour I was part of the twelve strong group to visit North America; seven were from the UK, and one each from China, India, Russia, Sri Lanka, and Ukraine. Our tour would involve thirty-two nights, twenty-three flights, and sixteen hotels, taking in Cuba, Jamaica, Canada, and the USA.

Our first day, 10 September, was a long day of travel and it set the pattern for the whole trip. We flew from London Heathrow to Paris, then to Caracas in Venezuela before going on to Havana in Cuba. This was the very first time that Cuba had accepted a visit from RCDS and we had been carefully briefed about the delicacy of our visit. Only a few weeks earlier, an aircraft belonging to one of the 'Free Cuba' organizations based in Florida was shot down by a Cuban Air Force Mig 29; the pilot had been killed. These aircraft occasionally flew over Havana dropping leaflets in a manner that was highly provocative to Fidel Castro's regime. This particular aircraft and its pilot had run the gauntlet once too often. So we were advised to stay well clear of this subject and any other that might strain relations during our short visit.

We were met by the British Ambassador, and he again emphasized 'no-go areas' during our discussions; such was his concern, and the importance and sensitivity of our visit, that he accompanied us on our first day.

We were subjected to a range of briefings by senior Cuban military officers covering foreign relations and the involvement of all Cubans in Cuba's national defence. At the end of the first session it was traditional for our group leader, or his deputy, to offer an appropriate RCDS thank you before leading off with a fairly innocuous question. On this occasion this task was handled by our Deputy Group Leader, a RN officer. The Ambassador looked on anxiously but then visibly relaxed as the RN officer began with a typically charming RCDS thank you. He went on to talk about relationships, particularly in the west, between the military and the civil power, and how they needed to interact when it came to decision making. We were all completely relaxed at this stage but we should have known better.

'So, a few weeks ago when an aircraft infringed your airspace, and the decision was taken to shoot it down, what coordination took place between your Air Force and your Government, and how did the decision process work?'

Our Deputy Group Leader then promptly sat down. You could have heard a pin drop. The Ambassador appeared to be in shock, while the rest of us sat up and listened carefully. The Cubans were stunned and they waffled; they were totally unprepared and we moved onto other topics.

Later that evening we attended a reception at the Ambassador's residence. For the first couple of hours everyone was on their best behaviour, but once all or most of the official guests had left, only our group and some British Embassy staff remained and we all began to relax on this first night of what would be a very long tour. The gin and tonics were strong and frequent, but it was idyllic standing on the patio overlooking a lovely garden of Her Britannic Majesty's Ambassador's Official Residence in Havana. I may even have been indulging in a cigar when someone behind me dug me sharply in the ribs. I turned around sharply only to see that it was our Group Leader, Air Vice-Marshal Sam Goddard.

'Paul,' he said, 'have you met Ramon Castro?'

What a silly question I thought, Ramon Castro was Fidel Castro's elder brother.

'No sir,' I replied.

With that, he turned around and said, 'Ramon, I'd like to introduce Wing Commander Paul McDonald.'

My hand was gripped firmly by a tall man with a beard and a beaming smile! He was charming.

Our busy programme covered visits to a scientific research institute, briefings on Cuba's economy, a visit to Old Havana, and meetings with the National Drugs Commission. We visited the Palacio de las Convenciones for briefings from the National Association of People's Power and also visited the Armed Forces Academy and College for National Defence Studies. At the end of the first day we were unexpectedly invited back to the Foreign Affairs Ministry to be given more information about the Mig 29 incident that had been raised on the first day. A nerve had clearly been touched, but we were very impressed with the way in which they returned to the question to give us a better answer.

On our final day we went to Cojimar, a fishing village to the east of Havana, and had lunch at The Old Man and The Sea Restaurant. It was here that Ernest Hemingway celebrated winning the Pulitzer Prize in 1953 with his fishermen friends and the captain of his yacht, Gregorio Fuentes, who was also the inspiration for the main character of his book *The Old Man and the Sea*. Later that day we visited Morro Castle, or to give it its proper title, Castillo de los Tres Reyes Magos Del Morro. The Spanish language added so much more to the old picturesque fortress guarding the entrance to Havana Bay; it had been built in 1589 when Cuba was under the control of Spain. Later, we visited the Museum of the Revolution which, perhaps appropriately, is located in what was the Presidential Palace of all former Cuban presidents.

At the end of our final day we were again invited to another briefing about the Mig 29 incident. For each of the briefings, a more senior Cuban officer had been present and this one was given, as far as I recall, by their Deputy Chief of Staff. Each briefing had offered more information, but for this final one they held little back. We were shown videos taken from 'Free Cuba' television and were given a map showing the route flown by the aircraft that was eventually shot down. It also showed the tracks taken by two Cuban Mig 29s which had been scrambled to intercept the aircraft. It was very clear that the Cubans wanted to answer our question and try to get their side of the story across. Post 9/11 not many countries would think for long before shooting down an intruding aircraft. So perhaps context counts for everything.

Cuba had proved to be a fascinating country to visit. The Cuban people seemed to have very good medical care and schooling but the economy was crippled by US sanctions. It also seemed as though, with investment, Cuba could become a 'jewel' of an island within the Caribbean, far more so than many.

One of our members compiled a video of the North American tour. One of the most memorable sequences shows our Chinese Army colleague, complete with a large Cuban cigar in one hand and a large brandy in the other, grinning broadly and saying, 'Do not think that you can corrupt me with your decadent imperialist ways!'

*   *   *

On 14 September we flew in a rather ancient Russian aircraft from Havana to Montego Bay in Jamaica. The aircraft only had sufficient seats for our group but it did have a stewardess. There was a time difference between Cuba and Jamaica and one of our number calculated that the sun would be almost over the yard arm when we arrived in Jamaica so it was appropriate that we enjoy some fine Jamaican rum on the way. We all agreed, but were shocked on arrival in Montego Bay to find that we had adjusted our clocks the wrong way and we actually arrived at 0930 hours in the morning!

The Jamaican visit was also interesting and we learnt something about foreign affairs, tourism, trade unionism and defence. We visited the University of West Indian Studies and enjoyed a 'meet the people' party organized by the Jamaican Tourist Board. One of 'the people' was the father of John Barnes, the England International Footballer. Jamaica was a fascinating country but it was a worry to see that all of the best hotels seemed to be within secure guarded compounds.

*   *   *

On 18 September we flew from Kingston to New York, and then to Ottowa. Air travel was the main feature of the Canadian leg of the tour as we moved first east and then west across this vast country, much of which is untouched wilderness.

Canada's cities were impressive. It's such a vast country, yet 90 per cent of Canada's population live within 100 miles of the US border. We attended briefings on Canada's Armed Forces, the system of regional government, and also talks about the Royal Canadian Mounted Police, and about native issues. In Ottowa we had a guided tour of the Parliament Buildings, and in Quebec City we visited La Citadelle and learnt something of its history. It is located on top of Cap Diamant, adjoining the Plains of Abraham and is part of the fortifications of Quebec City, the only city with surviving city walls in North America. In Halifax we all enjoyed magnificent Atlantic lobster and there was much to admire in the scenery of Nova Scotia.

In Toronto we had meetings at the Stock Exchange and the Board of Trade, and also visited the Toronto Globe and Mail for discussions with the editor. The view from the dining room atop the CN Tower was magnificent. It is 1,815 feet tall and, when it was completed in 1976, it became the tallest free-standing structure on land and tallest tower in the world for the next thirty-four years; it attracts more than 2 million international visitors each year. CN originally referred to Canadian National, the railway company that built the tower.

We were soon in Edmonton, and then flew north to the wilderness surrounding Yellowknife, where we were briefed on the Northern Area and dined at the Wildcat Café. On 26 September we flew to Vancouver where we learnt something of the huge forestry industry. The following day we flew to the beautiful city of Victoria for briefings on Maritime Pacific Command. Our return journey was by ferry and our RN Member 'blagged' our way onto the wheelhouse for a fascinating trip around the islands back to Vancouver. On 28 September we flew to Washington DC for the final leg of our tour.

*   *   *

The US trip took us from the east coast to the mid-west before we ended up in the south-east, so very close to where we had begun our tour thirty-one days earlier.

In Washington we visited CNN, the Pentagon, and the State Department. We also had a working breakfast with Senator Joseph B. Lieberman, who later ran for the White House. We also visited the National Defence University and Anacostia Senior High School before touring George Washington University Hospital. Following a metro liner train journey to New York, we were briefed on crime and social, economic and political trends in the city. We also visited the UN and had lunch with Kofi Annan a few months before he was appointed UN Secretary General. In 2012 he was appointed as the UN Special Envoy to Syria. Later, we visited a New York Police Department precinct and attended a number of seminars on education, US security, and housing in the South Bronx.

On 6 October we flew to Colorado Springs via Dallas, and the following day had briefings on the US space programme with Ronald M. Sega, one of the Mear Space Station astronauts. We then flew back to Denver and on to the Combined Arms Centre at Fort Leavenworth for tours of the National Simulation Centre and the Battle Command Laboratory and Staff College. Three days later we arrived in Miami where we were given an overview of Florida and especially their hurricane disaster contingencies. The following day we flew to Key West for our final overnight stop. In this picturesque town we heard about illegal immigration and anti drugs operations. It was in Key West that I saw at first hand the amazing flying skills of the pelican, that well known symbol of the Central Flying School.

With our return to the UK, my time at RCDS was coming to a close, and my tour ended on 23 November 1996. It would be the only time in thirty-four years RAF service that I would work in London.

Training Group, HQ Personnel and Training Command, 1996–1997
I commuted at weekends to and from RAF Innsworth, near Gloucester, until January 1997. My immediate boss was Group Captain Flying Training, a former Station Commander of RAF Valley and he and I got on well. I also had two capable staff officers, both of whom were squadron leaders; one was Andy Wyatt, a Hawk Instructor, and the other was Richard Graves, a Tucano Instructor. Another member of the flying training staff was Mike Napier, last seen on 14 Squadron at Bruggen; Mike was now a squadron leader but was soon to retire and join British Airways.

My role gave me good opportunities to visit Valley and Linton, and to fly both the Hawk and Tucano. I also jointly chaired the Fast-Jet Steering Group Sub-Committee, which was a committee involving staffs from all of the training units and the operational staffs within Strike Command. The meetings were held to discuss, and try to synchronize, output standards from the training pipeline, with minimum entry requirements demanded by the fast-jet operational conversion units.

Many fast-jet units felt that the output standard from the training pipeline, and notably from the Hawk course at RAF Valley, had reduced. Hawk students graduating from RAF Valley had previously moved onto the Hawk Tactical Weapons Unit at RAF Chivenor, a Strike Command Unit. However, as a cost saving measure, Chivenor had been closed and Hawk advanced flying training and weapons training had been combined at RAF Valley, a Training Group Unit. The combined course had been limited to a maximum of 100 flying hours per student, a loss of some twenty to thirty flying hours. While some reduction in hours could be justified to many, the new '100-hour course' was arbitrary, and most staff felt that a change in output standard from Valley was inevitable. In addition, engineering at Valley had been put out to contract, and the new company was struggling with recruitment, always an issue at Valley. While task achievement at Valley was an issue, Valley's customers were voicing concerns about standards.

In my view, it was inevitable that such a reduction in flying hours for such inexperienced pilots would affect the output standard of Valley's pilots. However, the *potential* of the graduating pilots had not changed. Some of the fast-jet units insisted that they would not in any way reduce their entry standard to match the output from Valley. If they did not, then they simply risked having empty places on their courses. While I had sympathy with their position, the only way that the system could work was for the input standard at each level to match the output standard of the lower level, even if that output standard had been adversely affected by a cut in flying hours. For the foreseeable future, increasing the Hawk course was simply a non-starter.

While all of this was going on the Air Officer Commanding was posted out and a new man arrived who set about making further drastic changes to a flying training system that had been the envy of many. There was no doubt that flying training was in need of reorganization and streamlining of process, especially within the HQ, but the changes that were imposed changed the RAF's pilot training system drastically. In fact so many changes had been introduced in rapid succession that it was impossible to determine the impact of each.

Fast-jet students had faced long delays during training, post Options for Change, with some being in backlog for two or three years; RAF elementary flying training with RAF instructors had ceased, with the task taken over by mainly civilian instructors in civil registered aircraft; student pilots were now to be subject to early streaming at the end of elementary flying training; this would mean that the one remaining traditional basic school (No. 1 Flying Training School) would only be concerned with meeting a fast-jet output target. Add to that the introduction of the '100 hour' Hawk course and it was little wonder that cause and effect could no longer be determined, and that concerns about standards were being expressed.

My job title was renamed Programme Development 1, whatever that meant, and I now worked for a Chief Executive. My job specification didn't change at all; at least as Flying Training 2, people could work out that I had something to do with flying training, but now? It also appeared as if the HQ staff were no longer valued. Morale plummeted. Even though Hawk flying training was going through something of a crisis, rather than focusing on the problems associated with the Hawk, attention seemed to be turned toward Linton, which was in good shape. Overall, I think that the next few years were very damaging for the RAF system of aircrew training and it would take the return of Chris Coville as Commander-in-Chief in 2001 to start putting things right.

I became increasingly frustrated, and I was not alone as a number of others sought their own 'escape tunnel' to an appointment elsewhere. It was probably the first time that I had been unhappy in my work since joining the RAF twenty-six years earlier. The only bright spots were being able to visit Linton and Valley regularly, and fly both the Tucano and the Hawk.

* * *

The promotion board came and went; I was not selected. While there was never any guarantee of how a promotion board would score candidates (four separate air vice-marshals score each candidate), as I had been very close to the 'cut' in 1996, the signs had been very good for the 1997 board. As I was approaching my forty-eighth birthday, I realized that the 1997 board had been my best chance if I harboured any hopes of command of a flying station. For whatever reason, I had probably reached my ceiling and therefore had to come to terms with spending the remaining eight years of my service in staff appointments, probably in or close to London; certainly my flying days would be over.

In an attempt to come to a decision about my future, I asked for an interview with my Desk Officer. He was very frank and helpful. As Chief Instructor at Linton I had spent two years under Air Vice-Marshal Coville's command when he had been AOC; I had also worked closely with him for two years before that. In June 1994 he had written that 'McDonald is the best Chief Instructor in my Group, has the strongest claim for command of Linton-on-Ouse in the next round, and shows clear potential for air rank.' I could not have asked for a better endorsement.

When I left Linton less than four months later, his successor, under whose command I had been for four weeks had other views, and commented that as far as JEFTS had been concerned I had 'perhaps persisted with a measure of micro-management'. That particular comment was very disappointing. But at least I now knew why things had not developed in the way that I had hoped and I could now make decisions accordingly.

I was fairly philosophical about the situation, but having to wait for almost three years before finding out what had actually been said about me in writing at the end of my Linton tour, spoke loudly about the limitations of the RAF's closed reporting system, thankfully now changed. As a reporting officer, I had always ensured that those under my command had been able to read exactly what I had written on their annual reports.

For the next promotion board, my fate would rest to a large extent on the views of my Chief Executive! Best if I didn't hold my breath then! I only met him once, and that was while walking to the HQ. But that was enough for him to comment in my 1997 report that while I was probably the sharpest wing commander on the staff that did not say a lot, although he did not discount promotion to group captain!

I joined the 'Escape Committee'; not surprisingly it was rather full!

* * *

Soon afterwards I was asked by my Desk Officer if I would be interested in a Loan Service appointment in Kuwait. I would first need to complete refresher flying on the Tucano, upgrading my 'Competent to Instruct' category to a full A2 instructor category, and also qualify as an Instrument Rating Examiner on the Tucano; that would at that time make me the only wing commander in the RAF with those qualifications. I had a weekend to think it over.

The job sounded interesting. Even though Kuwait was considered 'high risk' at the time, it was a condition of the appointment that I would be accompanied, so there was much to think about. Jackie was well aware of how frustrated I felt in my current job, perhaps more aware than I was, and she recognized that this move could be a good opportunity. We discussed it with Matthew, who had been living in California for three months, and with Hannah, who was in her first year at university; both agreed that this was an opportunity to grasp. So we did!

Matthew arrived back in September and announced his engagement to Dionne, an American girl; they would marry in Los Angeles two months later on his twenty-first birthday, and his new home would then be in Washington DC. Things then moved very quickly, with Hannah deciding to take a gap year from university to accompany us to Kuwait.

I only had a few days to clear my desk before heading to Linton. Shortly before leaving the HQ, I was invited out for lunch by my flying training colleagues. One of the other wing commanders, who had previously worked in the Middle East, said, 'You do realize that you will be working for a bunch of arrogant individuals who won't listen to a word you say!'

'Well, I won't need any pre-employment training then,' I replied.

*   *   *

In early summer I spent a memorable few days on an RAF Sailing Association yacht. Six of us, all colleagues who had worked together at Linton, hired a 32-foot yacht which was moored at Plymouth. The crew comprised of the skipper, Roger Clements, a very experienced yachtsman, Andy Shaw another experienced hand, two 'middle order batsmen', Nigel Gillingham and Dave Lewis, both of whom had been former General Service Training Officers at Linton, and bringing up the rear as sailing novices was Dave Taylor, my Deputy at Linton when I left, and me; neither of us had ever sailed before in a yacht.

We met up in Plymouth and spent the first day provisioning. Roger, very wisely, chose to spend the afternoon and evening within Plymouth Sound practicing some rudimentary sailing skills. That was just as well as a sister yacht, with another RAF crew, returned that evening having lost its mast outside the harbour in difficult conditions.

The following morning we set off for Salcombe. We followed the coastline east and the plan was to leave Salcombe at about 0200 hours the next morning to cross the English Channel, arriving in Guernsey's tidal harbour at high tide. We were split into two watches, and I joined Roger and Nigel for the departure. The trip down river was straightforward, but it was a very dark and cloudy night with the wind freshening as we reached the estuary. The heavens then opened and, as we cleared the headland, the swell increased markedly and the sea began to get very rough. Roger and Nigel went up top to take in sail while I held the tiller. It began to get most unpleasant. Roger, always calm in a crisis, and this was turning into something of a crisis, called for 'all hands on deck' as conditions worsened dramatically.

Afterwards, Dave Lewis described how, as he was coming up the rearward facing ladder, he had looked up to see me hanging on to the tiller for grim death. 'My word,' he thought, 'the sky is really dark!'

And then he realized that he was not looking at the sky above my head but at the sea! We were soon in the teeth of a Force 6 gale which quickly began to have an effect on the non-sailors amongst us. Roger judged that to try and turn about in such conditions would be too dangerous, so we pressed on towards the Channel Islands. Dave Taylor was the first to succumb to sea-sickness, but I wasn't far behind. Nigel seemed to have the remarkable knack of being able to 'heave' over the side and then carry on steering the yacht! I had no such constitution and soon headed for the cabin feeling absolutely wretched to join my equally wretched former Deputy. What a fine pair we made: the former Chief Instructor and Deputy of No. 1 Flying Training School 'out-retching' one another!

By dawn, the storm had abated but it was a tired and partially dispirited crew who entered the tidal harbour of Guernsey. Guernsey however proved to be delightful and for the next few days we enjoyed some good sailing, calling in at Sark and Alderney before returning to Plymouth. It was a fascinating experience but it was not one that I felt any urge to repeat.

*   *   *

In September I headed back to Linton for my refresher course, travelling back home each weekend. On 6 November 1997 I was awarded my A2 by the Central Flying School Examiner, Squadron Leader Brian Russell, and a few days later he also awarded me my Instrument Rating Examiner qualification. During the few weeks at Linton, I flew just over fifty-eight hours. I was pleased that three years after leaving Linton, I had been assessed as above the average in all disciplines.

My last few weeks in the UK were hectic: we travelled to Los Angeles for Matthew and Dionne's wedding and then back to the UK for Christmas and to pack. Tension with Iraq had been increasing and we were told to only take with us to Kuwait what we would be prepared to leave behind if we had to depart quickly. Therefore, the vast majority of our personal possessions went into storage. I was to travel first, so Jackie would again have to deal with the final packing arrangements as well as handing over the house to the RAF. I think that she was getting rather bored with that.

I would be going to a totally new appointment working directly for the Kuwait Air Force (KAF) in their HQ as the Senior RAF Advisor. Specifically I would be required to advise on STANEVAL, meaning standards and evaluation, which was very much about quality control, a role with which I was very familiar. To be a current instructor on at least one of the aircraft types operated by Kuwait would clearly be an enormous advantage and the KAF had a squadron of Tucanos; they also operated Hawks. The RAF was also very keen that I offered appropriate advice on flying training in Kuwait. That seemed to be fairly straightforward.

While on embarkation leave in January 1998, I was approached by a group captain from the HQ; he made me realize that there may be more to my new job than I had first thought. He showed me a signal from the British Ambassador in Kuwait that had arrived on his desk via the Foreign Office and the MOD. The Kuwaitis had formally asked the UK to provide twelve more RAF instructors and also to form a ground school. I knew that the RAF had no capacity whatsoever to provide such numbers. The RAF was often in a crisis with regard to pilot manning, and in early 1998 we had far too few. UK interests and in particular UK commercial interests, were then mentioned. The UK-built Hawks and Tucanos were being maintained in Kuwait by UK companies, and a number of British jobs in Kuwait and the UK depended on keeping the maintenance contracts for these aircraft in place. How that could be done was the key question, especially as the RAF could not provide the numbers of instructors requested. It would be up to me to try and find a solution.

At the time I didn't really give much thought to how I could do this while also acting as an impartial adviser to the KAF. In fact, I didn't really give the problem much thought at all, I had boxes to pack! But it was an interesting conversation and the problem and its solution would become the focus of my working life for the next four years.

*   *   *

A few days before my departure, I was contacted by Squadron Leader Euan Alexander who would be in my small team in Kuwait. He explained that as I would have diplomatic status I could purchase alcohol for home consumption, but only through the British Embassy. My six-monthly allowance was twenty-four cases, a case being a slab of beer (twenty-four cans), twelve bottles of wine or twelve bottles of spirits. It could not be brought home at the end of one's tour and you certainly weren't allowed to sell it. As Euan had not known who was going to fill my post when the last order had been submitted, he had ordered the full six-monthly allowance and it would arrive in Kuwait a few weeks after I did. He said that he would welcome a cheque from me as soon as possible.

'That's no problem' I said, 'how much is it likely to be?'

'Oh, not much' said Euan, 'about £1,000.'

As I looked outside at our thirteen-year old car, considered our mortgage which was virtually equal to the value of the house we had bought ten years earlier, and thought about two increasing student loans, I almost passed out!

Chapter 11

Desert Fox

Kuwait: Invasion and Occupation

Although I had met a number of RAF pilots who had served in Kuwait, I didn't know a great deal about the country before Iraq's invasion in 1991 brought this corner of the Gulf of Arabia into sharp focus. With the subsequent questions asked about the legality of Gulf War II over ten years later, it is easy to forget the cruelty, the brutality, and the sheer barbarism of Saddam Hussein, the man responsible for the invasion of Kuwait, Gulf War I, and for so much more.

While the invasion was a shock to many in the west, tension had been building up between the two countries for some time. The issue was mainly oil and the shared Rumailah oilfield. Saddam Hussein accused Kuwait of stealing Iraqi oil from the shared oilfield and then deliberately forcing down the oil price. A Kuwaiti delegation had been negotiating with Iraq and Kuwait's Crown Prince, who was also the Prime Minister, was due to attend further talks in Bagdad on 4 August 1990.

Kuwait's Armed Forces had been on high alert but, as the negotiations entered a crucial stage, they had been stood down to avoid antagonizing the Iraqis. Senior officers in Kuwait's 35 Brigade, the brigade nearest the border with Iraq, were convinced that Iraq would invade and argued strongly that they be allowed to deploy. They were ordered to do nothing. Against orders, the main armoured battalion was put on alert. When again ordered to stand-down, it did so, but very slowly.

The Kuwait Air Force (KAF) had three airbases. Abdullah Al-Mubarak was the transport base adjoining the KAF HQ and was part of the complex which housed Kuwait International Airport. Ali Al-Salem, home to the KAF's French-built air defence Mirage IIIs and helicopters, was about an hour's drive west; it was also within an hour's drive of Iraq. The other base was Ahmed Al-Jaber, an hour's drive to the south, and it was here that the KAF's British-built Hawk fast-jet trainers and American-built A6 Skyhawks fighter bombers were based. These bases were only fully manned when on alert, and most personnel lived in Kuwait City. So the KAF airbases, particularly the Mirage base in the west, were very vulnerable to surprise attack.

In the early hours of 2 August, with Kuwaiti's Armed Forces stood down, and two days before Kuwait's Crown Price was due in Baghdad for talks, Saddam made his move.

Many people in the west thought that the Kuwaitis did not put up much of a fight. Given their size, and the nature of the attack, there was no way that Kuwait could hold out for long, but fight they certainly did, and many brave Kuwaitis continued to fight from within during a cruel occupation. It is worth recording that after their country's occupation, the remnants of the KAF flew 2,662 missions from Saudi Arabia between September 1990, and the day of Kuwait's liberation. I was to learn much during our four years in Kuwait and would meet many who were directly involved in liberating their country.

* * *

Iraq attacked on two main routes, one from the north down the main road from Basrah and over the Mutla Ridge, the only high ground in Kuwait, while the other attack swung in from the north-west where the Iraq, Kuwait and Saudi borders met. The road across Mutla Ridge was to be the scene of carnage during the Iraqi's chaotic retreat the following spring. Within two years of our return from Kuwait in 2002, our daughter Hannah, by then an RAF air traffic controller, would drive down the same road from Basrah while she was serving on her first tour in Iraq after Gulf War II.

The routes converged on the small town of Jahra, east of the Mutla Ridge and west of Kuwait City. Ali Al-Salem was soon cut-off. The besieged Kuwaitis fought hard. Their Mirage fighters shot down a number of Iraqi helicopters while the Skyhawks from Ahmed Al-Jaber also had great success. The KAF Air Defence Brigade also took its toll.

Given their losses of helicopters, the Iraqi Air Force soon turned their attention to the airbases, and the main runways were bombed and put out of action. Most Mirages were airborne when Ali-Al-Salem was put out of action, and they were ordered to Ahmed-Al-Jaber only to find that its runways too were unusable. With insufficient fuel to reach Saudi Arabia they landed on a security road; it was a mere 4.5 metres wide. But these landings meant that the KAF could still fight. Shortly before Ali Al-Salem was captured, all their serviceable helicopters made their escape to Saudi Arabia, but not without loss.

Kuwait's 35 Armoured Brigade fought hard and with success as the Iraqis neared Jahra. Despite being heavily outnumbered, the Iraqi Republican Guard Divisions which spearheaded the invasion paid a heavy price. The Brigade only broke off and headed to Saudi Arabia when ammunition was low and it was about to be cut off.

In the city, large numbers of Iraqi Special Forces had been landed by sea with the aim of capturing the royal family, but the Emir was able to make his escape. However, his younger brother, the highly popular and globally respected Sheikh Fahad Al-Ahmed Al-Jaber Al-Sabah, was shot and killed at the Emir's Palace. Sheikh Fahad was the President of the Olympic Council of Asia and a member of the International Olympic Committee.

* * *

Many Kuwaiti servicemen only became aware of the invasion when Kuwait City was bombed. Some who tried to make it to Ali Al-Salem were captured en route. Those based at Ahmed Al-Jaber had a better chance.

I became close friends with one KAF Skyhawk pilot. Ahmed had trained as a pilot in the USA and he had also spent a year at the RAF Staff College at Bracknell where he and his family had lived in married quarters. At the time of the invasion he was a major and worked for the KAF Deputy Commander. Shortly before the HQ was overrun, Ahmed was ordered to try to make it to Ahmed-Al-Jaber and then on to Saudi Arabia. This order for Ahmed, and for many others, must have been very hard to follow as it meant leaving his family to a very uncertain fate. Ahmed subsequently described that frantic journey, at high speed, from the KAF HQ. He recalled driving along the 7th Ring Road and being passed by columns of Iraqi armour and troops heading in the opposite direction on their way into the city. As he turned left off the Ring Road to head south, he was waved down at an Iraqi roadblock, but he ignored it and drove quickly on. He successfully reached Ahmed-Al-Jaber and made his escape to Saudi Arabia in the back seat of the very last Hawk to get out of Kuwait.

I met a number of Kuwaiti pilots who did things that I wouldn't have dreamt of doing. One was another Skyhawk pilot, a quiet and unassuming man by the name of Majed. I heard from others what he did and when I eventually met him he was a colonel. In 1991 he was a major and had left home normally to go to work at Ahmed Al-Jaber to find that his country was at war. He was ordered to conduct a fighter reconnaissance sortie against any Iraqi forces. Such missions were normally conducted by pairs of aircraft, to provide mutual support, but he was surprised to learn that he would be on his own.

In normal circumstances such a mission when the enemy had control of the air would be unheard of; it would very likely be a one-way trip. But the circumstances were far from normal that day in Kuwait. He was then ordered to take-off from the narrow road which the Mirages had proven to be adequate, just. But Majed's aircraft was heavily laden with fuel and carried a full bomb load. He got airborne successfully to attack a column of Iraqi armour already in Kuwait, with Iraqi Mig 23 fighters on combat air patrol visible high above.

Our lone Skyhawk pilot didn't have any difficulty finding the Iraqis. Unbelievably, he completed separate dive-bombing attacks, dropping a single bomb each time. He did this to make every bomb count rather than risk straddling the target. The 'norm' is to drop all the bombs during a single attack and then exit 'stage left' as quickly and as low as you possibly could. After each attack Majed headed off into the desert to get away from the Iraqi anti-aircraft fire before climbing back up to find another target. To continually re-attack in this manner was an open invitation to be shot down, and he was well aware of the Iraqi fighters high above. On his last attack he was hit by anti-aircraft fire but was able to get his damaged aircraft back to Al-Jaber where he once again landed on the road. He was refuelled and then flew on to Saudi Arabia.

*   *   *

There was little publicity about what the Iraqis did in Kuwait, but there was very fierce resistance throughout the occupation. The Iraqis were merciless in their treatment of the people they caught. The most horrid torture imaginable was carried out with the victims being finally shot, or worse, outside their family home. Very little was ever said about how the Iraqis treated women, but rape was widespread with thousands of victims; this left a long term legacy. Publicity about this was much muted.

Some Kuwaiti friends of ours told us about their experiences. One, a KAF junior officer, stayed behind working in the resistance until his position became untenable. He made his escape over the roof at the back of his house as Iraqi soldiers entered through the front to search for him. A few days later his wife and four children made their escape across the desert in the family car, a saloon, not a 4x4. She was so 'matter of fact' in telling her story, and felt that the biggest challenge was not hurtling across the desert through Iraqi lines, but having to learn how to cope without her maid when she got to Saudi!

*   *   *

Colonel Bruce Duncan, Commander of the British Liaison Team in Kuwait in 1990, wrote an excellent account of life in Kuwait under Iraqi occupation. It was called *Cruelty and Compassion: An Englishman in Kuwait* and it was published in the Army Quarterly and Defence Journal in April 1991. There were sixty-six members of his team and 150 dependants in Kuwait at the time of the invasion, and within two days more than half of his team were picked up from the main families' complex. Their homes were broken into and looted and the women were harassed and molested.

He described the regular and conscript Iraqi soldiers (not the Republican Guard) as a wretched lot who were poorly led and ill equipped. He heard the story of a seventeen year old Iraqi conscript who had pleaded with the Iraqi recruiters that he couldn't enlist as his father and elder brothers had been killed fighting for Saddam Hussein in the war with Iran. He was now responsible for looking after his mother and four sisters. The following day his remaining family were lined up and executed. He was then required to enlist.

During the occupation, Colonel Duncan and his family moved into a vacant house in Mishref, the district that Jackie and I would live in. He described the manner in which his family were looked after by local Kuwaitis as an object lesson in all that is best in Islam. As far as the Kuwaitis were concerned, the British families were guests who had been outrageously treated by people of their faith, and a local committee kept Colonel Duncan's family supplied. Many Kuwaitis risked their lives to keep British families supplied with food.

He also described some of the activities of the Kuwaiti resistance. A number of young Kuwaitis died in their cars having attacked Iraqi armoured personnel carriers and ammunition trucks. The Resistance also shot down an Iraqi military transport aircraft, forcing the Iraqis to stop using the International Airport. The Iraqi response to these attacks was brutal. A number of Kuwaiti youths were seized at random and shot in front of their families. Two young boys, not even in their teens, were shot in front of their pleading parents in Mishref for distributing pro-Kuwaiti leaflets. Many Kuwaiti Palestinians also courageously refused to collaborate with the Iraqis. By mid-October only a dozen members of the team, plus Colonel Duncan's two sons, remained in hiding in Kuwait. The other captured servicemen had been sent to strategic sites in Iraq as human shields.

Sadly Bruce Duncan's family's experience ended in tragedy. During an evacuation brokered between the British Embassy and the Iraqi authorities, and while being transported by the Iraqis, his teenage sons were involved in a horrific accident. His elder son died while his younger son survived, though badly injured. For Colonel Duncan, his and his family's traumatic experience was over by late October, but for the Kuwaitis and those foreigners still in Kuwait, liberation was still four months away.

* * *

NATO's philosophy for air attack planning had been to use ingress and egress corridors to and from their targets. These corridors could be quite complex, as they changed direction to avoid friendly force concentrations and the worst of enemy defences. To use such corridors, Coalition aircraft needed good navigational equipment, as outside the corridor, often only five miles wide, there was a strong chance of being shot down by your own side!

I always found it most reassuring to have a navigator sitting behind me keeping me on track! When the air war against Saddam began, similar corridors were in place for Coalition aircraft. They jinked left and right before crossing the border. Ahmed and his fellow Skyhawk pilots looked at these in horror! They were flying single seat aircraft with fairly basic navigation equipment. They needed an alternative! And so the 'Kuwaiti Corridor' was born, a straight corridor, five miles wide from take-off to Kuwait and back again. No twists and turns, nothing fancy, just a nice straight line. And that's what they used.

Ahmed described his first mission as fairly straightforward with just the Kuwaiti Skyhawks using their own private corridor while the rest of the Coalition aircraft found their own tortuous way to and from the enemy. On the second mission, they were joined by some US A-10 attack aircraft that also chose to use the same simple route. By Day Three, a few US F-16s also joined in. And by Day Four it was like Piccadilly Circus, with dozens of Coalition aircraft all trying to use the 'Kuwaiti Corridor' in preference to the best that NATO's air planners could come up with!

It is difficult to truly understand how the Kuwaiti pilots felt leaving their families and their homes behind and then, within a few months, having to attack targets in their own country. While it was to take me a long time to become accepted amongst them, I came to admire their courage greatly and their regard for family.

Ahmed described something of what it was like; on some missions he could see his family home, but his biggest problem was one of fatigue and, once the air war began, he found it very difficult to sleep. Flying twice each day, by Day Three, he was very tired indeed. The following story was about the mission he flew when he had been tasked to lead a pair of Skyhawks to attack ground targets in Kuwait.

'Did you ever fly the Skyhawk, Paul?' he asked.

'No,' I replied.

'Well,' he said, 'it had an autopilot but not a very good one.'

At this point I wondered, slightly incredulously, what he was about to say.

'But I was so tired, I just had to close my eyes,' he said. 'So I engaged the autopilot, and closed my eyes. After probably only a few seconds, I was woken up by shouting on my radio.'

'Sir, sir, pull up!' shouted his No. 2.

Ahmed quickly pulled up as he was hurtling earthwards at great speed.

'What was your No. 2 doing at this point?' I asked him.

'Oh, he was still there,' said Ahmed with a smile, 'hanging on to my wing.'

As they continued on their way to the target, Ahmed's No. 2 asked, 'Sir, what was the problem? Are you ok? Have you been hit?'

'No', said Ahmed reassuringly, 'I was just having a nap!'

After a pause, Ahmed's No. 2 then went on, 'Sir, you were having a nap? In a couple of minutes, we will be at the target, soon we might be dead. Why were you bothering to have a nap?'

This story spread like wildfire throughout the KAF. Other Kuwaiti pilots told me the same story of Ahmed. He was a very cool customer! At the time that I knew him he was a colonel and very highly regarded within the KAF. He was promoted brigadier general not long after I left, and retired as a major general.

*   *   *

Given KAF pilots' clear intent to make every bomb count, their luck could not hold out for long. One Kuwaiti Skyhawk that was part of the KAF's third attack wave of eight aircraft during the opening day of the air war was shot down while climbing after completing his *third* bombing run against the same target. The pilot ejected successfully but he was captured immediately by Iraqi troops. He was later taken to Baghdad where he was imprisoned with downed RAF Tornado crews.

The brutal torture that all the prisoners-of-war received has been well documented, but the Iraqis reserved very special treatment for any Kuwaitis captured. Hundreds of Kuwaiti men and women taken to Iraq remain 'missing' to this day. A total of 605 went missing and the bodies of 236 were eventually recovered from mass graves in Iraq. Most had been lined up and ordered to kneel, blindfolded, and then they were shot twice in the head, women and men together. The remaining 369 are still open files with the International Committee of the Red Cross. The Kuwaitis attach huge importance to honouring and recovering their dead. There is a feeling of injustice even now, twenty years after the events of 1990 and 1991. That feeling will linger until all those still missing are returned home.

First Impressions
In early 1998, the escalating tension in the Gulf resulted in US and UK forces deploying to Kuwait only a few days before I arrived. I found that my old squadron from Bruggen, 14 Squadron, together with an RAF Regiment field squadron and some 500 RAF personnel were establishing themselves at Ali Al-Salem. From a family perspective this was slightly worrying, but I had two weeks to consider the situation before Jackie and Hannah were due to arrive.

*   *   *

Kuwait City is the country's only significant city, with the small town of Jahra to the west and the oil town of Ahmadi to the south. The weather is very hot all year round and temperatures often reached 50–55°C during the summer. Even in winter, temperatures rarely dropped much below 25–30°C. With the country being so rich everything is geared up for the high temperatures, with air conditioned shops, houses and cars. Before the 1960s it must have been very difficult to live and to work in such a climate. Humidity though was generally low, unlike the Gulf States of Bahrain and Dubai, so it was a very dry heat. Working hours were also adjusted to take the heat into account.

In winter, my working hours at the KAF HQ were 0730 to 1430 hours, and in summer 0700 to 1400 hours. When working at one of the KAF airbases in the desert, I began at the same time but finished an hour earlier. Weekends were Thursdays and Fridays, and shops closed during the afternoon, re-opening in the evening. This was very easy to adapt to, and eating out during the evening and then wandering around the shopping malls and souqs was a nice experience.

Kuwait isn't a pretty country, it's generally flat apart from the Mutla Ridge, and mostly it is a rocky, rather than sandy desert, but the city boasted lots of grand houses. It was very much the thing for the homes of rich Kuwaitis to be seen, so the largest and grandest of houses were on the main roads or on corners, whereas in the UK we often prefer more privacy and seclusion. Before oil was discovered, Kuwaitis were notable sailors and merchants, and pearl fishing was quite an industry. The discovery of oil changed all of that, and now Kuwait is considered to be one of the richest countries in the world per head of population.

In 1998 the population numbered about 1 million but only about a half were Kuwaiti. The rest, from the Philippines, India, and Bangladesh, did many of the jobs that Kuwaitis were no longer willing to do. Most Kuwaiti families would have three or four 'servants', including a driver and maids, and these were generally poorly paid. They were totally dependent on their employer to sponsor them for visa purposes, so if they lost their job they also lost their work permit and had to leave the country. There were stories of some having to leave Kuwait without being paid what was due to them. The Kuwaitis themselves though were a likeable people and I did not find them to be arrogant, although, as in most countries, there were exceptions. Like most Muslims they were also very family orientated. While the country was 'dry' (no alcohol), there were much fewer restrictions on westerners than existed in Saudi Arabia, and women could drive and work. While many Kuwaiti men and women wore traditional dress, a dish-dash for men (white robes) and abaya for women (black head-dress and gown to the floor, sometimes with faces covered), many others wore western dress.

*   *   *

The British Military Mission (BMM) was the successor to the earlier liaison team. Its HQ was in the basement of one of the main Kuwaiti MOD buildings on the western side of Kuwait City. BMM had about fifty personnel, including one RN advisor and nine RAF advisors, with the remainder being from the British Army. The majority of advisors were lieutenant colonels or majors, or equivalent. It was commanded by a British Army Brigadier and was divided into two groups, each headed by a colonel. The Deputy Commander coordinated those who worked directly for the various branches of the Kuwait Armed Forces, and it was this group that I joined; there was also a small team of administrative staff. The second colonel was the Director of Studies at the Kuwait Command and Staff College which had been set up by the UK and was now jointly run by UK and Kuwaiti staff. Three RAF wing commanders, one squadron leader, and one warrant officer were on the directing staff of the college.

Although my UK boss was BMM's Deputy Commander and I would report through him to the Brigadier commanding BMM, my boss on a daily basis would be a senior KAF officer within the KAF HQ. I soon developed a great deal of respect for the Brigadier who would command BMM for three years. He had led his Regiment to great success during Gulf War I. He was also the son of an air vice-marshal who had been a Spitfire squadron commander during the Battle of Britain. The Brigadier seemed to have a good understanding of what made the RAF 'tick'. A few weeks after I arrived he asked me to attend his weekly meetings with both colonels and the BMM administrative staff to discuss policy and other matters. As well as being the senior RAF advisor to the KAF, I now became the 'de-facto' senior RAF advisor on all RAF matters.

Two RAF advisors reported directly to me. The Helicopter Training Advisor, Euan Alexander, worked with a Master Aircrew Search and Rescue Advisor operating from Ali Al-Salem, flying Puma and Super Puma helicopters. Euan departed at the end of May and in August his successor, Andy Abbott, arrived. The Search and Rescue Advisor had a particularly challenging job: he was often at the bottom of the wire being winched up and down, while the helicopter was sometimes in the hands of a pilot of 'variable quality'. Ken Tucker filled this role extremely well from April 1998 and would stay in Kuwait for four years.

On a daily basis, I wore Kuwaiti rank, and had a Kuwaiti Military Identity Card in Arabic; my name badge was also in Arabic. I retained my RAF Identity Card and I had a Diplomatic Card too, which I always referred as my 'get out of jail free' card.

My task was to advise the KAF on flying standards, evaluation and flying training, while liaising closely with the Defence Attaché in the British Embassy. My presence in Kuwait, alongside the 500 RAF personnel so recently deployed there, was entirely coincidental. Whatever professional contact I would have with them would be on behalf of the KAF.

The three senior appointments within the KAF were the Commander, his Deputy and the Director of Operations and it was the latter who would be my immediate boss. One individual who, within a few months, would loom large in my life was Brigadier Nasser Abdul Rahman Al-Jehail. A lieutenant colonel in 1990, he escaped to Saudi Arabia to command all of the Kuwaiti helicopters during the ensuing war. He had long been recognized as being extremely able and by the time I arrived he was in command of Ahmed Al-Jaber airbase, the F18 base in southern Kuwait. It was very unusual in any air force to hear of a helicopter pilot commanding a fighter base, but that was the measure of Nasser, a man whom I came to admire greatly.

*   *   *

On arrival, I soon moved into a flat in Salwa and was issued with an old Nissan Patrol 4 × 4; it was very battered, had over 200,000 miles on the clock, and would rarely steer in a straight line, but it was great for driving anywhere on or off road, or in the city where most other drivers gave me a very wide berth. Kuwait's Armed Forces were on full alert as was the RAF at Ali Al-Salem. Even greater numbers of Americans were deployed to Ahmed Al-Jaber in the south. I couldn't fail to notice that there were a number of BMM dependents who just happened to be on 'holiday' out of the country. Was this a coincidence?

As the days unfolded, it seemed to me that much of the tension was actually being 'hyped up' by journalists enjoying a rather nice lifestyle in the luxurious five-star Sheraton Hotel. I often watched BBC World reporting panic buying in the shops and gas masks being issued throughout Kuwait. As far as I could see, life seemed to be perfectly normal; there was no evidence of panic, the shops were functioning normally and the only gas mask that I saw was mine. Perhaps the press were simply swopping copy. When Jackie and Hannah arrived a few days later they had been slightly concerned to be the ONLY passengers on the last leg of their flight into Kuwait City. When they had left Heathrow an immigration official had asked incredulously, 'You're going where?'

*   *   *

On my first day at the KAF HQ, on the southern side of Kuwait International Airport, the DA came with me to introduce me to my Kuwaiti Boss, the Director of Operations. He was a colonel and was quite nonplussed by my arrival; he also seemed more than a little uncertain about what to do with me. I was meant to work closely with the KAF STANEVAL Staff Officer within the STANEVAL Branch but my new boss wasn't very clear about what STANEVAL was all about as the branch had been the Air Force Commander's idea. He seemed to think that it was simply a staff job. I explained that STANEVAL was largely about flying standards and that it combined standardization and evaluation. The fact that the RAF had sent me on a three month refresher course involving sixty hours of refresher flying on the Tucano, a type of aircraft operated by the KAF, brought no response. While my job specification placed equal emphasis on advising on flying training, it did not appear as if anyone had actually discussed that aspect with my new boss.

There was one other rather large snag. The KAF STANEVAL Branch had been disbanded before I arrived and no one had been appointed as the KAF STANEVAL staff officer. So the idea of working hand-in-hand with a Kuwaiti opposite number was a non-starter.

After a rather unsatisfactory meeting, I was dispatched to the Operations Branch; I was not sure why. Two days later, I was given a free transfer to the Training Branch, much to the surprise of the Branch Chief who also had no idea what I was supposed to do. He was not alone.

My office had a table, a chair, and a telephone, but no windows. It was also without a computer (there was only one in the branch), or anything else that could have been useful. There was no one to ask for advice, no one to seek direction from, in fact there were few to even spend the time of day with. And, because of the crisis with Iraq, it would be some time before I would be able to meet the KAF Commander. So I was a little lost.

Given what else was going on, I had arrived at a bad time. The KAF had actually asked for my post to be filled more than a year earlier, so that by the time I got there I think that they had given up on the idea. Arriving in a new post, with no predecessor or handover, in the middle of a crisis, and as the sole 'Brit' and sole 'English as a first (and only!) language speaker', made for an interesting start. Over the next few weeks there was much evidence of crisis management, confusion, and misunderstanding. When the crisis ended, the crisis management continued. So did the confusion and many of the misunderstandings. What had I got myself into? Rightly or wrongly, we were in Kuwait for two years.

In April we moved into a villa in the district of Mishref. It was one of the more recent residential developments just inland from Salwa and north of the 6th Ring Road. It had easy access to the airport which was about fifteen minutes drive away.

Unlike Saudi Arabia, Jackie was allowed to drive. Hannah would also stay until she returned to university at the end of the summer. We were encouraged to buy a four wheel drive car for private use, and all the wives attended a desert driving course run by the British Army advisors. If things had escalated, the British military personnel would deploy with their Kuwaiti counterparts, so families had to be prepared to make their own way out on pre-planned routes across the desert to the Saudi border.

Within a few months my battered Nissan Patrol was replaced by a huge white Ford Mercury Grand Marquis – I called it my pimpmobile. It was very comfortable but, with a 4.5 litre engine, a huge air conditioning unit, and only a 60 litre petrol tank, I had to refuel virtually every day. Nor did other drivers give me quite as wide a berth as they had done in the past.

The Two-Step

In truth, I was quite lonely in the KAF HQ for at least a year. While many Kuwaitis spoke English there were few that I could relate to. Relationships in the Middle East need time, and I often thought that our American counterparts, who only spent a year in country, didn't really understand this.

At first meeting, under no circumstances should you talk 'shop'. There was an essential ritual to be followed whenever you entered an office. It began with *'salaam aleikum'* followed by the reply *'aleikum salaam'*. There was then an exchange of greetings followed by enquiries about family. You most definitely did not ask about the health of a Kuwaiti colleague's wife, unless you were extremely close friends; even then it would be frowned upon if overheard. Then there would be the inevitable chai, sweet tea, served without milk, usually brought by a Bangladeshi soldier; there were 5,000 such soldiers doing very similar tasks. And that would be it, no shop talk, not until the next meeting, which could be months away, but even then the same ritual would need to be followed.

The Director of Operations proved to be very hard going and it took some time before I began to suspect why. I would often go to try and see him but he always seemed much too busy with a constant stream of visitors. Whenever he did agree for me to make an office call he always had one or two other officers with him. When I discussed STANEVAL with him he was reluctant to accept that I needed to be able to fly if the STANEVAL concept was to have any hope of success.

The KAF had a squadron of Hawks and this was a type of aircraft that I had previously flown. They also had a squadron of Tucanos, so surely they could use my Tucano A2 instructor and examiner skills? But my boss seemed indifferent to the fact that he now had the RAF's most highly qualified wing commander on the Tucano as a member of his staff. And he appeared to have no intention of letting me near one of their Tucanos, or any other aircraft for that matter. Early on he said, 'Colonels don't fly.'

'They do in the RAF,' I replied.

But it was to no avail. He was never easy to talk to, and not for the first time I wondered if there was something personal between us. But what could it be?

* * *

After a few weeks I was able to meet the KAF Commander and he proved to be a charming man. He also knew what he wanted from STANEVAL. Everything!

He described my duties in some detail: I was to advise on all air matters, in particular on STANEVAL and flying training; I was to fly in all KAF aircraft, the F18, Hawk, Tucano, C130, Super Puma, Puma, and Gazelle; and I was to begin by examining the flying standards on KAF squadrons.

'What a breakthrough!' I thought.

Of course I assumed that he would inform his staff, and in particular my boss, as to my duties. The General then mentioned, almost as an afterthought that he would also welcome my advice on flight safety, engineering, air traffic control, fighter control, logistics, and administration, and anything else that I could think of! Where was the team of advisors that I would need to undertake such a task? And where was the STANEVAL Branch that I was to support?

But before I could even begin to grasp the enormity of the task, he went on to say that he wanted me to commence my work with the first ever STANEVAL visit to a KAF base at the beginning of the following week.

'Which base?' I asked.

'Ali Al-Salem,' he replied.

That was good; at least I could start with the aircraft types with which I was most familiar, the Tucanos of 19 Squadron, and the Hawks of 12 Squadron.

'Which squadron would you like my to begin with, sir?' I asked.

'32 Squadron,' he said.

'But that's a helicopter squadron, a Puma squadron,' I said slightly incredulously.

'Yes,' he replied, quite calmly.

'But, I'm a fixed-wing instructor, not a helicopter instructor,' I said.

'Yes,' said the General, 'but you are an instructor.'

I was well and truly trumped! But I couldn't say no, could I? I was a fixed-wing flying instructor with a fast-jet background and with virtually no experience of helicopters. This was a bit of a worry, but it did not appear to worry the KAF Commander at all.

* * *

Carrying out such a clear directive proved far from simple. I duly arrived at Ali Al-Salem and spoke to the Base Commander. He gave me verbal approval to fly on a routine air test in order that I could familiarize myself with procedures. This seemed like a good idea as it avoided arranging a special flight. The flight was duly authorized by the commanding officer of 32 Squadron. While I was airborne the Base Commander changed his mind and withdrew his approval, I suspect at the direction of my boss. The Base Commander then reprimanded the KAF Squadron Commander for allowing me to fly! When I landed, I couldn't quite work out what I had done wrong as no one would really explain what had happened. Off I went to see the Base Commander once more and he explained that a verbal directive from the KAF Commander was insufficient, I needed to have a letter of approval signed personally by the Air Force Commander.

'Welcome to Kuwait!' I thought.

* * *

Even though I was unable to resolve the issue over flying until I returned to the HQ, I completed the visit to 32 Squadron. I found the senior KAF crews and instructors very positive about the idea of STANEVAL. This gave me further ideas on how to develop a concept to suit the KAF; it would need a lot of work and the KAF would need to 'buy in' to my ideas. Back at KAF HQ I discussed the concept with the Director of Operations and he said that I was to write a manual to describe what STANEVAL was all about. I suspect he was trying to just keep me at arm's length. But why was this? What was the problem?

I borrowed an ancient laptop from the BMM to create this epic work from scratch. I had no reference documents and no printer, and over the next few weeks I spent a lot of time wandering around the HQ trying to find an unoccupied workstation, a task which became less difficult as summer grew nearer and the HQ emptied. I sought help from the RAF Training Group by asking for some documents on standardization and evaluation which I could then adapt. Meanwhile, I set to work writing, not flying, and slowly I began to put something together.

While many Kuwaitis had heard of the term STANEVAL, and associated it with improvements in capability, few had any understanding of what was involved. Units were already subject to inspections, lots of them, but that was all they seemed to be, inspections only, without any real attempt at analysis or assessment. Observations made during such inspections did not appear to be related to a unit's mission or its capabilities. Nor was there any mechanism to translate observations into lessons learnt, or for recommending action for commanders to take. Put simply, there was no effective or coherent internal or external system of quality control. And it showed.

A STANEVAL concept was needed that incorporated all the necessary functions but it needed to be seen by the units as not another meaningless inspection, implemented from on high, designed to find fault down below. Units had to realize that STANEVAL could help them, often simply, by getting the right message to where it mattered: to the commanders, without the delays, obstructions, and changes of interpretation caused so often by 'staffing'. The KAF Commander agreed with this, although I suspected that some of his senior officers thought that it might weaken their own position.

I was convinced that the fuss over my first flight in a Puma, which had been authorized and then wasn't, had been caused by the Director of Operations. In further discussion with the Base Commander at Ali-Al-Salem he said that he did not have a problem with me flying but it was essential that this should be authorized in writing by the KAF Commander. I had to wait a while before I got an appointment with the General and he agreed fully that I must fly and that he would authorize the sorties in writing.

Of course, I hadn't yet learnt that it was very impolite in the Arab world to say 'No', so invariably people said 'Yes' to my requests, all of my requests. Except that some 'Yes's' were actually 'No's' and it was a little difficult to spot which was which! But I eventually learned.

I trooped back and forward to the Air Force Commander's office over the course of a few weeks to see if the promised letter of authorization was ready. It wasn't. So I wrote it. It was all very formal, using the Air Force Commander's letterhead, and of course it was in English. I then gave it to his assistant and waited, and waited, and then waited some more. I called at his office one more time and lo and behold there it was, not quite as expected, but it was signed. He had actually written across the top of the letter 'I agree with this request' and then he had signed it. I couldn't really ask for much more.

So the very next morning I set off on the hour-long journey to Ali Al-Salem to go and see the Base Commander. After all of the appropriate and ritual preliminaries, I mentioned the subject and produced the letter which he read very carefully. He then read it again, and again. Then he said, 'I'm very sorry but I cannot accept this letter. The General has signed it at the top and he should have signed it at the bottom.'

I hadn't figured on that!

So back I trooped to Air Force HQ and to the General's outer office. His assistant, a lieutenant colonel, looked up as I entered and immediately said, 'Was there a problem with the letter?'

He clearly knew all along that there would be.

'Yes,' I replied.

'Was it because it was signed in the wrong place?' he asked.

'Welcome to Kuwait,' I thought, and not for the first time.

* * *

I called this 'the Kuwaiti Two-Step', two steps forward, then two back, and then repeat before thinking of something else.

I retyped the letter, took it back to the General and invited him to sign it at the bottom, which he duly did. The Ali Al-Salem Base Commander accepted the letter, so at last I had authority to fly. The small snag was that the KAF wanted me to evaluate their entire helicopter force, one squadron after the other, which involved visits to the Puma and Super Puma squadrons, the Gazelle training squadron, and then the two anti-tank squadrons. It looked as though it would be quite a while before I got close to a Tucano or Hawk. Maybe flying aircraft on which I was qualified was probably a little too much to ask for at this stage. I just hoped that the RAF would not find out what I was actually doing.

* * *

Just as I thought I was beginning to make some progress with the KAF, I received a setback from a most unlikely source. The Training Group refused my request for some basic documentary support citing 'intellectual property rights' and inferred that in making my request I had not gone through the 'proper channels'. I was appalled. I was directed to make a more formal request 'through the proper channels' and, once it had been considered, I would be advised how much the requested documents would cost. This response was simply unbelievable. What to do about it; that was the question?

I gave this matter some thought and then tried another tack. I was at last putting my experience working with the Kuwaitis to broader use.

I showed the letter to the Defence Attaché 'for his information.' He then used his 'proper channels' through the Foreign Office to the UK MOD, from there to HQ Personnel and Training Command and then on to the Training Group. Not long afterwards I received another letter from the Training Group enquiring if there was anything that they could do to help me in my work. That was one obstacle dealt with, but this would not be the first time that unnecessary obstacles from the UK would be put in my way in trying to complete the task that the UK had sent me to do.

* * *

I went back to Ali Al-Salem to complete a more formal visit to 32 Squadron and fly the Puma. It went well, although I was very selective about the pilots with whom I flew. The crews were interested and receptive, and above all, they hoped that at last someone would relay their concerns to the top. The lack of any Kuwaiti STANEVAL staff within the HQ was nevertheless a serious limitation. A team of KAF officers from the airbase had been assembled, so at least I could introduce them to the basic concept. Following my very first briefing, the only observation from the most senior Kuwaiti attached to the team for this groundbreaking visit was whether standardisation should have been spelt with a 'z' rather than with an 's'!

The visit resulted in me being able to put the finishing touches to the requested STANEVAL Manual, which I submitted at the end of May 1998, three months after I had arrived in country. It set out the aim, meaning, policy, and principles of STANEVAL and proposed a STANEVAL organization and programme. It also expanded on the concept and offered standardized questionnaires, reports, and assessments. I proposed a simple and easy to remember 'Noddy's Guide' to STANEVAL based on the word MASTER. This stood for Mission, Assets, Standards, Training, Evaluation, and Rules and Regulations, each of which was expanded to give appropriate guidance. The Kuwaiti response to the manual would be crucial in determining the way forward.

There was no response. It was as if the manual had disappeared into a black hole. And I heard nothing more about it for over a year.

* * *

By now I was becoming more and more convinced that my Kuwaiti boss was blocking much of my progress. Could we have actually met before? I began to suspect that maybe we had. Could he have been one of those young Kuwaiti lieutenants that I had met at RAF Upwood in the summer of 1972? If so, had he recognized me twenty-six years later? Did he think that I could, or would, embarrass him about anything? If he thought that there was, it might explain his attitude and why he kept me at a distance. RAF Upwood was never mentioned between us, nor did I raise the subject with anyone else.

It then dawned on me why I never seemed to be able to get an appointment to see anyone. It was because most Kuwaitis simply did not make appointments; they just walked into an office, went through the arrival ritual and sat down, regardless of who was there.

Most senior officers would have two rows of armchairs adjacent to their desks. When you entered someone's office, if there was no one else visiting you would be invited to sit on the chair nearest the desk on the right – the right hand man. If someone more important came in, you didn't leave, you just moved down one. If it was clear after you had sat down that there was a lot going on, you just made your excuses and left. This was often a chaotic way of doing business, especially as most senior officers would have CNN tuned in on their television.

This system of not making an appointment, or not waiting your turn, extended far beyond the military. It was a way of life. Whether you were trying to pay a telephone bill, or even going to see a doctor, you would wait at your peril, as others who considered themselves more important, or their time more precious, moved in ahead. It also occurred at the Kuwait Armed Forces Hospital which I used for my annual aircrew medical. At the end of one medical I was in the doctor's surgery undergoing examination when someone else entered and sat down. I assumed it was another member of the medical staff, but no, it turned out to be another patient simply jumping the queue outside.

*   *   *

The Search and Rescue Advisor, Ken Tucker, suggested that I accompany him to Ahmed Al-Jabber as he was in the process of planning sea survival courses for the Kuwaiti F18 pilots. This would be a good opportunity for my first visit to the base and also to see something of Ken's work. Crucially, Ken was confident that he could 'blag' my way into the Base Commander's office. Ken, as always, was successful and I met for the first time Brigadier Nasser Abdul Rahman Al-Jehail. Little did I realize just how important this brief introduction was to be? Ken went on to make a remarkable contribution during his four years in Kuwait and would be appointed MBE before the end of his tour.

The RAF in Kuwait

The RAF would maintain a fully operational detachment, including a Tornado GR1 squadron, at Ali Al-Salem throughout my time in Kuwait. It was known as Operation Bolton. I would have increasing contact with them on behalf of the KAF and there would be social contact too. Many of the crews were old friends and some had been students of mine at Linton-on-Ouse.

On 1 April 1998 we attended a sunset ceremony at Ali Al-Salem to mark the 80th Anniversary of the formation of the RAF. As the Last Post was played, and the RAF Ensign lowered, there was the most magnificent flypast I had seen in years.

At exactly the right moment a single 14 Squadron Tornado flew across the desert from behind us very, very low, not more than thirty or forty feet high, going well over 540 knots with full reheat selected on both engines. It was quite deafening. Directly over the parade, the aircraft pulled up climbing vertically, spiralling upwards as it went, firing a dozen anti-missile flares one after the other, until it disappeared out of sight into the very high haze above the desert! It was tremendous.

The ceremony ended with a march past by the RAF Regiment in their desert combat fatigues which brought into sharp focus why the RAF was there: this was no exercise; the RAF was on a war footing. Many of the aircraft would soon be shot at on a daily basis as they patrolled the skies in support of UN resolutions. There would be very little publicity about this in the UK.

Over the next four years, life and work for me was relatively comfortable, yet an hour's drive west things were very different, and I often thought of my existence as surreal when set against that of the RAF personnel of all ranks.

I would often visit Ali Al-Salem two or three times a week to fly with the Kuwaiti helicopter squadrons who also travelled to the base; they did not live there. And it was easy to understand why. Living conditions on base were poor with minimal facilities and very poor basic sanitation. And it was incredibly hot. When the RAF first arrived things were expected to be basic; they were on a short notice operational deployment to a war zone. The personnel were grateful to have barrack blocks rather than tents. However, as the months turned to years, nothing changed; many of the barrack blocks still did not have functioning toilets, and personnel made their own furniture and mattresses out of tri-wall cardboard boxes.

Once things had settled down, the facilities should have been improved to at least a basic standard. But they weren't, with the Kuwaitis assuming that the UK would look after its own, in the same way that the US did at Ahmed Al-Jaber. The UK Government seemed to spend as little as possible on improving the lot of the youngsters on the ground who were actually at war! Every day they were flying into Iraq in support of UN resolutions, and on most days they were being shot at. Often they would return to attack the facility that had fired at them the previous day. When they were not doing that, they were training at a very intense rate. And then they came back to very poor conditions. They did that for four months at a time, and within a year they would be back to do it again.

When 14 Squadron arrived back at Ali Al-Salem in 2000 for their third deployment they were saddened to recognize the same cardboard furniture that they had constructed two years earlier. The squadron commander on that deployment, who went on to become a most distinguished senior officer, returned to the UK from Kuwait to go to Buckingham Palace to receive a Distinguished Service Order, awarded for the manner in which he had lead the squadron in the field, not in Kuwait, but in Kosovo, which was where 14 Squadron, along with others, had been operating BETWEEN their deployments to Kuwait.

I met some RAF crews from Ali Al-Salem in the huge US Post Exchange facility at Camp Doha about twenty miles from Ali Al-Salem. I asked if they were there for shopping.

'No,' one of them replied, 'we have come for a shower!'

I have always felt that far too little was done to support our troops in Kuwait once it became clear that they would be staying for a number of years. It was to take nearly three years and ministerial intervention before conditions improved to a basic standard, and that was only because some RAF officers in Kuwait made sure that the Minister saw the conditions for himself.

I often visited Ali Al-Salem in the morning, occasionally chatted to the RAF aircrew (male and female alike), and then in the afternoon I went home for a gin and tonic while they went off to war! What they were doing rarely made the UK press, and they did it day in and day out for over four years. There was little that I could do to influence events except perhaps offer them some short, occasional, rest and relaxation, and that is what Jackie and I increasingly did by inviting groups of all ranks to our home in the city. They were superb and well-behaved guests, true ambassadors of a service on an operational footing, and we have many happy memories of these young men and women relaxing in our home for a few short hours. Many were complete strangers, although it was inevitable that many friends and colleagues from the past found themselves deployed to Kuwait. It was particularly good to see Al Vincent, ex-7 Squadron and now a group captain, Nigel Cookson now a squadron leader, and it was heart-warming to hear 'Bonnie Lad' being shouted by Herm Harper, now flying with 31 Squadron as a reservist.

* * *

In August 1998 I attended a lecture given by General Chuck Horner USAF. He had commanded all of the Coalition Air Forces during Gulf War I. During his two hour talk he also commanded the attention of his audience of senior Kuwaiti and British officers. In fact most of us were on the edges of our seats listening to his every word. He talked about the strategy of the air war and the tactics involved. He showed one slide which showed the Coalition aircraft by type, giving the numbers involved, the sorties flown, and the numbers lost. The Tornado GR1 stood out as far as casualties were concerned with eleven aircraft lost. However, the General was quick to point out that during the first few days of the war, when losses were particularly high, the Tornado was sent against the most difficult targets. He went on to say that the bravery of the Tornado crews was 'beyond belief'.

He mentioned that later during the air war, a number of pilot's returning from night missions reported seeing numerous 'hot spots' through their night vision goggles in the desert well away from known Iraqi installations. After analysis it was decided that each of these 'hot spots' were individual Iraqi tanks and armoured vehicles. So in a change of tactic, the Coalition mounted numerous air strikes targeting each 'hot-spot' with a laser guided bomb. The Iraqi tank crews soon learnt to sleep quite some distance from their tanks and this would have a marked impact on their ability to 'man up' when the ground war began. I was sitting next to BMM's Commander during the lecture.

'So that's why!' he exclaimed, 'I never understood until today why, when we attacked, we caught so many Iraqi tank crews in the open, midway between their trenches and their tanks.'

Air did 'good' in Gulf War I.

* * *

The KAF was keen to make the most of any training opportunities, given the number of US and RAF aircraft operating from KAF bases. They organized an exercise and asked me to seek support from the RAF Tornado squadron at Ali

Al-Salem. They wanted RAF Tornados and US F16s and A10s to simulate attacks against targets within Kuwait, defended by Kuwaiti F18s and the newly operational Kuwaiti Patriot ground-to-air missile system. Such an exercise would be routine for the RAF and USAF, but fairly major for the KAF, as it would be the first such exercise that they had been involved in since before the invasion. KAF senior officers would take a keen interest.

For the RAF, planning for such an exercise could easily be conducted over the telephone but the KAF wanted a series of face-to-face briefings at KAF HQ. General Nasser Al-Jehail intended to head up the briefings.

I spoke at length to the RAF Detachment Commander and explained the 'politics' that were at play here and I asked that the squadron, it was 14 Squadron again, provide a fairly senior crew for the first briefing. On the day of the briefing, all was ready. The US and the KAF provided their squadron commanders, both lieutenant colonels, and Kuwaiti senior officers appeared to be coming out of the woodwork in order to attend. Everything was ready, General Nasser was waiting. But there was no sign of the RAF crew. This was embarrassing. Had I not made it clear how important this exercise was to the KAF? And then they arrived, late. And they were both junior officers, both flight lieutenants. Not only that, but I recognized the pilot as a first tour pilot who had been a student of mine a few years earlier at Linton. As they sat down, General Nasser gave me a very sharp look. I was so disappointed, and felt that for once the RAF had made a major mis-judgement.

The briefing began, and went slowly. Then detailed discussion took place about the attack plan and some of the coordination that would be required. The US F16 squadron commander and the KAF colonels took the lead. Then the two junior RAF officers interrupted. The colonels looked a bit put out at first, and then they began to listen. Soon everyone, including General Nasser began to take careful note of the points that the RAF crew raised. Within a very short time everyone had deferred to the young RAF crew who clearly knew their business and knew it very well. General Nasser was well impressed and so was I. But I was also embarrassed; it had been my mis-judgement that day, not 14 Squadron's. Never again would I underestimate what these youngsters were capable of and went on to achieve in the months and years ahead.

*   *   *

On 3 February 2000, it was an honour for Jackie and I to join 14 Squadron at the Safir International Hotel in Kuwait City for an Anniversary Dinner, eighty-five years to the day after the Squadron had been formed at Shoreham in 1915. It was probably the only time that 14 Squadron has been toasted with fruit juice; it was the Squadron's third operational deployment to Kuwait in two years.

The Night of the Long Knives

Far-reaching changes occurred during the summer of 1998 which were to have a crucial impact on my future. It was the so-called 'Night of the Long Knives' (well, that's what I called it anyway), when within a twenty-four hour period most of the generals, except the Chief of Staff and his Deputy, were retired. Importantly, my immediate KAF superior, the Director of Operations, was replaced by the man I had met only a few weeks earlier, Nasser Al-Jehail. Now perhaps I might be able to make some real progress.

Nasser and I got on well. He had the very highest regard for the RAF and in particular for RAF training and had completed a Qualified Helicopter Instructor's course with the Central Flying School at RAF Shawbury in Shropshire. While I did not fully appreciate it at the time, General Nasser would prove to be fundamental in my work and my stay in Kuwait, and he was to be the main driving force behind the re-establishment of flying training in Kuwait.

It wasn't long before he made it clear that he intended to make much more use of me than his predecessor, and he asked me for a copy of my STANEVAL manual which he had heard about but had never seen. He also said that I was never to make an appointment to see him; I just had to walk into his office. Invariably I would sit at his right hand and whenever someone else entered the room I would rise to move to another chair. Sometimes Nasser let me do this but at other times he indicated that I was to sit down and the visitor had to sit elsewhere. This made it clear that I now had some influence.

In most areas of working life, promotion and ability usually go hand in hand, but in the Middle East, a couple of other factors came into play: family and influence, or 'wasta'. I once was sitting in a colonel's office when a corporal entered. The colonel stood up and was totally deferential to the young corporal because of the latter's family connection. However, I came across a number of British and American officers who consistently under-rated Kuwaiti officers, because they perceived that it was the Kuwaiti's family or influence which had been pivotal in their rise up the rank structure. What they failed to recognize was that some individuals would have reached high rank on ability alone in any other countries' military. Nasser Al-Jehail was one such man.

I also now had some 'wasta' and I rejoiced in it, and it was to make my life much easier in the months and years ahead. However, I was always careful not to abuse my position and would never simply visit Nasser's office or stay too long, and I would always have something to offer or discuss if the moment seemed right. Of course, being so closely linked to a single mentor brought with it risks. Woe betide the advisor whose sole mentor got the push! He might well find that his own days were numbered.

An important ritual was kissing between men. This was entirely normal and was often expected. It usually began with a handshake, which was continued while one or other, sometimes both, would initiate a movement towards the other which resulted in faces touching cheek to cheek. The 'more important' individual would initiate the ritual and control the number of 'touches', up to a maximum of four, which indicated that the individual was favoured.

One day when I got home, I told Jackie that I had just received my first kiss from a Kuwaiti officer – 'He won't do that again, I gave him a "Geordie" nut!'

*   *   *

General Nasser's appointment as Director of Operations, the No. 3 in the KAF, was crucial. He was a man of vision and influence and knew how to get things done. While he had the highest regard for RAF standards, above all else he sought Kuwaiti solutions to Kuwaiti requirements. Under his broad guidance STANEVAL was given a major push and I was asked to undertake more training visits. I was also asked to propose and then introduce an instructor categorization scheme similar to the one in use in the RAF. Nasser also began to talk more and more about flying training, but he would also task me with all sorts of things, some of which were well outside my experience.

One day Nasser asked me if I knew anyone who had been involved in officer training at Sandhurst, where a small number of Kuwaitis underwent officer training. I knew a sergeant major on the BMM staff that had come directly from Sandhurst to Kuwait. General Nasser asked me to arrange for him to visit KAF HQ. The sergeant major was greatly taken aback, as brigadiers tended not to be within his circle, but he agreed to come. While the sergeant major waited outside the General's office, I went inside. Nasser was delighted that the sergeant major had come and told me to bring him in. As I was leaving the office General Nasser said, 'Paul, what's his first name?'

'John,' I replied.

A very nervous sergeant major marched into the General's office, came crisply to attention, and gave an immaculate salute. Nasser returned the salute and walked across grinning broadly. As he shook hands with the sergeant major he said, 'Thank you very much for coming. It's John, isn't it?'

'Yes sir,' said a startled sergeant major.

General Nasser then turned towards me and said, 'Thank you Paul. That will be all.'

I was dismissed! As I left the office I couldn't help but smile at the adept way that General Nasser had dealt with the situation. By his manner and charm he had totally won over a mature and fairly hard-nosed British Army sergeant major. I have often thought that a number of British officers, especially senior officers, would have done well to emulate Nasser's approach to people and to leadership.

Desert Fox

Hannah returned to university in August 1998, but would come back to join us for a family holiday to Egypt at Christmas. We would fly to Cairo, stay in the same hotel in Giza where I had stayed with RCDS in 1995, before flying to Luxor for a six night cruise on the Nile to Aswan. It sounded too good to be true.

At one minute to midnight the night before our flight to Cairo, Kuwait was placed on alert and I was recalled. Tension with Iraq had escalated during the previous few weeks and there had been a significant build up of US forces. To witness how the US deployed was simply staggering. Awesome is the only word to describe that capability.

As for me, I wasn't really that sure what to do. I knew that I had to report to the KAF but my duties had not actually been covered. Once in my desert combats, complete with gas mask and helmet, I sped in my 'pimpmobile' to the BMM HQ within the Kuwait Armed Forces complex in the city. On arrival at about 0045 hours, I was almost shot by the very alert Kuwaiti guards clearly startled by this madman driving much to fast! After another fast drive to the KAF HQ I found it almost completely deserted; everyone had gone to their war locations. Where was mine, I wondered? I found a Kuwaiti friend of mine, a colonel, still in his office getting his equipment together.

'Where are you off to?' I asked.

'I'm going to the War Room,' he said.

A few seconds later he said, 'Would you like to come?'

Silly question! The next few days were to be quite an adventure.

*   *   *

When we entered the War Room, it caused something of a stir. The room comprised of three long tables in the form of a 'U' with the open end of the 'U' facing a huge screen. Senior Kuwaiti officers filled most of the seats and the Air Force Commander was at the centre of the top table facing the screen. As soon as I walked in he fired off a barrage of Arabic at my colleague. Whatever he replied seemed to satisfy the General and I was invited to sit down adjacent to the top table. I was 'in' and from that moment on I could come and go as I pleased.

Within a few hours the International Airport was closed to all traffic. Soon afterwards hostilities commenced and Coalition aircraft were launched against targets in Iraq. It was called Operation Desert Fox, clearly a sequel to Operation Desert Storm.

The large screen showed a computer generated radar picture covering the Arabian Gulf, Kuwait and Iraq, almost up to, but not including Baghdad. And very soon it was covered with radar traffic. The RAF Tornados were launched from Ali Al-Salem, the USAF F16s from Ahmed Al-Jaber, but all of these aircraft were soon dwarfed by an armada of F14s and F18s and others from USN carriers in the Gulf. It was an amazing sight and there I was, the only Brit, sitting watching it all unfold. I watched the very long-range B1s and B52s coming up the Gulf of Arabia from Diego Garcia in the Indian Ocean before they released their cruise missiles. The missiles could even be seen on the screen after they had been released. We all watched enthralled as the various attack aircraft headed north toward Baghdad. And then they disappeared off the top of the screen. Everyone then stood up, so I did too. What on earth was going on?

Everyone then left the room, so I tagged along trying to look as if I knew what was happening. We all went into the huge lounge next door, full of rather large leather chairs. We were all served tea and then someone switched on the television at the end of the room. It was CNN, live from Baghdad, and it showed various attacks taking place with lots of anti-aircraft fire and explosions. Eventually the anti-aircraft fire subsided, at which point everyone stood up, and we went back to our seats in the War Room just in time to see the radar tracks reappear as the Coalition aircraft headed home.

I watched, with some pride, as the RAF's Tornados recovered to Ali Al-Salem. I simply could not believe where I was and that I was able to witness this 'air war' from such a position. But then the bubble burst.

'Paul,' said the Air Force Commander. 'What time will the second wave of RAF Tornados get airborne?'

Oh b****r, I thought, how was I meant to answer that?

I did not know. I had no operational contact with the RAF and new nothing of their plans, although some Kuwaitis had doubts about that. If I gave an answer, and it was wrong, then I would lose credibility both with the General and with others. But if I gave an answer that was reasonably accurate then this might confirm to some that I was an 'RAF man' not a true 'Kuwaiti advisor'. A bit of a conundrum here then, and I had about a minute to come up with an answer.

I knew that the RAF did not have enough aircraft to launch a second wave immediately, so they would need to refuel and rearm. The second mission would have been pre-planned and there would be fresh crews as soon as the aircraft were ready. So how long would an operational turn-round take? I gave my best estimate to the General and hoped. About three minutes before the time that I had quoted, the second wave of RAF Tornados got airborne. The Commander looked across at me and nodded.

I stayed in the War Room throughout the air war (there was no ground war) but went home now and again to sleep. Yes, we had lost our dream holiday but at least Hannah was able to impress her friends no end when she got back to the UK. And maybe a seed had been sown in the back of her mind.

* * *

With Operation Desert Fox coming toward the end of my first year in country, my position had undoubtedly been strengthened. I had been a tiny and irrelevant part of the operation, but I had been seen to have been on alert with the KAF and I had shared aspects of the operation with them. And the senior Kuwaitis with whom I was to work had also witnessed their own Commander turning to me for advice. OK, I had given an educated guess, but they didn't know that. Maybe I could now start to make some real progress.

*   *   *

The Holy month of Ramadam had a major impact on every aspect of our lives, as it did throughout the Muslim world. No food or drink could be served or consumed in public during the hours of daylight. Westerners too were required to comply when in public. This placed a considerable limitation on everyone, especially with temperatures being so high.

Within a few days of Ramadam commencing, the number of people at work began to reduce and the hours they spent there also became less and less. The call to prayers which marked the end of daylight was also the time for families to get together to break their fast. The thirty minutes leading up to the evening call was also a time not to be on the roads, as driving deteriorated markedly as people desperately tried to get home. After the 'feast' which marked the end of the day's fasting, it was traditional for Kuwaiti men to then go visiting until the early hours of the morning.

Most homes had a dewaniya, a reception area where a man received his business colleagues and male guests. It refers both to a reception hall and the gathering held in it, and visiting or hosting a dewaniya is an indispensable feature of a Kuwaiti man's social life. Some claim that the term originally referred to the section of a Bedouin tent where the men folk and their visitors sat apart from the family.

After a long night of visiting, by normal start work time, many Kuwaitis were very tired. So they started late. And then, later still. Often many of the Kuwaitis with whom I worked would not come to work until after 1030 hours, and would leave shortly after 1300 hours, so very little was ever achieved. By the last week of Ramadam, some didn't come to work at all.

In true British tradition, the Commander BMM directed all UK personnel to work normal working hours throughout Ramadam. I didn't have a problem with that in principle, only in practice, although I would have very much enjoyed an even shorter working day. The problem in practice was that I couldn't get into the KAF HQ at the normal start time, it was locked. I explained my problem to General Nasser who, as always, listened very carefully.

'Yes Paul,' he said, 'I can see the problem. Leave it with me.'

A few days later I was given a set of keys. It reminded me of the wartime poster 'Sleep peacefully; your air force is awake.' Except for the sleeping population of Kuwait, their air force was in the hands of a Brit!

*   *   *

I was now happily ensconced within the Training Branch and very well accepted by the staff. I had at last been provided with a computer and printer courtesy of the BMM which had received some funding from the UK. It is difficult to imagine how advisors were meant to carry out their duties without such essential tools.

I shared my office with a KAF helicopter pilot, and we became good friends. Over the next few years we would occasionally go out for a meal, sometimes on our own, and sometimes with other Kuwaitis. He was very traditional in his outlook and in his dress. Off duty he was always immaculate in traditional dress, flowing white robes often edged with gold. Whenever he called to pick me up from home he would only ever come to our front gate, ring the bell and wait, even though I would leave the gate open for him. If he had gone further there was a risk that he might meet Jackie, and this in his eyes would have been inappropriate. He and I often talked about our families but there could never be any direct reference to one another's wives. He invited me to share a traditional Kuwaiti meal in the desert with him and others and these were very enjoyable occasions, a true Arabian night.

First a metal bin was buried in the sand up to the top and wooden debris from the desert was put inside. It was lit and left to burn until there were very hot embers at the bottom. Then lamb and chicken pieces were suspended from sticks which were laid across the open end of the bin. The lid was then replaced, covered in sand, and left to cook. We would then sit and talk before prayers, which were always interesting to watch. There would then be hand washing before prayers and the meal. The food was always good. I was always given a knife and fork to use but I insisted on eating the traditional way, using my right hand. But my struggles did not draw any smiles.

After a few months of working together I asked him what exactly his job was, I assumed he was just another staff officer working within the Training Branch and that his location in my office was simply a coincidence.

'I'm the STANEVAL staff officer,' he announced.

So after almost a year of working within the HQ, the KAF had now appointed a staff officer for me to work with, except no one happened to mention it! I learnt that STANEVAL officers had also been appointed at each of the airbases and also within the air defence brigade. Not long afterwards, he seemed to be incredibly busy, far busier than I had seen him before, typing on his computer. He was clearly working on a major staff paper. After a few days I asked him what he was doing.

'I'm translating your STANEVAL Manual into Arabic!' he said, with a grimace.

So almost a year after I had submitted it, the STANEVAL Manual had re-emerged from the black hole! Maybe I was making progress after all.

*   *   *

I continued to develop the STANEVAL concept and conducted visits to 62 Squadron (Super Puma) at Ali Al-Salem, and also to the Gazelle anti-tank and training squadrons based there. This was a good opportunity for me to fly, but it was slightly bizarre offering advice on flying standards to experienced helicopter pilots when I was totally unqualified to fly as captain on any of their aircraft.

I only ever flew with a Kuwaiti helicopter instructor in the other seat. I was very open about what I was trying to do and it gave them the opportunity to teach me, while I offered them advice on instructional technique and broader aspects of standardization and evaluation. I learnt to respect many of the KAF instructors who were certainly on a par with their RAF equivalents. I very much enjoyed this period and spent many days at a time at Ali Al-Salem practicing engine-off landings in the Gazelle, and low flying across the wide open desert. When I came across one of the vast dumps of destroyed Iraqi armour and vehicles from Gulf War I it brought home the realities of life in this part of the world. Meanwhile, overhead I would often see RAF Tornados departing into a very real and present danger a few miles to the north.

Having completed initial STANEVAL visits to all of the helicopter squadrons, much to my surprise, I was then asked personally by the Base Commander of Abdullah Al-Mubarak Air Base to conduct a visit there. The base was actually only a few hundred yards from my office in KAF HQ and it was the military part of Kuwait International Airport. It operated C130 Hercules transport aircraft, and I knew little about the aircraft, or its role. But, I could hardly refuse. I actually spent nine weeks there and the Base Commander said that he was happy with what I was able to offer. I also flew with him in a C130 to and from Bahrain on a training sortie.

I kept hoping that I would soon be invited to look at the Hawk and Tucano squadrons, but there seemed to be an unstated reluctance to let me near them, although flying training had not yet re-commenced. The Hawks had been sent back to the UK to the BAe facility at Dunsfold for major servicing, and they were gradually being returned to Kuwait. The Tucanos, and a Tucano flight simulator, had been purchased shortly before Iraq invaded Kuwait, and they had then been kept in storage in the UK until a slow delivery programme was set up to get them out to Kuwait. BAe had taken over control of Hawk and Tucano servicing and were very keen indeed to see flying training restart in Kuwait, as was the British Embassy, but as yet I was not in any position to influence matters. Until the KAF asked me to get involved I could not afford to push at a potentially closed door. But, the door would very soon be opened for me. And it was my relationship with General Nasser which was the key element.

Nasser Al-Jehail was appointed as the Deputy Commander of the KAF. This was very good news indeed for the KAF. He immediately asked to see me and told me that I was to continue to work directly for him; I was not to report to his successor as Director of Operations. Within days of taking over his new appointment, Nasser again asked me to call. He wanted my advice on flying training. Eureka!

A Flying School in the Desert

I had been giving a lot of thought as to how in-country flying training could be restarted and had also talked to many KAF officers and listened to their views. Kuwait did not have a pilot training strategy and there had been no coordinated vision or any drive, just lots of competing voices. Some favoured in-country training, others did not; some advocated RAF training, others preferred the USAF model. Disposal of the Kuwaiti Hawk and Tucano fleets and the loss of many British jobs were real possibilities with the consequent damage to UK prestige and interests.

However, my job was to offer the best possible advice, not simply to further UK interests. But I was not naive, nor were my hosts. Nasser Al-Jehail was certainly not naive, but he was a man who could provide drive, and he had vision. With the announcement that forty KAF pilot candidates would be selected from the Kuwait Military College in May 1999, the pressure was on to do something and do it quickly.

The best answer for Kuwait was not difficult to work out. The USAF solution was 'cradle to grave' training in the US with the KAF paying up front for the whole package of language training, elementary, basic, and then advanced flying training. They could not 'cherry-pick' items from the package. The USAF system was good and successful graduates would be well placed for the US-built F18s operated by the KAF, but it was also very expensive, and perhaps not cost effective. Nor did it make use of existing Kuwaiti aircraft during training, or improve the standards of KAF pilots by developing an instructor cadre. I thought that both of these aspects were important.

RAF training was also expensive, but the product was more suited to KAF requirements and failure rates were modest. RAF training was favoured by many Kuwaitis, and a number of senior officers, including General Nasser, had undergone flying courses with the RAF in the UK. However, years of cutbacks meant that the RAF no longer had the capacity to sell many places to overseas countries. Kuwait had previously asked the UK to provide RAF instructors to restart training, but the RAF no longer had the personnel to offer the numbers required. While I needed to be a little cautious in explaining the RAF's limitations lest it pushed the KAF towards a totally non-UK solution, my job was to provide best possible advice, was it not?

For some, cost effectiveness did not matter. A glance at Kuwait's military hardware gave a clue to the country's long-term defence strategy. They had tanks from the US, artillery from China, aircraft from the US, UK and France, missiles from the US and the UK, and naval vessels from France. In short, they had defence agreements with most of the Permanent Members of the UN

Security Council. It might be a political imperative when one lived next door to an unpredictable neighbour but it was a logistician's nightmare.

With two of the types of aircraft needed for flying training, both with engineering contracts in place, there was a basis on which to build. The KAF had some Hawk instructors, but no Tucano instructors. They also had a Tucano flight simulator, although this had been dismantled and in storage for years. What they needed was a package to link the various elements together, building on what already existed. This was feasible and it would be cost-effective.

What about a largely commercial solution but arranged through the UK MOD? General Nasser was receptive to this idea but it would need to involve the RAF in more ways than just from an administrative or organizational perspective. It would mean RAF bodies on the ground, in Kuwait, and not just mine. What was needed was a 'light-blue' veneer, even if very thin, to give the programme the RAF 'training standards stamp'. General Nasser saw this as essential.

So a mix of some training conducted in the UK and some in Kuwait, all designed to match closely the KAF requirement seemed to be the answer. However, moving towards this solution proved to be a tortuous and frustrating task beset with difficulties, many of which came from the most unlikely sources.

* * *

The Defence Attaché at the British Embassy was very supportive of what I was trying to achieve. He was very much the link with the UK MOD's Directorate of Military Assistance whose support was essential. I worked increasingly closely with the Defence Attaché and we both agreed that KAF pilot training could be achieved with the majority of UK support coming from industry, provided that the RAF would agree to 'buy-in' with a little more support than currently existed. This would have the benefit of furthering UK interests whilst avoiding having to turn down the KAF's original request for a significant increase in RAF manpower.

The KAF requirement had first been spelt out by the British Ambassador in December 1997, and it was his request through the Foreign Office that I had been briefed on when on embarkation leave in January 1998. The Ambassador had recognized that the RAF would be unlikely to provide the twelve instructors requested by the KAF and had suggested a compromise of one or two RAF officers as the senior instructors, assisted by contract officers provided by a commercial provider. This appeared to me to still be the best solution.

If the UK formally replied to the Kuwait MOD saying that it could not provide the number of RAF instructors requested, this could play right into the hands of those who advocated a non-UK supported package. If the UK could get this right, there was an opportunity to strengthen the UK's position and exert a level of influence with the KAF that had not existed for many years. While it was essential that we dealt with the art of the possible, not what was ideal, it seemed to me that the starting position had to be that the UK wished to support the KAF.

*   *   *

Within days of being appointed as the Deputy Commander, General Nasser asked me to write a flying training strategy. This was perfect timing, and I could now openly discuss the whole concept of regenerating flying training. General Nasser wanted a 'UK School' at Ali Al-Salem. The strategy that I suggested involved a course of English Language training in the UK, followed by RAF supervised elementary flying training, also in the UK. Students would then return to Kuwait for basic flying training on the Tucano using a mix of instructors, military and non-military, Kuwaiti and non-Kuwaiti. General Nasser, and the KAF at large, now seemed to accept that ex-service personnel provided by a contractor might be a more cost-effective solution than twelve RAF instructors, provided that an evident 'light blue veneer' remained. It was therefore essential that the UK provide some tangible RAF support.

The strategy was entitled *Strategy 2000* and it formed the basis of what was to follow. The BMM funded the first edition; it was good to know that I could at least get some financial support for my efforts. But when I revised and reprinted the strategy in February 2001, I had to pay for it out of my own pocket!

However, *Strategy 2000* on its own would not be enough to convince the Kuwait MOD. What was needed was an authoritative paper from the UK MOD on how the KAF may wish to regenerate its flying training capability. This could lend support and substance to what we already knew the KAF wanted. In other words a UK MOD version of *Strategy 2000* was needed.

The Central Flying School, with its worldwide reputation, would be the ideal author of such a paper and I set to work with the RAF's Training Group, and through the Defence Attaché, to arrange a CFS staff visit, which took place in February 1999. The CFS staff officer tasked with visiting Kuwait was an old friend from RAF Leeming and later 20 Squadron at RAF Laarbruch, Squadron Leader Bill Ramsay.

*   *   *

At the time I was focusing almost entirely on the competing voices between the KAF and the Kuwait MOD, where there were still some who advocated handing over the whole deal elsewhere, but I didn't realise that there might be competing voices within the UK that might cause problems.

Bill Ramsay and I had extensive discussions with General Nasser who made it very clear that the Central Flying School Report must include a requirement for some additional RAF support. Following his visit, Bill and I were in constant touch as drafts and re-drafts were sent back and forward.

The process seemed to take forever, and I had to continually apologize to General Nasser for the lack of a report. As May 1999 passed, the situation was getting desperate as forty prospective KAF student pilots were commissioned. They commenced language training in the UK, but I was well aware that my 'sticking plaster' solution of language training and some elementary flying training was not going to hold for long. However, there were other forces at play of which I was unaware.

At last I received the final draft of the report from the Embassy for comment. I was absolutely aghast! The all-important but relatively small RAF element contained within the previous drafts had been removed and replaced by a purely commercial element. The changes had been made without Bill's knowledge after the final draft had left his desk. I knew that this report, if submitted, would play right into the hands of those who did not advocate a UK solution. Rather than strengthen the UK commercial position that already existed, it would weaken it irrevocably, and could easily see the end of Hawk and Tucano flying and the whole package moving to another country. In a formal letter to the Embassy, I said that if the final draft was submitted I would have to disassociate myself from it altogether.

The UK response was particularly disappointing given the broad support offered by the RAF Chief of the Air Staff during a visit to the UK by the KAF Commander. The Commander BMM also realized what was at stake and offered to give up some army posts within BMM in favour of an additional RAF post. After a flurry of activity at the Embassy, I offered a carefully crafted, but fairly firm letter for the Embassy to send to the UK MOD, along with yet another revision to the CFS Report. That seemed to do the trick and our suggestions were accepted. On 2 August 1999, I was at last able to give General Nasser the report nearly six months after the CFS visit. Perhaps now some real progress could be made, or so I thought.

* * *

Over the next few weeks the programme of English Language training in the UK was extended and soon transferred to De Monteford University in Leicester, with the students boarding with local families to improve their language skills. While this was going on it gave me time to work out what should happen next.

All Kuwaiti officer candidates for all three services underwent officer training in Kuwait with a few being sent to Sandhurst. On commissioning, the air force officers were then selected. I attended some of the graduation ceremonies from the Kuwait Military College and these were grand affairs with the main tent, overlooking the parade, full of armchairs for the VIPs and main guests. This was, of course, a male preserve with no women in the main tent, not even the mothers of the graduating students. Within the tent, everyone was dressed in their very best uniforms with many Kuwaitis in the grandest of white robes with gold trimmings.

On the left of the tent, adjacent to the parade square, was a completely separate enclosure for the female guests, mostly wearing the full head to foot black abaya. At the end of the ceremony the women would begin ululation. This was a long, wavering, high-pitched sound, produced by making a vocal sound accompanied by a rapid movement of the tongue. It usually began quite softly and then gained momentum to be incredibly loud and quite eerie!

The first course of six to begin Elementary Flying Training (EFT) in the UK with the Joint Elementary Flying Training Squadron (JEFTS), at RAF Barkston Heath, included my boss's son, Thamer Al-Jehail, as well as the nephew of Kuwait's Defence Minister. If that wasn't enough it also included one of the Emir's sons. No pressure there then!

* * *

I could receive telephone calls from the UK in my office but I could not call overseas. Thankfully, I had an international mobile telephone but, with poor reception in the HQ, I would often be found outside in one of the car parks trying to find some shade whilst speaking to a UK staff officer in the comfort of his office.

Invariably UK staff officers would call me, usually toward the end of their week on a Thursday or a Friday, and of course, those days were my weekend so they often called me at home. I would often spend hours talking to the UK from home. I once suggested to one of the UK MOD staff that he give me his home telephone number so that I could call him over a weekend; he thought that I was most amusing.

* * *

As work continued putting together the various elements of the flying training package, I began to sense that all was still not well from a UK per-spective. Despite the hard fought agreement over the CFS Report there was still no coherent UK voice. What we seemed to have was a range of agencies with competing and often contradictory voices, all of whom seemed to have their own private agendas. There was more than a hint of arrogance and a 'we know best' attitude from some sources, especially those who had little direct or daily contact with the Kuwaitis.

My continual suggestions that trying to impose a fixed or template solution was not the way ahead were seen as interference that could be bypassed. I continued to receive very good support from the Commander BMM and from the Defence Attaché and suspected that the problem lay elsewhere. General Nasser was still totally on board but he wanted to see a tangible sign of what the RAF would deliver.

Matters came to a head when I paid a routine visit to the Embassy. It became clear that an element within the Embassy was taking an almost entirely commercial approach despite my advice to the contrary. The KAF did not want a purely commercial solution, a 'light-blue' veneer was essential, and I was in Kuwait to give the KAF my best advice, not to try and 'sell' them something they did not want. With my tact and diplomatic skills well and truly exhausted there was a heated exchange of views which was overheard by the Ambassador.

A few days later I was asked to accompany the Commander BMM to the Embassy for a meeting called by the Ambassador. After listening to the 'commercial view', the Ambassador offered broad support for the line suggested. My spirits sank. I was then invited to put forward my views. Nothing ventured, nothing gained, I thought.

I explained why it was essential to listen very carefully to what the KAF wanted and then to do our best to deliver it. Under no circumstances should we tell the KAF what they wanted. If we tried to do that, then everything that we had worked so hard to achieve could easily unravel. I spoke without interruption, at the end of which there was silence. There were no questions. After what seemed an eternity the Ambassador said, 'I agree with Wing Commander McDonald; that is the line that we will take.'

That was it. No further discussion, the meeting was over! During the drive back the Commander BMM said quietly, 'Well, I think that went rather well.'

After that things moved quickly. There were a couple of high-powered visits from the UK MOD and I also received very positive support from the international defence training staff within the Training Group.

Much to my delight, two new RAF Loan Service posts were established and quickly filled. I was joined by two squadron leaders, 'Fitz' Fitzgerald was a Tucano A2 instructor from Linton who joined the KAF Tucano Squadron at Ali Al-Salem, and Bob Farley, an A2 helicopter instructor, who set up the ground school. The speed with which this occurred was remarkable, and the timing could not have been better as it bought us more time to rally further UK support and develop the all-important next step – the first Flying Training contract, or Letter of Agreement as it was called.

BAe Systems, under Paul Kelly, soon provided a team of instructors who joined Dick Manning, a key test pilot and instructor who had kept the Tucano fleet going. Soon, in-country pilot training began in earnest. The KAF also began to move surprisingly quickly and new HQ buildings were completed for the Tucano and Hawk squadrons and a new ground school and simulator building was soon under construction. Getting the elderly simulator operational after it had been dismantled and in storage for some twelve years would be a major technical challenge; in the end it was to prove prohibitively expensive.

My role within the KAF had now changed completely and I became totally immersed in ensuring that the embryonic pilot training programme could be sustained. We soon had a regular flow of young Kuwaitis heading off for the UK before they returned to Kuwait for their Tucano training. It was particularly satisfying to welcome back from the UK, the first students to commence Tucano training in Kuwait, and these included Thamer Al-Jehail and the Emir's son, Sabah Al-Sabah.

* * *

I was soon into my fourth year in Kuwait. General Nasser was keen that I stay longer, but Jackie and I had decided four years in the Middle East was enough, and I made it clear to the RAF that at the end of my fourth year, in February 2002, we wanted to return to the UK or to Europe. We had experienced a wonderful tour but enough was enough. Our son was now living in Los Angeles, while our daughter had completely astounded us by announcing her intention to join the RAF as an air traffic control officer.

In April 2001, I received a message to telephone RAF Innsworth and Personnel Management Agency's Air Secretary 2; he dealt with all the appointments of group captains. I had long given up any thoughts or hopes of promotion. A few months earlier, as the Commander BMM was preparing to leave Kuwait he had said to me that, in his view, promotion in the RAF was something of a lottery, but if you went on Loan Service 'your ticket was taken out of the draw.' Maybe he was wrong.

I made the call, and yes, I was offered promotion to group captain. It was conditional on me accepting command of the Loan Service team in Oman. I had twenty-four hours to make up my mind and Air Secretary 2 asked that I call him back the following day. When I said that I didn't need to think about it he said, 'Good!'

He was a little taken aback when I said that my answer was 'no'.

'You're turning down promotion?' he asked.

'No,' I replied, 'I would be delighted to be promoted, but four years in the Middle East is enough for us, and if promotion is conditional on me going to Oman then I'm afraid I must decline.'

And it was conditional on the Oman appointment, so that was that. For months to come, the silence from the RAF as far as my future posting was concerned was deafening.

* * *

Over the remainder of my time in Kuwait I reflected on what had been a unique appointment; I had no regrets. I had been asked for lots of advice, some had been accepted, some not. The basis of STANEVAL had been introduced. The regeneration of KAF pilot training had the makings of a great success, although the momentum would have to be maintained once I left Kuwait. With General Nasser at the helm, and he was already tipped as the next KAF Commander, there was much to hope for. Also, the UK had at last realized the importance of supporting the KAF and I was to be replaced by two wing commanders. Much would depend on their flexibility and willingness to think 'outside the box' in keeping things going, but with four RAF personnel now well established at Ali Al-Salem, things looked promising.

After four years in post, Ken Tucker was also due a home posting. Also, a new and very able Helicopter Training Advisor, Chris Luck, had been in post for a year and was doing extremely well.

As far as flying KAF aircraft, my success had only been limited. I never did get near the Tucano or the Hawk, which were the only aircraft that I was qualified to fly. But I did fly the C130, Super Puma, Puma, and Gazelle, and I wasn't qualified on any of them! I had also 'examined' a number of KAF helicopter and crewmen instructors, and awarded them categories from the newly introduced KAF categorization scheme. I was also invited to take part in trial sorties in the Bell 430 helicopter and the Eurocopter; these were being evaluated for the Ministry of the Interior, which subsequently purchased two Eurocopters.

*   *   *

The most valuable lesson that I had learnt as an advisor was not to set targets or timescales that were unrealistic. In dealing with the local bureaucracy it was rare to be able to achieve more than one thing during a single day, even when it came to something as simple as paying a telephone bill. Work was often like that too. Sometimes you might be lucky and accomplish a couple of things on the same day, but usually if you tried you ended up frustrated and disappointed.

Whether an advisor's ideas were ever listened to, or considered, or implemented, depended on the personalities involved and, perhaps more importantly, on the approach used by the advisor. On arrival, with lots of doors to try, I quickly found that it was always best to go through those that were open, later it might be possible to open a door that was closed. It was never worthwhile asking for the key for a locked door. But if your Kuwaiti boss gave you the keys to the HQ, then you were in!

Above all else, advisors have to listen. Many officers in the host nation could recognize what was wrong; what they often needed was the advisor to offer a solution, or be supportive about something that they themselves were trying to push. It was important not to tell your host what you thought they wanted, but to be patient, listen, consider, then respond, even if that meant playing a rather long game. Once an advisor has proven that he can help with the 'how', he may eventually be asked about the 'what', but it was impossible to dictate the pace.

It had been suggested that working as an advisor was sometimes like pulling a brick with a piece of elastic. For a long time nothing happened, and then for no apparent reason the brick moved. You had no idea how long the brick would keep moving or where it would land but you needed to be ready to move with your ideas and suggestions because, when the brick stopped, usually so did you, and it could be a long time before you can get the wretched thing to move again.

Advisors needed to take time to establish their real local hierarchy – who was the 'office occupier' and who could get things done? Advisors needed to be able to identify who these people were and establish regular contact with them. But beware of only having one mentor; changes can happen with very little notice and you could so easily end up beached! But for my decision to leave Kuwait in 2002, I would have ended up beached. And no one could have seen it coming.

For me, the job was the nearest thing to being given a blank sheet of paper, and it was one of the most challenging and rewarding appointments that I have ever had.

* * *

During the summer of 2001 we spent a week in Oman, a beautiful country so very different to Kuwait. Our flight was direct, unlike a previous one earlier in our tour. On that occasion we had booked a week's holiday in Cyprus, staying in a hotel on the idyllic Pissouri Beach, flying to Larnaka with Kuwait Airways. While in the departures lounge I wondered around looking at the various departure details and came to a sudden standstill. Our flight was not direct. It was calling at Beirut in Lebanon first, and this was a location that was definitely 'off limits' at the time to a serving RAF officer. And for a serving RAF officer with an RAF identity card, a KAF identity card and a Diplomatic identity card, and two passports in his pocket? Thankfully, our intermediate stop passed without incident.

During our final afternoon in Oman we saw in a newspaper that the Red Arrows were there completing their work-up training, as the runways at their normal practice venue, RAF Akrotiri, were being resurfaced. That afternoon they were due to display over the beach immediately in front of our hotel. They were of course magnificent.

That evening as we sat in the large reception area in the hotel, a familiar figure walked past. It was Bill Ramsay, now promoted to wing commander since his last visit to Kuwait and filling the appointment of Wing Commander RAF Aerobatic Team. One of his duties involved him accompanying the team on deployment flying the spare Red Arrows Hawk, Red 10. He invited us to join him in the bar where the team were relaxing; two of the team members were former students of mine from Linton.

* * *

The advisory team did have a number of social get-togethers, mostly in one another's homes, and every few months we had more formal functions in one of Kuwait's many first class hotels. At one such function, all of the RAF advisors and their wives had been placed on the same table in the corner of the large room, not quite out of sight. Actually we had a great time! But, at the end of the meal, we decided to be 'offended' by being segregated to a back corner and, at a given signal, we moved the whole table, whilst still sitting, pushing between the other tables until we were at the front! Not a glass was spilt. That was the last occasion when RAF advisors were allowed to sit together.

On occasion, RN ships paid official visits to Kuwait. While they were there, a number of the ship's company would usually be given shore leave in a local hotel. When an RN aircraft carrier visited, some young seamen were accommodated in the beautiful Crown Plaza Hotel which was well known for its huge reception area and the glass lifts which operated from within the cavernous foyer. I can well imagine some experienced Chief Petty Officer 'persuading' these youngsters to take their shore leave in Kuwait rather than in Dubai or Muscat. However, the Manager was soon summoned by a worried member of staff as two young seamen were going from lift to lift and then ascending, stopping at each floor for a few minutes before re-embarking and moving on to the next floor. Up and down they went and this had been going on for some time. Eventually, the Manager caught up with them and asked if he could help.

'Yes,' they replied. 'Could you tell us which floor the bar is on?'

'Ah,' he said, with an understanding smile. 'If you are able to find it, could you let me know where it is?'

* * *

By November, I still had heard nothing about my future appointment. With a fixed departure date in February, and Ramadan approaching, followed soon afterwards by Christmas, I was anxious to make plans to move somewhere. Having turned down promotion, I wondered whether my name had actually been taken out of the posting lottery as well! I pressed the RAF once more, and it was suggested that a posting back to Innsworth for a short period might be a good idea as there was still a possibility of promotion. This sounded very much like what I had been told in 1997. I was older and wiser now, and indicated my lack of interest perhaps a little harshly.

Within a few days Air Secretary 2 phoned once more. He confirmed that I had been selected for substantive promotion. The first job that he suggested was a NATO appointment at Reitan in Norway, within the Arctic Circle. He then suggested another NATO appointment at Ramstein in Germany. As this would be my final tour it sounded ideal and within a few days the job was confirmed: I was to be Chief CJFACC Plans within the A5 Division of HQ AIRNORTH! What on earth was that I wondered?

There was more very good news: Ken Tucker was appointed MBE in the New Year Honours list. This was very well deserved recognition of the magnificent work that Ken had done over almost four years as the Search and Rescue Advisor in Kuwait.

Late one evening in early January 2002, I received a phone call from a Kuwaiti friend and colleague; he was very upset.

'Paul,' he said. 'General Nasser is dead!'

I was stunned. Nasser had been taken ill at home that evening, a heart attack, and he had died soon afterwards in the Military Hospital. He was about fifty years old.

As is normal in the Middle East, he was buried the following morning; there were vast crowds of mourners. The following day I visited the family home in Mishref to pay my respects. When I got there it was very difficult to park, all the streets were blocked with hundreds of cars all trying to park near Nasser's home. I joined the long line of male mourners; female mourners entered the house via a separate door to pay their respects to the female members of the family. The dewaniya was full. I offered my condolences to the new head of the Al-Jehail household, the very young Lieutenant Thamer Al-Jehail. Afterwards I sat on one of the many seats lining the walls of the large room. It was a solemn and very sad occasion.

Many years later I met a number of KAF officers undergoing simulator training at Linton-on-Ouse and they remembered General Nasser with great respect and much affection. They were all convinced that he would have become the next KAF Commander. He was a huge and irreplaceable loss.

With only days left before we departed, General Nasser's replacement as Deputy Commander of the KAF was announced. It was none other than my first boss who had been 'retired' but was now being brought back into service. So the timing of my departure was perfect.

Chapter 12

NATO and Finale

Ramstein, Germany, 2002–2004
In April 2002, we drove through France past Metz and then crossed into Germany just south of Saarbrucken. As we drove along the autobahn, I couldn't help but wonder where exactly 'Big X', one of my boyhood heroes, had so cruelly met his death. As any fan of the 1963 film *The Great Escape* will know, Big X was Squadron Leader Roger Bushell (played by Richard Attenborough), and he masterminded the escape of seventy-six allied airmen from *Stalag Luft III*. Only three made it to safety. A total of fifty were murdered by the Gestapo, not together as depicted in the film, but in one's or two's, shot by the roadside. Roger Bushell and his French partner Bernard Scheidhauer were captured at Saarbrucken railway station, and on 28 March 1944, on the road to Frankfurt somewhere very close to where we were now, they were murdered by Emil Schulz of the Gestapo, helped by others. Roger Bushell is buried at the Poznan Old Garrison Cemetery in Poland.

Near the small town of Landstuhl we turned north to the huge American airbase of Ramstein. Set in the middle of rolling forest covered hills, Ramstein was a huge USAF facility, the main US air transport hub in Europe, destined to become even larger when more USAF squadrons moved from Frankfurt Main. The base, its enormous aircraft ramp often full of Boeing 747s, C141 Starlifters, and C5 Galaxy aircraft, was testament to the USAF's huge airlift capability.

There was also an American Army hospital in Landstuhl and this would often be the first port of call for many personnel wounded in Iraq and Afghanistan. The nearest large town was Kaiserslautern, referred to by many Americans as 'K Town'. Over 100,000 US service personnel and their dependents lived there. By contrast, the British community numbered about 250.

For those with an interest in aviation, the name Ramstein will forever be associated with tragedy, as it was here during an air show that an awful mid-air collision occurred. On 28 August 1988 a crowd of 300,000 people were watching a display on a beautiful summer's day. The Italian Air Force display team, Frecce Tricolori, in their ten Aermacchi MB-339 aircraft were about halfway through their routine and were performing their 'pierced heart' formation. For this manoeuvre, two groups of aircraft create a heart shape with smoke in front of the crowd. As the lower part of the heart is completed, the two groups of four and five aircraft pass each other in front of the crowd line. The heart is then pierced by a single aircraft heading directly toward the very centre of the crowd. Whatever went wrong will never be known with certainty, but as the two heart-forming groups passed, the single heart-piercing aircraft collided with one aircraft which then hit another. All three pilots died. One aircraft crashed on the runway, one on a taxiway, while the third tumbled into the crowd. A total of sixty-seven spectators died and 346 sustained serious injuries. Such manoeuvres pointing directly at the crowd have since been banned, little comfort to the families of the victims and many more deeply affected by such a traumatic and very public disaster. The tragedy is commemorated by a memorial naming all the victims, in a quiet spot to the west of the airfield, next to a small footpath leading off to the left from the main road from Ramstein to Landstuhl.

*   *   *

A year before we arrived in Germany, our daughter Hannah had dumb-founded us by announcing her intention of joining the RAF. This surprise announcement was not untypical of Hannah, only letting us know after she had made up her mind. She was accepted for training as an air traffic control officer. She embarked on officer training at the RAF College Cranwell a few weeks before my tour began at Ramstein. When I visited Cranwell, she met me in the car park to the east of College Hall. It was a brilliant feeling to be able to acknowledge her immaculate salute.

*   *   *

We moved into US Bachelor Officers' Quarters until my predecessor vacated his house in Landstuhl-Melkerei, high on the hill overlooking the castle and the town. My predecessor was David Milne-Smith, my former Station Commander at Linton during my last six months in 1994.

Administration was in the hands of the UK Support Unit, which provided support for all RAF personnel filling NATO appointments throughout central and southern Germany, as there were no longer any RAF stations in Germany.

The key RAF figure at Ramstein, and arguably the driving force behind much needed change within the HQ, was its Chief of Staff, Air Marshal Sir 'Rocky' Goodall. It was really good to see Rocky and 'Lizzie', Lady Goodall, again. As a squadron leader, Rocky had posted me to Tornados in 1983, as a wing commander he commanded 16 Squadron at Laarbruch when I was on 20 Squadron, and as a group captain he was my Station Commander during the last and most important part of my Bruggen tour. Charismatic, with a renowned sense of humour, he was extremely popular with the international community at Ramstein and highly regarded by everyone who worked there.

It was Rocky who had approved my appointment to AIRNORTH, and determined that I would also wear two additional 'national' hats even though there were already to RAF group captains in the HQ: I would be the Senior

RAF Staff Officer with reporting and pastoral responsibility for all RAF personnel, and I would also be the UK Senior National Representative.

* * *

Since leaving Kuwait I had at least been able to find out that CJFACC stood for Combined Joint Force Air Component Command, and my task was to lead the small CJFACC Planning Branch within the A5/7/9 Division of HQ AIRNORTH. But what exactly was a CJFACC?

NATO's military structure in Europe had changed little since the end of the Cold War; change was long overdue and it was taking place, but slowly. A CJFACC was part of that change which revolved around the HQ becoming deployable, a unique and startling concept for some NATO nations.

For the moment our strategic HQ remained the Supreme Headquarters Allied Powers Europe in Brussels, with its two subordinate joint HQ: at Brunssum and at Naples. Each of these HQ had a subordinate air HQ: one at Ramstein and the other also at Naples. The structure and the names still reflected a static, defensive 'Euro-centric' philosophy, but this was changing with the accession of new former Warsaw Pact nations and a wider view that NATO needed to look beyond its borders. Nevertheless, it took some getting used to working so closely with personnel from the Czech Republic, Slovakia, Poland, and Hungary, all nations that many of us had previously studied as potential threats.

AIRNORTH was commanded by a US four-star general who also wore the US national 'hat' of Commander US Air Forces in Europe, a very large parish. The Deputy Commander was a German Lieutenant General. The No. 3 was the Chief of Staff, Sir Rocky, located in the main complex at the very heart of all activity within AIRNORTH.

Below Sir Rocky were the Assistant Chiefs of Staff who commanded a Division or a combination of Divisions. They varied in rank from colonel, or equivalent, to major general. A typical divisional structure included nine divisions with the letter 'A' denoting an Air HQ:

A1 – Administration
A2 – Intelligence
A3 – Operations
A4 – Logistics
A5 – Policy and Plans
A6 – Communications and Information Systems (CIS)
A7 – Exercises
A8 – Budgets and Finance
A9 – Military and Civilian Cooperation

Within our HQ, A5, A7 and A9 were combined into a single Division under a Norwegian brigadier general. The HQ had six generals, about fifteen colonels or equivalent, while lieutenant colonels were too numerous to count.

My Division included no less than six colonels. Not to put too fine a point on it, the HQ was grossly over-ranked and in that regard it was not dissimilar to the HQ that I had recently left in Kuwait.

With NATO's enlargement, everyone wanted a voice; the higher their rank, some thought, the louder their voice. Many of the 'older' nations were also reluctant to give up what they considered to be their traditional turf. Much needed change was being driven through, but it had taken far too long to recognize and to act, and this reflected the turgid bureaucracy that was NATO.

A CJFACC is a deployable Air HQ at the operational level of command which sometimes included a smaller tactical Air HQ that was deployable. We had one such tactical HQ at Ramstein, working within which was a good friend from Bruggen days, Doug Steer; we had flown together many times.

For a NATO operational HQ to consider deploying outside the NATO area was groundbreaking stuff for some nations, but not for the US or the UK. The emphasis was on determining what would be needed to deploy a full air HQ to a 'bare-base' location with no host nation support, in other words, planning for the worst eventuality. Circumstances might also dictate that the HQ might have to operate from a seaborne platform, in AIRNORTH's case this had been exercised in 2001.

The logistics involved in planning for the worst case were tremendous, especially when a joint – land and naval – HQ would probably need to be deployed too. That is why my Branch had been established, to plan for such an eventuality and to develop a concept of operations. This involved developing standard operating procedures, programmes, exercises, logistics, CIS, intelligence support manning, and infrastructure.

My Branch was small, comprising three lieutenant colonels (one Dutch, one German and one from the US), a RAF squadron leader logistics specialist, a Dutch major intelligence specialist and a Dutch corporal for administration. The Branch was only ever intended to be short-lived, and once the concept of mobility had been established, it would disband.

*   *   *

It took me a while to get to grips with my job but the more I thought about it my sense of unease increased. Planning for the worst case is a sound military maxim, but surely it would be more sensible to plan for the most likely scenario first? What chance was there of all of the various NATO nations, old and new alike, agreeing to the huge cost of funding for the worst case, especially when so many at the political level seemed to express disquiet about NATO going beyond its own borders?

I had seen at first hand during the 1980s just how capable NATO was as a defensive alliance: an attack on one would indeed have been an attack on all. I had never had any doubts that NATO could deliver a very real military capability and it still could as a defensive alliance. But, did an enlarged

NATO have the political will to consider going beyond its own borders? While some member nations were unwilling to articulate their doubts, would they put their hands deep into their pockets to fund the preparations necessary for a worst-case scenario that at best they might not support, or at worst they might wish to veto? NATO could be faced with a coalition of the unwilling.

While these questions were hopefully being asked at the highest level, would it not be sensible in the meantime to plan for the more likely scenarios, such as peace-keeping then peace-making, before peace enforcement?

I had watched from the sidelines in Kuwait in 1998 while the UK, at short notice, had deployed a formidable force which, within days, was capable of defending itself robustly and of delivering a potent offensive capability. Had this involved the establishment of a major HQ in Kuwait? No. Only the barest minimum of 'footprints' had been deployed forward. Support had also been sought from the host nation with much of the day-to-day logistics obtained from the local economy. The RAF detachment then used modern CIS to link to higher HQ. Could this not be a model for NATO?

From a planning and cost perspective, it always seemed to me that the first priority must be to plan for the most likely option first, before considering how to deploy a full HQ to a bare base and potentially hostile location to engage in war fighting. NATO should first consider deploying to supportive nations which could provide some basic infrastructure, and then only deploying a minimum footprint to the forward area. Why did the huge 'tail' of an Air or any other HQ have to deploy forward in the twenty-first century?

* * *

In October 2002, Jackie and I travelled back to the UK to see Hannah commissioned as an RAF officer. The parade, immediately in front of College Hall overlooking The Orange, was superb, and it ended with a first class flypast by a Tornado F3. It was a wonderful occasion and we were delighted to share in the success of a new generation of 'warriors'.

For them, the Cold War had long since been over; most of them would be involved in something much warmer. Within a year of completing her initial air traffic control course at RAF Shawbury, Hannah would find herself in Basrah in Iraq for her first operational tour. Three years later, she would be back there for her second. And in 2011, she would be at Camp Bastion, in Helmand Province, Afghanistan, for her third operational tour in less than eight years.

* * *

Command Post Exercises were held regularly with the HQ often deployed to its war location at the Ruppertsweiler Bunker, known as RUF, some miles to the south. Constructed during the 1930s for the Wehrmacht, RUF had been the home to many HQ after the Second World War. It was a large underground complex from which AIRNORTH would have fought in the event of hostilities with the Soviet Union. It had long been recognized that the bunker, large as it was, was too small, and between the mid-1980s and 1992 the equivalent of over €35 million was spent constructing RUF II, a much larger facility deep inside the same mountain. Construction came to an end when the Berlin Wall came down, leaving an immense and empty underground cavern, one more legacy of the Cold War. While the whole complex is now disused and has been sealed, in 2002, it was still operational and was used for one of the final times during Exercise Cannon Cloud. As my Branch did not have a war-role, we were ideally placed to act as an internal evaluation team to assess how the HQ performed. The experience was fascinating.

I had never worked in such a HQ on exercise so virtually everything that I saw was new. Many of my questions were therefore quite genuine, but most were perceived as being part of the evaluation. I would often ask, 'Why do you do that?'

Sometimes the answer was, 'We have always done it that way.'

Then I knew that it was time for a closer look.

Because of the limited size of RUF, some parts of the HQ had to be housed above ground, while others operated from their peacetime locations back at Ramstein. Given the capability and robustness of communications, these separated elements were nevertheless effective. That begged an important question. Instead of being a few miles away, why couldn't they have been 2,000 miles away? And if they could remain operationally effective, could not more elements of the HQ have been left 'at home' with only a small footprint deployed to RUF? Was that not the very CJFACC concept that we should be trying to develop, with a small but robust deployed HQ 'reaching back' for whatever support it needed?

Afterwards, I went to see Sir Rocky to discuss our initial observations. As always, he was in a cheerful and receptive mood. It seemed like a good opportunity to say what I thought about the CJFACC 'bare-base' concept, and I used Exercise Cannon Cloud as an example of how separation of elements of the HQ could be perfectly viable in many scenarios. Rocky simply smiled and said that he agreed. Clearly, far better minds than mine had been exercised for a lot longer in seeking a pragmatic solution to what was, to many, an intellectual concept. Circumstances in Afghanistan would soon test the veracity of the pragmatic solution.

*   *   *

One accidental but very pleasant addition to my job was to run the twice-yearly, week-long Introduction to NATO Joint Operational Air Campaign Planning Course, at the NATO School at Oberammergau in Bavaria. It was located within a German Army barracks built in 1935. In 1943, the Messerschmitt Company took over the site to develop its jet engines and twenty-two miles of tunnels were bored into the neighbouring Laber Mountain for engine production facilities. NATO established its principal operational training and education facility here in 1953.

The location was fabulous: beautiful high pastureland with the steep slopes of the Bavarian Alps rising on three sides. Every ten years, audiences from around the world flock to Oberammergau to see the village's famous passion play that had first been performed in 1634, following an outbreak of bubonic plague in the region. The inhabitants had vowed that if they were spared they would perform a passion play every ten years. The play involves over 2,000 actors, singers, instrumentalists, and technicians, all residents of the village. Not far from the village is Schloss Linderhof with its beautiful formal gardens, one of King Ludwig II's ornate and extravagant castles built in 1878. Often called the Swan King, he was probably best known for his fantasy castle of Neuschwanstein, now a huge tourist attraction, and an hour's drive from Oberammergau.

*   *   *

The nature of my NATO job very quickly became routine. Within a year, I was the senior colonel within my Division and often acted as the Assistant Chief of Staff, which added more interest. However, my two national 'hats' ensured that I was kept busy. I was the senior reporting officer for all the RAF personnel at Ramstein, and I ended up writing more annual confidential reports during my final tour than I had written in all of my previous tours combined. I also had two good national deputies during my tour; the first was a wing commander engineer from the A4 Division, and the second was AIRNORTH's extremely able Provost Marshal, Wing Commander John Whitmell. Whenever John came into my office for 'a quiet word', I always asked, 'Which hat are you wearing? Are you here as my Deputy or as a policeman?'

Once or twice he needed to see me as both! Within a year of my departure John would be promoted to group captain and he went on to become the RAF's senior police officer as Provost Marshal.

*   *   *

During 2004 I headed another evaluation team during a Command Post Exercise involving No. 2 Allied Tactical Operations Centre (ATOC) at Kalkar, not far from our 1985 home in nearby Goch. Until Day One of the exercise I had never set foot inside an ATOC. Thankfully, neither the German major general in command, nor any of his staff were aware of that.

The exercise was entirely computer generated and was due to last about four days. The computers went down on Day One, and I couldn't help but notice that there seemed to be a degree of quiet rejoicing amongst the permanent staff when this occurred. I was summoned to see the General who expressed his dismay and asked that I terminate the exercise; it would take about a year to reschedule. He was most put out when I declined saying, 'Computers might fail during a war, Sir. What would you do then?'

His staff were equally put out, and it was fascinating to watch the exercise unfold without the help of any computers. For about twenty-four hours, chaos reigned, but eventually the ATOC staff rediscovered long lost skills such as using chinagraph pencils, briefing boards and telephones. And, wonders to behold, they began talking to one another instead of sending emails.

I am sure that my being 'done' for speeding by the German civil police shortly after leaving Kalkar was a complete coincidence.

* * *

Although small, the UK community was very active. It had its own magazine called *The Britbull*, and a good social life. We had our own 'virtual' Mess called The George which was often to be found in one of the nearby restaurants, or sometimes we would take over the Ramstein Officers' Club. I was often involved in duty 'social' events which had taken on increased importance as new Eastern European nations were welcomed into NATO.

One of the highlights of the 2003 calendar for the RAF community was when we dined out Rocky Goodall immediately prior to his retirement from the RAF. To dine out an Air Officer from the RAF was a very rare privilege and, as the function would be a Ladies Guest Night in the Ramstein Officers' Club, it was a double privilege to also be able to say farewell to Lizzie, Lady Goodall. There were also two surprise guests. The evening before, I drove to Frankfurt-Hahn Airport to meet Sir Rocky's two daughters, who flew in for the occasion. When I dropped them off at Sir Rocky's residence, unusually, he was lost for words. I said that I had picked them up while they were hitchhiking on a nearby autobahn.

On Sir Rocky's final day, all of the NATO staff left the building and lined the sides of the large car park outside the HQ. When he came out of the HQ he was met with continuous applause as he made the very long walk down the car park. It was a very emotional farewell to a very popular and well-regarded Air Marshal.

I thoroughly enjoyed working for Sir Rocky who had been a key figure at some important times during my career. While he was well aware that I was also on my last tour of duty, I was pleased to read his comment that I 'could take on any demanding one star appointment now.' It was academic but nevertheless heartening.

* * *

During the months prior to Sir Rocky's departure, two much needed and linked concepts were being strongly pushed; my Branch was involved in both. The first was the introduction of a NATO Reaction Force aimed at adjusting NATO's previous focus to one of greater flexibility covering the full range of operations. This included planning for operations outside NATO territory. Interestingly, France was well on board with the concept, even though it had not been part of NATO's integrated military structure since the 1960s. France had observers attached to a number of NATO HQ, including AIRNORTH, and many of us considered it only a matter of time before France rejoined NATO's integrated military structure; they did so in 2009.

The other positive move was the acceptance that using the concept of 'reach-back' was not only viable, but had to be the way ahead in developing NATO's new concept of operations. It was not long before reach-back was tested for real, and that test was of course Afghanistan. By then a new RAF Chief of Staff, Air Marshal Phil Sturley was in post, and he continued to press forward in developing what were, to many nations, radical departures from NATO's previous stance. There was a new world out there and NATO had to adapt.

While many nations, and notably the new member nations, were enthusiastic about change and very much wanted to contribute, other nations were less so. We were soon faced with planning for Afghanistan and a small NATO air component HQ using reach-back was soon deployed to Kabul as part of the International Stabilization Augmentation Force, ISAF. The CJFACC Planning Branch had a role in ensuring that ISAF was manned appropriately.

Deploying NATO personnel from Ramstein to Kabul was a challenge, and this brought into sharp focus the difficulties in harnessing so many different nations toward a common military goal. The various senior national representatives had to agree national contributions for ISAF, and while some nations were willing to step forward, others were less so. This was demonstrated by one of my senior national representative colleagues, from one of the 'older' nations, when I asked him to nominate personnel for Afghanistan.

'Paul, you need to understand that it is very difficult. Some of my people have enrolled for night classes,' he said.

Such comments did make me wonder how serious some long-established NATO nations were in delivering a real military capability in the new world that we faced. During the Cold War I never had any doubts; now for the first time I had. Nevertheless, it was also heart-warming to form up outside the HQ as the national flag of a new member nation was raised to join those of the existing NATO nations. Harnessing so many voices for the common good had to be a good thing, but it would be an incredible challenge.

Thankfully, as far as ISAF was concerned, our first Air Component HQ capability was in the very safe hands of Group Captain Ian Stewart from the A3 Operations Division. Ian, a former Tornado F3 Squadron Commander, had flown the flypast at our daughter's graduation at Cranwell. He did an extremely good job in Kabul and after six months handed over to a very capable USAF officer. Only time would tell how effective all the NATO nations would be in delivering peace to the fledgling democracy in Kabul. Ian would later be promoted to air commodore and became Commandant of the Air Cadets. Ian had taken over at Ramstein from Russ Torbet, whom I had last served with on 14 Squadron at Bruggen; coincidentally, I had been flying with Russ's wife Nikki, an air traffic controller at the time, when I achieved my 1,000 flying hours on Tornados.

* * *

2004 saw many changes within the NATO HQ structure as, at long last, land, sea and air components downsized and restructured, to better reflect the changes in circumstances. HQ AIRNORTH was renamed Component Command Air (North) prior to a move into a new building at Ramstein.

My last national contribution was to agree which posts the UK would fill in the smaller and newly shaped HQ. I also oversaw the demise of my own Branch, and the disestablishment of my own post, prior to returning to the UK in October to prepare for my retirement from the RAF.

Was I leaving a coalition of the willing or a coalition of the unwilling? Only time would tell. But sometimes coalitions are the only way forward.

RAF Linton-on-Ouse, 2004

We drove into France, past Saarbrucken and Metz and on to the Channel Tunnel for the final time in October 2004. Then it was north to Linton-on-Ouse and the Officers' Mess, where Paul Medlicott had very kindly allocated us the VIP suite; on the wall was the picture of Wensleydale that I had presented to the Mess in 1994. Adjacent to the Mess entrance hall were framed photographs, that I had also presented, of the '75' Formation of Tucanos and their crews that I had led on 17 July 1994. Paul went on to become a first-class Mess Manager before handing over to the equally capable Bryan Griffiths. The following day we moved into a house on The Green, only a few doors from the one that we had occupied when I had been Chief Instructor. It felt as if we had come home.

Within a few days I joined three other aircrew group captains at RAF Innsworth, as members of the promotion board to select aircrew flight lieutenants for promotion to squadron leader. It was an interesting few weeks which gave me a good insight into how such boards worked.

All the officers eligible for promotion were considered separately by each board member who then scored an individual between 0 and 9; there was no discussion, no possibility of one board member influencing another. When everyone had been scored, if any two board member's scores were at variance by two points or more, then there was discussion and the individual was re-scored, but with board members being unaware of the score that they had previously awarded. The whole process was scrupulously fair and although observers were invited to attend, many more would have benefited by seeing how a promotion board went about its business.

Within twenty-four hours of my return to Linton I was recalled to act as President of a Board of Inquiry. The Inquiry had been convened to investigate the circumstances surrounding the sudden death of a serviceman whilst on duty. It was a very long and complex affair, necessarily so because of the personal tragedy involved. I hope that we were as thorough, that we showed the same understanding, the same careful and considered questioning, that I had experienced during the Gnat Board of Inquiry in 1979. It was a very distressing experience for the family who willingly gave evidence, and also for the colleagues of the individual concerned who had been with him when he died. The Inquiry lasted four months. It was my last official duty as a regular RAF officer, but as I signed it off I felt that it had probably been one of the most important tasks that I had been set in thirty-four years.

*   *   *

My final day of full-time RAF service was 30 June 2005, and I retired thirty-four years and one week after being commissioned at RAF Henlow. However, I wasn't yet finished with 'the light blue', and I dropped two ranks to be commissioned in the RAF Reserve as a squadron leader to work full time with the Air Cadets for three years. The Air Cadets had been a life changing experience for me and I was pleased to be able to give something back.

*   *   *

In late 2007 I bumped into Eric Constable, my first flight commander when I was an instructor at RAF Leeming in 1979. Eric was about to take over as Manager of the Tucano Flight Simulator at Linton for the French Company, Thales.

'Have you ever thought about being a Tucano simulator instructor?' he asked.

*   *   *

In May 2008, my time as an RAF officer ended as I rejoined that 'Centre of Excellence', No. 1 Flying Training School, wearing the uniform of Thales and doing once more what I had so much enjoyed in the past: teaching highly motivated and enthusiastic young men and women who were embarking on a long hard road that hopefully, would lead them to a fast-jet cockpit. Interestingly the three questions that they all still asked were: What is the 'chop' rate? Who is the instructor to avoid at all costs? Who is the 'natural pilot'?

This time I hoped that the students now welcomed a sortie with me, rather than perhaps fearing it as others may have done some fifteen years earlier.

*   *   *

However, my flying days were not yet over. I was approached by Squadron Leader Simon Johnston, who commanded 642 Volunteer Gliding Squadron, at RAF Linton-on-Ouse. He invited me to join his twenty-eight volunteer staff some forty-two years after my last 'official' gliding sortie.

On 30 November 2008, I was delighted to become a Grade One Glider Pilot on the Vigilant motor glider. 642 Squadron is one of sixteen units delivering basic gliding training to the Air Cadets, and very few of the volunteers have any regular RAF experience. They do a magnificent job at weekends giving cadets their very first air experience. They come from all walks of life, from plumbers to policemen, salesmen to surveyors, yet they all share a love of flying and are so very proud, deservedly so, of their association with 'the light blue'.

And, of course, they are very understanding of that grey-haired chap in the battered flying suit with faded badges of squadrons now disbanded, who helps out a couple of times a month. They even listen politely to his stories, although he is regularly misquoted, usually by 642's very able adjutant Ian Gilbert. Here, apparently, is but one example of one of my 'briefings':

> Try to stay in the middle of the air. Stay away from the edges. You can recognize the edges by the appearance of ground, buildings and trees. It is generally more difficult to fly in the edges.

* * *

The Tucano Simulator was another of the RAF's great 'crossroads', bringing together some of the most experienced of the RAF's former instructors. On arrival, I went into ground school with one-on-one tuition from the vastly experienced former RAF engineer Alf Akers. As well as having a great sense of humour, Alf was an oracle when it came to matters technical and I paid close attention to his lectures, as I had done on both of my previous visits to Linton. After a few days I then went into 'standards' under the 'gentle' guidance of Dave Guyatt. Coming some eleven years after my last Tucano sortie I found the learning curve to be rather steep.

Our crewroom, renamed by Rich Kimberley as 'Dinosaur's Den', was actually a welcoming environment for students, although Alf would always warn each new course that they were about to enter 'a banter-free zone' and that they should not try to take on the Simulator instructors at what was very much 'their game'.

All of the simulator instructors had known one another in the past, with many of our paths having crossed many times: Eric Constable, Steve Pepper, John Houlton, Alan Rayment, Rich Kimberley, Rod Leigh, Roger Clements, Mike Johnson, Dave Guyatt, Ken Jones, Steve Orwell, Dick Cole, and Brian Russell; all under the watchful eye of Anne Barker

Our combined RAF service was over 420 years and between us we had more than 70,000 flying hours. Of that total, 30,000 were flying instructional hours on aircraft ranging from current elementary trainers, through basic and fast-jet trainers, to operational front line aircraft such as the Tornado and F18.

We had also flown many aircraft types that were now museum pieces. But four of us were still active flying instructors. While reductions in the RAF task would reduce our numbers we were all inextricably marching toward 'a certain age' and would all have to come to terms with the fragility that comes with advancing years.

Rod Leigh, aged sixty-seven, such a great survivor and a true Cold War Warrior, succumbed after a short fight that he couldn't possibly win. On 14 March 2011, he was driven for the last time from his home to RAF Linton-on-Ouse where he had served for the best part of thirty years. At the Main Gate an RAF police car took the lead, escorting the cortège past the Officers' Mess where the President of the Mess Committee saluted Rod on his way to All Saints Church, Newton-on-Ouse. Rod's coffin, draped in the Union Flag, was carried into a packed church by six RAF pilots from Linton, under the careful direction of Warrant Officer Fred Dawson. The beautiful service was taken by a family friend, the Venerable Canon Brian Lucas, Archdeacon Emeritus of the RAF, and Honorary Chaplain of the Coastal Command Association.

Rod was buried on the gentle slope leading down to the Ouse, not far from his old friend 'Sir George', Squadron Leader Sir George Broadbent. Both Rod and George had served together on Standards Squadron at Linton and Rod had read the poem *High Flight* at George's funeral. This time the poem was read by Malcolm Tibble, Rod's navigator on Shackletons some forty years earlier. A single Tucano from Linton flew across the cemetery in final salute. Afterwards, everyone adjourned to the Officers' Mess at RAF Linton-on-Ouse to say farewell in the RAF aircrew way. The RAF had remembered Flight Lieutenant Rod Leigh very well.

* * *

1 March 2011 had been a sad day for 170 RAF student pilots, all at various stages of their training, some already proudly wearing their RAF wings. They were 'de-selected'; there were no cockpits for them. No less than twenty-four Linton students were given that most unwelcome news, nearly 50 per cent of the total undergoing training at Linton. This came only a few weeks after all navigator training in the RAF had ceased. I couldn't help but compare what was happening to these young men and women with exactly the same situation that had occurred in the early 1990s, post Options for Change, when the response by the RAF had been so very different. Was today's response a better way?

On the same day, it was also announced that not one but two of my former squadrons, XIII and 14, both now operating Tornado GR4s, were to be stood down by 1 June 2011. I had served on XIII Squadron from 1975 to 1978, and on 14 Squadron from 1985 until 1988. During the days leading up to the disbandment of these historic squadrons, it was ironic to watch their aircraft en route to Libya, in harms way once more until the very end of their service.

The loss of two more squadrons was perhaps an inevitable follow-on from what many considered to have been an all too rapid Strategic Defence Review. Coming so soon after the disbandment of all the RAF and RN Harrier squadrons, the termination of the RAF's anti-submarine and maritime patrol role, and the destruction of the Nimrod MR4, it seemed to be another case of 'short-termism'. We would have a capability gap, it was said. Did the general public have any real idea what that meant? In the meantime we would have to hope that we would have 'reliable' enemies who would not threaten in those areas where we had gaps.

These were difficult days for everyone in the UK and there was no doubt that the Armed Forces had to take their share of pain, but such terribly deep cuts would leave a lasting legacy, not least in the hearts and minds of the Armed Forces *most precious* asset, its people.

It looked as though the writing might also be on the wall for No. 1 Flying Training School and RAF Linton-on-Ouse, with the strong probability that basic fast-jet training would be transferred to RAF Valley. There had been hope that this would not take place until the demise of the Tucano, but it now appeared as if the financial imperative to close yet another RAF station might outweigh all other concerns. It would be a desperately sad day if the RAF was to leave Linton-on-Ouse, and heart-breaking if the world's first ever flying training school, No. 1 Flying Training School, was to be disbanded. I had no doubt that I had seen the very best of days.

*   *   *

I often think back to my regular RAF service. My flying hours currently total 4,970, not a huge amount compared with many, but all of my first pilot time was on single or twin engined aircraft and the average sortie length was less than ninety minutes. I had qualified on fourteen different aircraft types and I enjoyed them all. I hope that it will be on the Vigilant that I finally achieve 5,000 hours. Then maybe it will be time to hang up my 'green bag' for the final time.

I also think a lot about the places that we have been, the stations on which we lived, and the squadrons on which I served. But most of all, I think about the people. It was a privilege to serve with so many Cold War Warriors and I count myself as having been very lucky. There were no fatal accidents on squadrons on which I was serving at the time, although aircraft accidents were never far away and service funerals were all too frequent. A total of fourteen aircrew with whom I had flown were killed, and thirty-one others had to elect for a 'Martin Baker letdown' at least once during their careers. Yes, I had been very lucky.

County Durham, 2010

I drove through Consett once more on 10 May 2010, on my way to a friend's funeral in Blackhill. There had been many changes since 1971 but the office where I had worked was still an estate agents and the HQ of 1409 (Consett) Squadron was still in use. The Squadron was under the command of Flight Lieutenant David Parker; he and I had been cadets together for nearly six years and I had been the best man at his wedding.

I parked within the grounds of the church where the funerals of both of my paternal grandparents had taken place. After the service I spent a few minutes wandering around until I came across the War Memorial. There were so many names, but then there always are. Even though I knew none of those listed, I recognized so many of the surnames, so many Mc's and O's, it was like reading once more from my old school register.

While it had been sad saying farewell to a friend, I also felt that I was saying farewell to Consett. I had travelled quite a long way.

Postscript

Despite all the news of continual draw-downs and cutbacks within the RAF, there was at least some encouraging news about XIII and 14 Squadrons. They had not after all been consigned to the history books, but would re-emerge in very different guises to those that they had as Tornado GR4 squadrons.

During 2012, XIII Squadron was to re-form at RAF Waddington in Lincolnshire, with the MQ-9 Reaper unmanned aerial vehicle. For the very first time, these aircraft would be able to operate over Afghanistan while being 'flown' from the UK. When XIII Squadron does reform, I wonder whether they will find a place within their HQ for an ageing black and white photograph of a Soviet aircraft carrier called *Kiev*.

After a disbandment parade at RAF Lossiemouth, 14 Squadron was formally stood down after ninety-six years of unbroken service on 1 June 2011. According to the Air Force Board's own rules on squadron seniority, 14 Squadron should not have been selected for disbandment, but the unit which would have been chosen – according to those same rules – would have been on operations in Afghanistan when the decision was announced. This would have been politically embarrassing, so 14 Squadron was sacrificed instead. The Air Force Board soon agreed that 14 Squadron's number plate should be passed on to a new unit which, until then, had kept a very low public profile. The unit had been operating in the Intelligence, Surveillance, Target Acquisition and Reconnaissance role for two years and, on 1 October 2011, it formally became 14 Squadron flying Beechcraft Shadow R1 aircraft from RAF Waddington.

It was also time for Eric, Squadron Leader Eric Androvadi, to go too; now twenty-seven years old and twenty-two feet long, he was retired to a new home in 'Amazonia', an indoor tropical rainforest centre just outside Glasgow. Perhaps the RAF Police could now collect their picket post twenty-four years after it 'disappeared' from RAF Bruggen's Special Storage Area.

In February 2012, 14 Squadron hosted Air Marshal Tim Anderson in a formal visit. Air Marshal Anderson is a former 14 Squadron Commanding Officer and he is also President of the 14 Squadron Association. Air Marshal Anderson oversaw the presentation of the annual Grieve and Smith Memorial Trophy. This prestigious award is granted to the member of 14 Squadron who is judged to have made the most significant contribution to life during the year and the very deserving recipient was Corporal Rachel Mills. Well done Rachel!

The award honours the memory of Flight Lieutenants Mike Smith and Alan Grieve who were tragically killed in a mid-air collision on Friday 13 January 1989. Mike and Alan were extremely popular and professional airmen, and they are amongst so very many *Winged Warriors* who gave their lives for all of us. Long may we remember them.

July 2012

Record of Service

1964–1970	Air Cadet
1970	Civilian Instructor, Air Cadet Organization
Aug 1970 – Feb 1971	Pilot Officer, Royal Air Force Volunteer Reserve (Training), 1409 (Consett) Squadron, Air Training Corps
Feb 1971 – Jun 1971	Officer Cadet, Officer Cadet Training Unit (OCTU), RAF Henlow, Bedfordshire
Jul 1971 – Aug 1971	Course Member, Academic Training Squadron, RAF Church Fenton, North Yorkshire
Sep 1971 – Aug 1972	Student Pilot (Jet Provost), 3 Squadron, No. 3 Flying Training School (FTS), RAF Leeming, North Yorkshire
Oct 1972 – Mar 1973	Student Pilot (Gnat), 2 Squadron, No. 4 Flying Training School (FTS), RAF Valley, Anglesey, North Wales
Mar 1973 – Apr 1973	Course Member, Outdoor Activities Centre, Grantown-on-Spey, Scotland
May 1973 – Jun 1973	Refresher Pilot (Hunter), 3 Squadron, No. 4 Flying Training School, RAF Valley, Anglesey, North Wales
Jul 1973 – Oct 1973	Course Member (Canberra), 231 Operational Conversion Unit (OCU), RAF Cottesmore, Rutland
Oct 1973 – Aug 1975	Squadron Pilot (Canberra), 7 Squadron, RAF St Mawgan, Cornwall
Aug 1975 – Oct 1978	Squadron Pilot (Canberra), XIII (PR) Squadron, RAF Luqa, Malta
Dec 1978 – Jun 1979	Course Member (Jet Provost), Central Flying School (CFS), RAF Leeming, North Yorkshire
Jun 1979 – Feb 1983	Qualified Flying Instructor (QFI) (Jet Provost), Instrument Rating Examiner, Flight Commander, Deputy Squadron Commander, Standards Instructor, Refresher Flying Squadron (RFS), RAF Leeming, North Yorkshire

Mar 1980 – Sep 1981	Display Pilot (Meteor), Vintage Pair, Central Flying School, RAF Leeming, North Yorkshire
Mar 1983 – Apr 1983	Course Member (Hawk), 3 Squadron, No. 4 Flying Training School, RAF Valley, Anglesey, North Wales
May 1983 – Aug 1983	Course Member (Hawk), 151 Squadron, No. 2 Tactical Weapons Unit (TWU), RAF Chivenor, Devon
Oct 1983 – Feb 1984	Course Member (Tornado), C Squadron, Tornado Tri-national Training Establishment (TTTE), RAF Cottesmore, Rutland
Feb 1984 – May 1984	Course Member (Tornado), 45 (Reserve) Squadron, Tornado Weapons Conversion Unit (TWCU), RAF Honington, Suffolk
May 1984 – Jun 1985	Squadron Pilot (Tornado), 20 Squadron, RAF Laarbruch, West Germany
Jun 1985 – Sep 1988	Training Officer, Executive Officer (Tornado), 14 Squadron, RAF Bruggen, West Germany
Oct 1988 – Apr 1990	Central Region Specialist, Department of Air Warfare, RAF College Cranwell, Lincolnshire
Apr 1990 – Nov 1990	Course Member, Joint Services Defence College, Greenwich, London
Nov 1990 – Oct 1991	Personal Staff Officer to Air Officer Commanding (AOC) Training Group, RAF Brampton, Huntingdonshire
Oct 1991 – Feb 1992	Refresher Instructor (Jet Provost, Bulldog), Central Flying School (CFS), RAF Scampton, Lincolnshire
Mar 1992 – Nov 1994	Chief Instructor/OC Flying Training Wing (Jet Provost, Bulldog, Tucano, Firefly), No. 1 Flying Training School (FTS), RAF Linton-on-Ouse, North Yorkshire
Nov 1994 – Nov 1996	Directing Staff (Air), Royal College of Defence Studies, London
Nov 1996 – Aug 1997	Flying Training 2, Training Group, HQ Personnel and Training Command (HQ PTC), RAF Innsworth, Gloucestershire
Sep 1997 – Dec 1997	Refresher Instructor (Tucano), No. 1 Flying Training School, RAF Linton-on-Ouse, North Yorkshire
Feb 1998 – Feb 2002	Advisor, British Military Mission, Kuwait

Apr 2002 – Sep 2004	Chief Combined Joint Force Air Component Command (CJFACC) Plans, Senior RAF Staff Officer (SRAFSO), UK Senior National Representative (UK SNR), HQ AIRNORTH, Ramstein, Germany
Oct 2004 – Jun 2005	Supernumerary, RAF Linton-on-Ouse, North Yorkshire

Aircraft, Qualifications and Flying Hours

Canberra		1,470
Jet Provost	Instructor	1,460
Tornado	Instructor	1,100
Tucano	Instructor	270
Hawk		110
Bulldog	Instructor	100
Gnat		80
Vigilant		100
Meteor		70
Firefly	Instructor	60
Chipmunk		40
Cessna		35
Hunter		25
Other aircraft*		50
TOTAL		4,970

*Slingsby and Kirkby Cadet Gliders, Auster, Phantom, Gazelle, Puma, Harrier, Sea King, Super Puma, Eurocopter, Bell 430

UK Officer Ranks

Royal Air Force	Royal Navy	Army
Pilot Officer	Midshipman	Second Lieutenant
Flying Officer	Sub Lieutenant	Lieutenant
Flight Lieutenant	Lieutenant	Captain
Squadron Leader	Lieutenant Commander	Major
Wing Commander	Commander	Lieutenant Colonel
Group Captain	Captain	Colonel
Air Commodore	Commodore	Brigadier
Air Vice-Marshal	Rear Admiral	Major General
Air Marshal	Vice Admiral	Lieutenant General
Air Chief Marshal	Admiral	General
Marshal of the Royal Air Force	Admiral of the Fleet	Field Marshal

Index

Author's note: The ranks shown are the last known rank of the individuals mentioned.